D0450841

TEACHINGS
of the
PROPHET
JOSEPH SMITH

TEACHINGS
OF THE
PROPHET JOSEPH SMITH

*Taken from his sermons and writings as they are
found in the Documentary History and other
publications of the Church and written
or published in the days of the
Prophet's ministry*

Selected and arranged by the Historian, Joseph
Fielding Smith, and his Assistants in the Historian's Office of the Church of Jesus Christ
of Latter-day Saints.

Index and Concordance
prepared by Robert J. Matthews

DESERET BOOK COMPANY
SALT LAKE CITY, UTAH

First printing in paperbound edition, June 1989

Library of Congress Catalog Card Number 90-220999

ISBN 0-87747-626-8 (hardbound ed.)

ISBN 0-87579-243-X (paperbound ed.)

Printed in the United States of America

10   9   8   7   6   5   4   3

ABBREVIATIONS:
  MSS. — Manuscript History.
  J. H. — Journal History of the Church.
  D. H. C. — Documentary History of the Church.
  E. & M. S. — Evening and Morning Star.
  T. S. — Times and Seasons.
  F. W. R. — Far West Record.
  M. and A. — Messenger and Advocate.

INTRODUCTION

A quarter of a century ago, Elder Edwin F. Parry compiled and published a classified arrangement of excerpts from doctrinal sermons and writings of the Prophet Joseph Smith. These sayings were taken from the Documentary History of the Church. That little work filled an important mission, but left in the hearts and minds of all who were interested in the sayings of the great latter-day Prophet, a longing for more of his sayings, which longing was not satisfied. Many faithful members of the Church have expressed the desire that a more extensive work of this kind be published. The members of the Church quite generally desire to know what the Prophet Joseph Smith may have said on important subjects, for they look upon his utterances as coming through divine inspiration.

Many of these discourses and writings appear in the Documentary History of the Church, but others have not been included in these volumes, but are scattered through the early publications of the Church. It has been difficult even for the student to obtain these because the old publications are not accessible for general use.

In accordance with the many calls that have been made that there be a more extensive compilation of these discourses and sayings, the matter was taken up in the Historian's Office and such a compilation has been prepared, submitted to the First Presidency and passed by them for publication.

It should be remembered that this compilation contains some discourses and statements from the minutes of council and priesthood meetings, which are not verbatim reports of the Prophet's remarks, but which have been approved in those minutes. There has been no attempt to compile these sayings by subject, because frequently in the same article or discourse, several subjects are discussed. It has been thought best to give each article, or portion of article, chronologically, with an exhaustive index through which the various subjects may be found. Historical matters and incidental or unimportant matters have been eliminated. By the use of asterisks these portions left out are indicated in the body of the work.

Articles which are accessible, such as *Joseph Smith Tells His Own Story*, which has been published in tract form and also in the Pearl of Great Price, are not added to this work. References have been made to the revelations in the Doctrine and Covenants where necessary, but these revelations are not included in this work.

It is felt that this volume will meet a need and promote faith among the members of the Church. With this intent it is sent out on its mission as another testimony of the divine calling of the Prophet Joseph Smith.

JOSEPH FIELDING SMITH,
Church Historian.

SECTION ONE
1830 – 1834

TEACHINGS
OF THE
PROPHET JOSEPH SMITH

———————•———————

Title Page of the Book of Mormon

Meantime our translation drawing to a close, we went to Palmyra, Wayne County, New York, secured the copyright, and agreed with Mr. Egbert B. Grandin to print five thousand copies for the sum of three thousand dollars.

I wish to mention here, that the title-page of the Book of Mormon is a literal translation, taken from the very last leaf, on the left hand side of the collection or book of plates, which contained the record which has been translated, the language of the whole running the same as all Hebrew writing in general; and that said title-page is not by any means a modern composition, either of mine or of any other man who has lived or does live in this generation. Therefore, in order to correct an error which generally exists concerning it, I give below[1] that part of the title-page of the English version of the Book of Mormon, which is a genuine and literal translation of the title-page of the original Book of Mormon, as recorded on the plates.—D. H. C. 1:71. (1830.)

Value of the Revelations and Commandments

My time was occupied closely in reviewing the commandments and sitting in conference, for nearly two weeks, for from the first to the twelfth of November [1831] we held four special conferences. In the last which was held at Brother Johnson's, in Hiram, after deliberate consideration, in consequence of the Book of revelations, now to be printed,[2] being

---

[1]See the title-page of the Book of Mormon, the two paragraphs mentioned.

[2]At a conference of the Church held in November, 1831, the Prophet received the revelation known as Section One, or the Preface to the *Book of Commandments*. At this conference the Elders considered the question of publishing the revelations which had been given up to that time as the *Book of Commandments*. This action the Lord approved by revelation. It was decided that 10,000 copies should be published, but later this was

the foundation of the Church in these last days, and a benefit to the world, showing that the keys of the mysteries of the kingdom of our Savior are again entrusted to man; and the riches of eternity within the compass of those who are willing to live by every word that proceedeth out of the mouth of God—therefore the conference voted that they prize the revelations to be worth to the Church the riches of the whole earth, speaking temporally.   The great benefits to the world which result from the Book of Mormon and the revelations, which the Lord has seen fit in His infinite wisdom to grant unto us for our salvation, and for the salvation of all that will believe, were duly appreciated; and in answer to an inquiry, I received the following.[3] (Nov., 1831) D. H. C. 1:235-236.

Parting the Veil Through Perfect Faith

Brother Joseph Smith, Jr., said: We have assembled together to do the business of the Lord and it is through the great

---

changed to 3,000 copies. A number of the brethren, at this conference, arose and stated that they were willing to testify to the world that they knew that the revelations received by the Prophet were of the Lord. In due time the revelations were compiled by the Prophet, and at a conference held November 12, 1831, the revelations were received with thanksgiving. Oliver Cowdery, John Whitmer and William W. Phelps, were appointed to review the revelations for printing, and Oliver Cowdery and John Whitmer were appointed to carry them to Missouri where the printing was to be done. These brethren were "dedicated and consecrated with the sacred writings and all they have entrusted to their care to the Lord." The publication was commenced by William W. Phelps and Co. in Jackson County, Missouri, but before the work was completed the press and type were destroyed by a mob, July 20, 1833, and only a few of the printed forms were preserved; these were bound and used by those fortunate enough to secure them in the uncompleted condition as the *Book of Commandments*. Later, in the year 1835, the revelations, now greatly increased in number, were again compiled and ordered printed as *The Doctrine and Covenants*. This first edition, prepared under the care of the Prophet Joseph Smith, contained 254 pages and was printed by Frederick G. Williams and Co. in Kirtland, Ohio. The revelations ranged over a period from 1828 to 1834. Seven Lectures on Faith, which had been given before the School of the Elders in Kirtland were also added to the volume, not as revelations, but as stated by the brethren at that time "as profitable for doctrine." In this book there also appeared two articles written by Oliver Cowdery, one on *Marriage*, and the other on *Governments and Laws in General*. These were ordered printed in the volume with the revelations, but it should be remembered this was done in the absence and without the approval of the Prophet Joseph Smith, who with President Frederick G. Williams was in Michigan at the time this action was taken. Hence these articles are not, as some have supposed, revelations and were not so considered by the Church. It was on the occasion of the acceptance of the revelations for publication, November 12, 1831, when the Prophet wrote in his journal the comment on the value of the revelations.

[3]D. and C., Sec. 70.

mercy of our God that we are spared to assemble together, many of us have gone at the command of the Lord in defiance of everything evil, and obtained blessings unspeakable, in consequence of which our names are sealed in the Lamb's book of life, for the Lord has spoken it. It is the privilege of every Elder to speak of the things of God; and could we all come together with one heart and one mind in perfect faith the veil might as well be rent today as next week, or any other time, and if we will but cleanse ourselves and covenant before God, to serve Him, it is our privilege to have an assurance that God will protect us at all times.[4]—F. W. R., pp. 13-14. (Oct. 25, 1831.)

Perfect Love a Safeguard Against Falling from Grace

Brother Joseph Smith, Jr., said: That he intended to do his duty before the Lord and hoped that the brethren would be patient as they had a considerable distance (to go). Also said that the promise of God was that the greatest blessings which God had to bestow should be given to those who contributed to the support of his family while he was translating the fulness of the Scriptures. Until we have perfect love we are liable to fall and when we have a testimony that our names are sealed in the Lamb's book of life we have perfect love and then it is impossible for false Christs to deceive us; also said, that the Lord held the Church bound to provide for families of the absent Elders while proclaiming the Gospel; further, that God had often sealed up the heavens because of covetousness in the Church. The Lord would cut short his work in righteousness and except the Church receive the fulness of the Scriptures that they would yet fail.[5]—F. W. R., p. 16. (Oct. 25, 1831.)

Comment on Revision of the Scriptures

Upon my return from Amherst Conference, I resumed the translation of the Scriptures.[6] From sundry revelations which

---

[4]This is not a verbatim statement, but report in the minutes of the meeting of the conference held on that day.

[5]This is also a statement from the minutes of the Prophet's remarks as recorded by the scribe, not a verbatim report but a synopsis.

[6]Shortly after the organization of the Church the Lord commanded Joseph Smith to make a translation of the Bible by revelation. It had been made known in the translation of the Book of Mormon that because of iniquity "many plain and precious things" were "taken away from the book, which

had been received, it was apparent that many important points touching the salvation of men, had been taken from the Bible, or lost before it was compiled. It appeared from what truths were left, that if God rewarded every one according to the deeds

---

is the book of the Lamb of God." (I Nephi 13:28.) Moreover, because of the "many plain and precious things which have been taken out of the book, which were plain unto the understanding of the children of men, according to the plainness which is in the Lamb of God—because of these things which are taken away out of the gospel of the Lamb, an exceeding great many do stumble, yea, insomuch that Satan hath great power over them." (I Nephi 13:29.)

As early as April, 1829, the Lord declared that many of these plain and precious sayings were to be restored, not only through the Book of Mormon, but through a revision of the Bible. When Oliver Cowdery came to the Prophet Joseph Smith and commenced to write at the Prophet's dictation in the translation of the Book of Mormon, the Lord said unto him: "Verily verily, I say unto you, that there are records which contain much of my gospel, which have been kept back because of the wickedness of the people. And now I command you, that if you have good desires—a desire to lay up treasures for yourself in heaven—then shall you assist in bringing to light, with your gift, those parts of my scriptures which have been hidden because of iniquity." (D. and C. 6:26-27.) A few days later, in the same month of April, 1829, the Lord again referred to the coming forth of these scriptures in the following words: "I would that ye should continue until you have finished this record [i.e. the Book of Mormon], which I have entrusted unto him [Joseph Smith]. And then, behold, other records have I, that I will give unto you power that you may assist to translate." (D. and C. 9:1-2.) The earliest manuscripts of the Bible translation are in the handwriting of Oliver Cowdery. These bear the beginning date of June, 1830, and continue until October 21, the same year. This was done in Harmony, Pennsylvania, and Fayette, New York. Brother Cowdery then departed for Ohio and Missouri in response to a call from the Lord for missionary service among the Lamanites. (D. and C. 32:1-2.) At this juncture, John Whitmer served as scribe to the Prophet as the translation continued. In December, 1830, having recently joined the Church, Sidney Rigdon came to Fayette to see the Prophet Joseph and was called by revelation to do this writing in the following words: "And a commandment I give unto thee—that thou shalt write for him; and the scriptures shall be given, even as they are in mine own bosom, to the salvation of mine own elect." (D. and C. 35:20.) In February, 1831, the Lord spoke again, saying: "Thou shalt ask, and my scriptures shall be given as I have appointed, and they shall be preserved in safety; and it is expedient that thou shouldst hold thy peace concerning them, and not teach them until ye have received them in full. And I give unto you a commandment that then ye shall teach them unto all men; for they shall be taught unto all nations, kindreds, tongues and people." (D. and C. 42:56-58.)

From June, 1830, until March 7, 1831, the Brethren labored with the revision of the early chapters of Genesis. However, on the latter date they were instructed to begin a translation of the New Testament also. (D. and C. 45:60-61.) This they began the next day, March 8. The work continued through both the Old and New Testaments until July 2, 1833, when the Prophet finished the work as far as the Lord required of him at that time. In the remaining eleven years of his life the Prophet further revised some passages and attempted to prepare the manuscript for publication. However, because of persecution and a lack of financial means, this was not accomplished before his death. The original manuscripts came into the hands of his widow, Emma Smith, who refused to give them to the Church, although a request was made to her for them. The manuscripts subsequently came

done in the body the term "Heaven" as intended for the Saints' eternal home, must include more kingdoms than one. Accordingly, on the 16th of February, 1832, while translating St. John's Gospel, myself and Elder Rigdon saw the following vision.[7]—D. H. C. 1:245. (Feb. 16, 1832.)

The Prophet's Views on the Vision

Nothing could be more pleasing to the Saints upon the order of the Kingdom of the Lord, than the light which burst upon the world through the foregoing vision. Every law, every commandment, every promise, every truth, and every point touching the destiny of man, from Genesis to Revelation, where the purity of the Scriptures remains unsullied by the folly of men, go to show the perfection of the theory (of different degrees of glory in the future life) and witness the fact that the document is a transcript from the records of the eternal world. The sublimity of the ideas; the purity of the language; the scope for action; the continued duration for completion, in order that the heirs of salvation may confess the Lord and bow the knee; the rewards for faithfulness, and the punishments for sins, are so much beyond the narrow-mindedness of men, that every man is constrained to exclaim: "It came from God." (Feb., 1832.) D. H. C. 1:252-253.

Search the Revelations of God

The following excerpts are taken from the second number of the *Evening and Morning Star*, published in August, 1832. The article from which these thoughts are taken was prepared by the Prophet and published in this issue of the *Star*.

Search the scriptures—search the revelations which we publish, and ask your Heavenly Father, in the name of His Son Jesus Christ, to manifest the truth unto you, and if you do it with an eye single to His glory nothing doubting, He will answer you by the power of His Holy Spirit. You will then know for yourselves and not for another. You will not then be dependent on man for the knowledge of God; nor will there

into the possession of the Reorganized Church and were used for the publication of the "Inspired Version" of the Bible in 1867.

A partial copy of the manuscripts was made in the spring of 1845 by Dr. John M. Bernhisel and is now in the archives of the Church in Salt Lake City. Although it is an incomplete copy, it served to corroborate the accuracy of the printed editions insofar as its limited scope permits. The Prophet Joseph Smith's translation of the Bible is one of the greatest tangible evidences of his spiritual insight and divine calling.

[7]Section 76, D. and C.

be any room for speculation. No; for when men receive their instruction from Him that made them, they know how He will save them. Then again we say: Search the Scriptures, search the Prophets and learn what portion of them belongs to you and the people of the nineteenth century. You, no doubt, will agree with us, and say, that you have no right to claim the promises of the inhabitants before the flood; that you cannot found your hopes of salvation upon the obedience of the children of Israel when journeying in the wilderness, nor can you expect that the blessings which the apostles pronounced upon the churches of Christ eighteen hundred years ago, were intended for you. Again, if others' blessings are not your blessings, others' curses are not your curses; you stand then in these last days, as all have stood before you, agents unto yourselves, to be judged according to your works.

Every Man an Agent for Himself

Every man lives for himself. Adam was made to open the way of the world, and for dressing the garden. Noah was born to save seed of everything, when the earth was washed of its wickedness by the flood; and the Son of God came into the world to redeem it from the fall. But except a man be born again, he cannot see the kingdom of God. This eternal truth settles the question of all men's religion. A man may be saved, after the judgment, in the terrestrial kingdom, or in the telestial kingdom, but he can never see the celestial kingdom of God, without being born of water and the Spirit. He may receive a glory like unto the moon, [i. e. of which the light of the moon is typical], or a star, [i. e. of which the light of the stars is typical], but he can never come unto Mount Zion, and unto the city of the living God, the heavenly Jerusalem, and to an innumerable company of angels; to the general assembly and Church of the Firstborn, which are written in heaven, and to God the judge of all, and to the spirits of just men made perfect, and to Jesus the Mediator of the new covenant, unless he becomes as a little child, and is taught by the Spirit of God. Wherefore, we again say, search the revelations of God; study the prophecies, and rejoice that God grants unto the world Seers and Prophets. They are they who saw the mysteries of godliness; they saw the flood before it came; they saw angels ascending and descending upon a ladder that reached from earth to heaven: they saw the stone cut out of the mountain, which filled the whole earth; they saw the Son of God come from the regions of bliss and dwell with men on earth; they saw the deliverer come out of Zion, and turn away ungodliness from Jacob; they saw the glory of the Lord when he showed the transfiguration of the earth on the mount; they saw every mountain laid low and every valley exalted when the Lord was taking vengeance upon the wicked; they saw truth spring out of the earth, and righteousness look down from heaven in the last days, before the Lord came the second time to gather his elect; they saw the end of wickedness on earth, and the Sabbath of creation crowned with peace; they saw the end of the glorious thousand years, when Satan was loosed for a little season; they saw the day of judgment when all men received according to their works, and they saw the heaven and the earth flee away to make room for the city of God, when the righteous receive an inheritance in eternity. And, fellow sojourners upon earth, it is your privilege to purify yourselves and come up to the same glory, and see for yourselves, and know for yourselves. Ask, and it shall be given you; seek and ye shall find; knock, and it shall be opened unto you.— E. and M. S. August, 1832. D. H. C. 1:282-284.

Letter to Editor Seaton

January 4, 1833, the Prophet wrote to Mr. N. E. Seaton, an editor of a newspaper, the following words of counsel and warning concerning the state of the world and the purpose of the Lord in the restoration spoken of by the ancient prophets.

Kirtland, January 4th, 1833.

Mr. Editor:—Sir, Considering the liberal principles upon which your interesting and valuable paper is published, myself being a subscriber, and feeling a deep interest in the cause of Zion, and in the happiness of my brethren of mankind, I cheerfully take up my pen to contribute my mite at this very interesting and important period.

For some length of time I have been carefully viewing the state of things, as it now appears, throughout our Christian land; and have looked at it with feelings of the most painful anxiety. While upon one hand I behold the manifest withdrawal of God's Holy Spirit, and the veil of stupidity which seems to be drawn over the hearts of the people; upon the other hand, I behold the judgments of God that have swept, and are still sweeping hundreds and thousands of our race, and I fear unprepared, down to the shades of death. With this solemn and alarming fact before me, I am led to exclaim, "O that my head were waters, and mine eyes a fountain of tears, that I might weep day and night."

A Sleeping Christianity

I think that it is high time for a Christian world to awake out of sleep, and cry mightily to that God, day and night, whose anger we have justly incurred. Are not these things a sufficient stimulant to arouse the faculties, and call forth the energies of every man, woman or child, that possesses feelings of sympathy for their fellows, or that is in any degree endeared to the budding cause of our glorious Lord? I leave an intelligent community to answer this important question, with a confession, that this is what has caused me to overlook my own inability, and expose my weakness to a learned world; but, trusting in that God who has said that these things are hid from the wise and prudent and revealed unto babes, I step forth into the field to tell you what the Lord is doing, and what you must do, to enjoy the smiles of your Savior in these last days.

The Covenant with Israel

The time has at last arrived when the God of Abraham, of Isaac, and of Jacob, has set his hand again the second time to recover the remnants of his people, which have been left from Assyria, and from Egypt, and from Pathros, and from Cush, and from Elam, and from Shinar, and from Hamath, and from the islands of the sea, and with them to bring in the fulness of the Gentiles, and establish that covenant with them, which was promised when their sins should be taken away. See Isaiah xi; Romans xi:25, 26 and 27, and also Jeremiah xxxi:31, 32 and 33. This covenant has never been established with the house of Israel, nor with the house of Judah, for it requires two parties to make a covenant, and those two parties must be agreed, or no covenant can be made.

Christ, in the days of His flesh, proposed to make a covenant with them, but they rejected Him and His proposals, and in consequence thereof, they were broken off, and no covenant was made with them at that time.   But their unbelief has not rendered the promise of God of none effect: no, for there was another day limited in David, which was the day of His power; and then His people, Israel, should be a willing people;—and He would write His law in their hearts, and print it in their thoughts; their sins and their iniquities He would remember no more.

The Covenant to the Gentiles

Thus after this chosen family had rejected Christ and His proposals, the heralds of salvation said to them, "Lo we turn unto the Gentiles"; and the Gentiles received the covenant, and were grafted in from whence the chosen family were broken off; but the Gentiles have not continued in the goodness of God, but have departed from the faith that was once delivered to the Saints, and have broken the covenant in which their fathers were established (see Isaiah xxiv:5); and have become high-minded, and have not feared; therefore, but few of them will be gathered with the chosen family.   Have not the pride, high-mindedness, and unbelief of the Gentiles, provoked the Holy One of Israel to withdraw His Holy Spirit from them, and send forth His judgments to scourge them for their wickedness?   This is certainly the case.

The Earth Defiled

Christ said to His disciples (Mark xvi:17 and 18), that these signs should follow them that believe:—"In my name shall they cast out devils; they shall speak with new tongues; they shall take up serpents; and if they drink any deadly thing, it shall not hurt them; they shall lay hands on the sick, and they shall recover"; and also, in connection with this, read 1st Corinthians, 12th chapter.   By the foregoing testimonies we may look at the Christian world and see the apostasy there has been from the apostolic platform; and who can look at this and not exclaim, in the language of Isaiah, "The earth also is defiled under the inhabitants thereof; because they have transgressed the laws, changed the ordinances, and broken the everlasting covenant?"

The plain fact is this, the power of God begins to fall

upon the nations, and the light of the latter-day glory begins to break forth through the dark atmosphere of sectarian wickedness, and their iniquity rolls up into view, and the nations of the Gentiles are like the waves of the sea, casting up mire and dirt, or all in commotion, and they are hastily preparing to act the part allotted them, when the Lord rebukes the nations, when He shall rule them with a rod of iron, and break them in pieces like a potter's vessel. The Lord declared to His servants, some eighteen months since, that He was then withdrawing His Spirit from the earth; and we can see that such is the fact, for not only the churches are dwindling away, but there are no conversions, or but very few: and this is not all, the governments of the earth are thrown into confusion and division; and *Destruction*, to the eye of the spiritual beholder, seems to be written by the finger of an invisible hand, in large capitals, upon almost every thing we behold.

How to Escape Judgments

And now what remains to be done, under circumstances like these? I will proceed to tell you what the Lord requires of all people, high and low, rich and poor, male and female, ministers and people, professors of religion and non-professors, in order that they may enjoy the Holy Spirit of God to a fullness, and escape the judgments of God, which are almost ready to burst upon the nations of the earth. Repent of all your sins, and be baptized in water for the remission of them, in the name of the Father, and of the Son, and of the Holy Ghost, and receive the ordinance of the laying on of the hands of him who is ordained and sealed unto this power, that ye may receive the Holy Spirit of God; and this is according to the Holy Scriptures, and the Book of Mormon; and the only way that man can enter into the celestial kingdom. These are the requirements of the new covenant, or first principles of the Gospel of Christ: then "Add to your faith, virtue; and to virtue, knowledge; and to knowledge, temperance; and to temperance, patience; and to patience, godliness; and to godliness, brotherly kindness; and to brotherly kindness, charity [or love]; for if these things be in you, and abound, they make you that ye shall neither be barren nor unfruitful, in the knowledge of our Lord Jesus Christ."

Zion and Jerusalem

The Book of Mormon is a record of the forefathers of our western tribes of Indians; having been found through the ministration of an holy angel, and translated into our own language by the gift and power of God, after having been hid up in the earth for the last fourteen hundred years, containing the word of God which was delivered unto them.   By it we learn that our western tribes of Indians are descendants from that Joseph who was sold into Egypt, and that the land of America is a promised land unto them, and unto it all the tribes of Israel will come, with as many of the Gentiles as shall comply with the requisitions of the new covenant.   But the tribe of Judah will return to old Jerusalem.   The city of Zion spoken of by David, in the one hundred and second Psalm, will be built upon the land of America, "And the ransomed of the Lord shall return, and come to Zion with songs and everlasting joy upon their heads." (Isaiah xxxv:10); and then they will be delivered from the overflowing scourge that shall pass through the land. But Judah shall obtain deliverance at Jerusalem.   See Joel ii:32; Isaiah xxvi:20 and 21; Jeremiah xxxi:12; Psalms 1:5; Ezekiel xxxiv:11, 12 and 13.   These are testimonies that the Good Shepherd will put forth His own sheep, and lead them out from all nations where they have been scattered in a cloudy and dark day, to Zion, and to Jerusalem; besides many more testimonies which might be brought.

And now I am prepared to say by the authority of Jesus Christ, that not many years shall pass away before the United States shall present such a scene of *bloodshed* as has not a parallel in the history of our nation; pestilence, hail, famine, and earthquake will sweep the wicked of this generation from off the face of the land, to open and prepare the way for the return of the lost tribes of Israel from the north country.   The people of the Lord, those who have complied with the requirements of the new covenant, have already commenced gathering together to Zion, which is in the state of Missouri; therefore I declare unto you the warning which the Lord has commanded me to declare unto this generation, remembering that the eyes of my Maker are upon me, and that to Him I am accountable for every word I say, wishing nothing worse to my fellow-men than their eternal salvation; therefore, "Fear God, and give glory to Him, for the hour of His judgment is come." Repent ye, repent ye, and embrace the everlasting covenant, and flee to Zion, before the overflowing scourge overtake you, for there are those now living upon the earth whose eyes shall not be closed in death until they see all these things, which I have spoken, fulfilled. Remember these things; call upon the Lord while He is near, and seek Him while He may be found, is the exhortation of your unworthy servant.

(Signed) JOSEPH SMITH, JUN.

—D. H. C. 1:312-316.

Important Correspondence with the Brethren in Zion

The "Olive Leaf" is the name given by the Prophet to the wonderful revelation known as Sec. 88, in the *Doctrine and Covenants*. There are few, if any, revelations given to the Church—and to the world if the world will receive them—greater than this "Olive Leaf, plucked from the Tree of Paradise." In this letter to W. W. Phelps, one of the presiding brethren in Missouri, the Prophet raises a warning voice based upon the word of the Lord as revealed in the revelation and correspondence from Missouri.

Kirtland, January 14, 1833.

Brother William W. Phelps:

I send you the "olive leaf" which we have plucked from the Tree of Paradise, the Lord's message of peace to us; for though our brethren in Zion indulge in feelings towards us, which are not according to the requirements of the new covenant, yet, we have the satisfaction of knowing that the Lord approves of us, and has accepted us, and established His name in Kirtland for the salvation of the nations; for the Lord will have a place whence His word will go forth, in these last days, in purity; for if Zion will not purify herself, so as to be approved of in all things, in His sight, He will seek another people; for His work will go on until Israel is gathered, and they who will not hear His voice, must expect to feel His wrath. Let me say unto you, seek to purify yourselves, and also the inhabitants of Zion, lest the Lord's anger be kindled to fierceness.

A Warning to Zion

Repent, repent, is the voice of God to Zion; and strange as it may appear, yet it is true, mankind will persist in self-justification until all their iniquity is exposed, and their character past being redeemed, and that which is treasured up in their hearts be exposed to the gaze of mankind. I say to you (and what I say to you I say to all), hear the warning voice of God, lest Zion fall, and the Lord swear in His wrath the inhabitants of Zion shall not enter into His rest.

The brethren in Kirtland pray for you unceasingly, for, knowing the terrors of the Lord, they greatly fear for you. You will see that the Lord commanded us, in Kirtland, to build a house of God, and establish a school for the Prophets, this is the word of the Lord to us, and we must, yea, the Lord helping us, we will obey: as on conditions of our obedience He has promised us great things; yea, even a visit from the heavens to honor us with His own presence. We greatly fear before the Lord lest we should fail of this great honor, which our Master proposes to confer on us; we are seeking for humility and great faith lest we be ashamed in His presence. Our hearts are greatly grieved at the spirit which is breathed both in your letter and that of Brother Gilbert's, the very spirit which is wasting the strength of Zion like a pestilence; and if it is not detected and driven from you, it will ripen Zion for the threatened judgments of God. Remember God sees the secret springs of human action, and knows the hearts of all living.

Brother, suffer us to speak plainly, for God has respect to the feelings of His Saints, and He will not suffer them to be tantalized with impunity. * * * All we can say by way of conclusion is, if the fountain of our tears be not dried up, we will still weep for Zion. This from your brother who trembles for Zion, and for the wrath of heaven, which awaits her if she repents not.

(Signed) JOSEPH SMITH, JUN.

D. H. C. 1:316.

An Epistle

Of the First Presidency, to the Church of Christ in Thompson, Geauga County, Ohio.

Kirtland, February 6th, 1833.

Dear Brethren:

We salute you, by this our epistle, in the bonds of love, rejoicing in your steadfastness in the faith which is in Christ Jesus our Lord; and we desire your prosperity in the ways of truth and righteousness, praying for you continually, that your faith fail not, and that you may overcome all the evils with which you are surrounded, and become pure and holy before God, even our Father, to whom be glory for ever and ever. Amen.

It has seemed good unto the Holy Spirit and unto us, to send this our epistle to you by the hand of our beloved Brother Salmon Gee, your messenger, who has been ordained by us, in obedience to the commandments of God, to the office of Elder to preside over the Church in Thompson, taking the oversight thereof, to lead you and to teach the things which are according to godliness; in whom we have great confidence, as we presume also you have, we therefore say to you, yea, not us only, but the Lord also, receive him as such, knowing that the Lord has appointed him to this office for your good, holding him up by your prayers, praying for him continually that he may be endowed with wisdom and understanding in the knowledge of the Lord, that through him you may be kept from evil spirits, and all strifes and dissensions, and grow in grace and in the knowledge of our Lord and Savior Jesus Christ.

Brethren beloved, continue in brotherly love, walk in meekness, watching unto prayer, that you be not overcome. Follow after peace, as said our beloved brother Paul, that you may be the children of our Heavenly Father, and not give occasion for stumbling, to Saint or sinner. Finally, brethren, pray for us, that we may be enabled to do the work whereunto we are called, that you may enjoy the mysteries of God, even a fullness; and may the grace of our Lord Jesus Christ be with you all. Amen.

JOSEPH SMITH, JUN.
SIDNEY RIGDON,
FREDERICK G. WILLIAMS.
—D. H. C. 1:324, 325.

Order for Instruction in the Church

Kirtland, April 13, 1833.

Dear Brother Carter:—Your letter to Brother Jared is just put into my hand, and I have carefully perused its contents, and embrace this opportunity to answer it. We proceed to answer your questions: first concerning your labor in the region where you live; we acquiesce in your feelings on this subject until the mouth of the Lord shall name. Respecting the vision you speak of we do not consider ourselves bound to receive any revelation from any one man or woman without his being legally constituted and ordained to that authority, and giving sufficient proof of it.

Order by Which Revelation Comes

I will inform you that it is contrary to the economy of God for any member of the Church, or any one, to receive instruction for those in authority, higher than themselves; therefore you will see the impropriety of giving heed to them; but if any person have a vision or a visitation from a heavenly messenger, it must be for his own benefit and instruction; for the fundamental principles, government, and doctrine of the Church are vested in the keys of the kingdom. Respecting an apostate, or one who has been cut off from the Church, and who wishes to come in again, the law of our Church expressly says that such shall repent, and be baptized, and be admitted as at the first.

The duty of a High Priest is to administer in spiritual and holy things, and to hold communion with God; but not to exercise monarchial government, or to appoint meetings for the Elders without their consent. And again, it is the High Priests' duty to be better qualified to teach principles and doctrines, than the Elders; for the office of Elder is an appendage to the High Priesthood, and it concentrates and centers in one. And again, the process of laboring with members: We are to deal with them precisely as the Scriptures direct. If thy brother trespass against thee, take him between him and thee alone; and, if he make thee satisfaction, thou hast saved thy brother; and if not, proceed to take another with thee, etc., and when there is no Bishop, they are to be tried by the voice of the Church; and if an Elder, or a High Priest be present, he is to take the lead in managing the business; but if not, such as have the highest authority should preside.

With respect to preparing to go to Zion:—First it would be pleasing to the Lord that the church or churches going to Zion should be organized, and a suitable person appointed who is well acquainted with the condition of the church, and he be sent to Kirtland to inform the Bishop, and procure a license from him agreeable to the revelation: by so doing you will prevent confusion and disorder, and escape many difficulties that attend an unorganized band in journeying in the last days.

And again, those in debt, should in all cases pay their debts; and the rich are in no wise to cast out the poor, or leave them behind, for it is said that the poor shall inherit the earth.

You quoted a passage in Jeremiah, with regard to journeying to Zion; the word of the Lord stands sure, so let it be done.

There are two paragraphs in your letter which I do not commend, as they are written blindly. Speaking of the Elders being sent like lightning from the bow of Judah; the second, no secret in the councils of Zion. You mention these as if fear rested upon your mind, otherwise we cannot understand it. And again we never inquire at the hand of God for special revelation only in case of their being no previous revelation to suit the case; and that in a council of High Priests. * * *

It is a great thing to inquire at the hands of God, or to come into His presence; and we feel fearful to approach Him on subjects that are of little or no consequence, to satisfy the queries of individuals, especially about things the knowledge of which men ought to obtain in all sincerity, before God, for themselves, in humility by the prayer of faith; and more especially a teacher or a High Priest in the Church. I speak these things not by way of reproach, but by way of instruction; and I speak as if acquainted with you, whereas we are strangers to each other in the flesh.

I love your soul, and the souls of the children of men, and pray and do all I can for the salvation of all.

I now close by sending you a salutation of peace in the name of the Lord Jesus Christ. Amen.

The blessing of our Lord Jesus Christ be and abide with you all. Amen.

JOSEPH SMITH, JUN.

—D. H. C. 1:338, 339.

Items of Instruction Concerning the Consecration of Property

Brother Edward Partridge:

Sir:—I proceed to answer your questions, concerning the consecration of property:—First, it is not right to condescend to very great particulars in taking inventories. The fact is this, a man is bound by the law of the Church, to consecrate to the Bishop, before he can be considered a legal heir to the kingdom of Zion; and this, too, without constraint; and unless he does this, he cannot be acknowledged before the Lord on the Church Book; therefore, to condescend to particulars, I will tell you that every man must be his own judge how much he should receive, and how much he should suffer to remain in the hands of the Bishop. I speak of those who consecrate more than they need for the support of themselves and their families.

By Mutual Consent

The matter of consecration must be done by the mutual consent of both parties; for to give the Bishop power to say how much every man shall have, and he be obliged to comply with the Bishop's judgment, is giving to the Bishop more power than a king has; and, upon the other hand, to let every man say how much he needs, and the Bishop be obliged to comply with his judgment, is to throw Zion into confusion, and make a slave of the Bishop. The fact is, there must be a balance or equilibrium of power, between the Bishop and the people; and thus harmony and good-will may be preserved among you.

Therefore, those persons consecrating property to the Bishop in Zion, and then receiving an inheritance back, must reasonably show to the Bishop that they need as much as they claim. But in case the two parties cannot come to a mutual agreement, the Bishop is to have nothing to do about receiving such consecrations; and the case must be laid before a council of twelve High Priests, the Bishop not being one of the council, but he is to lay the case before them.

* * *

We were not a little surprised to hear that some of our letters of a public nature, which we sent for the good of Zion, have been kept back from the Bishop. This is conduct which we highly disapprobate.

Answers to Queries to Brother Phelps' Letter of June 4th

First, in relation to the poor: When the Bishops are appointed according to our recommendation, it will devolve upon them to see to the poor, according to the laws of the Church.

* * *

Say to the brothers Hulet and to all others, that the Lord never authorized them to say that the devil, his angels, or the sons of perdition, should ever be restored; for their state of destiny was not revealed to man, is not revealed, nor ever shall be revealed, save to those who are made partakers thereof; consequently those who teach this doctrine have not received it of the Spirit of the Lord. Truly Brother Oliver declared it to be the doctrine of devils. We, therefore, command that this doctrine be taught no more in Zion. We sanction the decision of the Bishop and his council, in relation to this doctrine being a bar to communion.

* * *

We conclude our letter by the usual salutation, in token of the new and everlasting covenant. We hasten to close, because the mail is just going.

JOSEPH SMITH, JUN.,
SIDNEY RIGDON,
F. G. WILLIAMS.

P. S.—We feel gratified with the way in which Brother William W. Phelps is conducting the *Star* at present, we hope he will seek to render it more and more interesting. In relation to the size of Bishoprics: When Zion is once properly regulated there will be a Bishop to each square of the size of the one we send you with this; but at present it must be done according to wisdom. It is needful, brethren, that you should be all of one heart, and of one mind, in doing the will of the Lord.

There should exist the greatest freedom and familiarity among the rulers in Zion.

We were exceedingly sorry to hear the complaint that was made in Brother Edward Partridge's letter, that the letters attending the Olive Leaf had been kept from him, as it is meet that he should know all things in relation to Zion, as the Lord has appointed him to be a judge in Zion. We hope, dear brethren, that the like occurrence will not take place again. When we direct letters to Zion to any of the High Priests, which pertain to the regulation of her affairs, we always design that they should be laid before the Bishop, so as to enable him to perform his duty. We say so much hoping it will be received in kindness; and our brethren will be careful of one another's feelings, and walk in love, honoring one another more than themselves, as is required by the Lord.

Yours as ever,

J. S.,
S. R.,
F. G. W.

—D. H. C. 1:364-368.

Excerpts from the Second Communication to the Brethren in Zion

Kirtland, July 2nd, 1833.

To the Brethren in Zion:

*   *   *

The Gift of Tongues

We are engaged in writing a letter to Eugene [branch] respecting the two Smiths, as we have received two letters from them; one from John Smith, the other from the Elder of the Church [Eden Smith]. As to the gift of tongues, all we can say is, that in this place we have received it as the ancients did: we wish you, however, to be careful, lest in this you be deceived. Guard against evils which may arise from any accounts given by women, or otherwise; be careful in all things lest any root of bitterness spring up among you, and thereby many be defiled. Satan will no doubt trouble you about the gift of tongues, unless you are careful; you cannot watch him too closely, nor pray too much. May the Lord give you wisdom in all things. In a letter mailed last week, you will doubtless, before you receive this, have obtained information about the New Translation. Consign the box of the Book of Commandments to N. K. Whitney & Co., Kirtland, Geauga county, Ohio, care of Kelly and Walworth, Cleveland, Cuyahoga county, Ohio.

*   *   *

We conclude by giving our heartiest approbation to every measure calculated for the spread of the truth, in these last days; and our strongest desires, and sincerest prayers for the prosperity of Zion. Say to all the brethren and sisters in Zion, that they have our hearts, our best wishes, and the strongest desires of our spirits for their welfare, temporal, spiritual, and

eternal. As ever, we salute you in the name of the Lord Jesus.
Amen.

JOSEPH SMITH, JUN.,
SIDNEY RIGDON,
F. G. WILLIAMS.

—D. H. C. 1:368-370.

Minor Events in Zion and Kirtland—an Appeal to the Governor of Missouri

* * *

Letter to Vienna Jaques

September 4.—I wrote as follows to Sister Vienna Jaques,
at Independence, Missouri:

Dear Sister:—Having a few leisure moments, I sit down
to communicate to you a few words, which I know I am under
obligation to improve for your satisfaction, if it should be a
satisfaction for you to receive a few words from your unworthy
brother in Christ. I received your letter some time since, containing a history of your journey and your safe arrival, for
which I bless the Lord; I have often felt a whispering since I
received your letter, like this: "Joseph, thou art indebted to thy
God for the offering of thy Sister Vienna, which proved a savor
of life as pertaining to thy pecuniary concerns. Therefore she
should not be forgotten of thee, for the Lord hath done this,
and thou shouldst remember her in all thy prayers and also by
letter, for she oftentimes calleth on the Lord, saying, O Lord,
inspire thy servant Joseph to communicate by letter some word
to thine unworthy handmaiden, and say all my sins are forgiven,
and art thou not content with the chastisement where-with
thou hast chastised thy handmaiden?" Yes, sister, this seems
to be the whispering of a spirit, and judge ye what spirit it is.
I was aware when you left Kirtland that the Lord would chasten
you, but I prayed fervently in the name of Jesus that you might
live to receive your inheritance, agreeable to the commandment
which was given concerning you. I am not at all astonished
at what has happened to you, neither to what has happened
to Zion, and I could tell all the whys and wherefores of all
these calamities. But alas, it is in vain to warn and give precepts, for all men are naturally disposed to walk in their own
paths as they are pointed out by their own fingers, and are not

willing to consider and walk in the path which is pointed out by another, saying, This is the way, walk ye in it, although he should be an unerring director, and the Lord his God sent him. Nevertheless I do not feel disposed to cast any reflections, but I feel to cry mightily unto the Lord that all things which have happened may work together for good; yea, I feel to say, O Lord, let Zion be comforted, let her waste places be built up and established an hundred fold; let Thy Saints come unto Zion out of every nation; let her be exalted to the third heavens, and let Thy judgment be sent forth unto victory; and after this great tribulation, let Thy blessing fall upon Thy people, and let Thy handmaid live till her soul shall be satisfied in beholding the glory of Zion; for notwithstanding her present affliction, she shall yet arise and put on her beautiful garments, and be the joy and glory of the whole earth. Therefore let your heart be comforted; live in strict obedience to the commandments of God, and walk humbly before Him, and He will exalt thee in His own due time. I will assure you that the Lord has respect unto the offering you made. Brother David W. Patten has just returned from his tour to the east, and gives us great satisfaction as to his ministry. He has raised up a church of about eighty-three members in that part of the country where his friends live—in the state of New York. Many were healed through his instrumentality, several cripples were restored. As many as twelve that were afflicted came at a time from a distance to be healed; he and others administered in the name of Jesus, and they were made whole. Thus you see that the laborers in the Lord's vineyard are laboring with their might, while the day lasts, knowing "the night soon cometh when no man can work."   (Signed) JOSEPH SMITH.
          —D. H. C. 1:407-409.

Remembrance of Canada Saints—Correspondence and Petition Relative to Missouri Affairs

November 19.—I wrote as follows, from Kirtland, to Moses C. Nickerson, Mount Pleasant, Upper Canada:

Anxiety for Afflicted Saints

Brother Moses:—We arrived at this place on the fourth ultimo, after a fatiguing journey, during which we were blessed with usual health. We parted with Father and Mother Nickerson at Buffalo, in good health, and they expressed a degree of satisfaction for the prosperity and blessings of their journey.

Since our arrival here, Brother Sidney has been afflicted with sore eyes, which is probably the reason why you have not previously heard from us, as he was calculating to write you immediately. But though I expect he will undoubtedly write you soon, as his eyes are evidently better, yet, lest you should be impatient to learn something concerning us, I have thought that perhaps a few lines from me, though there may be a lack of fluency according to the *literati* of the age, might be received with a degree of satisfaction on your part, at least, when you call to mind the near relation with which we are united by the everlasting ties of the Gospel of our Lord Jesus Christ.

We found our families and the Church in this place well, generally. Nothing of consequence happened while we were absent, except the death of one of our brethren—David Johnson —a young man of great worth as a private citizen among us, the loss of whom we justly mourn.

We are favored with frequent intelligence from different sections of our country, respecting the progress of the Gospel, and our prayers are daily to our Father, that it may greatly spread, even till all nations shall hear the glorious news and come to a knowledge of the truth.

We have received letters from our brethren in Missouri of late, but we cannot tell, from their contents, the probable extent to which those persons who are desirous to expel them from that country will carry their unlawful and unrighteous purposes. Our brethren have applied to the executive of the state, who has promised them all the assistance that the civil law can give; and in all probability a suit has been commenced ere this.

We are informed, however, that those persons are very violent, and threaten immediate extermination upon all those who profess our doctrine. How far they will be suffered to execute their threats, we know not, but we trust in the Lord, and leave the event with Him to govern in His own wise providence.

I shall expect a communication from you on receipt of

this, and hope you will give me information concerning the brethren, their health, faith, etc., also inform me concerning our friends with whom we formed acquaintance.

You are aware, no doubt, dear brother, that anxieties inexpressible crowd themselves continually upon my mind for the Saints, when I consider the many temptations to which we are subject, from the cunning and flattery of the great adversary of our souls: and I can truly say, with much fervency have I called upon the Lord for our brethren in Canada. And when I call to mind with what readiness they received the word of truth by the ministry of Brother Sidney and myself, I am truly under great obligations to humble myself before Him.

Coming of the Son of Man

When I contemplate the rapidity with which the great and glorious day of the coming of the Son of Man advances, when He shall come to receive His Saints unto Himself, where they shall dwell in His presence, and be crowned with glory and immortality: when I consider that soon the heavens are to be shaken, and the earth tremble and reel to and fro; and that the heavens are to be unfolded as a scroll when it is rolled up; and that every mountain and island are to flee away, I cry out in my heart, What manner of persons ought we to be in all holy conversation and godliness!

You remember the testimony which I bore in the name of the Lord Jesus, concerning the great work which He has brought forth in the last days. You know my manner of communication, how that in weakness and simplicity, I declared to you what the Lord had brought forth by the ministering of His holy angels to me for this generation. I pray that the Lord may enable you to treasure these things in your mind, for I know that His Spirit will bear testimony to all who seek diligently after knowledge from Him. I hope you will search the Scriptures to see whether these things are not also consistent with those things which the ancient Prophets and Apostles have written.

I remember Brother Freeman and wife, Ransom also, and Sister Lydia, and little Charles, with all the brethren and sisters. I entreat for an interest in all your prayers before the throne of mercy, in the name of Jesus. I hope the Lord will grant

that I may see you all again, and above all that we may overcome, and sit down together in the kingdom of our Father.

Your brother, etc.

JOSEPH SMITH.

—D. H. C. 1:441-443.

The Prophet's Reflections Concerning Sidney Rigdon

The character of Sidney Rigdon is here vividly portrayed, followed
by an earnest prayer for his salvation and a prophecy concerning his
posterity. It is true that his generations have been hunted for, and some of
them found. His son, John W., joined the Church many years ago after
wandering in the wilderness of darkness. More recently one of his grandsons,
now an old man, joined the Church and another grandson has expressed
himself favorably towards the Church. In this way, in part at least, we see
the fulfilment of this earnest plea by the Prophet Joseph Smith.

Nothing of note occurred from the falling of the stars
on the 13th, to this date, November 19th, when my heart is
somewhat sorrowful, but I feel to trust in the Lord, the God
of Jacob. I have learned in my travels that man is treacherous
and selfish, but few excepted.

Sidney Rigdon

Brother Sidney is a man whom I love, but he is not capable
of that pure and steadfast love for those who are his benefactors that should characterize a President of the Church of
Christ. This, with some other little things, such as a selfishness
and independence of mind, which too often manifested destroy
the confidence of those who would lay down their lives for
him—these are his faults. But notwithstanding these things,
he is a very great and good man; a man of great power of
words, and can gain the friendship of his hearers very quickly.
He is a man whom God will uphold, if he will continue faithful
to his calling. O God, grant that he may, for the Lord's sake.
Amen.

And again, blessed be Brother Sidney: notwithstanding
he shall be high and lifted up, yet he shall bow down under
the yoke like unto an ass that croucheth beneath his burden,
that learneth his master's will by the stroke of the rod; thus
saith the Lord: yet, the Lord will have mercy on him, and he
shall bring forth much fruit, even as the vine of the choice
grape, when her clusters are ripe, before the time of the gleaning

of the vintage; and the Lord shall make his heart merry as with sweet wine, because of Him who putteth forth His hand, and lifteth him up out of deep mire, and pointeth him out the way, and guideth his feet when he stumbles, and humbleth him in his pride. Blessed are his generations: nevertheless one shall hunt after them as a man hunteth after an ass that has strayed in the wilderness, and straightway findeth him and bringeth him into the fold. Thus shall the Lord watch over his generation, that they may be saved. Even so, Amen.

The Prophet's Maxims

The man who willeth to do well, we should extol his virtues, and speak not of his faults behind his back. A man who wilfully turneth away from his friend without a cause, is not easily forgiven. The kindness of a man should never be forgotten. That person who never forsaketh his trust, should ever have the highest place of regard in our hearts, and our love should never fail, but increase more and more, and this is my disposition and these my sentiments.
—D. H. C. 1:443-444.

Instructions on Sale of Land in Zion

The following is an excerpt taken from a communication to the Saints in Zion, who had been driven from their homes and basely persecuted by a mob in Jackson County, Missouri.

Kirtland, December 5, 1833.
*   *   *

I wish, when you receive this letter, that you would collect every particular, concerning the mob, from the beginning, and send us a correct statement of facts, as they occurred from time to time, that we may be enabled to give the public correct information on the subject; and inform us also of the situation of the brethren, with respect to their means of sustenance.

I would inform you that it is not the will of the Lord for you to sell your lands in Zion, if means can possibly be procured for your sustenance without. Every exertion should be made to maintain the cause you have espoused, and to contribute to the necessities of one another, as much as possible, in this your great calamity, and remember not to murmur at the dealings of God with his creatures. You are not as yet brought into as trying circumstances as were the ancient Prophets and Apostles. Call to mind Daniel, the three Hebrew children, Jeremiah, Paul, Stephen, and many others, too numerous to mention, who were stoned, sawn asunder, tempted, slain with the sword, and wandered about in sheep skins and goat skins, being destitute, afflicted, tormented, of whom the world was not worthy. They wandered in deserts and in mountains, and hid in dens, and caves of the earth; yet they all obtained a good report through faith; and amidst all their afflictions they rejoiced that they were counted worthy to receive persecution for Christ's sake.

We know not what we shall be called to pass through before Zion is delivered and established; therefore, we have great need to live near to God, and always be in strict obedience to all His commandments, that we may have a conscience void of offense toward God and man. It is your privilege to use every lawful means in your power to seek redress for your grievances from your enemies, and prosecute them to the extent of the law; but it will be impossible for us to render you any temporal assistance, as our means are already exhausted, and we are deeply in debt, and know of no means whereby we shall be able to extricate ourselves.

The inhabitants of this county threaten our destruction, and we know not how soon they may be permitted to follow the example of the Missourians; but our trust is in God, and we are determined, His grace assisting us, to maintain the cause and hold out faithful unto the end, that we may be crowned with crowns of celestial glory, and enter into the rest that is prepared for the children of God.

We are now distributing the type, and intend to commence setting today, and issue a paper the last of this week, or beginning of next. We wrote to Elder Phelps some time since, and also sent by Elder Hyde, for the list of names of subscribers to the *Star,* which we have not yet received; and, until we receive it, the most of the subscribers will be deprived of the paper; and when you receive this, if you have not sent the list, I wish you to attend to it immediately, as much inconvenience will follow a delay.

*   *   *

We learn by Elder Phelps, that the brethren have surrendered their arms to the Missourians, and are fleeing across the river. If that is the case, it is not meet that they should recommence hostilities with them; but, if not, you should maintain the ground as long as there is a man left, as the spot of ground upon which you were located, is the place appointed of the Lord for your inheritance, and it is right in the sight of God that you contend for it to the last.

You will recollect that the Lord has said, that Zion should not be removed out of her place; therefore the land should not be sold, but be held by the Saints, until the Lord in His wisdom shall open a way for your return; and until that time, if you can purchase a tract of land in Clay county, for present emergencies, it is right you should do so, if you can do it, and not sell your land in Jackson county. It is not safe for us to send you a written revelation on the subject, but what is stated above is according to wisdom. I haste to a close to give room for Brother Oliver, and remain yours in the bonds of the everlasting covenant,   Joseph Smith, Jun.
—D. H. C. 1:448-451.

A Letter from the Prophet Joseph Smith to the Exiled Saints in Missouri

This letter depicts the tenderness and sympathy of the Prophet towards the Saints in Missouri, and his desire to encourage and strengthen them by faith and hope in this great hour of their deep affliction.

Kirtland Mills, Ohio,
December 10, 1833.

Edward Partridge, W. W. Phelps, John Whitmer, A. S. Gilbert, John Corrill, Isaac Morley, and all the Saints whom it may concern:

Beloved Brethren:—This morning's mail brought letters from Bishop Partridge, and Elders Corrill and Phelps, all mailed at Liberty, November 19th, which gave us the melancholy intelligence of your flight from the land of your inheritance, having been driven before the face of your enemies in that place.

From previous letters we learned that a number of our brethren had been slain, but we could not learn from the letters referred to above, that there had been more than one killed, and that one Brother Barber; and that Brother Dibble was wounded in the bowels. We were thankful to learn that no more had been slain, and our daily prayers are that the Lord will not suffer His Saints, who have gone up to His land to keep His commandments, to stain His holy mountain with their blood.

Zion to Suffer Affliction

I cannot learn from any communication by the Spirit to me, that Zion has forfeited her claim to a celestial crown, notwithstanding the Lord has caused her to be thus afflicted, except it may be some individuals, who have walked in disobedience, and forsaken the new covenant; all such will be made manifest by their works in due time. I have always expected that Zion would suffer some affliction, from what I could learn from the commandments which have been given. But I would remind you of a certain clause in one which says, that after much tribulation cometh the blessing. By this, and also others, and also one received of late, I know that Zion, in the due time of the Lord, will be redeemed; but how many will be the days of her purification, tribulation, and affliction, the Lord has kept hid from my eyes; and when I inquire concerning this subject, the voice of the Lord is: Be still, and know that I am God; all those who suffer for my name shall reign with me, and he that layeth down his life for my sake shall find it again.

Now, there are two things of which I am ignorant; and the Lord will not show them unto me, perhaps for a wise purpose in Himself—I mean in some respects—and they are these: Why God has suffered so great a calamity to come upon Zion, and what the great moving cause of this great affliction is; and again, by what means He will return her back to her inheritance, with songs of everlasting joy upon her head. These two things, brethren, are in part kept back that they are not plainly shown unto me; but there are some things that are plainly manifest which have incurred the displeasure of the Almighty.

The Righteous Suffer with the Guilty

When I contemplate upon all things that have been manifested, I am aware that I ought not to murmur, and do not murmur, only in this, that those who are innocent are compelled to suffer for the iniquities of the guilty; and I cannot account for this, only on this wise, that the saying of the Savior has not been strictly observed: "If thy right eye offend thee, pluck it out, and cast it from thee; or if thy right arm offend thee, cut it off, and cast it from thee." Now the fact is, if any of the members of our body is disordered, the rest of our body will be affected with it, and then all are brought into bondage together; and yet, notwithstanding all this, it is with difficulty that I can restrain my feelings when I know that you, my brethren, with whom I have had so many happy hours—sitting, as it were, in heavenly places in Christ Jesus; and also, having the witness which I feel, and ever have felt, of the purity of your motives— are cast out, and are as strangers and pilgrims on the earth, exposed to hunger, cold, nakedness, peril, sword—I say when I contemplate this, it is with difficulty that I can keep from complaining and murmuring against this dispensation; but I am sensible that this is not right, and may God grant that not-withstanding your great afflictions and sufferings, there may not anything separate us from the love of Christ.

Brethren, when we learn your sufferings, it awakens every sympathy of our hearts; it weighs us down; we cannot refrain from tears, yet, we are not able to realize, only in part, your sufferings: and I often hear the brethren saying, they wish they were with you, that they might bear a part of your suffer-ings; and I myself should have been with you, had not God prevented it in the order of His providence, that the yoke of affliction might be less grievous upon you, God having fore-warned me, concerning these things, for your sake; and also, Elder Cowdery could not lighten your afflictions by tarrying longer with you, for his presence would have so much the more enraged your enemies; therefore God hath dealt mercifully with us. O brethren, let us be thankful that it is as well with us as it is, and we are yet alive and peradventure, God hath laid up in store great good for us in this generation, and may grant that we may yet glorify His name.

The Value of an Inheritance

I feel thankful that there have no more denied the faith; I pray God in the name of Jesus that you all may be kept in the faith unto the end: let your sufferings be what they may, it is better in the eyes of God that you should die, than that you should give up the land of Zion, the inheritances which you have purchased with your moneys; for every man that giveth not up his inheritance, though he should die, yet, when the Lord shall come, he shall stand upon it, and with Job, in his flesh he shall see God. Therefore, this is my counsel, that you retain your lands, even unto the uttermost, and employ every lawful means to seek redress of your enemies; and pray to God, day and night, to return you in peace and in safety to the lands of your inheritance: and when the judge fail you, appeal unto the executive; and when the executive fail you, appeal unto the president; and when the president fail you, and all laws fail you, and the humanity of the people fail you, and all things else fail you but God alone, and you continue to weary Him with your importunings, as the poor woman did the unjust judge, He will not fail to execute judgment upon your enemies, and to avenge His own elect that cry unto Him day and night.

Behold, He will not fail you! He will come with ten thousand of His Saints, and all His adversaries shall be destroyed with the breath of His lips! All those who keep their inheritances, notwithstanding they should be beaten and driven, shall be likened unto the wise virgins who took oil in their lamps. But all those who are unbelieving and fearful, will be likened unto the foolish virgins, who took no oil in their lamps: and when they shall return and say unto the Saints, Give us of your lands—behold, there will be no room found for them. As respects giving deeds, I would advise you to give deeds as far as the brethren have legal and just claims for them, and then let every man answer to God for the disposal of them.

I would suggest some ideas to Elder Phelps, not knowing that they will be of any real benefit but suggest them for consideration. I would be glad if he were here, were it possible for him to come, but dare not advise, not knowing what shall befall us, as we are under very heavy and serious threatenings from a great many people in this place.

But, perhaps, the people in Liberty may feel willing, God having power to soften the hearts of all men, to have a press established there; and if not, in some other place; any place where it can be the most convenient, and it is possible to get to it; God will be willing to have it in any place where it can be established in safety. We must be wise as serpents and harmless as doves. Again, I desire that Elder Phelps should collect all the information, and give us a true history of the beginning and rise of Zion, and her calamities.

A Prayer for the Afflicted Saints

Now hear the prayer of your unworthy brother in the new and everlasting covenant:—O my God! Thou who hast called and chosen a few, through Thy weak instrument by commandment, and sent them to Missouri, a place which Thou didst call Zion, and commanded Thy servants to consecrate it unto Thyself for a place of refuge and safety for the gathering of Thy Saints, to be built up a holy city unto Thyself; and as Thou hast said that no other place should be appointed like unto this, therefore, I ask Thee in the name of Jesus Christ, to return Thy people unto their houses and their inheritances, to enjoy the fruit of their labors; that all the waste places may be built up; that all the enemies of Thy people, who will not repent and turn unto Thee, may be destroyed from off the face of the land; and let a house be built and established unto Thy name; and let all the losses that Thy people have sustained, be rewarded unto them, even more than four-fold, that the borders of Zion may be enlarged forever; and let her be established no more to be thrown down; and let all Thy Saints, when they are scattered as sheep, and are persecuted, flee unto Zion, and be established in the midst of her; and let her be organized according to Thy law; and let this prayer ever be recorded before Thy face. Give Thy Holy Spirit unto my brethren, unto whom I write; send Thine angels to guard them, and deliver them from all evil; and when they turn their faces toward Zion, and bow down before Thee and pray, may their sins never come up before Thy face; neither have place in the book of Thy remembrance; and may they depart from all their iniquities. Provide food for them as Thou doest for the ravens; provide clothing to cover their nakedness, and houses that they may dwell therein; give unto them friends in abundance, and let their names be recorded in the Lamb's book of life, eternally before Thy face. Amen.

Finally, brethren, the grace of our Lord Jesus Christ be with you all until His coming in His kingdom. Amen.

—D. H. C. 1:453-456.   JOSEPH SMITH, JUN.

Blessings Given to Oliver Cowdery and the Prophet's Family

On the eighteenth day of December, 1833, the Prophet and a number of the leading Elders of the Church assembled in the printing office which had just been built and that office was dedicated by the Prophet Joseph Smith. Following this ceremony the Prophet proceeded to bless Oliver Cowdery and several members of the Smith family, after having conferred upon Joseph Smith, Sen., the office and Priesthood of Patriarch of the Church. The blessings follow.

Blessing of Oliver Cowdery

Blessed of the Lord is Brother Cowdery, nevertheless there are two evils in him that he must needs forsake, or he cannot altogether escape the buffetings of the adversary. If he forsake these evils he shall be forgiven, and shall be made like unto the bow which the Lord hath set in the heavens; and shall be a sign and an ensign unto the nations. Behold, he is blessed of the Lord for his constancy and steadfastness in the work of the Lord; wherefore, he shall be blessed in his generation, and they shall never be cut off, and he shall be helped out of many troubles; and if he keep the commandments, and hearken unto the counsel of the Lord, his rest shall be glorious.

The Prophet's Blessing to His Father and Mother

Thus spoke the Seer, and these are the words which fell from his lips while the visions of the Almighty were open to his view, saying:

Blessed of the Lord is my father, for he shall stand in the midst of his posterity and shall be comforted by their blessings when he is old and bowed down with years, and shall be called a prince over them, and shall be numbered among those who hold the right of Patriarchal Priesthood, even the keys of that ministry: for he shall assemble together his posterity like unto Adam; and the assembly which he called shall be an example for my father, for thus it is written of him:

Three years previous to the death of Adam, he called Seth, Enos, Cainan, Mahalaleel, Jared, Enoch and Methuselah, who were High Priests, with the residue of his posterity, who were righteous, into the valley of Adam-ondi-Ahman, and there bestowed upon them his last blessing. And the Lord appeared unto them, and they rose up and blessed Adam, and called

him Michael, the Prince, the Archangel. And the Lord administered comfort unto Adam, and said unto him, I have set
thee to be at the head: a multitude of nations shall come of
thee, and thou art a Prince over them forever.

So shall it be with my father: he shall be called a prince
over his posterity, holding the keys of the patriarchal Priesthood over the kingdom of God on earth, even the Church of
the Latter-day Saints, and he shall sit in the general assembly
of Patriarchs, even in council with the Ancient of Days when
he shall sit and all the Patriarchs with him and shall enjoy
his right and authority under the direction of the Ancient of
Days.

And blessed also, is my mother, for she is a mother in
Israel, and shall be a partaker with my father in all his patriarchal blessings.

And blessed, also, are my brothers and my sisters, for they
shall yet find redemption in the house of the Lord, and their
offsprings shall be a blessing, a joy and a comfort unto them.

Blessed is my mother, for her soul is ever filled with benevolence and philanthropy; and notwithstanding her age, she
shall yet receive strength and be comforted in the midst of her
house: and thus saith the Lord. She shall have eternal life.

And again, blessed is my father, for the hand of the Lord
shall be over him, and he shall be full of the Holy Ghost; for
he shall predict whatsoever shall befall his posterity unto the
latest generation, and shall see the affliction of his children pass
away, and their enemies under their feet: and when his head
is fully ripe he shall behold himself as an olive tree whose
branches are bowed down with much fruit. Behold, the blessings of Joseph by the hand of his progenitor, shall come upon
the head of my father and his seed after him, to the uttermost,
even he shall be a fruitful bough; he shall be as a fruitful bough,
even a fruitful bough by a well whose branches run over the
wall, and his seed shall abide in strength, and the arms of their
hands shall be made strong by the hands of the mighty God of
Jacob, and the God of his fathers: even the God of Abraham,
Isaac and Jacob, shall help him and his seed after him: even
the Almighty shall bless him with blessings of heaven above
and his seed after him, and the blessings of the deep that lieth
under: and his seed shall rise up and call him blessed. He shall
be as the vine of the choice grape when her clusters are fully

ripe: and he shall also possess a mansion on high, even in the Celestial Kingdom. His counsel shall be sought for by thousands, and he shall have place in the house of the Lord; for he shall be mighty in the council of the elders, and his days shall yet be lengthened out: and when he shall go hence he shall go in peace, and his rest shall be glorious; and his name shall be had in remembrance to the end. Amen.

Oliver Cowdery, Clerk and Recorder.
—MSS., Dec. 18, 1833.

The Prophet's Blessing to His Brother Hyrum

Blessed of the Lord is my brother Hyrum for the integrity of his heart; he shall be girt about with strength, truth and faithfulness shall be the strength of his loins. From generation to generation he shall be a shaft in the hand of his God to execute judgment upon his enemies: and he shall be hid by the hand of the Lord that none of his secret parts shall be discovered unto his enemies, unto his hurt. His name shall be called a blessing among men. His acquaintance shall be among kings, and he shall be sought for that he may sit in council, by nations and kings that are afar off; and thousands of souls shall he be an instrument in the hand of his God in bringing unto salvation. And when he is in trouble, and great tribulation has come upon him, he shall remember the God of Jacob, and he shall shield him from the power of Satan. He shall receive counsel in the house of the Most High that he may be strengthened in hope. He shall be as a cooling spring that breaketh forth at the foot of the mountain, overshadowed with choice trees bowed down with ripe fruit, that yieldeth both nourishment to the appetite and quencheth the thirst, thereby yielding refreshment to the weary traveller: and the goings of his feet shall ever be by streams of living water. He shall not fail nor want for knowledge, for the Lord his God shall put forth his hand and lift him up and shall call upon him with his voice in the way wherein he is travelling, that he may be established forever. He shall stand in the tracks of his father and be numbered among those who hold the right of Patriarchal Priesthood, even the Evangelical Priesthood and power shall be upon him, that in his old age his name may be magnified on the earth. Behold he shall be blessed with an abundance of riches of the earth—gold, silver, and treasures of precious stones, of diamonds and platina. His chariots shall be numerous, and his cattle shall multiply abundantly: horses, mules, asses, camels, dromedaries, and swift beasts, that he may magnify the name of the Lord and benefit the poor. Yea, this shall be the desire of his soul, to comfort the needy and bind up the broken in heart. His children shall be many and his posterity numerous, and they shall rise up and call him blessed. And he shall have eternal life. Amen.

Oliver Cowdery, Clerk and Recorder.
Given in Kirtland, December 18, 1833.

Blessing to Samuel and William Smith

Blessed of the Lord is my brother Samuel, because the Lord shall say unto him, Samuel, Samuel; therefore he shall be made a teacher in the house of the Lord, and the Lord shall mature his mind in judgment, and thereby he shall obtain the esteem and fellowship of his brethren, and his soul shall be established and he shall benefit the house of the Lord, because he shall obtain answer to prayer in his faithfulness.

Brother William is as the fierce lion, which divideth not the spoil because of his strength; and in the pride of his heart he will neglect the more weighty matters until his soul is bowed down in sorrow; and then he shall return and call on the name of his God, and shall find forgiveness, and shall wax valiant, therefore, he shall be saved unto the uttermost; and as the roaring lion of the forest in the midst of his prey, so shall the hand of his generation be lifted up against those who are set on high, that fight against the God of Israel; fearless and undaunted shall they be in battle, in avenging the wrongs of the innocent, and relieving the oppressed; therefore, the blessings of the God of Jacob shall be in the midst of his house, notwithstanding his rebellious heart.

And now, O God, let the residue of my father's house ever come up in remembrance before Thee, that Thou mayest save them from the hand of the oppressor, and establish their feet upon the Rock of Ages, that they may have place in Thy house, and be saved in Thy kingdom; and let all things be even as I have said, for Christ's sake. Amen.

—D. H. C. 1:466-467.

Counsel and Admonition

Dear Brethren in Christ, and Companions in Tribulation:—
It seemeth good unto us to drop a few lines to you giving you
some instruction relative to conducting the affairs of the kingdom of God, which has been committed unto us in these latter
times, by the will and testament of our Mediator, whose inter-
cessions in our behalf are lodged in the bosom of the Eternal
Father, and ere long will burst with blessings upon the heads
of all the faithful.

We have all been children, and are too much so at the
present time; but we hope in the Lord that we may grow in
grace and be prepared for all things which the bosom of futurity may disclose unto us. Time is rapidly rolling on, and the
prophecies must be fulfilled. The days of tribulation are fast
approaching, and the time to test the fidelity of the Saints has
come. Rumor with her ten thousand tongues is diffusing her
uncertain sounds in almost every ear; but in these times of sore
trial, let the Saints be patient and see the salvation of God.
Those who cannot endure persecution, and stand in the day
of affliction, cannot stand in the day when the Son of God
shall burst the veil, and appear in all the glory of His Father,
with all the holy angels.

The Evils of Hasty Ordinations

On the subject of ordination, a few words are necessary.
In many instances there has been too much haste in this thing,
and the admonition of Paul has been too slightingly passed over,
which says, "Lay hands suddenly upon no man." Some have
been ordained to the ministry, and have never acted in that
capacity, or magnified their calling at all. Such may expect
to lose their appointment, except they awake and magnify their
office. Let the Elders abroad be exceedingly careful upon this
subject, and when they ordain a man to the holy ministry, let
him be a faithful man, who is able to teach others also; that
the cause of Christ suffer not. It is not the multitude of preachers
that is to bring about the glorious millennium! but it is those
who are "called, and chosen, and faithful."

Avoiding Disputes

Let the Elders be exceedingly careful about unnecessarily disturbing and harrowing up the feelings of the people. Remember that your business is to preach the Gospel in all humility and meekness, and warn sinners to repent and come to Christ.

Avoid contentions and vain disputes with men of corrupt minds, who do not desire to know the truth. Remember that "it is a day of warning, and not a day of many words." If they receive not your testimony in one place, flee to another remembering to cast no reflections, nor throw out any bitter sayings. If you do your duty, it will be just as well with you, as though all men embraced the Gospel.

Be careful about sending boys to preach the Gospel to the world; if they go let them be accompanied by some one who is able to guide them in the proper channel, lest they become puffed up, and fall under condemnation, and into the snare of the devil. Finally, in these critical times, be careful; call on the Lord day and night; beware of pride; beware of false brethren, who will creep in among you to spy out your liberties. Awake to righteousness, and sin not; let your light shine, and show yourselves workmen that need not be ashamed, rightly dividing the word of truth. Apply yourselves diligently to study, that your minds may be stored with all necessary information.

We remain your brethren in Christ, anxiously praying for the day of redemption to come, when iniquity shall be swept from the earth, and everlasting righteousness brought in. Farewell. (Dec., 1833.) D. H. C. 1:467-469.

SECTION TWO
1834-1837

SECTION TWO

———◆———

Dear Brethren in Christ, and Companions in Tribulation:

*   *   *

Spiritual Darkness

Consider for a moment, brethren, the fulfillment of the
words of the prophet; for we behold that darkness covers the
earth, and gross darkness the minds of the inhabitants thereof
—that crimes of every description are increasing among men
—vices of great enormity are practiced—the rising generation
growing up in the fullness of pride and arrogance—the aged
losing every sense of conviction, and seemingly banishing
every thought of a day of retribution—intemperance, immorality, extravagance, pride, blindness of heart, idolatry, the loss
of natural affection; the love of this world, and indifference
toward the things of eternity increasing among those who profess a belief in the religion of heaven, and infidelity spreading
itself in consequence of the same—men giving themselves up
to commit acts of the foulest kind, and deeds of the blackest
dye, blaspheming, defrauding, blasting the reputation of neighbors, stealing, robbing, murdering; advocating error and opposing the truth, forsaking the covenant of heaven, and denying
the faith of Jesus—and in the midst of all this, the day of the
Lord fast approaching when none except those who have won
the wedding garment will be permitted to eat and drink in the
presence of the Bridegroom, the Prince of Peace!

The World's Deplorable Condition

Impressed with the truth of these facts what can be the
feelings of those who have been partakers of the heavenly gift
and have tasted the good word of God, and the powers of the
world to come? Who but those that can see the awful precipice

upon which the world of mankind stands in this generation, can labor in the vineyard of the Lord without feeling a sense of the world's deplorable situation? Who but those who have duly considered the condescension of the Father of our spirits, in providing a sacrifice for His creatures, a plan of redemption, a power of atonement, a scheme of salvation, having as its great objects, the bringing of men back into the presence of the King of heaven, crowning them in the celestial glory, and making them heirs with the Son to that inheritance which is incorruptible, undefiled, and which fadeth not away—who but such can realize the importance of a perfect walk before all men, and a diligence in calling upon all men to partake of these blessings? How indescribably glorious are these things to mankind! Of a truth they may be considered tidings of great joy to all people; and tidings, too, that ought to fill the earth and cheer the heart of every one when sounded in his ears. The reflection that everyone is to receive according to his own diligence and perseverance while in the vineyard, ought to inspire everyone who is called to be a minister of these glad tidings, to so improve his talent that he may gain other talents, that when the Master sits down to take an account of the conduct of His servants, it may be said, Well done, good and faithful servant: thou hast been faithful over a few things; I will now make thee ruler over many things: enter thou into the joy of thy Lord.

Some may pretend to say that the world in this age is fast increasing in righteousness; that the dark ages of superstition and blindness have passed, when the faith of Christ was known and held only by a few, when ecclesiastical power had an almost universal control over Christendom, and the consciences of men were bound by the strong chains of priestly power: but now, the gloomy cloud is burst, and the Gospel is shining with all the resplendent glory of an apostolic day; and that the kingdom of the Messiah is greatly spreading, that the Gospel of our Lord is carried to divers nations of the earth, the Scriptures translating into different tongues; the ministers of truth crossing the vast deep to proclaim to men in darkness a risen Savior, and to erect the standard of Emmanuel where light has never shone; and that the idol is destroyed, the temple of images forsaken; and those who but a short time previous followed the traditions of their fathers and sacrificed their own flesh to appease the wrath of some imaginary god, are now raising their voices in the worship of the Most High, and are lifting their thoughts up to Him with the full expectation that one day they will meet with a joyful reception in His everlasting kingdom!

The Law of Free Agency

But a moment's candid reflection upon the principles of these systems, the manner in which they are conducted, the individuals employed, the apparent object held out as an inducement to cause them to act, we think, is sufficient for every candid man to draw a conclusion in his own mind whether this is the order of heaven or not. We deem it a just principle, and it is one the force of which we believe ought to be duly considered by every individual, that all men are created equal, and that all have the privilege of thinking for themselves upon all matters relative to conscience. Consequently, then, we are not disposed, had we the power, to deprive any one of exercising that free independence of mind which heaven has so graciously bestowed upon the human family as one of its choicest gifts; but we take the liberty (and this we have a right to do) of looking at this order of things a few moments, and contrasting it with the order of God as we find it in the sacred Scriptures. In this review, however, we shall present the points as we consider they were really designed by the great Giver to be understood, and the happy results arising from a performance of the requirements of heaven as revealed to every one who obeys them; and the consequence attending a false construction, a misrepresentation, or a forced meaning that was never designed in the mind of the Lord when He condescended to speak from the heavens to men for their salvation.

*   *   *

Obedience to Governments Necessary

All regularly organized and well established governments have certain laws by which, more or less, the innocent are protected and the guilty punished. The fact admitted that certain laws are good, equitable and just, ought to be binding upon the individual who admits this, and lead him to observe in the strictest manner an obedience to those laws. These laws when violated, or broken by the individual, must, in justice, convict his mind with a double force, if possible, of the extent and magnitude of his crime; because he could have no plea of ignorance to produce; and his act of transgression was openly committed against light and knowledge. But the individual who may be ignorant and imperceptibly transgresses or violates laws, though the voice of the country requires that he should suffer, yet he will never feel that remorse of conscience that the other will, and that keen, cutting reflection will never rise in his breast that otherwise would, had he done the deed, or committed the offense in full conviction that he was breaking the law of his country, and having previously acknowledged the same to be just. It is not our intention by these remarks, to attempt to place the law of man on a parallel with the law of heaven; because we do not consider that it is formed in the same wisdom and propriety; neither do we consider that it is sufficient in itself to bestow anything on man in comparison with the law of heaven, even should it promise it. The laws of men may guarantee to a people protection in the honorable pursuits of this life, and the temporal happiness arising from a protection against unjust insults and injuries; and when this is said, all is said, that can be in truth, of the power, extent, and influence of the laws of men, exclusive of the law of God. The law of heaven is presented to man, and as such guarantees to all who obey it a reward far beyond any earthly considera- tion; though it does not promise that the believer in every age should be exempt from the afflictions and troubles arising from different sources in consequence of the acts of wicked men on earth. Still in the midst of all this there is a promise predicated upon the fact that it is the law of heaven, which transcends the law of man, as far as eternal life the temporal; and as the bless- ings which God is able to give, are greater than those which can be given by man. Then, certainly, if the law of man is binding upon man when acknowledged, how much more must the law of heaven be! And as much as the law of heaven is more perfect than the law of man, so much greater must be the reward if obeyed. The law of man promises safety in temporal life; but the law of God promises that life which is eternal, even an inheritance at God's own right hand, secure from all the powers of the wicked one.

As Man Approaches God He Is Enlightened

We consider that God has created man with a mind capable of instruction, and a faculty which may be enlarged in proportion to the heed and diligence given to the light communicated from heaven to the intellect; and that the nearer man approaches perfection, the clearer are his views, and the greater his enjoyments, till he has overcome the evils of his life and lost every desire for sin; and like the ancients, arrives at that point of faith where he is wrapped in the power and glory of his Maker and is caught up to dwell with Him. But we consider that this is a station to which no man ever arrived in a moment: he must have been instructed in the government and laws of that kingdom by proper degrees, until his mind is capable in some measure of comprehending the propriety, justice, equality, and consistency of the same. For further instruction we refer you to Deut. xxxii, where the Lord says, that Jacob is the lot of His inheritance. He found him in a desert land, and in the waste, howling wilderness; He led him about, He instructed him, He kept him as the apple of His eye, etc.; which will show the force of the last item advanced, that it is necessary for men to receive an understanding concerning the laws of the heavenly kingdom, before they are permitted to enter it: we mean the celestial glory. So dissimilar are the governments of men, and so divers are their laws, from the government and laws of heaven, that a man, for instance, hearing that there was a country on this globe called the United States of North America, could take his journey to this place without first learning the laws of governments; but the conditions of God's kingdom are such, that all who are made partakers of that glory, are under the necessity of learning something respecting it previous to their entering into it. But the foreigner can come to this country without knowing a syllable of its laws, or even subscribing to obey them after he arrives. Why? Because the government of the United States does not require it: it only requires an obedience to its laws after the individual has arrived within its jurisdiction.

Laws of Man Not on Parallel with Laws of Heaven

As we previously remarked, we do not attempt to place the law of man on a parallel with the law of heaven; but we will bring forward another item, to further urge the propriety of yielding obedience to the law of heaven, after the fact is admitted, that the laws of man are binding upon man. Were a king to extend his dominion over the habitable earth, and send forth his laws which were the most perfect kind, and command his subjects one and all to yield obedience to the same, and add as a reward to those who obeyed them, that at a certain period they should be called to attend the marriage of his son, who in due time was to receive the kingdom, and they should be made equal with him in the same; and fix as a penalty for disobedience that every individual guilty of it should be cast out at the marriage feast, and have no part nor portion with his government, what rational mind could for a moment accuse the king with injustice for punishing such rebellious subjects? In the first place his laws were just, easy to be complied with, and perfect: nothing of a tyrannical nature was required of them; but the very construction of the laws was equity and beauty; and when obeyed would produce the happiest condition possible to all who adhered to them, beside the last great benefit of sitting down with a royal robe in the presence of the king at the great, grand marriage supper of his son, and be made equal with him in all the affairs of the kingdom.

"Thus Saith the King"

When these royal laws were issued, and promulgated throughout the vast dominion, every subject, when interrogated whether he believed them to be from his sovereign or not, answered, Yes; I know they are, I am acquainted with the signature, for it is as usual. *Thus saith the King!* This admitted, the subject is bound by every consideration of honor to his country, his king, and his own personal character, to observe in the strictest sense every requisition in the royal edict. Should any escape the search of the ambassadors of the king, and never hear these last laws, giving his subjects such exalted privileges, an excuse might be urged in their behalf, and they escape the censure of the king. But for those who had heard, who had admitted, and who had promised obedience to these just laws no excuse could be urged, and when brought into the presence of the king certainly, justice would require that they should suffer a penalty. Could that king be just in admitting these rebellious individuals into the full enjoyment and privileges with his son, and those who had been obedient to his commandments? Certainly not. Because they disregarded the voice of their lawful king; they had no regard for his virtuous laws, for his dignity, nor for the honor of his name; neither for the honor of their country, nor their private virtue. They regarded not his authority enough to obey him, neither did they regard the immediate advantages and blessings arising from these laws if kept, so destitute were they of virtue and goodness; and above all, they regarded so little the joy and satisfaction of a legal seat in the presence of the king's only son, and to be made equal with him in all the blessings, honors, comforts, and felicities of his kingdom, that they turned away from a participation in them, and considered that they were beneath their present notice, though they had no doubt as to the real authenticity of the royal edict.

*   *   *

How could a government be conducted with harmony if its administrators were possessed with such different dispositions and different principles? Could it prosper? Could it flourish? Would harmony prevail? Would order be established, and could justice be executed in righteousness in all branches of its departments? No! In it were two classes of men as dissimilar as light and darkness, virtue and vice, justice and injustice, truth and falsehood, holiness and sin. One class were perfectly harmless and virtuous: they knew what virtue was for they had lived in the fullest enjoyment of it, and their fidelity to truth had been fairly tested by a series of years of faithful obedience to all its heavenly precepts. They knew what good order was, for they had been orderly and obedient to the laws imposed on them by their wise sovereign, and had experienced the benefits arising from a life spent in his government till he has now seen proper to make them equal with his son. Such individuals would indeed adorn any court where perfection was one of its main springs of action, and shine far more fair than the richest gem in the diadem of the prince.

*   *   *

God Speaks from Heaven

We take the sacred writings into our hands, and admit that they were given by direct inspiration for the good of man. We believe that God condescended to speak from the heavens and declare His will concerning the human family, to give them just and holy laws, to regulate their conduct, and guide them in a direct way, that in due time He might take them to Himself, and make them joint heirs with His Son. But when this fact is admitted, that the immediate will of heaven is contained in the Scriptures, are we not bound as rational creatures to live in accordance to all its precepts? Will the mere admission, that this is the will of heaven ever benefit us if we do not comply with all its teachings? Do we not offer violence to the Supreme Intelligence of heaven, when we admit the truth of its teachings, and do not obey them? Do we not descend below our own knowledge, and the better wisdom which heaven has endowed us with, by such a course of conduct? For these reasons, if we have direct revelations given us from heaven, surely those revelations were never given to be trifled with, without the trifler's incurring displeasure and vengeance upon his own head, if there is any justice in heaven; and that there is must be admitted by every individual who admits the truth and force of God's teachings, His blessings and cursings, as contained in the sacred volume.

The Faithful to Receive Celestial Rest

Here, then, we have this part of our subject immediately before us for consideration: God has in reserve a time, or period appointed in His own bosom, when He will bring all His subjects, who have obeyed His voice and kept His commandments, into His celestial rest. This rest is of such perfection and glory, that man has need of a preparation before he can, according to the laws of that kingdom, enter it and enjoy its blessings. This being the fact, God has given certain laws to the human family, which, if observed, are sufficient to prepare them to inherit this rest. This, then, we conclude, was the purpose of God in giving His laws to us: if not, why, or for what were they given? If the whole family of man were as well off without them as they might be with them, for what purpose or intent were they ever given? Was it that God wanted to merely show that He could talk? It would be nonsense to suppose that He would condescend to talk in vain: for it would be in vain, and to no purpose whatever (if the law of God were of no benefit to man): because, all the commandments contained in the law of the Lord, have the sure promise annexed of a reward to all who obey, predicated upon the fact that they are really the promises of a Being who cannot lie, One who is abundantly able to fulfill every tittle of His word: and if man were as well prepared, or could be as well prepared, to meet God without their ever having been given in the first instance, why were they ever given? for certainly, in that case they can now do him no good.

All Governments Have Laws

As we previously remarked, all well established and properly organized governments have certain fixed and prominent laws for the regulation and management of the same. If man has grown to wisdom and is capable of discerning the propriety of laws to govern nations, what less can be expected from the Ruler and Upholder of the universe? Can we suppose that He has a kingdom without laws? Or do we believe that it is composed of an innumerable company of beings who are entirely beyond all law? Consequently have need of nothing to govern or regulate them? Would not such ideas be a reproach to our Great Parent, and at variance with His glorious intelligence? Would it not be asserting that man had found out a secret beyond Deity? That he had learned that it was good to have laws, while God after existing from eternity and having power to create man, had not found out that it was proper to have laws for His government? We admit that God is the great source and fountain from whence proceeds all good; that He is perfect intelligence, and that His wisdom is alone sufficient to govern and regulate the mighty creations and worlds which shine and blaze with such magnificence and splendor over our heads, as though touched with His finger and moved by His Almighty word. And if so, it is done and regulated by law; for without law all must certainly fall into chaos. If, then, we admit that God is the source of all wisdom and understanding, we must admit that by His direct inspiration He has taught man that law is necessary in order to govern and regulate His own immediate interest and welfare; for this reason, that law is beneficial to promote peace and happiness among men. And as before remarked, God is the source from whence proceeds all good; and if man is benefited by law, then certainly, law is good; and if law is good, then law, or the principle of it emanated from God; for God is the source of all good;

consequently, then, he was the first Author of law, or the principle of it, to mankind.

★   ★   ★

What Is the Purpose of Existence?

Think for a moment, of the greatness of the Being who created the Universe; and ask, could He be so inconsistent with His own character, as to leave man without a law or rule by which to regulate his conduct, after placing him here, where, according to the formation of his nature he must in a short period sink into the dust? Is there nothing further; is there no existence beyond this veil of death which is so suddenly to be cast over all of us? If there is, why not that Being who had power to place us here, inform us something of the hereafter? If we had power to place ourselves in this present existence, why not have power to know what shall follow when that dark veil is cast over our bodies? If in this life we receive our all; if when we crumble back to dust we are no more, from what source did we emanate, and what was the purpose of our existence? If this life were all, we should be led to query, whether or not there was really any substance in existence, and we might with propriety say, "Let us eat, drink, and be merry, for to-morrow we die!" But if this life is all, then why this constant toiling, why this continual warfare, and why this unceasing trouble? But this life is not all; the voice of *reason,* the language of *inspiration,* and the Spirit of the living God, our Creator, teaches us, as we hold the record of truth in our hands, that this is not the case, that this is not so; for, the heavens declare the glory of a God, and the firmament showeth His handiwork; and a moment's reflection is sufficient to teach every man of common intelligence, that all these are not the mere productions of *chance,* nor could they be supported by any power less than an Almighty hand; and He that can mark the power of Omnipotence, inscribed upon the heavens, can also see God's own handwriting in the sacred volume: and he who reads it oftenest will like it best, and he who is acquainted with it, will know the hand wherever he can see it; and when once discovered, it will not only receive an acknowledgment, but an obedience to all its heavenly precepts. For a moment reflect: what could have been the purpose of our Father in giving to us a law? Was it that it might be obeyed, or disobeyed? And think further, too, not only of the propriety, but of the importance of attending to His laws in every particular. If, then, there is an importance in this respect, is there not a responsibility of great weight resting upon those who are called to declare these truths to men? Were we capable of laying any thing before you as a just comparison, we would cheerfully do it; but in this our ability fails, and we are inclined to think that man is unable, without assistance beyond what has been given to those before, of expressing in words the greatness of this important subject. We can only say, that if an anticipation of the joys of the celestial glory, as witnessed to the hearts of the humble is not sufficient, we will leave to yourselves the result of your own diligence; for God ere long, will call all His servants before Him, and there from His own hand they will receive a just recompense and a rightous reward for all their labors.

* * *

Man Departed from the Lord's Government

It is reasonable to suppose that man departed from the first teachings, or instructions which he received from heaven in the first age, and refused by his disobedience to be governed by them. Consequently, he formed such laws as best suited his own mind, or as he supposed, were best adapted to his situation. But that God has influenced man more or less since that time in the formation of law for His benefit we have no hesitancy in believing; for, as before remarked, being the source of all good, every just and equitable law was in a greater or less degree influenced by Him. And though man in his own supposed wisdom would not admit the influence of a power superior to his own, yet for wise and great purposes, for the good and happiness of His creatures, God has instructed man to form wise and wholesome laws, since he had departed from Him and refused to be governed by those laws which God had given by His own voice from on high in the beginning. But notwithstanding the transgression, by which man had cut himself off from an immediate intercourse with his Maker without a Mediator, it appears that the great and glorious plan of His redemption was previously provided; the sacrifice prepared;

the atonement wrought out in the mind and purpose of God,
even in the person of the Son, through whom man was now
to look for acceptance and through whose merits he was now
taught that he alone could find redemption, since the word had
been pronounced, Unto dust thou shalt return.

The Law of Sacrifice

But that man was not able himself to erect a system, or
plan with power sufficient to free him from a destruction which
awaited him is evident from the fact that God, as before remarked, prepared a sacrifice in the gift of His own Son who
should be sent in due time, to prepare a way, or open a door
through which man might enter into the Lord's presence,
whence he had been cast out for disobedience. From time to
time these glad tidings were sounded in the ears of men in
different ages of the world down to the time of Messiah's
coming. By faith in this atonement or plan of redemption,
Abel offered to God a sacrifice that was accepted, which was
the firstlings of the flock. Cain offered of the fruit of the
ground, and was not accepted, because he could not do it in
faith, he could have no faith, or could not exercise faith contrary
to the plan of heaven. It must be shedding the blood of the
Only Begotten to atone for man; for this was the plan of redemption; and without the shedding of blood was no remission; and
as the sacrifice was instituted for a type, by which man was to
discern the great Sacrifice which God had prepared; to offer
a sacrifice contrary to that, no faith could be exercised, because
redemption was not purchased in that way, nor the power of
atonement instituted after that order; consequently Cain could
have no faith; and whatsoever is not of faith, is sin. But Abel
offered an acceptable sacrifice, by which he obtained witness
that he was righteous, God Himself testifying of his gifts.
Certainly, the shedding of the blood of a beast could be beneficial to no man, except it was done in imitation, or as a type,
or explanation of what was to be offered through the gift of
God Himself; and this performance done with an eye looking
forward in faith on the power of that great Sacrifice for a
remission of sins. But however various may have been, and
may be at the present time, the opinions of men respecting
the conduct of Abel, and the knowledge which he had on the

subject of atonement, it is evident in our minds, that he was instructed more fully in the plan than what the Bible speaks of, for how could he offer a sacrifice in faith, looking to God for a remission of his sins in the power of the great atonement, without having been previously instructed in that plan? And further, if he was accepted of God, what were the ordinances performed further than the offering of the firstlings of the flock?

The Lord Spake to Abel

It is said by Paul in his letter to the Hebrew brethren, that Abel obtained witness that he was righteous, God testifying of his gifts. To whom did God testify of the gifts of Abel, was it to Paul? We have very little on this important subject in the forepart of the Bible. But it is said that Abel himself obtained witness that he was righteous. Then certainly God spoke to him: indeed, it is said that God talked with him; and if He did, would He not, seeing that Abel was righteous deliver to him the whole plan of the Gospel? And is not the Gospel the news of the redemption? How could Abel offer a sacrifice and look forward with faith on the Son of God for a remission of his sins, and not understand the Gospel? The mere shedding of the blood of beasts or offering anything else in sacrifice, could not procure a remission of sins, except it were performed in faith of something to come; if it could, Cain's offering must have been as good as Abel's. And if Abel was taught of the coming of the Son of God, was he not taught also of His ordinances? We all admit that the Gospel has ordinances, and if so, had it not always ordinances, and were not its ordinances always the same?

Gospel Ordinances from the Beginning

Perhaps our friends will say that the Gospel and its ordinances were not known till the days of John, the son of Zacharias, in the days of Herod, the king of Judea. But we will here look at this point: For our own part we cannot believe that the ancients in all ages were so ignorant of the system of heaven as many suppose, since all that were ever saved, were saved through the power of this great plan of redemption, as much before the coming of Christ as since; if not, God has had different plans in operation (if we may so express it), to bring men back to dwell with Himself; and this we cannot believe, since there has been no change in the constitution of man since he fell; and the ordinance or institution of offering blood in sacrifice, was only designed to be performed till Christ was offered up and shed His blood—as said before—that man might look forward in faith to that time. It will be noticed that, according to Paul, (see Gal. iii:8) the Gospel was preached to Abraham. We would like to be informed in what name the Gospel was then preached, whether it was in the name of Christ or some other name. If in any other name, was it the Gospel? And if it was the Gospel, and that preached in the name of Christ, had it any ordinances? If not, was it the Gospel? And if it had ordinances what were they? Our friends may say, perhaps, that there were never any ordinances except those of offering sacrifices before the coming of Christ, and that it could not be possible before the Gospel to have been administered while the law of sacrifices of blood was in force. But we will recollect that Abraham offered sacrifice, and notwithstanding this, had the Gospel preached to him. That the offering of sacrifice was only to point the mind forward to Christ, we infer from these remarkable words of Jesus to the Jews: "Your Father Abraham rejoiced to see my day: and he saw it, and was glad" (John viii:56). So, then, because the ancients offered sacrifice it did not hinder their hearing the Gospel; but served, as we said before, to open their eyes, and enable them to look forward to the time of the coming of the Savior, and rejoice in His redemption. We find also, that when the Israelites came out of Egypt they had the Gospel preached to them, according to Paul in his letter to the Hebrews, which says: "For unto us was the Gospel preached, as well as unto them: but the word preached did not profit them, not being mixed with faith in them that heard it" (see Heb. iv:2). It is said again, in Gal. iii:19, that the law (of Moses, or the Levitical law) was "added" because of transgression. What, we ask, was this law added to, if it was not added to the Gospel? It must be plain that it was added to the Gospel, since we learn that they had the Gospel preached to them. From these few facts, we conclude that whenever the Lord revealed Himself to men in ancient days, and commanded them to offer sacrifice to Him, that it was done that they might look forward in faith to the time of His coming, and rely upon the power of that atonement for a remission of their sins. And this they have done, thousands who have gone before us, whose garments are spotless, and who are, like Job, waiting with an assurance like his, that they will see Him in the *latter day* upon the earth, even in their flesh.

We may conclude, that though there were different dispensations, yet all things which God communicated to His people were calculated to draw their minds to the great object, and to teach them to rely upon God alone as the author of their salvation, as contained in His law.

Not All Revelation Is in the Bible

From what we can draw from the Scriptures relative to the teaching of heaven, we are induced to think that much instruction has been given to man since the beginning which we do not possess now. This may not agree with the opinions of some of our friends who are bold to say that we have everything written in the Bible which God ever spoke to man since the world began, and that if He had ever said anything more we should certainly have received it. But we ask, does it remain for a people who never had faith enough to call down one scrap of revelation from heaven, and for all they have now are indebted to the faith of another people who lived hundreds and thousands of years before them, does it remain for them to say how much God has spoken and how much He has not spoken? We have what we have, and the Bible contains what it does contain: but to say that God never said anything more to man than is there recorded, would be saying at once that we have at last received a revelation: for it must require one to advance thus far, because it is nowhere said in that volume by the mouth of God, that He would not, after giving what is there contained, speak again; and if any man has found out for a fact that the Bible contains all that God ever revealed to man he has ascertained it by an immediate revelation, other than has been previously written by the prophets and apostles. But through the kind providence of our Father a portion of His word which he delivered to His ancient saints, has fallen into our hands, is presented to us with a promise of a reward if obeyed, and with a penalty if disobeyed. That all are deeply interested in these laws or teachings, must be admitted by all who acknowledge their divine authenticity.

Blessings for the Faithful—The Resurrection

It may be proper for us to notice in this place a few of the many blessings held out in this law of heaven as a reward to those who obey its teachings. God has appointed a day in which He will judge the world, and this He has given an assurance of in that He raised up His Son Jesus Christ from the dead—the point on which the hope of all who believe the inspired record is found for their future happiness and enjoyment; because, "If Christ be not raised," said Paul to the Corinthians, "your faith is vain; ye are yet in your sins. Then they also which are fallen asleep in Christ are perished" (see I Cor. xv). If the resurrection from the dead be not an important point, or item in our faith, we must confess that we know nothing about it; for if there be no resurrection from the dead, then Christ has not risen; and if Christ has not risen He was not the Son of God; and if He was not the Son of God, there is not nor cannot be a Son of God, if the present book called the Scriptures is true; because the time has gone by when, according to that book, He was to make His appearance. On this subject, however, we are reminded of the words of Peter to the Jewish Sanhedrin, when speaking of Christ, he says that God raised Him from the dead, and we (the apostles) are His witnesses of these things, and so is the Holy Ghost, whom God had given to them that obey Him (see Acts v). So that after the testimony of the Scriptures on this point, the assurance is given by the Holy Ghost, bearing witness to those who obey Him, that Christ Himself has assuredly risen from the dead; and if He has risen from the dead, He will by His power, bring all men to stand before Him; for if He has risen from the dead the bands of the temporal death are broken that the grave has no victory. If then, the grave has no victory, those who keep the sayings of Jesus and obey His teachings have not only a promise of a resurrection from the dead, but an assurance of being admitted into His glorious kingdom; for, He Himself says, "Where I am, there shall also my servant be" (see John xii).

The Marriage Supper

In the 22nd chapter of Matthew's account of the Messiah, we find the kingdom of heaven likened unto a king who made a marriage for his son. That this son was the Messiah will not be disputed, since it was the kingdom of heaven that was represented in the parable; and that the Saints, or those who are found faithful to the Lord, are the individuals who will be found worthy to inherit a seat at the marriage supper, is evident from the sayings of John in the Revelation where he represents the sound which he heard in heaven to be like a great multitude, or like the voice of mighty thunderings, saying, the Lord God Omnipotent reigneth. Let us be glad and rejoice, and give honor to Him; for the marriage of the Lamb is come, and His wife hath made herself ready. And to her was granted that she should be arrayed in fine linen, clean and white: For the fine linen is the righteousness of Saints (Rev. xix).

They Who Endure to the End

That those who keep the commandments of the Lord and walk in His statutes to the end, are the only individuals permitted to sit at this glorious feast, is evident from the following items in Paul's last letter to Timothy, which was written just previous to his death,—he says: "I have fought a good fight, I have finished my course, I have kept the faith: henceforth there is laid up for me a crown of righteousness, which the Lord, the righteous Judge, shall give me at that day: and not to me only, but unto all them also that love His appearing." No one who believes the account, will doubt for a moment this assertion of Paul which was made, as he knew, just before he was to take his leave of this world. Though he once, according to his own word, persecuted the Church of God and wasted it, yet after embracing the faith, his labors were unceasing to spread the glorious news: and like a faithful soldier, when called to give his life in the cause which he had espoused, he laid it down, as he says, with an assurance of an eternal crown. Follow the labors of this Apostle from the time of his conversion to the time of his death, and you will have a fair sample of industry and patience in promulgating the Gospel of Christ. Derided, whipped, and stoned, the moment he escaped the hands of his persecutors he as zealously as ever proclaimed the doctrine of the Savior. And all may know that he did not embrace the faith for honor in this life, nor for the gain of earthly goods. What, then, could have induced him to undergo all this toil? It was, as he said, that he might obtain the crown of righteousness from the hand of God. No one, we presume, will doubt the faithfulness of Paul to the end. None will say that he did not keep the faith, that he did not fight the good fight, that he did not preach and persuade to the last. And what was he to receive? A crown of righteousness. And what shall others receive who do not labor faithfully, and continue to the end? We leave such to search out their own promises if any they have; and if they have any they are welcome to them, on our part, for the Lord says that every man is to receive according to his works. Reflect for a moment, brethren, and enquire, whether you would consider yourselves worthy a seat at the marriage feast with Paul and others like him, if you had been unfaithful? Had you not fought the good fight, and kept the faith, could you expect to receive? Have you a promise of receiving a crown of righteousness from the hand of the Lord, with the Church of the Firstborn? Here then, we understand, that Paul rested his hope in Christ, because he had kept the faith, and loved His appearing and from His hand he had a promise of receiving a crown of righteousness.

A Crown for the Righteous

If the Saints are not to reign, for what purpose are they crowned? In an exhortation of the Lord to a certain Church in Asia, which was built up in the days of the Apostles, unto whom He communicated His word on that occasion by His servant John, He says, "Behold, I come quickly: hold that fast which thou hast, that no man take thy crown." And again, "To him that overcometh will I grant to sit with Me in My throne, even as I also overcame, and am set down with My Father in His Throne" (see Rev. iii). And again, it is written, "Beloved, now are we the sons of God, and it doth not yet appear what we shall be: but we know that, when He shall appear, we shall be like Him; for we shall see Him as He is. And every man that hath this hope in him purifieth himself, even as He is pure" (I John iii:2, 3). How is it that these old Apostles should say so much on the subject of the coming of Christ? He certainly had once come; but Paul says, To all who love His appearing, shall be given the crown: and John says, When He shall appear, we shall be like Him; for we shall see Him as He is. Can we mistake such language as this? Do we not offer violence to our own good judgment when we deny the second coming of the Messiah? When has He partaken of the fruit of the vine new with His ancient Apostles in His Father's kingdom, as He promised He would just before he was crucified? In Paul's epistle to the Philippians (iii:20, 21) he says: "For our conversation is in heaven; from whence also we look for the Savior, the Lord Jesus Christ: who shall change our vile body, that it may be fashioned like unto His glorious body, according to the working whereby He is able even to subdue all things unto Himself." We find another promise to individuals living in the Church at Sardis who had not defiled their garments: "And they shall walk with me in white: for they are worthy. He that overcometh, the same shall be clothed in white raiment; and I will not blot out his name out of the book of life, but I will confess his name before my Father, and before His angels." John represents the sound which he heard from heaven, as giving thanks and glory to God, saying that the Lamb was worthy to take the book and to open its seals; because he was slain, and had made them kings and priests unto God: and they should reign on the earth (see Rev. v). In the 20th chapter we find a length of time specified, during which Satan is to be confined in his own place, and the Saints reign in peace, all these promises and blessings we find contained in the law of the Lord, which the righteous are to enjoy: and we might enumerate many more places where the same or similar promises are made to the faithful, but we do not deem it of importance to rehearse them here, as this epistle is now lengthy; and our brethren, no doubt, are familiar with them all.

The Ancient Saints Obtained Promises

Most assuredly it is, however, that the ancients, though persecuted and afflicted by men, obtained from God promises of such weight and glory, that our hearts are often filled with gratitude that we are even permitted to look upon them while we contemplate that there is no respect of persons in His sight, and that in every nation, he that feareth God and worketh righteousness, is acceptable with Him. But from the few items previously quoted we can draw the conclusion that there is to be a day when all will be judged of their works, and rewarded according to the same; that those who have kept the faith will be crowned with a crown of righteousness; be clothed in white raiment; be admitted to the marriage feast; be free from every affliction, and reign with Christ on the earth, where, according to the ancient promise, they will partake of the fruit of the vine new in the glorious kingdom with Him; at least we find that such promises were made to the ancient Saints. And though we cannot claim these promises which were made to the ancients for they are not our property, merely because they were made to the ancient Saints, yet if we are the children of the Most High, and are called with the same calling with which they were called, and embrace the same covenant that they embraced, and are faithful to the testimony of our Lord as they were, we can approach the Father in the name of Christ as they approached Him, and for ourselves obtain the same promises. These promises, when obtained, if ever by us, will not be because Peter, John, and the other Apostles, with the churches at Sardis, Pergamos, Philadelphia, and elsewhere, walked in the fear of God, and had power and faith to prevail and obtain them; but it will be because we, ourselves, have faith and approach God in the name of His Son Jesus Christ, even as they did; and when these promises are obtained, they will be promises directly to us, or they will do us no good. They will be communicated for our benefit, being our own property (through the gift of God), earned by our own diligence in keeping His commandments and walking uprightly before Him. If not, to what end serves the Gospel of our Lord Jesus Christ, and why was it ever communicated to us?

*   *   *

Apostates Excluded from Fellowship

The Messiah's kingdom on earth is of that kind of government, that there has always been numerous apostates, for the reason that it admits of no sins unrepented of without excluding the individual from its fellowship. Our Lord said, "Strive to enter in at the strait gate: for many, I say unto you, will seek to enter in, and shall not be able." And again, many are called, but few are chosen. Paul said to the elders of the Church at Ephesus, after he had labored three years with them, that he knew that some of their own number would turn away from the faith, and seek to lead away disciples after them. None, we presume, in this generation will pretend that he has the experience of Paul in building up the Church of Christ and yet, after his departure from the Church at Ephesus, many, even of the elders turned away from the truth; and what is almost always the case, sought to lead away disciples after them. Strange as it may appear at first thought, yet it is no less strange than true, that notwithstanding all the professed determination to live godly, apostates after turning from the faith of Christ, unless they have speedily repented, have sooner or later fallen into the snares of the wicked one, and have been left destitute of the Spirit of God, to manifest their wickedness in the eyes of multitudes. From apostates the faithful have received the severest persecutions. Judas was rebuked and immediately betrayed his Lord into the hands of His enemies, because Satan entered into him. There is a superior intelligence bestowed upon such as obey the Gospel with full purpose of heart, which, if sinned against, the apostate is left naked and destitute of the Spirit of God, and he is, in truth, nigh unto cursing, and his end is to be burned. When once that light which was in them is taken from them, they become as much darkened as they were previously enlightened, and then, no marvel, if all their power should be enlisted against the truth, and they, Judas like, seek the destruction of those who were their greatest benefactors. What nearer friend on earth, or in heaven, had Judas than the Savior? And his first object was to destroy Him. Who, among all the Saints in these last days can consider himself as good as our Lord? Who is as perfect? Who is as pure? Who is as holy as He was? Are they to be found? He never transgressed or broke a commandment or law of heaven—no deceit was in His mouth, neither was guile found in His heart. And yet one that ate with Him, who had often drunk of the same cup, was the first to lift up his heel against Him. Where is one like Christ? He cannot be found on earth. Then why should His followers complain, if from those whom they once called brethren, and considered as standing in the nearest relation in the everlasting covenant they should receive persecution? From what source emanated the principle which has ever been manifested by apostates from the true Church to persecute with double diligence, and seek with double perseverance, to destroy those whom they once professed to love, with whom they once communed, and with whom they once covenanted to strive with every power in righteousness to obtain the rest of God? Perhaps our brethren will say the same that caused Satan to seek to overthrow the kingdom of God, because he himself was evil, and God's kingdom is holy.

* * *

Gift of Salvation

The great plan of salvation is a theme which ought to occupy our strict attention, and be regarded as one of heaven's best gifts to mankind. No consideration whatever ought to deter us from showing ourselves approved in the sight of God, according to His divine requirement. Men not unfrequently forget that they are dependent upon heaven for every blessing which they are permitted to enjoy, and that for every opportunity granted them they are to give an account. You know, brethren, that when the Master in the Savior's parable of the stewards called his servants before him he gave them several talents to improve on while he should tarry abroad for a little season, and when he returned he called for an accounting. So it is now. Our Master is absent only for a little season, and at the end of it He will call each to render an acount; and where the five talents were bestowed, ten will be required; and he that has made no improvement will be cast out as an unprofitable servant, while the faithful will enjoy everlasting honors. Therefore we earnestly implore the grace of our Father to rest upon you, through Jesus Christ His Son, that you may not faint in the hour of temptation, nor be overcome in the time of persecution. (January 22, 1834) D. H. C. 2:4-24.

Duties of Seventies

The Seventies are to constitute traveling quorums, to go into all the earth, whithersoever the Twelve Apostles shall call them. (Feb. 8, 1834.) D. H. C. 2:202.

Orders in Councils

At a council of the High Priests and Elders, (Orson Hyde, clerk), at my house in Kirtland, on the evening of the 12th of February (1834), I remarked that I should endeavor to set before the council the dignity of the office which had been conferred on me by the ministering of the angel of God, by His own voice, and by the voice of this Church; that I had never set before any council in all the order in which it ought to be conducted, which, perhaps, has deprived the councils of some or many blessings.

And I continued and said, no man is capable of judging a matter, in council, unless his own heart is pure; and that we frequently are so filled with prejudice, or have a beam in our own eye, that we are not capable of passing right decisions.

But to return to the subject of order; in ancient days councils were conducted with such strict propriety, that no one was allowed to whisper, be weary, leave the room, or get uneasy in the least, until the voice of the Lord, by revelation, or the voice of the council by the Spirit, was obtained, which has not been observed in this Church to the present time. It was understood in ancient days, that if one man could stay in council, another could; and if the president could spend his time, the members could also; but in our councils, generally, one will be uneasy, another asleep; one praying, another not; one's mind on the business of the council, and another thinking on something else.

Our Acts Are Recorded

Our acts are recorded, and at a future day they will be laid before us, and if we should fail to judge right and injure our fellow-beings, they may there, perhaps, condemn us; there they are of great consequence, and to me the consequence appears to be of force, beyond anything which I am able to express. Ask yourselves, brethren, how much you have exercised yourselves in prayer since you heard of this council; and if you are now prepared to sit in council upon the soul of your brother.

I then gave a relation of my situation at the time I obtained the record [Book of Mormon], the persecutions I met with, and prophesied that I would stand and shine like the sun in the firmament, when my enemies and the gainsayers of my testimony shall be put down and cut off, and their names blotted out from among men.—D. H. C. 2:25-26.

Covenant of Tithing

On the evening of the 29th of November, I united in prayer with Brother Oliver for the continuance of blessings. After giving thanks for the relief which the Lord had lately sent us by opening the hearts of the brethren from the east, to loan us $430; after commencing and rejoicing before the Lord on this occasion, we agreed to enter into the following covenant with the Lord, viz:

That if the Lord will prosper us in our business and open the way before us that we may obtain means to pay our debts, that we be not troubled nor brought into disrepute before the world, nor His people; after that, of all that He shall give unto us, we will give a tenth to be bestowed upon the poor in His Church, or as He shall command; and that we will be faithful over that which he has entrusted to our care, that we may obtain much; and that our children after us shall remember to observe this sacred and holy covenant; and that our children, and our children's children, may know of the same, we have subscribed our names with our own hands. (March 29, 1834.) D. H. C. 2:174-175.

(Signed) JOSEPH SMITH, JUN.,
OLIVER COWDERY.

Importance of Revelation

At a conference of the Elders of the Church held at the home of Jared Carter, April 21, 1834, the Prophet read the second chapter of Joel and then made the following remarks:

It is very difficult for us to communicate to the churches all that God has revealed to us, in consequence of tradition; for we are differently situated from any other people that ever existed upon this earth; consequently those former revelations cannot be suited to our conditions; they were given to other people, who were before us; but in the last days, God was to call a remnant, in which was to be deliverance, as well as in Jerusalem and Zion. Now if God should give no more revela-

tions, where will we find Zion and this remnant? The time is near when desolation is to cover the earth, and then God will have a place of deliverance in his remnant, and in Zion,
* * *

Take away the Book of Mormon and the revelations, and where is our religion? We have none; for without Zion, and a place of deliverance, we must fall; because the time is near when the sun will be darkened, and the moon turn to blood, and the stars fall from heaven, and the earth reel to and fro. Then, if this is the case, and if we are not sanctified and gathered to the places God has appointed, with all our former professions and our great love for the Bible, we must fall; we cannot stand; we cannot be saved; for God will gather out his Saints from the Gentiles, and then comes desolation and destruction, and none can escape except the pure in heart who are gathered.—D. H. C. 2:52.

Kindness to Animals Required of Man

The following incidents occurred while Zion's Camp was on the march from Kirtland to Missouri.

In pitching my tent we found three massasaugas or prairie rattlesnakes, which the brethren were about to kill, but I said, "Let them alone—don't hurt them! How will the serpent ever lose its venom, while the servants of God possess the same disposition, and continue to make war upon it? Men must become harmless before the brute creation, and when men lose their viscious dispositions and cease to destroy the animal race, the lion and the lamb can dwell together, and the sucking child can play with the serpent in safety." The brethren took the serpents carefully on sticks and carried them across the creek. I exhorted the brethren not to kill a serpent, bird, or an animal of any kind during our journey unless it became necessary in order to preserve ourselves from hunger. (May 26, 1834.) D. H. C. 2:71.

Never Trifle with Promises of God

Martin Harris having boasted to the brethren that he could handle snakes with perfect safety, while fooling with a black snake with his bare feet, he received a bite on his left foot. The fact was communicated to me, and I took occasion to reprove him, and exhort the brethren never to trifle with the promises of God. I told them it was presumption for any one to provoke a serpent to bite him, but if a man of God was accidentally bitten by a poisonous serpent, he might have faith, or his brethren might have faith for him, so that the Lord would hear his prayer and he might be healed; but when a man designedly provokes a serpent to bite him, the principle is the same as when a man drinks deadly poison knowing it to be such. In that case no man has any claim on the promises of God to be healed. (June 16, 1834.) D. H. C. 2:95-96.

Important Items of Instruction to the Twelve

Kirtland, February 27, 1835.

This evening, nine of the Twelve, viz., Lyman Johnson, Brigham Young, Heber C. Kimball, Orson Hyde, David W. Patten, Luke Johnson, William E. M'Lellin, John F. Boynton, and William Smith, assembled at the house of President Joseph Smith, Jun., who was present, with Frederick G. Williams, Sidney Rigdon, Bishop Whitney, and three Elders. Parley P. Pratt had gone to New Portage, and Orson Pratt and Thomas B. Marsh had not yet arrived to receive their ordination.

Importance of Records

After prayer by President Joseph Smith, Jun., he said, if we heard patiently, he could lay before the council an item which would be of importance. He had for himself, learned a fact by experience, which, on recollection, always gave him deep sorrow. It is a fact, if I now had in my possession, every decision which had been had upon important items of doctrine and duties since the commencement of this work, I would not part with them for any sum of money; but we have neglected to take minutes of such things, thinking, perhaps, that they would never benefit us afterwards; which, if we had them now, would decide almost every point of doctrine which might be agitated. But this has been neglected, and now we cannot bear record to the Church and to the world, of the great and glorious manifestations which have been made to us with that degree of power and authority we otherwise could, if we now had these things to publish abroad.

Since the Twelve are now chosen, I wish to tell them a course which they may pursue, and be benefited thereafter, in a point of light of which they are not now aware. If they will, every time they assemble, appoint a person to preside over them during the meeting, and one or more to keep a record of their proceedings, and on the decision of every question or item, be it what it may, let such decision be written, and such decision will forever remain upon record, and appear an item of covenant or doctrine. An item thus decided may appear, at the time, of little or no worth, but should it be published, and one of you lay hands on it after, you will find it of infinite worth, not only to your brethren, but it will be a feast to your own souls.

Records a Protection Against Evil

Here is another important item. If you assemble from time to time, and proceed to discuss important questions, and pass decisions upon the same, and fail to note them down, by and by you will be driven to straits from which you will not be able to extricate yourselves, because you may be in a situation not to bring your faith to bear with sufficient perfection or power to obtain the desired information; or, perhaps, for neglecting to write these things when God had revealed them, not esteeming them of sufficient worth, the Spirit may withdraw, and God may be angry; and there is, or was, a vast knowledge, of infinite importance, which is now lost. What was the cause of this? It came in consequence of slothfulness, or a neglect to appoint a man to occupy a few moments in writing all these decisions.

Here let me prophesy. The time will come, when, if you neglect to do this thing, you will fall by the hands of unrighteous men. Were you to be brought before the authorities, and be accused of any crime or misdemeanor, and be as innocent as the angels of God, unless you can prove yourselves to have been somewhere else, your enemies will prevail against you; but if you can bring twelve men to testify that you were in a certain place, at that time, you will escape their hands. Now, if you will be careful to keep minutes of these things, as I have said, it will be one of the most important records ever seen: for all such decisions will ever after remain as items of doctrine and covenants. (From minutes of Instruction to the Council of the Twelve, Feb. 27, 1835. D. H. C. 2:198-199.)

Calling of the Apostles

President Smith proposed the following question: What importance is there attached to the calling of the Twelve Apostles, different from the other callings or officers of the Church?

After the question was discussed by Councilors Patten, Young, Smith, and M'Lellin, President Joseph Smith, Jun., gave the following decision:

They are the Twelve Apostles, who are called to the office of the Traveling High Council, who are to preside over the churches of the Saints, among the Gentiles, where there is no presidency established; and they are to travel and preach among the Gentiles, until the Lord shall command them to go to the Jews. They are to hold the keys of this ministry, to unlock the door of the Kingdom of heaven unto all nations, and to preach the Gospel to every creature. This is the power, authority, and virtue of their apostleship.

OLIVER COWDERY, Clerk.

(Feb. 27, 1835. D. H. C. 2:200.)

Items of Instruction to the Twelve and the Seventy

Order of Councils

President Joseph Smith stated that the Twelve will have no right to go into Zion, or any of the stakes, and there undertake to regulate the affairs thereof, where there is a standing high council; but it is their duty to go abroad and regulate all matters relative to the different branches of the Church. When the Twelve are together, or a quorum of them, in any church, they will have authority to act independently, and make decisions, and those decisions will be valid. But where there is not a quorum, they will have to do business by the voice of the Church. No standing High Council has authority to go into the churches abroad, and regulate the matters thereof, for this belongs to the Twelve. No standing High Council will ever be established only in Zion, or one of her stakes. When the Twelve pass a decision, it is in the name of the Church, therefore it is valid.

No official member of the Church has authority to go into any branch thereof, and ordain any minister for that church, unless it is by the voice of that branch. No Elder has authority to go into any branch of the Church, and appoint meetings, or attempt to regulate the affairs of the Church, without the advice and consent of the presiding Elder of that branch.

Calling of Seventies

If the first Seventy are all employed, and there is a call for more laborers, it will be the duty of the seven presidents of the first Seventy to call and ordain other Seventy and send them forth to labor in the vineyard, until, if needs be, they set apart seven times seventy, and even until there are one hundred and forty-four thousand thus set apart for the ministry.

The Seventy are not to attend the conferences of the Twelve, unless they are called upon or requested so to do by the Twelve. The Twelve and the Seventy have particularly to depend upon their ministry for their support, and that of their families; and they have a right, by virtue of their offices, to call upon the churches to assist them.

*   *   *

The circumstances of the presidents of the Seventy were severally considered, relative to their traveling in the vineyard; and it was unanimously agreed that they should hold themselves in readiness to go, at the call of the Twelve when the Lord opens the way. Twenty-seven of the Seventy were also considered, and it was decided they should hold themselves in readiness to travel in the ministry, at the call of the president of the Seventy, as the Lord opens the way.

*   *   *

Voted, that all the Elders of the Church are bound to travel in the world to preach the Gospel, with all their might, mind, and strength, when their circumstances will admit of it; and that the door is now opened.

Voted, that Elders Brigham Young, John P. Greene, and Amos Orton be appointed to go and preach the Gospel to the remnants of Joseph, the door to be opened by Elder Brigham Young; and this will open the door to the whole house of Joseph. Voted, that when another Seventy is required, the presidency of the first Seventy shall choose, ordain, and set them apart from among the most experienced of the Elders of the Church.—From the Minutes of a General Priesthood Meeting held May 2, 1835.—D. H. C. 2:220-222.

Epistle to the Saints Scattered Abroad

Love for One Another

Dear Brethren:—It is a duty which every Saint ought to render to his brethren freely—to always love them, and ever succor them. To be justified before God we must love one another: we must overcome evil; we must visit the fatherless and the widow in their affliction, and we must keep ourselves unspotted from the world: for such virtues flow from the great fountain of pure religion, strengthening our faith by adding every good quality that adorns the children of the blessed Jesus, we can pray in the season of prayer; we can love our neighbor as ourselves, and be faithful in tribulation, knowing that the reward of such is greater in the kingdom of heaven. What a consolation! What a joy! Let me live the life of the righteous, and let my reward be like his!

Duty of the High Council and Elders

According to the order of the kingdom begun in the last days, to prepare men for the rest of the Lord, the Elders in Zion, or in her immediate region, have no authority or right to meddle with her spiritual affairs, to regulate her concerns, or hold councils for the expulsion of members in her unorganized condition. The High Council has been expressly organized to administer in all her spiritual affairs; and the Bishop and his council, are set over her temporal matters: so that the Elders' acts are null and void. Now the Lord wants the tares and wheat to grow together: for Zion must be redeemed with judgment, and her converts with righteousness. Every Elder that can, after providing for his family (if he has any) and paying his debts, must go forth and clear his skirts from the blood of this generation. While they are in that region instead of trying members for transgressions, or offenses, let every one labor to prepare himself for the vineyard, sparing a little time to comfort the mourners; to bind up the broken-hearted; to reclaim the backslider; to bring back the wanderer; to re-invite into the kingdom such as have been cut off, by encouraging them to lay to while the day lasts, and to work righteousness, and, with one heart and one mind, prepare to help redeem Zion, that goodly land of promise, where the willing and the obedient shall be blessed. Souls are as precious in the sight of God as they ever were; and the Elders were never called to drive any down to hell, but to persuade and invite all men everywhere to repent, that they may become the heirs of salvation. It is the acceptable year of the Lord: liberate the captives that they may sing hosanna. The Priests, too, should not be idle: their duties are plain, and unless they do them diligently, they cannot expect to be approved. Righteousness must be the aim of the Saints in all things, and when the covenants are published, they will learn that great things must be expected from them. Do good and work righteousness with an eye single to the glory of God, and you shall reap your reward when the Lord recompenses every one according to his work. The Teachers and Deacons are the standing ministers of the Church, and in the absence of other officers, great things and holy walk are required of them. They must strengthen the members' faith; persuade such as are out of the way to repent, and turn to God and live; meekly persuade and urge every one to forgive one another all their trespasses, offenses and sins, that they may work out their own salvation with fear and trembling.

Seek to Save Souls

Brethren, bear and forbear one with another, for so the Lord does with us. Pray for your enemies in the Church and curse not your foes without: for vengeance is mine, saith the Lord, and I will repay. To every ordained member, and to all, we say, be merciful and you shall find mercy. Seek to help save souls, not to destroy them: for verily you know, that "there is more joy in heaven, over one sinner that repents, than there is over ninety and nine just persons that need no repentance." Strive not about the mysteries of the kingdom; cast not your pearls before swine, give not the bread of the children to dogs, lest you and the children should suffer, and you thereby offend your righteous Judge. Your brethren who leave their families, with whom they have enjoyed an earthly measure of peace and joy, to carry glad tidings around the world, expect great things of you, while you are privileged to enjoy the bless-ings of the Saints' society. They pray our heavenly Father that you may be very prayerful, very humble, and very char-itable; working diligently, spiritually and temporally for the redemption of Zion, that the pure in heart may return with songs of everlasting joy to build up her waste places, and meet the Lord when He comes in His glory. Brethren, in the name of Jesus Christ, we entreat you to live worthy of the blessings that shall follow, after much tribulation, to satiate the souls of them that hold out faithful to the end—M. and A. 1:137-138.

The substance of the foregoing article from the Messenger and Advocate is also contained, according to John Whitmer's history (manuscript, page 52) in a letter to Hezekiah Peck, signed by Joseph Smith, Jun., Oliver Cowdery, Sidney Rigdon, Frederick G. Williams, W. W. Phelps and John Whitmer; the opening paragraph of which is as follows:

Officers in Transgression

"The Presidency of Kirtland and Zion say that the Lord has manifested by revelation of His Spirit, that the High Priests, Teachers, Priests, and Deacons, or in other words, all the officers in the land of Clay County, Missouri, belonging to the Church, are more or less in transgression, because they have not enjoyed the Spirit of God sufficiently to be able to comprehend their duties respecting themselves and the welfare of Zion; thereby having been left to act in a manner that is detrimental to the interest, and also a hindrance to the redemption of Zion. Now if they will be wise, they will humble themselves in a peculiar manner that God may open the eyes of their under-standing. It will be clearly manifested what the design and purposes of the Almighty are with regard to them, and the children of Zion, that they should let the High Council, which is appointed of God and ordained for that purpose, make and regulate all the affairs of Zion, and that it is the will of God that her children should stand still and see the salvation of redemption." Then follows the substance of the Messenger and Advocate article. This letter has the following postscript written personally by the Prophet, to Brother Peck, and is a gem which manifests the profound sympathy of the Prophet for the faithful in Israel:

P. S.—Brother Hezekiah Peck: We remember your family with all the first families of the Church who first embraced the truth. We remember your losses and sorrows; our first ties are not broken; we participate with you in the evil as well as the good, in the sorrows as well as the joys; our union, we trust, is stronger than death, and shall never be severed. Remember us unto all who believe in the fulness of the Gospel of our Lord and Savior Jesus Christ. We hereby authorize you, Hezekiah Peck, our beloved brother, to read this epistle and communicate it unto all the brotherhood in that region of country.

Dictated by me, your unworthy brother, and fellow laborer in the testimony of the Book of Mormon, Signed by my own hand in the token of the everlasting covenant. JOSEPH SMITH, JUN.—M. and A., June, 1835, also D. H. C. 2:229-231.

Excerpts from an Epistle to the Elders of the Church of Latter-day Saints

After so long a time, and after so many things have been said, I feel it my duty to drop a few hints, that perhaps the Elders traveling through the world, to warn the inhabitants of the earth to flee the wrath to come, and save themselves from this untoward generation—may be aided in a measure, in doctrine, and in the way of their duty. I have been laboring in this cause for eight years, during which time I have traveled much, and have had much experience. I removed from Seneca County, New York, to Geauga County, Ohio, in February, 1831.

The Prophet's Commandment to Go to Missouri

I received, by a heavenly vision, a commandment in June following, to take my journey to the western boundaries of the State of Missouri, and there designate the very spot which was to be the central place for the commencement of the gathering together of those who embrace the fullness of the everlasting Gospel. Accordingly I undertook the journey, with certain ones of my brethren, and after a long and tedious journey, suffering many privations and hardships, arrived in Jackson County, Missouri, and after viewing the country, seeking diligently at the hand of God, He manifested Himself unto us, and designated, to me and others, the very spot upon which he designed to commence the work of the gathering, and the upbuilding of an "holy city," which should be called Zion— Zion, because it is a place of righteousness, and all who build thereon are to worship the true and living God, and all believe in one doctrine, even the doctrine of our Lord and Savior Jesus Christ. "Thy watchmen shall lift up the voice; with the voice together shall they sing: for they shall see eye to eye, when the Lord shall bring again Zion" (Isaiah lii:8).

* * *

Location of Zion

After having ascertained the very spot, and having the happiness of seeing quite a number of the families of my brethren comfortably situated upon the land, I took leave of them and journeyed back to Ohio, and used every influence and argument that lay in my power to get those who believed in the everlasting covenant, whose circumstances would admit, and whose families were willing to remove to the place which I had designated to be the land of Zion; and thus the sound of the gathering, and of the doctrine, went abroad into the world; and many, having a zeal not according to knowledge, and not understanding the pure principles of the doctrine of the Church, have, no doubt, in the heat of enthusiasm, taught and said many things which are derogatory to the genuine character and principles of the Church; and for these things we are heartily sorry, and would apologize, if apology would do any good.

Principles of the Gospel

But we pause here, and offer a remark upon the saying which we learn has gone abroad, and has been handled in a manner detrimental to the cause of truth, by saying, "that in preaching the doctrine of gathering, we break up families, and give license for men to leave their families, women their husbands, children their parents and slaves their masters, thereby deranging the order and breaking up the harmony and peace of society." We shall here show our faith, and thereby, as we humbly trust, put an end to these false and wicked misrepresentations, which have caused, we have every reason to believe, thousands to think they were doing God's service, when they were persecuting the children of God; whereas, if they could have enjoyed the true light, and had a just understanding of our principles, they would have embraced them with all their hearts, and been rejoicing in the love of the truth. And now to show our doctrine on this subject, we shall commence with the first principles of the Gospel, which are faith, repentance, and baptism for the remission of sins, and the gift of the Holy Ghost by the laying on of the hands. This we believe to be our duty—to teach to all mankind the doctrine of repentance, which we shall endeavor to show from the following quotations:

"Then opened He their understanding, that they might understand the scriptures, and said unto them, Thus it is written, and thus it behooved Christ to suffer, and to rise from the dead the third day: and that repentance and remission of sins should be preached in His name among all nations, beginning at Jerusalem" (Luke xxiv:45, 46, 47).

By this we learn that it behooved Christ to suffer, and to be crucified, and rise again on the third day for the express purpose that repentance and remission of sins should be preached to all nations.

Repentance

"Then Peter said unto them, Repent, and be baptized every one of you in the name of Jesus Christ for the remission of sins, and ye shall receive the gift of the Holy Ghost. For the promise is unto you, and to your children, and to all that are afar off, even as many as the Lord our God shall call" (Acts ii:38, 39).

By this we learn that the promise of the Holy Ghost is made unto as many as those to whom the doctrine of repentance was to be preached, which was unto all nations. And we discover also, that the promise was to extend by lineage; for Peter says, not only unto you, but "to your children, and to all that are afar off." From this we infer, that the promise was to continue unto their children's children, and even unto as many as the Lord their God should call. We discover here that we are blending two principles together in these quotations. The first is the principle of repentance, and the second is the principle of the remission of sins; and we learn from Peter that remission of sins is to be obtained by baptism in the name of the Lord Jesus Christ; and the gift of the Holy Ghost follows inevitably, for, says Peter, "you shall receive the Holy Ghost."

Therefore we believe in preaching the doctrine of repentance in all the world, both to old and young, rich and poor, bond and free, as we shall endeavor to show hereafter how, and in what manner, and how far, it is binding on the consciences of mankind, making proper distinctions between old and young, men, women, children and servants. But we discover, in order to be benefited by the doctrine of repentance, we must believe in obtaining the remission of sins. And in order to obtain the remission of sins, we must believe in the doctrine of baptism in the name of the Lord Jesus Christ. And if we believe in baptism for the remission of sins, we may expect a fulfillment of the promise of the Holy Ghost, for the promise extends to all whom the Lord our God shall call; and hath He not surely said, as you will find in the last chapter of Revelation—"And the Spirit and the bride say, Come. And let him that heareth say, Come. And let him that is athirst come. And whosoever will let him take the water of life freely" (Rev. xxii:17).

Again, the Savior says, "Come unto me, all ye that labor, and are heavy laden, and I will give you rest. Take my yoke upon you, and learn of me; for I am meek and lowly in heart: and ye shall find rest unto your souls. For my yoke is easy, and my burden is light" (Matt. xi:28, 29, 30).

Again, Isaiah says, "Look unto me, and be ye saved, all the ends of the earth: for I am God, and there is none else. I have sworn by myself, the word is gone out of my mouth in righteousness, and shall not return. That unto me every knee shall bow, every tongue shall swear. Surely shall one say, in the Lord have I righteousness and strength: even to Him shall men come; and all that are incensed against Him shall be ashamed" (Isaiah xlv:22-24).

*　*　*

Not Leaving the First Principles

"Therefore, leaving the principles of the doctrine of Christ, let us go on unto perfection; not laying again the foundation of repentance from dead works, and of faith toward God, of the doctrine of baptisms, and of laying on of hands, and of resurrection of the dead, and of eternal judgment. And this will we do, if God permit. For it is impossible for those who were once enlightened, and have tasted of the heavenly gift, and were made partakers of the Holy Ghost, and have tasted the good word of God, and the powers of the world to come, if they shall fall away, to renew them again unto repentance, seeing they crucify to themselves the Son of God afresh, and put Him to an open shame." (Heb. vi:1-6).

* * *

JOSEPH SMITH, JUN.
M. and A., Sept. 1, 1835, also D. H. C. 2:253-259.

To the Elders of the Church of the Latter-day Saints

At the close of my letter in the September number of the *Messenger and Advocate* I promised to continue the subject there commenced. I do so with a hope that it may be a benefit and a means of assistance in the labors of the Elders, while they are combating the prejudices of a crooked and perverse generation, by having in their possession the facts of my religious principles, which are misrepresented by almost all those whose crafts are in danger by the same; and also, to aid those who are anxiously inquiring, and have been excited to do so from rumor, to ascertain correctly what my principles are. I have been drawn into this course of proceeding by persecution, that is brought upon us from false rumors and misrepresentations concerning my sentiments.

Righteousness to Sweep the Earth

But to proceed. In the letter alluded to, the principles of repentance and baptism for the remission of sins were not only set forth, but many passages of scripture were quoted, clearly elucidating the subject; let me add, I do positively rely upon the truth of those principles inculcated in the New Testament, and then pass on from the above-named items, to the item or subject of the gathering, and show my views upon this point. It is a principle I esteem to be of the greatest importance to those who are looking for salvation in this generation, or in these, that may be called, "the latter times." All that the prophets that have written, from the days of righteous Abel, down to the last man that has left any testimony on record for our consideration, in speaking of the salvation of Israel in the last days, goes directly to show that it consists in the work of the gathering.

First, I shall begin by quoting from the prophecy of Enoch, speaking of the last days: "Righteousness will I send down out of heaven, and truth will I send forth out of the earth, to bear testimony of mine Only Begotten, His resurrection from the dead (this resurrection I understand to be the corporeal body); yea, and also the resurrection of all men; righteousness and truth will I cause to sweep the earth as with a flood, to gather out mine own elect from the four quarters of the earth, unto a place which I shall prepare, a holy city, that my people may gird up their loins, and be looking forth for the time of my coming, for there shall be my tabernacle, and it shall be called Zion a new Jerusalem." (Moses 7:62, 1902 edition.)

The Glorious Resurrection

Now I understand by this quotation, that God clearly manifested to Enoch the redemption which He prepared, by offering the Messiah as a Lamb slain from before the foundation of the world; and by virtue of the same, the glorious resurrection of the Savior, and the resurrection of all the human family, even a resurrection of their corporeal bodies, is brought to pass; and also righteousness and truth are to sweep the earth as with a flood. And now, I ask, how righteousness and truth are going to sweep the earth as with a flood? I will answer. Men and angels are to be co-workers in bringing to pass this great work, and Zion is to be prepared, even a new Jerusalem, for the elect that are to be gathered from the four quarters of the earth, and to be established an holy city, for the tabernacle of the Lord shall be with them.

The Elect Must Be Gathered

Now Enoch was in good company in his views upon this subject: "And I heard a great voice out of heaven, saying, Behold, the tabernacle of God is with men, and He will dwell with them, and they shall be His people and God Himself shall be with them, and be their God" (Revelation xxi:3).

I discover by this quotation, that John upon the isle of Patmos, saw the same things concerning the last days, which Enoch saw. But before the tabernacle can be with men, the elect must be gathered from the four quarters of the earth. And to show further upon this subject of the gathering, Moses, after having pronounced the blessing and cursing upon the children of Israel, for their obedience or disobedience, says thus:

"And it shall come to pass, when all these things are come upon thee, the blessing and the curse which I have set before thee, and thou shalt call them to mind, among all the nations whither the Lord thy God hath driven thee, and shalt return unto the Lord thy God, and shalt obey His voice, according to all that I command thee, this day, thou and thy children, with all thine heart, and with all thy soul, that then the Lord thy God will turn thy captivity, and have compassion upon thee, and will return and gather thee from all the nations whither the Lord thy God hath scattered thee. If any of thine be driven out unto the outmost parts of heaven, from thence will the Lord thy God gather thee, and from thence will He fetch thee (Deut. xxx:1-4).

The New Jerusalem

It has been said by many of the learned and wise men, or historians, that the Indians or aborigines of this continent, are of the scattered tribes of Israel. It has been conjectured by many others, that the aborigines of this continent are not of the tribes of Israel, but the ten tribes have been led away into some unknown regions of the north. Let this be as it may, the prophecy I have just quoted "will fetch them," in the last days, and place them in the land which their fathers possessed. And you will find in the 7th verse of the 30th chapter, quoted, "And the Lord thy God will put all these curses upon thine enemies, and on them that hate thee, which persecuted thee."

Many may say that this scripture is fulfilled, but let them mark carefully what the prophet says: "If any are driven out unto the outmost parts of heaven," (Which must mean the breadth of the earth). Now this promise is good to any, if there should be such, that are driven out, even in the last days, therefore, the children of the fathers have claim unto this day. And if these curses are to be laid over on the heads of their enemies, wo be unto the Gentiles. (See Book of Mormon, III Nephi, Ch. xvi, current edition). "Wo unto the unbelieving of the Gentiles, saith the Father." And again (see Book of Mormon, III Nephi xx:22, current edition, which says), "Behold this people will I establish in this land, unto the fulfilling of the covenant which I made with your father Jacob, and it shall be a New Jerusalem." Now we learn from the Book of Mormon the very identical continent and spot of land upon which the New Jerusalem is to stand, and it must be caught up according to the vision of John upon the isle of Patmos.

Now many will feel disposed to say, that this New Jerusalem spoken of, is the Jerusalem that was built by the Jews on the eastern continent. But you will see, from Revelation xxi:2, there was a New Jerusalem coming down from God out of heaven, adorned as a bride for her husband; that after this, the Revelator was caught away in the Spirit, to a great and high mountain, and saw the great and holy city descending out of heaven from God. Now there are two cities spoken of here. As everything cannot be had in so narrow a compass as a letter, I shall say with brevity, that there is a New Jerusalem to be established on this continent, and also Jerusalem shall be rebuilt on the eastern continent (see Book of Mormon, Ether xiii:1-12). "Behold, Ether saw the days of Christ, and he spake also concerning the house of Israel, and the Jerusalem from whence Lehi should come; after it should be destroyed, it should be built up again, a holy city unto the Lord, wherefore it could not be a New Jerusalem, for it had been in a time of old." This may suffice, upon the subject of gathering, until my next.

Duties of Elders

I now proceed, at the close of my letter, to make a few remarks on the duty of Elders with regard to their teaching parents and children, husbands and wives, masters and slaves, or servants, as I said I would in my former letter.

And first, it becomes an Elder when he is traveling through the world, warning the inhabitants of the earth to gather together, that they may be built up an holy city unto the Lord, instead of commencing with children, or those who look up to parents or guardians to influence their minds, thereby drawing them from their duties, which they rightfully owe these legal guardians, they should commence their labors with parents, or guardians; and their teachings should be such as are calculated to turn the hearts of the fathers to the children, and the hearts of children to the fathers; and no influence should be used with children, contrary to the consent of their parents or guardians; but all such as can be persuaded in a lawful and righteous manner, and with common consent, we should feel it our duty to influence them to gather with the people of God. But otherwise let the responsibility rest upon the heads of parents or guardians, and all condemnation or consequences be upon their heads, according to the dispensation which he hath committed unto us; for God hath so ordained, that His work shall be cut short in righteousness, in the last days; therefore, first teach the parents, and then, with their consent, persuade the children to embrace the Gospel also. And if children embrace the Gospel, and their parents or guardians are unbelievers, teach them to stay at home and be obedient to their parents or guardians, if they require it; but if they consent to let them gather with the people of God, let them do so, and there shall be no wrong; and let all things be done carefully and righteously and God will extend to all such His guardian care.

And secondly, it is the duty of Elders, when they enter into any house, to let their labors and warning voice be unto the master of that house; and if he receive the Gospel, then he may extend his influence to his wife also, with consent, that peradventure she may receive the Gospel: but if a man receive not the Gospel, but gives his consent that his wife may receive it, and she believes, then let her receive it. But if a man forbid his wife, or his children, before they are of age, to receive the Gospel, then it should be the duty of the Elder to go his way, and use no influence against him, and let the responsibility be upon his head; shake off the dust of thy feet as a testimony against him, and thy skirts shall then be clear of their souls. Their sins are not to be answered upon such as God hath sent to warn them to flee the wrath to come, and save themselves from this untoward generation. The servants of God will not have gone over the nations of the Gentiles, with a warning voice, until the destroying angel will commence to waste the inhabitants of the earth, and as the prophet hath said, "It shall be a vexation to hear the report." I speak thus because I feel for my fellow men; I do it in the name of the Lord, being moved upon by the Holy Spirit. Oh, that I could snatch them from the vortex of misery, into which I behold them plunging themselves, by their sins; that I might be enabled by the warning voice, to be an instrument of bringing them to unfeigned repentance, that they might have faith to stand in the evil day!

Thirdly, it should be the duty of an Elder, when he enters into a house, to salute the master of that house, and if he gain his consent, then he may preach to all that are in that house; but if he gain not his consent, let him not go unto his slaves, or servants, but let the responsibility be upon the head of the master of that house, and the consequences thereof, and the guilt of that house is no longer upon his skirts, he is free; therefore, let him shake off the dust of his feet, and go his way. But if the master of that house give consent, the Elder may preach to his family, his wife, his children and his servants, his man-servants, or his maid-servants, or his slaves; then it should be the duty of the Elder to stand up boldly for the cause of Christ, and warn that people with one accord to repent and be baptized for the remission of sins, and for the Holy Ghost, always commanding them in the name of the Lord, in the spirit of meekness, to be kindly affectionate one toward another, that the fathers should be kind to their children, husbands to their wives, masters to their slaves or servants, children obedient to their parents, wives to their husbands, and slaves or servants to their masters.

Love of Husbands and Wives

"Wives, submit yourselves unto your own husbands, as unto the Lord, for the husband is the head of the wife, even as Christ is the head of the Church; and He is the Savior of the body. Therefore, as the Church is subject unto Christ, so let the wives be to their own husbands, in everything. Husbands, love your wives, even as Christ also loved the Church and gave Himself for it, that He might sanctify and cleanse it with the washing of water by the Word, that He might present it to Himself a glorious Church, not having spot or wrinkle, or any such thing, but that it should be holy and without blemish, so ought men to love their own wives as their own bodies. He that loveth his wife, loveth himself, for no man ever yet hated his own flesh, but nourisheth and cherisheth it, even as the Lord the Church, for we are members of His body, of His flesh, and His bones. For this cause shall a man leave his father and mother, and shall be joined unto his wife, and they two shall be one flesh" (Ephesians v:22-31).

"Wives, submit yourselves unto your own husbands, as it is fit in the Lord. Husbands, love your wives, and be not bitter against them. Children, obey your parents in all things, for this is well pleasing unto the Lord. Fathers, provoke not your children to anger, lest they be discouraged. Servants, obey in all things your masters, according to the flesh, not with eye-service, as men-pleasers, but in singleness of heart, fearing God" (Colossians iii:18-22).

But I must close this letter, and resume the subject in another number.

In the bonds of the New and Everlasting Covenant,

JOSEPH SMITH, JUN.

M. and A., November, 1835; also D. H. C. 2:259-264.

Reflections

Friday, November 6.—At home. Attended school during school hours, returned and spent the evening at home. I was this morning introduced to a man from the east. After hearing my name, he remarked that I was nothing but a man, indicating by this expression, that he had supposed that a person to whom the Lord should see fit to reveal His will, must be something more than a man. He seemed to have forgotten the saying that fell from the lips of St. James, that Elias was a man subject to like passions as we are, yet he had such power with God, that He, in answer to his prayers, shut the heavens that they gave no rain for the space of three years and six months; and again, in answer to his prayer, the heavens gave forth rain, and the earth gave forth fruit. Indeed, such is the darkness and ignorance of this generation, that they look upon it as incredible that a man should have any intercourse with his Maker. (Nov. 6, 1835). D. H. C., Vol. 2:302.

The Prophet's Remarks to the Twelve

At six o'clock, Nov. 12, 1835, the Apostles met with the First Presidency in council and on this occasion the Prophet made the following remarks:

I am happy in the enjoyment of this opportunity of meeting with this Council on this occasion. I am satisfied that the Spirit of the Lord is here, and I am satisfied with all the brethren present; and I need not say that you have my utmost confidence, and that I intend to uphold you to the uttermost, for I am well aware that you have to sustain my character against the vile calumnies and reproaches of this ungodly generation, and that you delight in so doing.

Darkness prevails at this time as it did at the time Jesus Christ was about to be crucified. The powers of darkness strove to obscure the glorious Sun of righteousness, that began to dawn upon the world, and was soon to burst in great blessings upon the heads of the faithful; and let me tell you, brethren, that great blessings await us at this time, and will soon be poured out upon us, if we are faithful in all things, for we are even entitled to greater spiritual blessings than they were, because they had Christ in person with them, to instruct them in the great plan of salvation. His personal presence we have not, therefore we have need of greater faith, on account of our peculiar circumstances; and I am determined to do all that I can to uphold you, although I may do many things inadvertently that are not right in the sight of God.

Special Ordinances

You want to know many things that are before you, that you may know how to prepare yourselves for the great things that God is about to bring to pass. But there is one great deficiency or obstruction in the way, that deprives us of the greater blessings; and in order to make the foundation of this Church complete and permanent, we must remove this obstruction, which is, to attend to certain duties that we have not as yet attended to. I supposed I had established this Church on a permanent foundation when I went to Missouri, and indeed I did so, for if I had been taken away, it would have been enough, but I yet live, and therefore God requires more at my hands. The item to which I wish the more particularly to call your attention to-night, is the ordinance of washing of feet. This we have not done as yet, but it is necessary now, as much as it was in the days of the Savior; and we must have a place prepared, that we may attend to this ordinance aside from the world.

We have not desired as much from the hand of the Lord through faith and obedience, as we ought to have done, yet we have enjoyed great blessings, and we are not so sensible of this as we should be. When or where has God suffered one of the witnesses or first Elders of this Church to fall? Never, and nowhere. Amidst all the calamities and judgments that have befallen the inhabitants of the earth, His almighty arm has sustained us, men and devils have raged and spent their malice in vain. We must have all things prepared, and call our solemn assembly as the Lord has commanded us, that we may be able to accomplish His great work, and it must be done in God's own way. The house of the Lord must be prepared, and the solemn assembly called and organized in it, according to the order of the house of God; and in it we must attend to the ordinance of washing of feet. It was never intended for any but official members. It is calculated to unite our hearts, that we may be one in feeling and sentiment, and that our faith may be strong, so that Satan cannot overthrow us, nor have any power over us here.

Order in House of God Always the Same

The endowment you are so anxious about, you cannot comprehend now, nor could Gabriel explain it to the understanding of your dark minds; but strive to be prepared in your hearts, be faithful in all things, that when we meet in the solemn assembly, that is, when such as God shall name out of all the official members shall meet, we must be clean every whit. Let us be faithful and silent, brethren, and if God gives you a manifestation, keep it to yourselves; be watchful and prayerful, and you shall have a prelude of those joys that God will pour out on that day. Do not watch for iniquity in each other, if you do you will not get an endowment, for God will not bestow it on such. But if we are faithful, and live by every word that proceeds forth from the mouth of God, I will venture to prophesy that we shall get a blessing that will be worth remembering, if we should live as long as John the Revelator; our blessings will be such as we have not realized before, nor received in this generation. The order of the house of God has been, and ever will be, the same, even after Christ comes; and after the termination of the thousand years it will be the same; and we shall finally enter into the celestial kingdom of God, and enjoy it forever.

Endowment Necessary

You need an endowment, brethren, in order that you may be prepared and able to overcome all things; and those that reject your testimony will be damned. The sick will be healed, the lame made to walk, the deaf to hear, and the blind to see, through your instrumentality. But let me tell you, that you will

not have power, after the endowment to heal those that have
not faith, nor to benefit them, for you might as well expect to
benefit a devil in hell as such as are possessed of his spirit, and
are willing to keep it: for they are habitations for devils, and
only fit for his society. But when you are endowed and prepared to preach the Gospel to all nations, kindreds, and tongues,
in their own languages, you must faithfully warn all, and bind
up the testimony, and seal up the law, and the destroying angel
will follow close at your heels, and exercise his tremendous
mission upon the children of disobedience; and destroy the
workers of iniquity, while the Saints will be gathered out from
among them, and stand in holy places ready to meet the Bridegroom when he comes.

I feel disposed to speak a few words more to you, my
brethren, concerning the endowment: All who are prepared,
and are sufficiently pure to abide the presence of the Savior,
will see Him in the solemn assembly.

The brethren expressed their gratification for the instruction I had given them. We then closed by prayer, when I
returned home and retired to rest.—D. H. C. 2:308-310.

High Councils and the Twelve

I decided that the High Council had nothing to do with
the Twelve, or the decisions of the Twelve. But if the Twelve
erred they were accountable only to the General Council of
the authorities of the whole Church, according to the revelations. (Sept. 26, 1835). D. H. C., Vol. 2:285.

Indians of Israel

Remarks by the Prophet at a meeting of the High Council at Kirtland.

Gathering of Israel

Much has been said and done of late by the general government in relation to the Indians (Lamanites) within the terri-
torial limits of the United States. One of the most important
points in the faith of the Church of the Latter-day Saints,
through the fullness of the everlasting Gospel, is the gathering
of Israel (of whom the Lamanites constitute a part) that happy
time when Jacob shall go up to the house of the Lord, to worship
Him in spirit and in truth, to live in holiness; when the Lord

will restore His judges as at the first, and His counselors as at
the beginning; when every man may sit under his own vine and
fig tree, and there will be none to molest or make afraid; when
He will turn to them a pure language, and the earth will be
filled with sacred knowledge, as the waters cover the great
deep; when it shall no longer be said, the Lord lives that brought
up the children of Israel out of the land of Egypt, but the Lord
lives that brought up the children of Israel from the land of
the north, and from all the lands whither He has driven them.
That day is one, all important to all men.

In view of its importance, together with all that the prophets have said about it before us, we feel like dropping a few
ideas in connection with the official statements from the government concerning the Indians. In speaking of the gathering,
we mean to be understood as speaking of it according to scripture, the gathering of the elect of the Lord out of every nation
on earth, and bringing them to the place of the Lord of Hosts,
when the city of righteousness shall be built, and where the
people shall be of one heart and one mind, when the Savior
comes: yea, where the people shall walk with God like Enoch,
and be free from sin. The word of the Lord is precious; and
when we read that the veil spread over all nations will be
destroyed, and the pure in heart see God, and reign with Him
a thousand years on earth, we want all honest men to have
a chance to gather and build up a city of righteousness, where
even upon the bells of the horses shall be written *"Holiness to
the Lord."*

The Book of Mormon has made known who Israel is, upon
this continent. And while we behold the government of the
United States gathering the Indians, and locating them upon
lands to be their own, how sweet it is to think that they may
one day be gathered by the Gospel! (Jan. 6, 1836). D. H. C.
2:357.

Orders in Councils

From the minutes of a Priesthood meeting in Kirtland Temple.

In the investigation of the subject [i. e. The Government
of the House of the Lord], it was found that many who
had deliberated upon it, were darkened in their minds, which
drew forth some remarks from President Smith respecting the
privileges of the authorities of the Church, that each should

speak in his turn and in his place, and in his time and season, that there may be perfect order in all things; and that every man, before he makes an objection to any item that is brought before a council for consideration, should be sure that he can throw light upon the subject rather than spread darkness, and that his objection be founded in righteousness, which may be done by men applying themselves closely to study the mind and will of the Lord, whose spirit always makes manifest and demonstrates the truth to the understanding of all who are in possession of the Spirit. (Jan. 15, 1836). D. H. C., Vol. 2:370.

To the Elders of the Church of Latter-day Saints

Parable of the Sower

I have shown unto you, in my last, that there are two Jerusalems spoken of in holy writ, in a manner I think satisfactory to your minds; at any rate I have given my views upon the subject, I shall now proceed to make some remarks from the sayings of the Savior, recorded in the 13th chapter of His Gospel according to St. Matthew, which, in my mind, afforded us as clear an understanding upon the important subject of the gathering, as anything recorded in the Bible. At the time the Savior spoke these beautiful sayings and parables contained in the chapter above quoted, we find Him seated in a ship on account of the multitude that pressed upon Him to hear His words; and He commenced teaching them, saying:

"Behold, a sower went forth to sow, and when he sowed, some seeds fell by the way side, and the fowls came and devoured them up: some fell upon stony places, where they had not much earth; and forthwith they sprang up because they had no deepness of earth: and when the sun was up they were scorched: and because they had no root they withered away. And some fell among thorns; and the thorns sprung up and choked them: but other fell in good ground, and brought forth fruit, some an hundred fold, some sixty fold, some thirty fold. Who hath ears to hear, let him hear.

He Who Will Not Receive Light Shall Lose Light

"And the disciples came and said unto Him, Why speakest thou unto them in parables? [I would here remark, that the 'them' made use of in this interrogation, is a personal pronoun, and refers to the multitude.] He answered and said unto them, [that is unto the disciples] because it is given unto you, to know the mysteries of the Kingdom of Heaven, but to them, [that is, unbelievers] it is not given; for whosoever hath, to him shall be given, and he shall have more abundance; but whosoever hath not, from him shall be taken away even that he hath."

We understand from this saying, that those who had been previously looking for a Messiah to come, according to the testimony of the prophets, and were then, at that time looking for a Messiah, but had not sufficient light, on account of their unbelief, to discern Him to be their Savior; and He being the true Messiah, consequently they must be disappointed, and lose even all the knowledge, or have taken away from them all the light, understanding, and faith which they had upon this sub-ject; therefore he that will not receive the greater light, must have taken away from him all the light which he hath; and if the light which is in you become darkness, behold, how great is that darkness! "Therefore," says the Savior, "speak I unto them in parables because they, seeing, see not, and hearing, they hear not, neither do they understand; and in them is ful-filled the prophecy of Esaias, which saith, By hearing ye shall hear, and shall not understand; and seeing ye shall see, and not perceive."

Now we discover that the very reason assigned by this prophet, why they would not receive the Messiah, was, because they did not or would not understand; and seeing, they did not perceive; "for this people's heart is waxed gross, and their ears are dull of hearing, and their eyes they have closed, lest at any time they should see with their eyes, and hear with their ears, and understand with their heart, and should be converted, and I should heal them." But what saith He to His disciples? "Blessed are your eyes for they see, and your ears for they hear; for verily I say unto you, that many prophets and right-eous men have desired to see those things which ye see, and have not seen them; and to hear those things which ye hear, and have not heard them."

Darkness the Condemnation of the World

We again make remark here—for we find that the very principle upon which the disciples were accounted blessed, was because they were permitted to see with their eyes and hear with their ears—that the condemnation which rested upon the multitude that received not His saying, was because they were not willing to see with their eyes, and hear with their ears; not because they could not, and were not privileged to see and hear, but because their hearts were full of iniquity and abominations; "as your fathers did, so do ye." The prophet, foreseeing that they would thus harden their hearts, plainly declared it; and herein is the condemnation of the world; that light hath come into the world, and men choose darkness rather than light, because their deeds are evil. This is so plainly taught by the Savior, that a wayfaring man need not mistake it.

And again—hear ye the parable of the sower. Men are in the habit, when the truth is exhibited by the servants of God, of saying, All is mystery; they have spoken in parables, and, therefore, are not to be understood. It is true they have eyes to see, and see not, but none are so blind as those who will not see; and, although the Savior spoke this to such characters, yet unto His disciples he expounded it plainly; and we have reason to be truly humble before the God of our fathers, that He hath left these things on record for us, so plain, that notwithstanding the exertions and combined influence of the priests of Baal, they have not power to blind our eyes, and darken our understanding, if we will but open our eyes, and read with candor, for a moment.

Explanation of the Parable of the Sower

But listen to the explanation of the parable of the Sower: "When any one heareth the word of the Kingdom, and understandeth it not, then cometh the wicked one, and catcheth away that which was sown in his heart." Now mark the expression—that which was sown in his heart. This is he which receiveth seed by the way side. Men who have no principle of righteousness in themselves, and whose hearts are full of iniquity, and have no desire for the principles of truth, do not understand the word of truth when they hear it. The devil taketh away the word of truth out of their hearts, because there is no desire for righteousness in them. "But he that receiveth seed in stony places, the same is he that heareth the word, and anon, with joy receiveth it; yet hath he not root in himself, but dureth for a while: for when tribulation or persecution ariseth because of the word, by and by, he is offended. He also that receiveth seed among the thorns, is he that heareth the word; and the care of this world, and the deceitfulness of riches choke the word, and he becometh unfruitful. But he that received seed into the good ground, is he that heareth the word, and understandeth it, which also beareth fruit, and bringeth forth, some an hundred fold, some sixty, some thirty." Thus the Savior Himself explains unto His disciples the parable which He put forth, and left no mystery or darkness upon the minds of those who firmly believe on His words.

We draw the conclusion, then, that the very reason why the multitude, or the world, as they were designated by the Savior, did not receive an explanation upon His parables, was because of unbelief. To you, He says (speaking to His disciples) it is given to know the mysteries of the Kingdom of God. And why? Because of the faith and confidence they had in Him. This parable was spoken to demonstrate the effects that are produced by the preaching of the word; and we believe that it has an allusion directly, to the commencement, or the setting up of the Kingdom in that age; therefore we shall continue to trace His sayings concerning this Kingdom from that time forth, even unto the end of the world.

Parable of the Tares

"Another parable put He forth unto them, saying, [which parable has an allusion to the setting up of the Kingdom, in that age of the world also], The Kingdom of Heaven is likened unto a man which sowed good seed in his field, but while men slept, his enemy came and sowed tares among the wheat, and went his way. But when the blade was sprung up, and brought forth fruit, then appeared the tares also; so the servants of the householder came and said unto him, Sir, didst not thou sow good seed in thy field? From whence, then, hath it tares? He said unto them, An enemy hath done this. The servants said unto him, Wilt thou then that we go and gather them up? But he said, Nay; lest while ye gather up the tares, ye root up also the wheat with them. Let both grow together until the harvest: and in the time of harvest I will say to the reapers, Gather ye together first the tares, and bind them in bundles to burn them, but gather the wheat into my barn."

Now we learn by this parable, not only the setting up of

the Kingdom in the days of the Savior, which is represented by the good seed, which produced fruit, but also the corruptions of the Church, which are represented by the tares, which were sown by the enemy, which His disciples would fain have plucked up, or cleansed the Church of, if their views had been favored by the Savior. But He, knowing all things, says, Not so. As much as to say, your views are not correct, the Church is in its infancy, and if you take this rash step, you will destroy the wheat, or the Church, with the tares; therefore it is better to let them grow together until the harvest, or the end of the world, which means the destruction of the wicked, which is not yet fulfilled, as we shall show hereafter, in the Savior's explanation of the parable, which is so plain that there is no room left for dubiety upon the mind, notwithstanding the cry of the priests—"parables, parables! figures, figures! mystery, mystery! all is mystery!" But we find no room for doubt here, as the parables were all plainly elucidated.

Parable of the Church in Last Days

And again, another parable put He forth unto them, having an allusion to the Kingdom that should be set up, just previous to or at the time of the harvest, which reads as follows—"The Kingdom of Heaven is like a grain of mustard seed, which a man took and sowed in his field: which indeed is the least of all seeds: but, when it is grown, it is the greatest among herbs, and becometh a tree, so that the birds of the air come and lodge in the branches thereof." Now we can discover plainly that this figure is given to represent the Church as it shall come forth in the last days. Behold, the Kingdom of Heaven is likened unto it. Now, what is like unto it?

Let us take the Book of Mormon, which a man took and hid in his field, securing it by his faith, to spring up in the last days, or in due time; let us behold it coming forth out of the ground, which is indeed accounted the least of all seeds, but behold it branching forth, yea, even towering, with lofty branches, and God-like majesty, until it, like the mustard seed, becomes the greatest of all herbs. And it is truth, and it has sprouted and come forth out of the earth, and righteousness begins to look down from heaven, and God is sending down His powers, gifts and angels, to lodge in the branches thereof.

The Kingdom of Heaven is like unto a mustard seed. Behold, then is not this the Kingdom of Heaven that is raising its head in the last days in the majesty of its God, even the Church of the Latter-day Saints, like an impenetrable, immovable rock in the midst of the mighty deep, exposed to the storms and tempests of Satan, but has, thus far, remained steadfast, and is still braving the mountain waves of opposition, which are driven by the tempestuous winds of sinking crafts, which have [dashed] and are still dashing with tremendous foam across its triumphant brow; urged onward with redoubled fury by the enemy of righteousness, with his pitchfork of lies, as you will see fairly represented in a cut contained in Mr. Howe's *Mormonism Unveiled?* And we hope that this adversary of truth will continue to stir up the sink of iniquity, that the people may the more readily discern between the righteous and the wicked.

Modern Sons of Sceva

We also would notice one of the modern sons of Sceva, who would fain have made people believe that he could cast out devils, by a certain pamphlet, the *Millennial Harbinger,* that went the rounds through our country; who felt so fully authorized to brand "Jo" Smith with the appellation of Elymas the sorcerer, and to say with Paul, "O full of all subtlety, and all mischief, thou child of the devil, thou enemy of all righteousness, wilt thou not cease to pervert the right ways of the Lord?" We would reply to this gentleman, Paul we know, and Christ we know, but who are ye? And with the best of feeling would say to him, in the language of Paul to those who said they were John's disciples, but had not so much as heard there was a Holy Ghost—to repent and be baptized for the remission of sins, by those who have legal authority, and under their hands you shall receive the Holy Ghost, according to the Scriptures:

"Then laid they their hands upon them, and they received the Holy Ghost" (Acts viii:17). "And when Paul had laid his hands upon them the Holy Ghost came on them and they spake with tongues and prophesied" (Acts xix:6). "Of the doctrine of baptism, and of laying on of hands, and of resurrection of the dead and of eternal judgment" (Hebrews vi:2). "How, then, shall they call on him in whom they have not believed? And how shall they believe in him of whom they have not heard? And how shall they hear without a preacher? And how shall they preach, except they be sent? As it is written, How beautiful are the feet of them that preach the Gospel of peace, and bring glad tidings of good things" (Romans x:14, 15). But if this man will not take our admonition, but will persist in his wicked course, we hope that he will continue trying to cast out devils, that we may have the clearer proof that the kingdom of Satan is divided against itself, and consequently cannot stand; for a kingdom divided against itself, speedily hath an end.

* * *

Parable of the Leaven

"And another parable spake He unto them. The Kingdom of Heaven is like unto leaven which a woman took and hid in three measures of meal till the whole was leavened." It may be understood that the Church of the Latter-day Saints has taken its rise from a little leaven that was put into three witnesses. Behold, how much this is like the parable! It is fast leavening the lump, and will soon leaven the whole. But let us pass on.

"All these things spake Jesus unto the multitude in parables; and without a parable spake He not unto them: that it might be fulfilled which was spoken by the prophet, saying, I will open my mouth in parables; I will utter things which have been kept secret from the foundation of the world. Then Jesus sent the multitude away, and went into the house: and His disciples came unto Him, saying, Declare unto us the parable of the tares of the field. He answered and said unto them, He that soweth the good seed is the Son of Man; the field is the world; the good seed are the children of the Kingdom; but the tares are the children of the wicked one." Now let our readers mark the expression—"the field is the world, the tares are the children of the wicked one, the enemy that sowed them is the devil, the harvest is the end of the world, [let them carefully mark this expression—the end of the world] and the reapers are the angels."

Destruction of the Wicked the End of the World

Now men cannot have any possible grounds to say that this is figurative, or that it does not mean what it says: for He is now explaining what He had previously spoken in parables; and according to this language, the end of the world is the destruction of the wicked, the harvest and the end of the world have an allusion directly to the human family in the last days, instead of the earth, as many have imagined; and that which shall precede the coming of the Son of Man, and the restitution of all things spoken of by the mouth of all the holy prophets since the world began; and the angels are to have something to do in this great work, for they are the reapers. As, therefore, the tares are gathered and burned in the fire, so shall it be in the end of the world; that is, as the servants of God go forth warning the nations, both priests and people, and as they harden their hearts and reject the light of truth, these first being delivered over to the buffetings of Satan, and the law and the testimony being closed up, as it was in the case of the Jews, they are left in darkness, and delivered over unto the day of burning; thus being bound up by their creeds, and their bands being made strong by their priests, are prepared for the fulfilment of the saying of the Savior—"The Son of Man shall send forth His angels, and gather out of His Kingdom all things that offend, and them which do iniquity, and shall cast them into a furnace of fire, there shall be wailing and gnashing of teeth." We understand that the work of gathering together of the wheat into barns, or garners, is to take place while the tares are being bound over, and preparing for the day of burning; that after the day of burnings, the righteous shall shine forth like the sun, in the Kingdom of their Father. Who hath ears to hear, let him hear.

The Treasure Hid in a Field

But to illustrate more clearly this gathering: We have another parable—"Again, the Kingdom of Heaven is like a treasure hid in a field, the which, when a man hath found, he hideth, and for joy thereof, goeth and selleth all that he hath, and buyeth that field!" The Saints work after this pattern. See the Church of the Latter-day Saints, selling all that they have, and gathering themselves together unto a place that they may purchase for an inheritance, that they may be together and bear each other's afflictions in the day of calamity.

"Again, the Kingdom of Heaven is like unto a merchant-man seeking goodly pearls, who, when he had found one pearl of great price, went and sold all that he had, and bought it." The Saints again work after this example. See men traveling to find places for Zion and her stakes or remnants, who, when they find the place for Zion, or the pearl of great price, straightway sell that they have, and buy it.

The Net Cast in the Sea

"Again, the Kingdom of Heaven is like unto a net that was cast into the sea, and gathered of every kind, which when it was full they drew to shore, and sat down, and gathered the good into vessels, but cast the bad away." For the work of this pattern, behold the seed of Joseph, spreading forth the Gospel net upon the face of the earth, gathering of every kind, that the good may be saved in vessels prepared for that purpose, and the angels will take care of the bad. So shall it be at the end of the world—the angels shall come forth and sever the wicked from among the just, and cast them into the furnace of fire, and there shall be wailing and gnashing of teeth.

"Jesus saith unto them, Have ye understood all these things? They say unto Him, Yea, Lord." And we say, yea, Lord; and well might they say, yea, Lord; for these things are so plain and so glorious, that every Saint in the last days must respond with a hearty Amen to them.

"Then said He unto them, therefore every scribe which is instructed in the kingdom of heaven, is like unto a man that is an householder, which bringeth forth out of his treasure things that are new and old."

For the works of this example, see the Book of Mormon coming forth out of the treasure of the heart. Also the covenants given to the Latter-day Saints, also the translation of the Bible—thus bringing forth out of the heart things new and old, thus answering to three measures of meal undergoing the purifying touch by a revelation of Jesus Christ, and the ministering of angels, who have already commenced this work in the last days, which will answer to the leaven which leavened the whole lump. Amen.

So I close, but shall continue the subject in another number. In the bonds of the New and Everlasting Covenant,

JOSEPH SMITH, JUN.

—Messenger and Advocate, Dec. 1835, also D. H. C. 2:264-272.

False Doctrines of Joshua the Jewish Minister

While sitting in my house, between ten and eleven this morning, a man came in and introduced himself to me by the name of "Joshua, the Jewish Minister." His appearance was something singular, having a beard about three inches in length, quite grey; also his hair was long and considerably silvered with age; I thought him about fifty or fifty-five years old; tall, straight, slender built, of thin visage, blue eyes, and fair complexion; wore a sea-green frock coat and pantaloons, black fur hat with narrow brim; and, while speaking, frequently shut his eyes, with a scowl on his countenance. I made some inquiry after his name, but received no definite answer. We soon commenced talking on the subject of religion, and, after I had made some remarks concerning the Bible, I commenced giving him a relation of the circumstances connected with the coming forth of the Book of Mormon, as recorded in the former part of this history.

While I was relating a brief history of the establishment of the Church of Christ in the last days, Joshua seemed to be highly entertained. When I had closed my narration, I observed that the hour of worship and dinner had arrived, and invited him to tarry, to which he consented. After dinner, the conversation was resumed, and Joshua proceeded to make some remarks on the prophecies, as follows—he observed that he was aware that I could bear stronger meat than many others, therefore he should open his mind the more freely:

Daniel has told us that he is to stand in his proper lot, in the latter days; according to his vision he had a right to shut it up, and also to open it again after many days, or in latter times. Daniel's image, whose head was gold, and body, arms, legs and feet, were composed of the different materials described in his vision, represents different governments. The golden head was to represent Nebuchadnezzar, King of Babylon; the other parts, other kings and forms of governments which I shall not now mention in detail, but confine my remarks more particularly to the feet of the image. The policy of the wicked spirit is to separate what God has joined together, and unite what He has separated, which the devil has succeeded in doing to admiration in the present state of society, which is like unto iron and clay.

There is confusion in all things, both political and religious; and notwithstanding all the efforts that are made to bring about a union, society remains disunited, and all attempts to unite it are as fruitless as to attempt to unite iron and clay. The feet of the image are the government of these United States. Other nations and kingdoms are looking up to her for an example of union, freedom, and equal rights, and therefore worship her as Daniel saw in the vision; although they are beginning to lose confidence in her, seeing the broils and discord that rise on her political and religious horizon. This image is characteristic of all governments.

We should leave Babylon. Twenty-four hours of improvement now, are worth as much as a year a hundred years ago. The spirits of the fathers that were cut down, or those that were under the altar, are now rising; this is the first resurrection. The Elder that falls first will rise last. We should not form any opinion only for the present, and leave the result of futurity with God. I have risen up out of obscurity, but was looked up to in temporal things when but a youth. It is not necessary that God should give us all things in His first commission to us, but in His second. John saw the angel deliver the Gospel in the last days. The small lights that God has given are sufficient to lead us out of Babylon; when we get out, we shall have the greater light.

Transmigration a Doctrine of the Devil

I told Joshua I did not understand his remarks on the resurrection, and wished him to explain. He replied that he did not feel impressed by the Spirit to unfold it further at present, but perhaps he might at some future time.

I then withdrew to transact some business with a gentleman who had called to see me, when Joshua informed my scribe that he was born in Cambridge, Washington County, New York. He says that all the railroads, canals, and other improvements are projected by the spirits of the resurrection. The silence spoken of by John the Revelator, which is to be in heaven for the space of half an hour, is between 1830 and 1851, during which time the judgments of God will be poured out, after that time there will be peace. * * *

Suspicions were entertained that the said Joshua was the noted Matthias of New York, spoken so much of in the public prints, on account of the trials he endured in that place, before a court of justice, for murder, man-slaughter, contempt of court, whipping his daughter, etc.; for the last two crimes he was imprisoned and came out about four months since. After some equivocating, he confessed that he really was Matthias.

After supper I proposed that he should deliver a lecture to us. He did so, sitting in his chair.

He commenced by saying, God said, let there be light, and there was light, which he dwelt upon throughout his discourse. He made some very excellent remarks, but his mind was evidently filled with darkness. * * *

I resumed conversation with Matthias, and desired him to enlighten my mind more on his views respecting the resurrection.

He said that he possessed the spirit of his fathers, that he was a literal descendant of Matthias, the Apostle, who was chosen in the place of Judas that fell; that his spirit was resurrected in him; and that this was the way or scheme of eternal life—this transmigration of soul or spirit from father to son.

I told him that his doctrine was of the devil, that he was in reality in possession of a wicked and depraved spirit, although he professed to be the Spirit of truth itself; and he said also that he possessed the soul of Christ.

He tarried until Wednesday, 11th, when, after breakfast, I told him, that my God told me, that his god was the devil, and I could not keep him any longer, and he must depart. And so I, for once, cast out the devil in bodily shape, and I believe a murderer. (Nov. 9, 1835.) D. H. C. 2:304-307.

Authority of the Twelve

From the minutes of a special meeting with the Twelve Apostles.

President Smith next proceeded to explain the duty of the Twelve, and their authority, which is next to the present Presidency, and that the arrangement of the assembly in this place, on the 15th instant, in placing the High Councils of Kirtland next the Presidency, was because the business to be transacted, was business relating to that body in particular, which was to fill the several quorums in Kirtland, not because they were first in office, and that the arrangements were the most judicious that could be made on the occasion; also the

Twelve are not subject to any other than the First Presidency, viz., "myself," said the Prophet, "Sidney Rigdon, and Frederick G. Williams, who are now my Counselors, and where I am not, there is no First Presidency over the Twelve."

The Prophet also stated to the Twelve that he did not countenance the harsh language of President Cowdery to them, neither would he countenance it in himself nor in any other man, "although," said he, "I have sometimes spoken too harshly from the impulse of the moment, and inasmuch as I have wounded your feelings, brethren, I ask your forgiveness, for I love you and will hold you up with all my heart in all righteousness, before the Lord, and before all men; for be assured, brethren, I am willing to stem the torrent of all opposition, in storms and in tempests, in thunders and in lightnings, by sea and by land, in the wilderness or among false brethren, or mobs, or wherever God in His providence may call us. And I am determined that neither heights nor depths, principalities nor powers, things present or things to come, or any other creature, shall separate me from you. And I will now covenant with you before God, that I will not listen to or credit any derogatory report against any of you, nor condemn you upon any testimony beneath the heavens, short of that testimony which is infallible, until I can see you face to face, and know of a surety; and I do place unremitted confidence in your word, for I believe you to be men of truth. And I ask the same of you, when I tell you anything, that you place equal confidence in my word, for I will not tell you I know anything that I do not know. But I have already consumed more time than I intended when I commenced, and I will now give way to my colleagues." (January 16, 1836.) D. H. C. 2:373-374.

Vision of the Celestial Kingdom

On the twenty-first day of January, 1836, the First Presidency, and a number of the presiding brethren in the Church, assembled in the Kirtland Temple where they engaged in the ordinances of the endowment, as far as it had at that time been revealed. After this was done the Prophet states that "All of the Presidency laid their hands upon me, and pronounced upon my head many prophecies and blessings, many of which I shall not notice at this time." "All of the Presidency" included Oliver Cowdery and Father Joseph Smith as well as the two counselors, Sidney Rigdon and Frederick G. Williams. Following this ordinance the following vision and revelation were given to the Prophet, making known to him and through him to the

Church one of the most important principles pertaining to the salvation of men.

The heavens were opened upon us, and I beheld the celestial kingdom of God, and the glory thereof, whether in the body or out I cannot tell. I saw the transcendent beauty of the gate through which the heirs of that kingdom will enter, which was like unto circling flames of fire; also the blazing throne of God, whereon was seated the Father and the Son. I saw the beautiful streets of that kingdom, which had the appearance of being paved with gold. I saw Father Adam and Abraham, and my father and my mother, my brother, Alvin, that has long since slept, and marvelled how it was that he had obtained an inheritance in that kingdom, seeing that he had departed this life before the Lord had set his hand to gather Israel the second time, and had not been baptized for the remission of sins.

Thus came the voice of the Lord unto me, saying—

Revelation

All who have died without a knowledge of this Gospel, who would have received it if they had been permitted to tarry, shall be heirs of the celestial kingdom of God; also all that shall die henceforth without a knowledge of it, who would have received it with all their hearts, shall be heirs of that kingdom, for I, the Lord, will judge all men according to their works, according to the desire of their hearts. And I also beheld that all children who die before they arrive at the years of accountability, are saved in the celestial kingdom of heaven. —D. H. C. 2:380-381.

Vision of the Apostles

I saw the Twelve Apostles of the Lamb, who are now upon the earth, who hold the keys of this last ministry, in foreign lands, standing together in a circle, much fatigued, with their clothes tattered and feet swollen, with their eyes cast downward, and Jesus standing in their midst, and they did not behold Him. The Savior looked upon them and wept. (January 21, 1836.) D. H. C. 2:381.

The Prophet's Vision of the Twelve

I also beheld Elder M'Lellin in the south, standing upon a hill, surrounded by a vast multitude, preaching to them, and a lame man standing before him supported by his crutches; he threw them down at his word and leaped as a hart, by the mighty power of God. Also, I saw Elder Brigham Young standing in a strange land, in the far south and west, in a desert place, upon a rock in the midst of about a dozen men of color, who appeared hostile. He was preaching to them in their own tongue, and the angel of God standing above his head, with a drawn sword in his hand, protecting him, but he did not see it. And I finally saw the Twelve in the celestial kingdom of God. I also beheld the redemption of Zion, and many things which the tongue of men cannot describe in full. (Jan. 21, 1836.) D. H. C. 2:381.

The Prophet's Draft of Resolutions

First. Resolved—That no one be ordained to any office in the Church in this stake of Zion, at Kirtland, without the unanimous voice of the several bodies that constitute this quorum, who are appointed to do Church business in the name of said Church, viz., the Presidency of the Church; the Twelve Apostles of the Lamb; the twelve High Councilors of Kirtland; the twelve High Councilors of Zion; the Bishop of Kirtland and his counselors; the Bishop of Zion and his counselors; and the seven presidents of Seventies; until otherwise ordered by said quorums.

Second. And further Resolved—That no one be ordained in the branches of said Church abroad, unless they are recommended by the voice of the respective branches of the Church to which they belong, to a general conference appointed by the heads of the Church, and from that conference receive their ordination. The foregoing resolutions were concurred in by the presidents of the Seventies. (Feb. 12, 1836.) D. H. C. 2:394.

Evils of Intemperance

I was informed today that a man by the name of Clark, who was under the influence of ardent spirits froze to death last night, near this place. How long, O Lord, will this monster intemperance find its victims on the earth! I fear until the earth is swept with the wrath and indignation of God, and Christ's kingdom becomes universal. O, come, Lord Jesus, and cut short Thy work in righteousness. (March 12, 1836.) D. H. C. 2:406.

The Twelve as Revelators

I then called upon the quorums and congregation of Saints to acknowledge the Twelve Apostles, who were present, as Prophets, Seers, Revelators, and special witnesses to all the nations of the earth, holding the keys of the kingdom, to unlock it, or cause it to be done, among them, and uphold them by their prayers, which they assented to by rising. (March 27, 1836.) D. H. C. 2:417.

Priesthood and Church Organization

While waiting, [i. e. for preparations for the observance of the Sacrament] I made the following remarks: that the time that we were required to tarry in Kirtland to be endowed, would be fulfilled in a few days, and then the Elders would go forth, and each must stand for himself, as it was not necessary for them to be sent out, two by two, as in former times, but to go in all meekness, in sobriety, and preach Jesus Christ and Him crucified; not to contend with others on account of their faith, or systems of religion, but pursue a steady course. This I delivered by way of commandment; and all who observe it not, will pull down persecution upon their heads, while those who do, shall always be filled with the Holy Ghost; this I pronounced as a prophecy, and sealed with hosanna and amen. Also that the Seventies are not called to serve tables, or preside over churches, to settle difficulties, but are to preach the Gospel and build them up, and set others, who do not belong to these quorums, to preside over them, who are High Priests. The Twelve also are not to serve tables, but to bear the keys of the Kingdom to all nations, and unlock the door of the Gospel to them, and call upon the Seventies to follow after them, and assist them. The Twelve are at liberty to go wheresoever they will, and if any one will say, I wish to go to such a place, let all the rest say amen.

Revelation of Necessary Ceremonies

The Seventies are at liberty to go to Zion if they please, or go wheresoever they will, and preach the Gospel; and let the redemption of Zion be our object, and strive to effect it by sending up all the strength of the Lord's house, wherever we find them; and I want to enter into the following covenant, that if any more of our brethren are slain or driven from their lands in Missouri, by the mob, we will give ourselves no rest, until we are avenged of our enemies to the uttermost. This covenant was sealed unanimously, with a hosanna and an amen.

I then observed to the quorums, that I had now completed the organization of the Church, and we had passed through all the necessary ceremonies,[1] that I had given them all the instruction they needed, and that they now were at liberty, after obtaining their licenses, to go forth and build up the Kingdom of God, and that it was expedient for me and the Presidency to retire, having spent the night previously in waiting upon the Lord in His Temple, and having to attend another dedication on the morrow, or conclude the one commenced on the last Sabbath, for the benefit of those of my brethren and sisters who could not get into the house on the former occasion, but that it was expedient for the brethren to tarry all night and worship before the Lord in His house. (March 29, 1836.) D. H. C. 2:431-432.

High Priests Not to Be Seventies

At an early hour on Thursday, the 6th of April, the official members assembled in the House of the Lord, when

---

[1]In speaking here of the completion of the organization of the Church, the Prophet had reference to the organizations of the Priesthood quorums; and the reference to the bestowal of "all the necessary ceremonies," and that he had given the brethren "all the instruction they needed," had reference to their setting apart and the receiving of all the necessary blessings to enable them to go forth and preach the Gospel in all the world. They were now prepared by instruction and endowment sufficiently to carry the message acceptably to the world. This remark by the Prophet did not have any reference to other ceremonies which were revealed later, as set forth in the Doctrine and Covenants, Section 124, 127, 128 and 132.

In 1834 (see *D. and C.* 105:33) the Elders who had been preaching the Gospel were instructed to gather at Kirtland and there they were to be endowed. This is the commandment: "Verily I say unto you, it is expedient in me that the first elders of my church should receive their endowment from on high in my house, which I have commanded to be built unto my name in the land of Kirtland." In the month of March, 1836, these endowment ceremonies were given. These ceremonies were not as complete as are the endowment ceremonies given in the Church today, but they were sufficient for the needs of that time and in keeping with the commandment of the Lord herein stated.

the time for the first two or three hours was spent by the different quorums in washing of feet, singing, praying, and preparing to receive instructions from the Presidency. The Presidents, together with the Seventies and their presidents, repaired to the west room in the attic story, where, for want of time the preceding evening, it became necessary to seal the anointing of those who had recently been anointed and not sealed.

Another subject of vital importance to the Church, was the establishing of the grades of the different quorums. It was ascertained that all but one or two of the presidents of the Seventies were High Priests, and when they had ordained and set apart any from the quorum of Elders, into the quorum of Seventies, they had conferred upon them the High Priesthood also. This was declared to be wrong, and not according to the order of heaven. New presidents of the Seventies were accordingly ordained to fill the places of such of them as were High Priests, and the ex-officio presidents, and such of the Seventies as had been legally ordained to be High Priests, were directed to unite with the High Priests' quorum. (Apr. 6, 1837.) D. H. C. 2:475-476.

Instruction on Priesthood

A solemn assembly of the official members of the Church was held in the Kirtland Temple commencing Monday, April 3rd, and continuing each day until Thursday the 6th. On the latter day, after these official members had received their endowment as far as it was revealed in the Kirtland Temple, the Prophet addressed them on many subjects, a synopsis of which in relation to the Priesthood he recorded in his journal as follows—

How and By Whom Revelation Comes

President Joseph Smith, Jun., addressed the assembly and said, the Melchizedek High Priesthood was no other than the Priesthood of the Son of God; that there are certain ordinances which belong to the Priesthood, from which flow certain results; and the Presidents or Presidency are over the Church; and revelations of the mind and will of God to the Church, are to come through the Presidency. This is the order of heaven, and the power and privilege of this Priesthood. It is also the privilege of any officer in this Church to obtain revelations, so far as relates to his particular calling and duty in the Church. All are bound by the principles of virtue and happiness, but one great privilege of the Priesthood is to obtain revelations of the mind and will of God.   It is also the privilege of the Melchizedek Priesthood, to reprove, rebuke, and admonish, as well as to receive revelation.   If the Church knew all the commandments, one-half they would condemn through prejudice and ignorance.

Offices in the Priesthood

A High Priest is a member of the same Melchizedek Priesthood with the Presidency, but not of the same power or authority in the Church.   The Seventies are also members of the same Priesthood, [i. e. the High Priesthood], are a sort of traveling council or Priesthood, and may preside over a church or churches, until a High Priest can be had.   The Seventies are to be taken from the quorum of Elders, and are not to be High Priests.   They are subject to the direction and dictation of the Twelve, who have the keys of the ministry. All are to preach the Gospel, by the power and influence of the Holy Ghost; and no man can preach the Gospel without the Holy Ghost.

The Bishop is a High Priest, and necessarily so, because he is to preside over that particular branch of Church affairs, that is denominated the Lesser Priesthood, and because we have no direct lineal descendant of Aaron, to whom it would of right belong.   This is the same, or a branch of the same, Priesthood, which may be illustrated by the figure of the human body, which has different members, which have different offices to perform; all are necessary in their place, and the body is not complete without all the members.

From a retrospect of the requirements of the servants of God to preach the Gospel, we find few qualified even to be Priests, and if a Priest understands his duty, his calling, and ministry, and preaches by the Holy Ghost, his enjoyment is as great as if he were one of the Presidency; and his services are necessary in the body, as are also those of Teachers and Deacons.   Therefore, in viewing the Church as a whole, we may strictly denominate it one Priesthood.   President Smith also said:

Value of a Righteous Rebuke

"I frequently rebuke and admonish my brethren, and that because I love them, not because I wish to incur their displeasure, or mar their happiness.   Such a course of conduct is not calculated to gain the good will of all, but rather the ill will of many; therefore, the situation in which I stand is an important one; so, you see, brethren, the higher the authority, the greater the difficulty of the station; but these rebukes and admonitions become necessary, from the perverseness of the brethren, for their temporal as well as spiritual welfare. They actually constitute a part of the duties of my station and calling. Others have other duties to perform, that are important, and far more enviable, and may be just as good, like the feet and hands, in their relation to the human body—neither can claim priority, or say to the other, I have no need of you. After all that has been said, the greatest and most important duty is to preach the Gospel.

"There are many causes of embarrassment, of a pecuniary nature, now pressing upon the heads of the Church. They began poor; were needy, destitute, and were truly afflicted by their enemies; yet the Lord commanded them to go forth and preach the Gospel, to sacrifice their time, their talents, their good name, and jeopardize their lives; and in addition to this, they were to build a house for the Lord, and prepare for the gathering of the Saints. Thus it is easy to see this must [have] involved them [in financial difficulties]. They had no temporal means in the beginning commensurate with such an undertaking; but this work must be done; this place [Kirtland] had to be built up. Large contracts have been entered into for lands on all sides, where our enemies have signed away their rights. We are indebted to them but our brethren from abroad have only to come with their money, take these contracts, relieve their brethren from the pecuniary embarrassments under which they now labor, and procure for themselves a peaceable place of rest among us. This place must and will be built up, and every brother that will take hold and help secure and discharge those contracts that have been made, shall be rich." (April 6, 1837.) D. H. C. 2:477-479.

SECTION THREE
1838-1839

SECTION THREE

---◇---

The Political Motto of the Church of Latter-day Saints

The Constitution of our country formed by the Fathers of liberty. Peace and good order in society. Love to God, and good will to man. All good and wholesome laws, virtue and truth above all things, and aristarchy, live forever! But woe to tyrants, mobs, aristocracy, anarchy, and toryism, and all those who invent or seek out unrighteous and vexatious law suits, under the pretext and color of law, or office, either religious or political. Exalt the standard of Democracy! Down with that of priestcraft, and let all the people say Amen! that the blood of our fathers may not cry from the ground against us. Sacred is the memory of that blood which bought for us our liberty.

JOSEPH SMITH, JUN.,
THOMAS B. MARSH,
DAVID W. PATTEN,
BRIGHAM YOUNG,
SAMUEL H. SMITH,
GEORGE M. HINKLE,
JOHN CORRILL,
GEORGE W. ROBINSON.

—D. H. C. 3:9.)   (March, 1838).

The Word of Wisdom

President Joseph Smith, Jr., next made a few remarks on the Word of Wisdom, giving the reason of its coming forth, saying it should be observed.[1] (April 7, 1838.) F. W. R., p. 111.

---

[1]This statement by the Prophet is in accord with the action of the High Council of the Church shortly after its organization in February, 1834. At one of the earliest meetings of this council over which the Presidency of the Church presided, the following action was taken: The question was asked: "Whether disobedience to the word of wisdom was a transgression sufficient to deprive an official member from holding office in the Church, after having it sufficiently taught him?" After a free and full discussion, Joseph Smith the Prophet gave the following decision which was unanimously accepted by the council: "No official member in this Church is worthy to hold an office after having the word of wisdom properly taught him; and he, the official member, neglecting to comply with and obey it."

Revelation Given to Brigham Young at Far West

Verily, thus saith the Lord, let my servant Brigham Young go unto the place which he has bought, on Mill Creek, and there provide for his family until an effectual door is opened for the support of his family, until I shall command him to go hence, and not to leave his family until they are amply provided for. Amen. (April 17, 1838.) D. H. C. 3:23.

Evils of Hasty Judgment

Sunday, May 6, 1838—I preached to the Saints, setting forth the evils that existed, and that would exist, by reason of hasty judgment, or decisions upon any subject given by any people, or in judging before they had heard both sides of a question. I also cautioned the Saints against men who came amongst them whining and growling about their money, because they had kept the Saints, and borne some of the burden with others, and thus thinking that others, who are still poorer, and have borne greater burdens than they themselves, ought to make up their losses. I cautioned the Saints to beware of such, for they were throwing out insinuations here and there, to level a dart at the best interests of the Church, and if possible destroy the character of its Presidency. I also gave some instructions in the mysteries of the kingdom of God; such as the history of the planets, Abraham's writings upon the planetary systems, etc.[2]

---

*There is a prevalent notion in the world today that before the time of Columbus, Galileo, and Copernicus, all ancient people believed that the earth was flat and the center of the universe. From the writings of the Scriptures, and more especially those which have come to us in this dispensation, we know that the ancient peoples, when they were guided by the Spirit of the Lord, had the true conception of the universe. The Lord revealed to Abraham great truths about the heavenly bodies, their revolutions, times and seasons, and these were published by the Prophet Joseph Smith before modern astronomers were familiar with these facts. From the writings of Abraham we learn that the Egyptians understood the nature of the planets. Moses also recorded much about this and other worlds, but because of the unbelief and apostasy from truth, these writings were eliminated from his writings. In the Book of Abraham we find the following:

"But the records of the fathers, even the patriarchs concerning, the right of Priesthood the Lord my God preserved in mine own hands; therefore a knowledge of the beginning of the creation, and also of the planets, and of the stars, as they were made known unto the fathers, have I kept even unto this day, and I shall endeavor to write some of these things upon this record, for the benefit of my posterity that shall come after me."

We learn from the Book of Mormon (Helaman 12:13-15) that the Ne-

In the afternoon I spoke again on different subjects: the principle of wisdom, and the Word of Wisdom. (May 6, 1838.) D. H. C. 3:27.

The Prophet's Answer to Sundry Questions

I answered the questions which were frequently asked me, while on my last journey but one from Kirtland to Missouri, as printed in the Elders' Journal, Vol. I, Number II, pages 28 and 29, as follows:

First—"Do you believe the Bible?"

If we do, we are the only people under heaven that does, for there are none of the religious sects of the day that do.

Second—"Wherein do you differ from other sects?"

In that we believe the Bible, and all other sects profess to believe their interpretations of the Bible, and their creeds.

Third—"Will everybody be damned, but Mormons?"

Yes, and a great portion of them, unless they repent, and work righteousness.

Fourth—"How and where did you obtain the Book of Mormon?"

Moroni, who deposited the plates in a hill in Manchester, Ontario County, New York, being dead and raised again therefrom, appeared unto me, and told me where they were, and gave me directions how to obtain them. I obtained them, and the Urim and Thummim with them, by the means of which I translated the plates; and thus came the Book of Mormon.

Fifth—"Do you believe Joseph Smith, Jun., to be a Prophet?"

Yes, and every other man who has the testimony of Jesus. For the testimony of Jesus is the spirit of prophecy.—Revelation, xix:10th verse.

Sixth—"Do the Mormons believe in having all things in common?"

No.

Seventh—"Do the Mormons believe in having more wives than one?"

No, not at the same time. But they believe that if their companion dies, they have a right to marry again. But we do

---

phites understood the nature of the planets. It was not until apostasy and rebellion against the things of God that the true knowledge of the universe, as well as the knowledge of other truths, became lost among men.

disapprove of the custom, which has gained in the world, and has been practiced among us, to our great mortification, in marrying in five or six weeks, or even in two or three months, after the death of their companion. We believe that due respect ought to be had to the memory of the dead, and the feelings of both friends and children.[3]

Eighth—"Can they [the Mormons] raise the dead?"

No, nor can any other people that now lives, or ever did live. But God can raise the dead, through man as an instrument.

Ninth—"What signs does Joseph Smith give of his divine mission?"

The signs which God is pleased to let him give, according as His wisdom thinks best, in order that He may judge the world agreeably to His own plan.

Tenth—"Was not Joseph Smith a money digger?"

Yes, but it was never a very profitable job for him, as he only got fourteen dollars a month for it.

Eleventh—"Did not Joseph Smith steal his wife?"

Ask her, she was of age, she can answer for herself."

Twelfth—"Do the people have to give up their money when they join his Church?"

No other requirement than to bear their proportion of the expenses of the Church, and support the poor.

Thirteenth—"Are the Mormons abolitionists?"

No, unless delivering the people from priestcraft, and the priests from the power of Satan, should be considered abolition. But we do not believe in setting the negroes free.

Fourteenth—"Do they not stir up the Indians to war, and to commit depredations?"

No, and they who reported the story knew it was false when they put it in circulation. These and similar reports are

---

[3]Nothwithstanding this remark about due respect for both the living and the dead, the Prophet varied from this view in counseling his brother Hyrum. Hyrum Smith's wife Jerusha, died in October, 1837, leaving an infant daughter and a large family of small children. The Prophet told his brother Hyrum that it was the will of the Lord that he should marry without delay and take as a wife a young English girl, named Mary Fielding, who had joined the Church through the preaching of Elder Parley P. Pratt in Toronto, Canada. Hyrum accepted this counsel from the Prophet and Mary Fielding became his wife and the mother of President Joseph F. Smith, who was born November 13, 1838.

palmed upon the people by the priests, and this is the only reason why we ever thought of answering them.

Fifteenth—"Do the Mormons baptize in the name of 'Joe' Smith?"

No, but if they did, it would be as valid as the baptism administered by the sectarian priests.

Sixteenth—"If the Mormon doctrine is true, what has become of all those who died since the days of the Apostles?"

All those who have not had an opportunity of hearing the Gospel, and being administered unto by an inspired man in the flesh, must have it hereafter, before they can be finally judged.

Seventeenth—"Does not 'Joe' Smith profess to be Jesus Christ?"

No, but he professes to be His brother, as all other Saints have done and now do: Matt. xii:49, 50, "And He stretched forth His hand toward His disciples and said, Behold my mother and my brethren; for whosoever shall do the will of my Father, which is in heaven, the same is my brother, and sister, and mother."

Eighteenth—"Is there anything in the Bible which licenses you to believe in revelation now-a-days?"

Is there anything that does not authorize us to believe so? If there is, we have, as yet, not been able to find it.

Nineteenth—"Is not the canon of the Scriptures full?"

If it is, there is a great defect in the book, or else it would have said so.

Twentieth—"What are the fundamental principles of your religion?"

The fundamental principles of our religion are the testimony of the Apostles and Prophets, concerning Jesus Christ, that He died, was buried, and rose again the third day, and ascended into heaven; and all other things which pertain to our religion are only appendages to it. But in connection with these, we believe in the gift of the Holy Ghost, the power of faith, the enjoyment of the spiritual gifts according to the will of God, the restoration of the house of Israel, and the final triumph of truth.

I published the foregoing answers to save myself the trouble of repeating the same a thousand times over and over again. (May 8, 1838.) D. H. C. 3:28-30.

The Prophet and Party at Tower Hill or Adam-ondi-Ahman

Saturday, 19—This morning we struck our tents and formed a line of march, crossing Grand River at the mouth of Honey Creek and Nelson's Ferry. Grand River is a large, beautiful, deep and rapid stream, during the high waters of Spring, and will undoubtedly admit of navigation by steamboat and other water craft. At the mouth of Honey Creek is a good landing. We pursued our course up the river, mostly through timber, for about eighteen miles, when we arrived at Colonel Lyman Wight's home. He lives at the foot of Tower Hill (a name I gave the place in consequence of the remains of an old Nephite altar or tower that stood there), where we camped for the Sabbath.

In the afternoon I went up the river about half a mile to Wight's Ferry, accompanied by President Rigdon, and my clerk, George W. Robinson, for the purpose of selecting and laying claim to a city plat near said ferry in Daviess County, township 60, ranges 27 and 28, and sections 25, 36, 31, and 30, which the brethren called "Spring Hill," but by the mouth of the Lord it was named Adam-ondi-Ahman, because, said He, it is the place where Adam shall come to visit his people, or the Ancient of Days shall sit, as spoken of by Daniel the Prophet. (May 19, 1838.) D. H. C. 3:34-35.

The Prophet's Letter to the Church Written from Liberty Jail

December 16, 1838.

To the Church of Jesus Christ of Latter-day Saints in Caldwell county, and all the Saints who are scattered abroad, who are persecuted, and made desolate, and who are afflicted in divers manners for Christ's sake and the Gospel's, by the hands of a cruel mob and the tyrannical disposition of the authorities of this state; and whose perils are greatly augmented by the wickedness and corruption of false brethren, greeting:

May grace, mercy, and the peace of God be and abide with you; and notwithstanding all your sufferings, we assure you that you have our prayers and fervent desires for your welfare, day and night. We believe that that God who seeth us in this solitary place, will hear our prayers, and reward you openly.

In Bonds for the Testimony of Jesus

Know assuredly, dear brethren, that it is for the testimony of Jesus that we are in bonds and in prison. But we say unto you, that we consider that our condition is better (notwithstanding our sufferings) than that of those who have persecuted us, and smitten us, and borne false witness against us; and we most assuredly believe that those who do bear false witness against us, do seem to have a great triumph over us for the present. But we want you to remember Haman and Mordecai: you know that Haman could not be satisfied so long as he saw Mordecai at the king's gate, and he sought the life of Mordecai and the destruction of the people of the Jews. But the Lord so ordered it, that Haman was hanged upon his own gallows.

So shall it come to pass with poor Haman in the last days, and those who have sought by unbelief and wickedness and by the principle of mobocracy to destroy us and the people of God, by killing and scattering them abroad, and wilfully and maliciously delivering us into the hands of murderers, desiring us to be put to death, thereby having us dragged about in chains and cast into prison. And for what cause? It is because we were honest men, and were determined to defend the lives of the Saints at the expense of our own. I say unto you, that those who have thus vilely treated us, like Haman, shall be hanged upon their own gallows; or, in other words, shall fall into their own gin, and snare, and ditch, and trap, which they have prepared for us, and shall go backwards and stumble and fall, and their name shall be blotted out, and God shall reward them according to all their abominations.

Though in Prison, Yet Hearts Not Faint

Dear brethren, do not think that our hearts faint, as though some strange thing had happened unto us, for we have seen and been assured of all these things beforehand, and have an assurance of a better hope than that of our persecutors. Therefore God hath made broad our shoulders for the burden. We glory in our tribulation, because we know that God is with us, that He is our friend, and that He will save our souls. We do not care for them that can kill the body; they cannot harm our souls. We ask no favors at the hands of mobs, nor of the world, nor of the devil, nor of his emissaries the dissenters, and those who love, and make, and swear falsehoods, to take away our lives. We have never dissembled, nor will we for the sake of our lives.

Forasmuch, then, as we know that we have been endeavoring with all our mind, might, and strength, to do the will of God, and all things whatsoever He has commanded us; and as to our light speeches, which may have escaped our lips from time to time, they have nothing to do with the fixed purposes of our hearts; therefore it sufficeth us to say, that our souls were vexed from day to day. We refer you to Isaiah, who considers those who make a man an offender for a word, and lay a snare for him that reproveth in the gate. We believe that the old Prophet verily told the truth: and we have no retraction to make. We have reproved in the gate, and men have laid snares for us. We have spoken words, and men have made us offenders. And notwithstanding all this, our minds are not yet darkened, but feel strong in the Lord. But behold the words of the Savior: "If the light which is in you become darkness, behold how great is that darkness." Look at the dissenters. Again, "If you were of the world the world would love its own."

*　*　*

Blessed Are the Persecuted

Perhaps our brethren will say, because we thus write, that we are offended at these characters. If we are, it is not for a word, neither because they reproved in the gate—but because they have been the means of shedding innocent blood. Are they not murderers then at heart? Are not their consciences seared as with a hot iron? We confess that we are offended; but the Savior said, "It must needs be that offenses come, but woe unto them by whom they come." And again, "Blessed are ye when men shall revile you, and persecute you, and shall say all manner of evil against you falsely for my sake; rejoice and be exceeding glad, for great is your reward in heaven, for so persecuted they the Prophets which were before you."

Now, dear brethren, if any men ever had reason to claim this promise, we are the men; for we know that the world not only hate us, but they speak all manner of evil of us falsely, for no other reason than that we have been endeavoring to teach the fullness of the Gospel of Jesus Christ.

After we were bartered away by Hinkle, and were taken into the militia camp, we had all the evidence we could have asked for that the world hated us. If there were priests among them of all the different sects, they hated us, and that most cordially too. If there were generals, they hated us; if there were colonels, they hated us; and the soldiers, and officers of every kind, hated us; and the most profane, blasphemous, and drunkards; and whoremongers, hated us—they all hated us, most cordially. And now what did they hate us for? Purely because of the testimony of Jesus Christ. Was it because we were liars? We know that it has been so reported by some, but it has been reported falsely. Was it because we have committed treason against the government in Daviess county, or burglary, or larceny, or arson, or any other unlawful act in Daviess county? We know that we have been so reported by priests, and certain lawyers, and certain judges, who are the instigators, aiders, and abettors of a certain gang of murderers and robbers, who have been carrying on a scheme of mobocracy to uphold their priestcraft, against the Saints of the last days; and for a number of years have tried, by a well contemplated and premeditated scheme, to put down by physical power a system of religion that all the world, by their mutual attainments, and by any fair means whatever, were not able to resist.

Accused by False Witnesses

Hence mobbers were encouraged by priests and Levites, by the Pharisees, by the Sadducees, and Essenes, and Herodians, and the most worthless, abandoned, and debauched, lawless, and inhuman, and the most beastly set of men that the earth can boast of—and indeed a parallel cannot be found anywhere else—to gather together to steal, to plunder, to starve, and to exterminate, and burn the houses of the "Mormons."

These are characters that, by their treasonable and overt acts, have desolated and laid waste Daviess county. These are the characters that would fain make all the world believe that we are guilty of the above named acts. But they represent us falsely; we stood in our own defense, and we believe that no man of us acted only in a just, a lawful, and a righteous retaliation against such marauders.

We say unto you, that we have not committed treason, nor any other unlawful act in Daviess county. Was it for murder in Ray county, against mob-militia; who was as a wolf in the first instance, hide and hair, teeth, legs and tail, who afterwards put on a militia sheep skin with the wool on; who could sally forth, in the day time, into the flock, and snarl and show his teeth, and scatter and devour the flock, and satiate himself upon his prey, and then sneak back into the bramble in order that he might conceal himself in his well tried skin with the wool on?

We are well aware that there is a certain set of priests and satellites, and mobbers that would fain make all the world believe that we were guilty of the doings of this howling wolf that made such havoc among the sheep, who, when he retreated, howled and bleated at such a desperate rate, that if one could have been there, he would have thought that all the wolves, whether wrapped up in sheep skins or in goat skins, or in some other skins, and in fine all the beasts of the forest, were awfully alarmed, and catching the scent of innocent blood, they sallied forth with one tremendous howl and crying of all sorts; and such a howling, and such a tremendous havoc never was known before; such inhumanity, and relentless cruelty and barbarity as were practiced against the Saints in Missouri can scarcely be found in the annals of history.

Now those characters if allowed to would make the world believe that we had committed murder, by making an attack upon this howling wolf, while the fact is we were at home and in our bed, and asleep, and knew nothing of that transaction any more than we know what is going on in China while we are within these walls. Therefore we say again unto you, we are innocent of these things, and they have represented us falsely.

Was it for committing adultery that we were assailed? We are aware that that false slander has gone abroad, for it has been reiterated in our ears. These are falsehoods also. Renegade "Mormon" dissenters are running through the world and spreading various foul and libelous reports against us, thinking thereby to gain the friendship of the world, because they know that we are not of the world, and that the world hates us; therefore they [the world] make a tool of these fellows [the dissenters]; and by them try to do all the injury they can, and after that they hate them worse than they do us, because they find them to be base traitors and sycophants.

Consecrated Lives

Such characters God hates; we cannot love them. The world hates them, and we sometimes think that the devil ought to be ashamed of them.

We have heard that it is reported by some, that some of us should have said, that we not only dedicated our property, but our families also to the Lord; and Satan, taking advantage of this, has perverted it into licentiousness, such as a community of wives, which is an abomination in the sight of God.

When we consecrate our property to the Lord it is to administer to the wants of the poor and needy, for this is the law of God; it is not for the benefit of the rich, those who have no need; and when a man consecrates or dedicates his wife and children, he does not give them to his brother, or to his neighbor, for there is no such law: for the law of God is, Thou shalt not commit adultery. Thou shalt not covet thy neighbor's wife. He that looketh upon a woman to lust after her, has committed adultery already in his heart. Now for a man to consecrate his property, wife and children, to the Lord, is nothing more nor less than to feed the hungry, clothe the naked, visit the widow and fatherless, the sick and afflicted, and do all he can to administer to their relief in their afflictions, and for him and his house to serve the Lord. In order to do this, he and all his house must be virtuous, and must shun the very appearance of evil.

Now if any person has represented anything otherwise than what we now write, he or she is a liar, and has represented us falsely—and this is another manner of evil which is spoken against us falsely.

We have learned also since we have been prisoners, that many false and pernicious things, which were calculated to lead the Saints far astray and to do great injury, have been taught by Dr. Avard as coming from the Presidency, and we have reason to fear that many other designing and corrupt characters like unto himself, have been teaching many things which the Presidency never knew were being taught in the Church by anybody until after they were made prisoners. Had they known of such things they would have spurned them and their authors as they would the gates of hell. Thus we find that there have been frauds and secret abominations and evil works of darkness going on, leading the minds of the weak and unwary

into confusion and distraction, and all the time palming it off
upon the Presidency, while the Presidency were ignorant as
well as innocent of those things which those persons were practicing in the Church in their name.   Meantime the Presidency
were attending to their own secular and family concerns,
weighed down with sorrow, in debt, in poverty, in hunger,
essaying to be fed, yet finding [i.e. supporting] themselves.
They occasionally received deeds of charity, it is true; but these
were inadequate to their subsistence; and because they received
those deeds, they were envied and hated by those who professed
to be their friends.

But notwithstanding we thus speak, we honor the Church,
when we speak of the Church as a Church, for their liberality,
kindness, patience, and long-suffering, and their continual kindness towards us.

★   ★   ★

Wilful Sin Unpardonable

Again, if men sin wilfully after they have received the
knowledge of the truth, there remaineth no more sacrifice for
sin, but a certain fearful looking for of judgment and fiery
indignation to come, which shall devour these adversaries. For
he who despised Moses' law died without mercy under two or
three witnesses. Of how much more severe punishment suppose
ye, shall he be thought worthy, who hath sold his brother, and
denied the new and everlasting covenant by which he was
sanctified, calling it an unholy thing, and doing despite to the
Spirit of grace.

And again we say unto you, that inasmuch as there is
virtue in us, and the Holy Priesthood has been conferred upon
us—and the keys of the kingdom have not been taken from us,
for verily thus saith the Lord, "Be of good cheer, for the keys
that I gave unto you are yet with you"—therefore we say unto
you, dear brethren, in the name of the Lord Jesus Christ, we
deliver these characters unto the buffetings of Satan until the
day of redemption, that they may be dealt with according to
their works; and from henceforth their works shall be made
manifest.

A Word of Exhortation

And now dear and well beloved brethren—and when we
say brethren, we mean those who have continued faithful in

Christ, men, women and children—we feel to exhort you in the name of the Lord Jesus, to be strong in the faith in the new and everlasting covenant, and nothing frightened at your enemies. For what has happened unto us is an evident token to them of damnation; but unto us, of salvation, and that of God. Therefore hold on even unto death; for "he that seeks to save his life shall lose it; and he that loses his life for my sake, and the Gospel's, shall find it," saith Jesus Christ.

Brethren, from henceforth, let truth and righteousness prevail and abound in you; and in all things be temperate; abstain from drunkenness, and from swearing, and from all profane language, and from everything which is unrighteous or unholy; also from enmity, and hatred, and covetousness, and from every unholy desire. Be honest one with another, for it seems that some have come short of these things, and some have been uncharitable, and have manifested greediness because of their debts towards those who have been persecuted and dragged about with chains without cause, and imprisoned. Such characters God hates—and they shall have their turn of sorrow in the rolling of the great wheel, for it rolleth and none can hinder. Zion shall yet live, though she seem to be dead.

Remember that whatsoever measure you mete out to others, it shall be measured to you again. We say unto you, brethren, be not afraid of your adversaries; contend earnestly against mobs, and the unlawful works of dissenters and of darkness.

And the very God of peace shall be with you, and make a way for your escape from the adversary of your souls. We commend you to God and the word of His grace, which is able to make us wise unto salvation. Amen.

JOSEPH SMITH, JUN.

—D. H. C. 3:226-233.

The Prophet's Epistle to the Church, Written in Liberty Prison, Clay County, Missouri, March 25, 1839

To the Church of Latter-day Saints at Quincy, Illinois, and scattered abroad, and to Bishop Partridge in particular;[4]

---

[4]The following important communication written by the Prophet and signed by all of his fellow prisoners, to the Church at large, and to Bishop Edward Partridge in particular, was written between the 20th and 25th of March. In the Prophet's history as published many years ago in current issues of the *Deseret News* and *Millennial Star* the communication is divided

Your humble servant, Joseph Smith, Jun., prisoner for the Lord Jesus Christ's sake, and for the Saints, taken and held by the power of mobocracy, under the exterminating reign of his excellency, the governor, Lilburn W. Boggs, in company with his fellow prisoners and beloved brethren, Caleb Baldwin, Lyman Wight, Hyrum Smith, and Alexander McRae, send unto you all greeting. May the grace of God the Father, and of our Lord and Savior Jesus Christ, rest upon you all, and abide with you forever. May knowledge be multiplied unto you by the mercy of God. And may faith and virtue, and knowledge and temperance, and patience and godliness, and brotherly kindness and charity be in you and abound, that you may not be barren in anything, nor unfruitful.

The Sustaining Love of God

For inasmuch as we know that the most of you are well acquainted with the wrongs and the high-handed injustice and cruelty that are practiced upon us; whereas we have been taken prisoners charged falsely with every kind of evil, and thrown into prison, enclosed with strong walls, surrounded with a strong guard, who continually watch day and night as indefatigable as the devil does in tempting and laying snares for the people of God.

Therefore, dearly beloved brethren, we are the more ready and willing to lay claim to your fellowship and love. For our circumstances are calculated to awaken our spirits to a sacred remembrance of everything, and we think that yours are also, and that nothing therefore can separate us from the love of God and fellowship one with another; and that every species of wickedness and cruelty practiced upon us will only tend to bind our hearts together and seal them together in love. We have no need to say to you that we are held in bonds without cause, neither is it needful that you say unto us, We are driven from

near the middle of it by reciting the few incidents happening between the 20th and 25th of March—the former being the date on which the letter was begun, the latter the date on which it was completed; but in this publication it is thought desirable that the letter be given without this division, and hence it appears under the date on which it was completed, viz., the 25th of March, 1839. The parts of the communication enclosed in brackets were regarded of such special value that they were taken from this communication, and placed in the *Doctrine and Covenants* and comprise sections 121, 122 and 123 of that work.

our homes and smitten without cause. We mutually understand that if the inhabitants of the state of Missouri had let the Saints alone, and had been as desirable of peace as they were, there would have been nothing but peace and quietude in the state unto this day; we should not have been in this hell, surrounded with demons (if not those who are damned, they are those who shall be damned) and where we are compelled to hear nothing but blasphemous oaths, and witness a scene of blasphemy, and drunkenness and hypocrisy, and debaucheries of every description.

The Persecution of the Saints

And again the cries of orphans and widows would not have ascended up to God against them. Nor would innocent blood have stained the soil of Missouri. But oh! the unrelenting hand! The inhumanity and murderous disposition of this people! It shocks all nature; it beggars and defies all description; it is a tale of woe; a lamentable tale; yea a sorrowful tale; too much to tell; too much for contemplation; too much for human beings; it cannot be found among the heathens; it cannot be found among the nations where kings and tyrants are enthroned; it cannot be found among the savages of the wilderness; yea, and I think it cannot be found among the wild and ferocious beasts of the forest—that a man should be mangled for sport! women be robbed of all that they have—their last morsel for subsistence, and then be violated to gratify the hellish desires of the mob, and finally left to perish with their helpless offspring clinging around their necks.

But this is not all. After a man is dead, he must be dug up from his grave and mangled to pieces, for no other purpose than to gratify their spleen against the religion of God.

They practice these things upon the Saints, who have done them no wrong, who are innocent and virtuous; who loved the Lord their God, and were willing to forsake all things for Christ's sake. These things are awful to relate, but they are verily true. It must needs be that offenses come, but woe unto them by whom they come.

A Righteous Appeal to Heaven

[Oh God! where art Thou? And where is the pavilion that covereth Thy hiding place? How long shall Thy hand be stayed, and Thine eye, yea Thy pure eye, behold from the eternal heavens, the wrongs of Thy people, and of Thy servants, and Thy ear be penetrated with their cries? Yea, O Lord, how long shall they suffer these wrongs and unlawful oppressions, before Thine heart shall be softened towards them?

O Lord God Almighty, Maker of Heaven, Earth and Seas, and of all things that in them are, and who controllest and subjectest the devil, and the dark and benighted dominion of Sheol! Stretch forth Thy hand, let Thine eye pierce; let Thy pavilion be taken up; let Thy hiding place no longer be covered; let Thine ear be inclined; let Thine heart be softened, and Thy bowels moved with compassion towards us; let Thine anger be kindled against our enemies; and in the fury of Thine heart, with Thy sword avenge us of our wrongs; remember Thy suffering Saints, O our God! and Thy servants will rejoice in Thy name forever.]

Perilous Times

Dearly and beloved brethren, we see that perilous times have come, as was testified of. We may look, then, with most perfect assurance, for the fulfillment of all those things that have been written, and with more confidence than ever before, lift up our eyes to the luminary of day, and say in our hearts, Soon thou wilt veil thy blushing face. He that said "Let there be Light," and there was light, hath spoken this word. And again, Thou moon, thou dimmer light, thou luminary of night, shalt turn to blood.

We see that everything is being fulfilled; and that the time shall soon come when the Son of Man shall descend in the clouds of heaven. Our hearts do not shrink, neither are our spirits altogether broken by the grievous yoke which is put upon us. We know that God will have our oppressors in derision; that He will laugh at their calamity, and mock when their fear cometh.

O that we could be with you, brethren, and unbosom our feelings to you! We would tell, that we should have been liberated at the time Elder Rigdon was, on the writ of habeas corpus, had not our own lawyers interpreted the law, contrary to what it reads, against us; which prevented us from introducing our evidence before the mock court.

They have done us much harm from the beginning. They have of late acknowledged that the law was misconstrued, and tantalized our feelings with it, and have entirely forsaken us, and have forfeited their oaths and their bonds; and we have a come-back on them, for they are co-workers with the mob.

Change of Public Opinion

As nigh as we can learn, the public mind has been for a long time turning in our favor, and the majority is now friendly; and the lawyers can no longer browbeat us by saying that this or that is a matter of public opinion, for public opinion is not willing to brook it; for it is beginning to look with feelings of indignation against our oppressors, and to say that the "Mormons" were not in the fault in the least. We think that truth, honor, virtue and innocence will eventually come out triumphant. We should have taken a habeas corpus before the high judge and escaped the mob in a summary way; but unfortunately for us, the timber of the wall being very hard, our auger handles gave out, and hindered us longer than we expected; we applied to a friend, and a very slight incautious act gave rise to some suspicions, and before we could fully succeed, our plan was discovered; we had everything in readiness, but the last stone, and we could have made our escape in one minute, and should have succeeded admirably, had it not been for a little imprudence or over-anxiety on the part of our friend.

The sheriff and jailer did not blame us for our attempt; it was a fine breach, and cost the county a round sum; but public opinion says that we ought to have been permitted to have made our escape; that then the disgrace would have been on us, but now it must come on the state; that there cannot be any charge sustained against us; and that the conduct of the mob, the murders committed at Haun's Mills, and the exterminating order of the governor, and the one-sided, rascally proceedings of the legislature, have damned the state of Missouri to all eternity. I would just name also that General Atchison has proved himself as contemptible as any of them.

We have tried for a long time to get our lawyers to draw us some petitions to the supreme judges of this state, but they utterly refused. We have examined the law, and drawn the petitions ourselves, and have obtained abundance of proof to counteract all the testimony that was against us, so that if the supreme judge does not grant us our liberty, he has to act without cause, contrary to honor, evidence, law or justice, sheerly to please the devil, but we hope better things and trust before many days God will so order our case, that we shall be set at liberty and take up our habitation with the Saints.

The Sympathy of Friends

We received some letters last evening—one from Emma, one from Don C. Smith, and one from Bishop Partridge—all breathing a kind and consoling spirit. We were much gratified with their contents. We had been a long time without information; and when we read those letters they were to our souls as the gentle air is refreshing, but our joy was mingled with grief, because of the sufferings of the poor and much injured Saints. And we need not say to you that the floodgates of our hearts were lifted and our eyes were a fountain of tears, but those who have not been enclosed in the walls of prison without cause or provocation, can have but little idea how sweet the voice of a friend is; one token of friendship from any source whatever awakens and calls into action every sympathetic feeling; it brings up in an instant everything that is passed; it seizes the present with the avidity of lightning; it grasps after the future with the fierceness of a tiger; it moves the mind backward and forward, from one thing to another, until finally all enmity, malice and hatred, and past differences, misunderstandings and mismanagements are slain victorious at the feet of hope; and when the heart is sufficiently contrite, then the voice of inspiration steals along and whispers—

The Value of Tribulation

[My son, peace be unto thy soul; thine adversity and thine afflictions shall be but a small moment; and then if thou endure it well, God shall exalt thee on high; thou shalt triumph over all thy foes; thy friends do stand by thee, and they shall hail thee again, with warm hearts and friendly hands; thou art not yet as Job; thy friends do not contend against thee, neither charge thee with transgression, as they did Job; and they who do charge thee with transgression, their hope shall be blasted and their prospects shall melt away as the hoar frost melteth before the burning rays of the rising sun; and also that God hath set His hand and seal to change the times and seasons, and to blind their minds, that they may not understand His marvelous workings, that He may prove them also and take them in their own craftiness; also because their hearts are corrupted, and the things which they are willing to bring upon others, and love to have others suffer, may come upon themselves to the very uttermost; that they may be disappointed also; and their hopes may be cut off; and not many years hence, that they and their posterity shall be swept from under heaven, saith God, that not one of them is left to stand by the wall. Cursed are all those that shall lift up the heel against mine anointed, saith the Lord, and cry they have sinned when they have not sinned before me, saith the Lord, but have done that which was meet in mine eyes, and which I commanded them; but those who cry transgression do it because they are the servants of sin and are the children of disobedience themselves; and those who swear falsely against my servants, that they might bring them into bondage and death; wo unto them; because they have offended my little ones; they shall be severed from the ordinances of mine house; their basket shall not be full, and their houses and their barns shall perish, and they themselves shall be despised by those that flattered them; they shall not have right to the Priesthood, nor their posterity after them, from generation to generation; it had been better for them that a millstone had been hanged about their necks, and they drowned in the depth of the sea.

Wo unto all those that discomfort my people, and drive and murder, and testify against them, saith the Lord of Hosts; a generation of vipers shall not escape the damnation of hell. Behold mine eyes see and know all their works, and I have in reserve a swift judgment in the season thereof, for them all; for there is a time appointed for every man according as his work shall be.]

A Tried People

And now, beloved brethren, we say unto you, that inasmuch as God hath said that He would have a tried people, that He would purge them as gold, now we think that this time He has chosen His own crucible, wherein we have been tried;

and we think if we get through with any degree of safety, and shall have kept the faith, that it will be a sign to this generation, altogether sufficient to leave them without excuse; and we think also, it will be a trial of our faith equal to that of Abraham, and that the ancients will not have whereof to boast over us in the day of judgment, as being called to pass through heavier afflictions; that we may hold an even weight in the balance with them; but now, after having suffered so great sacrifice and having passed through so great a season of sorrow, we trust that a ram may be caught in the thicket speedily, to relieve the sons and daughters of Abraham from their great anxiety, and to light up the lamp of salvation upon their countenances, that they may hold on now, after having gone so far unto everlasting life.

A Location for the Saints

Now, brethren, concerning the places for the location of the Saints, we cannot counsel you as we could if we were present with you; and as to the things that were written heretofore, we did not consider them anything very binding, therefore we now say once for all, that we think it most proper that the general affairs of the Church, which are necessary to be considered, while your humble servant remains in bondage, should be transacted by a general conference of the most faithful and the most respectable of the authorities of the Church, and a minute of those transactions may be kept, and forwarded from time to time, to your humble servant; and if there should be any corrections by the word of the Lord, they shall be freely transmitted, and your humble servant will approve all things whatsoever is acceptable unto God. If anything should have been suggested by us, or any names mentioned, except by commandment, or thus saith the Lord, we do not consider it binding; therefore our hearts shall not be grieved if different arrangements should be entered into. Nevertheless we would suggest the propriety of being aware of an aspiring spirit, which spirit has oftentimes urged men forward to make foul speeches, and influence the Church to reject milder counsels, and has eventually been the means of bringing much death and sorrow upon the Church.

Beware of Pride

We would say, beware of pride also; for well and truly hath the wise man said, that pride goeth before destruction, and a haughty spirit before a fall.   And again, outward appearance is not always a criterion by which to judge our fellow man; but the lips betray the haughty and overbearing imaginations of the heart; by his words and his deeds let him be judged. Flattery is also a deadly poison.   A frank and open rebuke provoketh a good man to emulation; and in the hour of trouble he will be your best friend; but on the other hand, it will draw out all the corruptions of corrupt hearts, and lying and the poison of asps is under their tongues; and they do cause the pure in heart to be cast into prison, because they want them out of their way.

A fanciful and flowery and heated imagination beware of; because the things of God are of deep import; and time, and experience, and careful and ponderous and solemn thoughts can only find them out.   Thy mind, O man! if thou wilt lead a soul unto salvation, must stretch as high as the utmost heavens, and search into and contemplate the darkest abyss, and the broad expanse of eternity—thou must commune with God. How much more dignified and noble are the thoughts of God, than the vain imaginations of the human heart! None but fools will trifle with the souls of men.

How vain and trifling have been our spirits, our conferences, our councils, our meetings, our private as well as public conversations—too low, too mean, too vulgar, too condescending for the dignified characters of the called and chosen of God, according to the purposes of His will, from before the foundation of the world! We are called to hold the keys of the mysteries of those things that have been kept hid from the foundation of the world until now.   Some have tasted a little of these things, many of which are to be poured down from heaven upon the heads of babes; yea, upon the weak, obscure and despised ones of the earth.   Therefore we beseech of you, brethren, that you bear with those who do not feel themselves more worthy than yourselves, while we exhort one another to a reformation with one and all, both old and young, teachers and taught, both high and low, rich and poor, bond and free, male and female; let honesty, and sobriety, and candor, and solemnity, and virtue, and pureness, and meekness, and simplicity crown our heads in every place; and in fine, become as little children, without malice, guile or hypocrisy.

Revelation of Eternal Truth

And now, brethren, after your tribulations, if you do these things, and exercise fervent prayer and faith in the sight of God always, [He shall give unto you knowledge by His Holy Spirit, yea by the unspeakable gift of the Holy Ghost, that has not been revealed since the world was until now; which our forefathers have waited with anxious expectation to be revealed in the last times, which their minds were pointed to by the angels, as held in reserve for the fullness of their glory; a time to come in the which nothing shall be withheld, whether there be one God or many Gods, they shall be manifest; all thrones and dominions, principalities and powers, shall be revealed and set forth upon all who have endured valiantly for the Gospel of Jesus Christ; and also if there be bounds set to the heavens, or to the seas; or to the dry land, or to the sun, moon or stars; all the times of their revolutions; all the appointed days, months and years, and all the days of their days, months and years, and all their glories, laws, and set times, shall be revealed, in the days of the dispensation of the fullness of times, according to that which was ordained in the midst of the Council of the Eternal God of all other Gods, before this world was, that should be reserved unto the finishing and the end thereof, when every man shall enter into His eternal presence, and into His immortal rest].

Ignorance Retards the Church

But I beg leave to say unto you, brethren, that ignorance, superstition and bigotry placing itself where it ought not, is oftentimes in the way of the prosperity of this Church; like the torrent of rain from the mountains, that floods the most pure and crystal stream with mire, and dirt, and filthiness, and obscures everything that was clear before, and all rushes along in one general deluge; but time weathers tide; and notwithstanding we are rolled in the mire of the flood for the time being, the next surge peradventure, as time rolls on, may bring to us the fountain as clear as crystal, and as pure as snow; while the filthiness, flood-wood and rubbish is left and purged out by the way.

The Hand of the Lord Cannot Be Stayed

[How long can rolling water remain impure? What power shall stay the heavens? As well might man stretch forth his puny arm to stop the Missouri river in its decreed course, or to turn it up stream, as to hinder the Almighty from pouring down knowledge from heaven, upon the heads of the Latter-day Saints].

What is Boggs or his murderous party, but wimbling willows upon the shore to catch the flood-wood? As well might we argue that water is not water, because the mountain torrents send down mire and roil the crystal stream, although afterwards render it more pure than before; or that fire is not fire, because it is of a quenchable nature, by pouring on the flood; as to say that our cause is down because renegades, liars, priests, thieves and murderers, who are all alike tenacious of their crafts and creeds, have poured down, from their spiritual wickedness in high places, and from their strongholds of the devil, a flood of dirt and mire and filthiness and vomit upon our heads.

No! God forbid. Hell may pour forth its rage like the burning lava of Mount Vesuvius, or of Etna, or of the most terrible of the burning mountains; and yet shall "Mormonism" stand. Water, fire, truth and God are all realities. Truth is "Mormonism." God is the author of it. He is our shield. It is by Him we received our birth. It was by His voice that we were called to a dispensation of His Gospel in the beginning of the fullness of times. It was by Him we received the Book of Mormon; and it is by Him that we remain unto this day; and by Him we shall remain, if it shall be for our glory; and in His Almighty name we are determined to endure tribulation as good soldiers unto the end.

But brethren, we shall continue to offer further reflections in our next epistle. You will learn by the time you have read this, and if you do not learn it, you may learn it, that walls and irons, doors and creaking hinges, and half-scared-to-death guards and jailers, grinning like some damned spirits, lest an innocent man should make his escape to bring to light the damnable deeds of a murderous mob, are calculated in their very nature to make the soul of an honest man feel stronger than the powers of hell.

But we must bring our epistle to a close. We send our

respects to fathers, mothers, wives and children, brothers and sisters; we hold them in the most sacred remembrance.

We feel to inquire after Elder Rigdon; if he has not forgotten us, it has not been signified to us by his writing. Brother George W. Robinson also; and Elder Cahoon, we remember him, but would like to jog his memory a little on the fable of the bear and the two friends who mutually agreed to stand by each other. And perhaps it would not be amiss to mention uncle John [Smith], and various others. A word of consolation and a blessing would not come amiss from anybody, while we are being so closely whispered by the bear. But we feel to excuse everybody and everything, yea the more readily when we contemplate that we are in the hands of persons worse than a bear, for the bear would not prey upon a dead carcass.

Our respects and love and fellowship to all the virtuous Saints. We are your brethren and fellow-sufferers, and prisoners of Jesus Christ for the Gospel's sake, and for the hope of glory which is in us. Amen.

Continued Reflections

We continue to offer further reflections to Bishop Partridge, and to the Church of Jesus Christ of Latter-day Saints, whom we love with a fervent love, and do always bear them in mind in all our prayers to the throne of God.

It still seems to bear heavily on our minds that the Church would do well to secure to themselves the contract of the land which is proposed to them by Mr. Isaac Galland, and to cultivate the friendly feelings of that gentleman, inasmuch as he shall prove himself to be a man of honor and a friend to humanity; also Isaac Van Allen, Esq., the attorney-general of Iowa Territory, and Governor Lucas, that peradventure such men may be wrought upon by the providence of God, to do good unto His people. We really think that Mr. Galland's letter breathes that kind of a spirit, if we may judge correctly. Governor Lucas' also. We suggest the idea of praying fervently for all men who manifest any degree of sympathy for the suffering children of God.

We think that the United States Surveyor of the Iowa Territory may be of great benefit to the Church, if it be the will of God to this end; and righteousness should be manifested as the girdle of our loins.

Preparation Against the Wrath of God

It seems to be deeply impressed upon our minds that the Saints ought to lay hold of every door that shall seem to be opened unto them, to obtain foothold on the earth, and be making all the preparation that is within their power for the terrible storms that are now gathering in the heavens, "a day of clouds, with darkness and gloominess, and of thick darkness," as spoken of by the Prophets which cannot be now of a long time lingering, for there seems to be a whispering that the angels of heaven who have been entrusted with the counsel of these matters for the last days, have taken counsel together; and among the rest of the general affairs that have to be transacted in their honorable council, they have taken cognizance of the testimony of those who were murdered at Haun's Mills, and also those who were martyred with David W. Patten, and elsewhere, and have passed some decisions peradventure in favor of the Saints, and those who were called to suffer without cause.

These decisions will be made known in their time; and the council will take into consideration all those things that offend.

We have a fervent desire that in your general conferences everything should be discussed with a great deal of care and propriety, lest you grieve the Holy Spirit, which shall be poured out at all times upon your heads, when you are exercised with those principles of righteousness that are agreeable to the mind of God, and are properly affected one toward another, and are careful by all means to remember, those who are in bondage, and in heaviness, and in deep affliction for your sakes.   And if there are any among you who aspire after their own aggrandizement, and seek their own opulence, while their brethren are groaning in poverty, and are under sore trials and temptations, they cannot be benefited by the intercession of the Holy Spirit, which maketh intercession for us day and night with groanings that cannot be uttered.

We ought at all times to be very careful that such high-mindedness shall never have place in our hearts; but condescend to men of low estate, and with all long-suffering bear the infirmities of the weak.

Many Called But Few Chosen

[Behold, there are many called, but few are chosen. And why are they not chosen? Because their hearts are set so much upon the things of this world, and aspire to the honors of men, that they do not learn this one lesson—that the rights of the Priesthood are inseparably connected with the powers of heaven, and that the powers of heaven cannot be controlled nor handled only upon the principles of righteousness. That they may be conferred upon us, it is true; but when we undertake to cover our sins, or to gratify our pride, our vain ambition, or to exercise control, or dominion, or compulsion, upon the souls of the children of men, in any degree of unrighteousness, behold, the heavens withdraw themselves; the Spirit of the Lord is grieved; and when it is withdrawn, *Amen to the Priesthood,* or the authority of that man. Behold! ere he is aware, he is left unto himself, to kick against the pricks; to persecute the Saints, and to fight against God.

We have learned by sad experience that it is the nature and disposition of almost all men, as soon as they get a little authority, as they suppose, they will immediately begin to exercise unrighteous dominion. Hence many are called, but few are chosen.

The Priesthood Gentle and Long-suffering

No power or influence can or ought to be maintained by virtue of the Priesthood, only by persuasion, by long-suffering, by gentleness, and meekness, and by love unfeigned; by kindness, and pure knowledge, which shall greatly enlarge the soul without hypocrisy, and without guile, reproving betimes with sharpness, when moved upon by the Holy Ghost, and then showing forth afterwards an increase of love toward him whom thou hast reproved, lest he esteem thee to be his enemy; that he may know that thy faithfulness is stronger than the cords of death; let thy bowels also be full of charity towards all men, and to the household of faith, and let virtue garnish thy thoughts unceasingly, then shall thy confidence wax strong in the presence of God, and the doctrine of the Priesthood shall distil upon thy soul as the dews from heaven. The Holy Ghost shall be thy constant companion, and thy sceptre an unchanging sceptre of righteousness and truth, and thy dominion shall be an everlasting dominion, and without compulsory means it shall flow unto thee forever and ever.]

[The ends of the earth shall inquire after thy name, and fools shall have thee in derision, and hell shall rage against thee, while the pure in heart, and the wise, and the noble, and the virtuous, shall seek counsel, and authority and blessings constantly from under thy hand, and thy people shall never be turned against thee by the testimony of traitors; and although their influence shall cast thee into trouble, and into bars and walls, thou shalt be had in honor, and but for a small moment and thy voice shall be more terrible in the midst of thine enemies, than the fierce lion, because of thy righteousness; and thy God shall stand by thee forever and ever.

Experience Through Suffering

If thou art called to pass through tribulations; if thou art in perils among false brethren; if thou art in perils among robbers; if thou art in perils by land or by sea; if thou art accused with all manner of false accusations; if thine enemies fall upon thee; if they tear thee from the society of thy father and mother and brethren and sisters; and if with a drawn sword thine enemies tear thee from the bosom of thy wife, and of thine offspring, and thine elder son, although but six years of age, shall cling to thy garments, and shall say, My father, my father, why can't you stay with us? O, my father, what are the men going to do with you? and if then he shall be thrust from thee by the sword, and thou be dragged to prison, and thine enemies prowl around thee like wolves for the blood of the lamb; and if thou shouldst be cast into the pit, or into the hands of murderers, and the sentence of death passed upon thee; if thou be cast into the deep, if the billowing surge conspire against thee; if fierce winds become thine enemy; if the heavens gather blackness, and all the elements combine to hedge up the way; and above all, if the very jaws of hell shall gape open the mouth wide after thee, know thou, my son, that all these things shall give thee experience, and shall be for thy good. The Son of Man hath descended below them all; art thou greater than he?

Gathering of the Saints

Therefore, hold on thy way, and the Priesthood shall remain with thee, for their bounds are set, they cannot pass. Thy days are known, and thy years shall not be numbered less; therefore, fear not what man can do, for God shall be with you forever and ever.]

Now, brethren, I would suggest for the consideration of the conference, its being carefully and wisely understood by the council or conferences that our brethren scattered abroad, who understood the spirit of the gathering, that they fall into the places and refuge of safety that God shall open unto them, between Kirtland and Far West. Those from the east and from the west, and from far countries, let them fall in somewhere between those two boundaries, in the most safe and quiet places they can find; and let this be the present understanding, until God shall open a more effectual door for us for further considerations.

And again, we further suggest for the considerations of the Council, that there be no organization of large bodies upon common stock principles, in property, or of large companies of firms, until the Lord shall signify it in a proper manner, as it opens such a dreadful field for the avaricious, the indolent, and the corrupt hearted to prey upon the innocent and virtuous, and honest.

We have reason to believe that many things were introduced among the Saints before God had signified the times; and notwithstanding the principles and plans may have been good, yet aspiring men, or in other words, men who had not the substance of godliness about them, perhaps undertook to handle edged tools. Children, you know, are fond of tools, while they are not yet able to use them.

Time and experience, however, are the only safe remedies against such evils. There are many teachers, but, perhaps, not many fathers. There are times coming when God will signify many things which are expedient for the well-being of the Saints; but the times have not yet come, but will come, as fast as there can be found place and reception for them.

The Gathering of False Reports

[And again, we would suggest for your consideration the propriety of all the Saints gathering up a knowledge of all the facts and sufferings and abuses put upon them by the people of this state; and also of all the property and amount of damages which they have sustained, both of character and personal injuries, as well as real property; and also the names of all persons that have had a hand in their oppressions, as far as they can get hold of them and find them out; and perhaps a committee can be appointed to find out these things, and to take statements, and affidavits, and also to gather up the libelous publications that are afloat, and all that are in the magazines, and in the encyclopædias, and all the libelous histories that are published, and are writing, and by whom, and present the whole concatenation of diabolical rascality, and nefarious and murderous impositions that have been practiced upon this people, that we may not only publish to all the world, but present them to the heads of government in all their dark and hellish hue, as the last effort which is enjoined on us by our Heavenly Father, before we can fully and completely claim that promise which shall call Him forth from His hiding place, and also that the whole nation may be left without excuse before He can send forth the power of His mighty arm.

A Duty to Wives and Children

It is an imperative duty that we owe to God, to angels, with whom we shall be brought to stand, and also to ourselves, to our wives and children, who have been made to bow down with grief, sorrow, and care, under the most damning hand of murder, tyranny, and oppressions, supported and urged on and upheld by the influence of that spirit which has so strongly riveted the creeds of the fathers, who have inherited lies, upon the hearts of the children, and filled the world with confusion, and has been growing stronger and stronger, and is now the very main-spring of all corruption, and the whole earth groans under the weight of its iniquity.

It is an iron yoke, it is a strong band; they are the very hand-cuffs, and chains, and shackles, and fetters of hell.

Therefore it is an imperative duty that we owe, not only to our own wives and children, but to the widows and fatherless, whose husbands and fathers have been murdered under its iron hand; which dark and blackening deeds are enough to make hell itself shudder, and to stand aghast and pale, and the hands of the very devil to tremble and palsy. And also it is an imperative duty that we owe to all the rising generation, and to all the pure in heart, (for there are many yet on the earth among all sects, parties, denominations, who are blinded by the subtle craftiness of men, whereby they lie in wait to deceive, and who are only kept from the truth because they know not where to find it); therefore, that we should waste and wear out our lives in bringing to light all the hidden things of darkness, wherein we know them; and they are truly manifest from heaven.

These should then be attended to with great earnestness. Let no man count them as small things; for there is much which lieth in futurity, pertaining to the Saints, which depends upon these things. You know, brethren, that a very large ship is benefited very much by a very small helm in the time of a storm, by being kept workways with the wind and the waves.

Therefore, dearly beloved brethren, let us cheerfully do all things that lie in our power, and then may we stand still with the utmost assurance, to see the salvation of God, and for His arm to be revealed.]

Counsel Against Secrecies

And again, I would further suggest the impropriety of the organization of bands or companies, by covenant or oaths, by penalties or secrecies; but let the time past of our experience and sufferings by the wickedness of Doctor Avard suffice and let our covenant be that of the Everlasting Covenant, as is contained in the Holy Writ and the things that God hath revealed unto us. Pure friendship always becomes weakened the very moment you undertake to make it stronger by penal oaths and secrecy.

Your humble servant or servants, intend from henceforth to disapprobate everything that is not in accordance with the fullness of the Gospel of Jesus Christ, and is not of a bold, and frank, and upright nature. They will not hold their peace— as in times past when they see iniquity beginning to rear its head—for fear of traitors, or the consequences that shall follow by reproving those who creep in unawares, that they may get something with which to destroy the flock. We believe that the experience of the Saints in times past has been sufficient, that they will from henceforth be always ready to obey the truth without having men's persons in admiration because of advantage. It is expedient that we should be aware of such things; and we ought always to be aware of those prejudices which sometimes so strangely present themselves, and are so congenial to human nature, against our friends, neighbors, and brethren of the world, who choose to differ from us in opinion and in matters of faith. Our religion is between us and our God. Their religion is between them and their God.

There is a love from God that should be exercised toward those of our faith, who walk uprightly, which is peculiar to itself, but it is without prejudice; it also gives scope to the mind, which enables us to conduct ourselves with greater liberality towards all that are not of our faith, than what they exercise towards one another. These principles approximate nearer to the mind of God, because it is like God, or Godlike.

The Principle of Religious Freedom

Here is a principle also, which we are bound to be exercised with, that is, in common with all men, such as governments, and laws, and regulations in the civil concerns of life. This principle guarantees to all parties, sects, and denominations, and classes of religion, equal, coherent, and indefeasible rights; they are things that pertain to this life; therefore all are alike interested; they make our responsibilities one towards another in matters of corruptible things, while the former principles do not destroy the latter, but bind us stronger, and make our responsibilities not only one to another, but unto God also. Hence we say, that the Constitution of the United States is a glorious standard; it is founded in the wisdom of God. It is a heavenly banner; it is to all those who are privileged with the sweets of liberty, like the cooling shades and refreshing waters of a great rock in a thirsty and weary land. It is like a great tree under whose branches men from every clime can be shielded from the burning rays of the sun.

We, brethren, are deprived of the protection of its glorious principles, by the cruelty of the cruel, by those who only look for the time being, for pasturage like the beasts of the field, only to fill themselves; and forget that the "Mormons," as well as the Presbyterians, and those of every other class and description, have equal rights to partake of the fruits of the great tree of our national liberty. But notwithstanding we see what we see, and feel what we feel, and know what we know, yet that fruit is no less precious and delicious to our taste; we cannot be weaned from the milk, neither can we be driven from the breast;

neither will we deny our religion because of the hand of oppression; but we will hold on until death.

We say that God is true; that the Constitution of the United States is true; that the Bible is true; that the Book of Mormon is true; that the Book of Covenants is true; that Christ is true; that the ministering angels sent forth from God are true, and that we know that we have an house not made with hands eternal in the heavens, whose builder and maker is God; a consolation which our oppressors cannot feel, when fortune, or fate, shall lay its iron hand on them as it has on us. Now, we ask, what is man? Remember, brethren, that time and chance happen to all men.

We shall continue our reflections in our next.

We subscribe ourselves, your sincere friends and brethren in the bonds of the everlasting Gospel, prisoners of Jesus Christ, for the sake of the Gospel and the Saints.

We pronounce the blessings of heaven upon the heads of the Saints who seek to serve God with undivided hearts, in the name of Jesus Christ. Amen.

JOSEPH SMITH, JUN.,
HYRUM SMITH,
LYMAN WIGHT,
CALEB BALDWIN,
ALEXANDER McRAE.

—D. H. C. 3:289-305.

The Prophet's Instruction on Various Doctrines

Faith comes by hearing the word of God, through the testimony of the servants of God; that testimony is always attended by the Spirit of prophecy and revelation.

Repentance is a thing that cannot be trifled with every day. Daily transgression and daily repentance is not that which is pleasing in the sight of God.

Baptism is a holy ordinance preparatory to the reception of the Holy Ghost; it is the channel and key by which the Holy Ghost will be administered.

The Gift of the Holy Ghost by the laying on of hands, cannot be received through the medium of any other principle than the principle of righteousness, for if the proposals are not complied with, it is of no use, but withdraws.

Tongues were given for the purpose of preaching among

those whose language is not understood; as on the day of Pentecost, etc., and it is not necessary for tongues to be taught to the Church particularly, for any man that has the Holy Ghost, can speak of the things of God in his own tongue as well as to speak in another; for faith comes not by signs, but by hearing the word of God.

Doctrines of Resurrection and Election

The Doctrines of the Resurrection of the Dead and the Eternal Judgment are necessary to preach among the first principles of the Gospel of Jesus Christ.

The Doctrine of Election. Peter exhorts us to make our calling and election sure. This is the sealing power spoken of by Paul in other places.

"13. In whom ye also trusted, that after ye heard the word of truth, the Gospel of your salvation: in whom also after that ye believed, ye were sealed with that Holy Spirit of promise,

"14. Which is the earnest of our inheritance until the redemption of the purchased possession, unto the praise of His glory, that we may be sealed up unto the day of redemption."— Ephesians, 1st chapter.

This principle ought (in its proper place) to be taught, for God hath not revealed anything to Joseph, but what He will make known unto the Twelve, and even the least Saint may know all things as fast as he is able to bear them, for the day must come when no man need say to his neighbor, Know ye the Lord; for all shall know Him (who remain) from the least to the greatest. How is this to be done? It is to be done by this sealing power, and the other Comforter spoken of, which will be manifest by revelation.

The Two Comforters

There are two Comforters spoken of. One is the Holy Ghost, the same as given on the day of Pentecost, and that all Saints receive after faith, repentance, and baptism. This first Comforter or Holy Ghost has no other effect than pure intelligence. It is more powerful in expanding the mind, enlightening the understanding, and storing the intellect with present knowledge, of a man who is of the literal seed of Abraham, than one that is a Gentile, though it may not have half as much visible effect upon the body; for as the Holy Ghost falls upon one of the literal seed of Abraham, it is calm and serene; and his whole soul and body are only exercised by the pure spirit of intelligence; while the effect of the Holy Ghost upon a Gentile, is to purge out the old blood, and make him actually of the seed of Abraham. That man that has none of the blood of Abraham (naturally) must have a new creation by the Holy Ghost. In such a case, there may be more of a powerful effect upon the body, and visible to the eye, than upon an Israelite, while the Israelite at first might be far before the Gentile in pure intelligence.

The Second Comforter

The other Comforter spoken of is a subject of great interest, and perhaps understood by few of this generation. After a person has faith in Christ, repents of his sins, and is baptized for the remission of his sins and receives the Holy Ghost, (by the laying on of hands), which is the first Comforter, then let him continue to humble himself before God, hungering and thirsting after righteousness, and living by every word of God, and the Lord will soon say unto him, Son, thou shalt be exalted. When the Lord has thoroughly proved him, and finds that the man is determined to serve Him at all hazards, then the man will find his calling and his election made sure, then it will be his privilege to receive the other Comforter, which the Lord hath promised the Saints, as is recorded in the testimony of St. John, in the 14th chapter, from the 12th to the 27th verses.

Note the 16, 17, 18, 21, 23 verses:

"16. And I will pray the Father, and He shall give you another Comforter, that he may abide with you forever;

"17. Even the Spirit of Truth; whom the world cannot receive, because it seeth him not, neither knoweth him; but ye know him; for he dwelleth with you, and shall be in you.

"18. I will not leave you comfortless: I will come to you. * *

"21. He that hath my commandments, and keepeth them he it is that loveth me: and he that loveth me shall be loved of my Father, and I will love him, and will manifest myself to him.

"23. If a man love me, he will keep my word: and my Father will love him, and we will come unto him, and make our abode with him."

Now what is this other Comforter? It is no more nor less

than the Lord Jesus Christ Himself; and this is the sum and substance of the whole matter; that when any man obtains this last Comforter, he will have the personage of Jesus Christ to attend him, or appear unto him from time to time, and even He will manifest the Father unto him, and they will take up their abode with him, and the visions of the heavens will be opened unto him, and the Lord will teach him face to face, and he may have a perfect knowledge of the mysteries of the Kingdom of God; and this is the state and place the ancient Saints arrived at when they had such glorious visions—Isaiah, Ezekiel, John upon the Isle of Patmos, St. Paul in the three heavens, and all the Saints who held communion with the general assembly and Church of the Firstborn.

The Spirit of Revelation

The Spirit of Revelation is in connection with these blessings. A person may profit by noticing the first intimation of the spirit of revelation; for instance, when you feel pure intelligence flowing into you, it may give you sudden strokes of ideas, so that by noticing it, you may find it fulfilled the same day or soon; (i.e.) those things that were presented unto your minds by the Spirit of God, will come to pass; and thus by learning the Spirit of God and understanding it, you may grow into the principle of revelation, until you become perfect in Christ Jesus.

The Evangelist

An Evangelist is a Patriarch, even the oldest man of the blood of Joseph or of the seed of Abraham. Wherever the Church of Christ is established in the earth, there should be a Patriarch for the benefit of the posterity of the Saints, as it was with Jacob in giving his patriarchal blessing unto his sons, etc. (June 27, 1839.) D. H. C. 3:379-381.

SECTION FOUR
1839 – 1842

SECTION FOUR

---◆---

The Prophet's Address to the Twelve

In the afternoon of Monday, July 2, 1839, the Prophet met with the apostles and some of the Seventies who were about to depart on their mission to Great Britain in fulfilment of the revelation of the Lord, and instructed them. A synopsis of his remarks he placed in his journal and this is here reproduced in full as they are given in the History of the Church.

Beware of Pride

Ever keep in exercise the principle of mercy, and be ready to forgive our brother on the first intimations of repentance, and asking forgiveness; and should we even forgive our brother, or even our enemy, before he repent or ask forgiveness, our heavenly Father would be equally as merciful unto us.

Again, let the Twelve and all Saints be willing to confess all their sins, and not keep back a part; and let the Twelve be humble, and not be exalted, and beware of pride, and not seek to excel one above another, but act for each other's good, and pray for one another, and honor our brother or make honorable mention of his name, and not backbite and devour our brother. Why will not man learn wisdom by precept at this late age of the world, when we have such a cloud of witnesses and examples before us, and not be obliged to learn by sad experience everything we know. Must the new ones that are chosen to fill the places of those that are fallen, of the quorum of the Twelve, begin to exalt themselves, until they exalt themselves so high that they will soon tumble over and have a great fall, and go wallowing through the mud and mire and darkness, Judas-like, to the buffetings of Satan, as several of the quorum have done, or will they learn wisdom and be wise? O God! give them wisdom, and keep them humble, I pray.

When the Twelve or any other witnesses stand before the congregations of the earth, and they preach in the power and demonstration of the Spirit of God, and the people are astonished and confounded at the doctrine, and say, "That man has preached a powerful discourse, a great sermon," then let that man or those men take care that they do not ascribe the glory unto themselves, but be careful that they are humble, and ascribe the praise and glory to God and the Lamb; for it is by the power of the Holy Priesthood and the Holy Ghost that they have power thus to speak. What art thou, O man, but dust? And from whom receivest thou thy power and blessings, but from God?

Not Sent to Be Taught

Then, O ye Twelve! notice this Key, and be wise for Christ's sake, and your own soul's sake. Ye are not sent out to be taught, but to teach. Let every word be seasoned with grace. Be vigilant; be sober. It is a day of warning, and not of many words. Act honestly before God and man. Beware of Gentile sophistry; such as bowing and scraping unto men in whom you have no confidence. Be honest, open, and frank in all your intercourse with mankind.

Do Not Betray the Brethren

O ye Twelve! and all Saints! profit by this important Key—that in all your trials, troubles, temptations, afflictions, bonds, imprisonments and death, see to it, that you do not betray heaven; that you do not betray Jesus Christ; that you do not betray the brethren; that you do not betray the revelations of God, whether in Bible, Book of Mormon, or Doctrine and Covenants, or any other that ever was or ever will be given and revealed unto man in this world or that which is to come. Yea, in all your kicking and flounderings, see to it that you do not this thing, lest innocent blood be found upon your skirts, and you go down to hell. All other sins are not to be compared to sinning against the Holy Ghost, and proving a traitor to the brethren.

A Key to Mysteries

I will give you one of the Keys of the mysteries of the Kingdom. It is an eternal principle, that has existed with God from all eternity: That man who rises up to condemn others, finding fault with the Church, saying that they are out of the way, while he himself is righteous, then know assuredly, that that man is in the high road to apostasy; and if he does not repent, will apostatize, as God lives. The principle is as correct as the one that Jesus put forth in saying that he who seeketh a sign is an adulterous person; and that principal is eternal, undeviating, and firm as the pillars of heaven; for whenever you see a man seeking after a sign, you may set it down that he is an adulterous man.

The Prophet on Priesthood

The Priesthood was first given to Adam; he obtained the First Presidency, and held the keys of it from generation to generation. He obtained it in the Creation, before the world was formed, as in Genesis 1:26, 27, 28. He had dominion given him over every living creature. He is Michael the Archangel, spoken of in the Scriptures. Then to Noah, who is Gabriel: he stands next in authority to Adam in the Priesthood; he was called of God to this office, and was the father of all living in this day, and to him was given the dominion. These men held keys first on earth, and then in heaven.

Priesthood Everlasting

The Priesthood is an everlasting principle, and existed with God from eternity, and will to eternity, without beginning of days or end of years. The keys have to be brought from heaven whenever the Gospel is sent. When they are revealed from heaven, it is by Adam's authority.

Adam the Oldest Man

Daniel in his seventh chapter speaks of the Ancient of Days; he means the oldest man, our Father Adam, Michael, he will call his children together and hold a council with them to prepare them for the coming of the Son of Man. He (Adam) is the father of the human family, and presides over the spirits of all men, and all that have had the keys must stand before him in this grand council. This may take place before some of us leave this stage of action. The Son of Man stands before him, and there is given him glory and dominion. Adam delivers up his stewardship to Christ, that which was delivered to him as holding the keys of the universe, but retains his standing as head of the human family.

The Spirit of Man

The spirit of man is not a created being;[5] it existed from eternity, and will exist to eternity. Anything created cannot be eternal; and earth, water, etc., had their existence in an elementary state, from eternity. Our Savior speaks of children and says, Their angels always stand before my Father. The Father called all spirits before Him at the creation of man, and organized them. He (Adam) is the head, and was told to multiply. The keys were first given to him, and by him to others. He will have to give an account of his stewardship, and they to him.

Keys Given to Peter, James and John

The Priesthood is everlasting. The Savior, Moses, and Elias, gave the keys to Peter, James and John, on the mount, when they were transfigured before him. The Priesthood is everlasting—without beginning of days or end of years; without father, mother, etc. If there is no change of ordinances, there is no change of Priesthood. Wherever the ordinances of the Gospel are administered, there is the Priesthood.

Descent of Priesthood

How have we come at the Priesthood in the last days? It came down, down, in regular succession. Peter, James, and John had it given to them and they gave it to others. Christ is the Great High Priest; Adam next. Paul speaks of the Church coming to an innumerable company of angels—to God the Judge of all—the spirits of just men made perfect; to Jesus the Mediator of the new covenant. (Hebrews 12:22-24.)

I saw Adam in the valley of Adam-ondi-Ahman. He called together his children and blessed them with a patriarchal blessing. The Lord appeared in their midst, and he (Adam) blessed them all, and foretold what should befall them to the latest generation.

---

[5]In saying the spirit of man is not created the Prophet without any doubt had in mind the intelligence as explained in the *Doctrine and Covenants,* Sec. 93:29: "Man was also in the beginning with God. Intelligence, or the light of truth, was not created or made, neither indeed can be." From this we gather that the intelligence in man was not created, but the Prophet taught very clearly that man is in very deed the offspring of God, and that the spirits of men were born in the spirit world the children of God. See Doctrine and Covenants 76:24.

This is why Adam blessed his posterity; he wanted to bring them into the presence of God. They looked for a city, etc., "whose builder and maker is God." (Hebrews 11:10.) Moses sought to bring the children of Israel into the presence of God, through the power of the Priesthood, but he could not. In the first ages of the world they tried to establish the same thing; and there were Eliases raised up who tried to restore these very glories, but did not obtain them; but they prophesied of a day when this glory would be revealed. Paul spoke of the dispensation of the fullness of times, when God would gather together all things in one, etc.; and those men to whom these keys have been given, will have to be there; and they without us cannot be made perfect.

These men are in heaven, but their children are on the earth. Their bowels yearn over us. God sends down men for this reason. "And the Son of Man shall send forth His angels, and they shall gather out of His kingdom all things that give offense and them that do iniquity." (Matthew 13:41.) All these authoritative characters will come down and join hand in hand in bringing about this work.

We Cannot Be Perfect Without Our Dead

The Kingdom of Heaven is like a grain of mustard seed. The mustard seed is small, but brings forth a large tree, and the fowls lodge in the branches. The fowls are the angels. Thus angels come down, combine together to gather their children, and gather them. We cannot be made perfect without them, nor they without us; when these things are done, the Son of Man will descend, the Ancient of Days sit; we may come to an innumerable company of angels, have communion with and receive instruction from them. Paul told about Moses' proceedings; spoke of the children of Israel being baptized. (I Cor. 10:1-4.) He knew this, and that all the ordinances and blessings were in the Church. Paul had these things, and we may have the fowls of heaven lodge in the branches, etc.

The "Horn" made war with the Saints and overcame them, until the Ancient of Days came; judgment was given to the Saints of the Most High from the Ancient of Days; the time came that the Saints possessed the Kingdom. This not only makes us ministers here, but in eternity.

No Salvation Without Revelation

Salvation cannot come without revelation; it is in vain for anyone to minister without it. No man is a minister of Jesus Christ without being a Prophet. No man can be a minister of Jesus Christ except he has the testimony of Jesus; and this is the spirit of prophecy. Whenever salvation has been administered, it has been by testimony. Men of the present time testify of heaven and hell, and have never seen either; and I will say that no man knows these things without this.

Signs of Second Coming Have Commenced

Men profess to prophesy. I will prophesy that the signs of the coming of the Son of Man are already commenced. One pestilence will desolate after another. We shall soon have war and bloodshed. The moon will be turned into blood. I testify of these things, and that the coming of the Son of Man is nigh, even at your doors. If our souls and our bodies are not looking forth for the coming of the Son of Man; and after we are dead, if we are not looking forth, we shall be among those who are calling for the rocks to fall upon them.

Hearts of Children Turn to Fathers

The hearts of the children of men will have to be turned to the fathers, and the fathers to the children, living or dead, to prepare them for the coming of the Son of Man. If Elijah did not come, the whole earth would be smitten.

There will be here and there a Stake [of Zion] for the gathering of the Saints. Some may have cried peace, but the Saints and the world will have little peace from henceforth. Let this not hinder us from going to the Stakes; for God has told us to flee, not dallying, or we shall be scattered, one here, and another there. There your children shall be blessed, and you in the midst of friends where you may be blessed. The Gospel net gathers of every kind.

I prophesy, that that man who tarries after he has an opportunity of going, will be afflicted by the devil. Wars are at hand; we must not delay; but are not required to sacrifice. We ought to have the building up of Zion as our greatest object. When wars come, we shall have to flee to Zion. The cry is to make haste. The last revelation says, Ye shall not have time to have gone over the earth, until these things come. It will come as did the cholera, war, fires, and earthquakes; one pestilence after another, until the Ancient of Days comes, then judgment will be given to the Saints.

No Peace But in Zion

Whatever you may hear about me or Kirtland, take no notice of it; for if it be a place of refuge, the devil will use his greatest efforts to trap the Saints. You must make yourselves acquainted with those men who like Daniel pray three times a day toward the House of the Lord. Look to the Presidency and receive instruction. Every man who is afraid, covetous, will be taken in a snare. The time is soon coming, when no man will have any peace but in Zion and her stakes.

I saw men hunting the lives of their own sons, and brother murdering brother, women killing their own daughters, and daughters seeking the lives of their mothers. I saw armies arrayed against armies. I saw blood, desolation, fires. The Son of Man has said that the mother shall be against the daughter, and the daughter against the mother. These things are at our doors. They will follow the Saints of God from city to city. Satan will rage, and the spirit of the devil is now enraged. I know not how soon these things will take place; but with a view of them, shall I cry peace? No; I will lift up my voice and testify of them. How long you will have good crops, and the famine be kept off, I do not know; when the fig tree leaves, know then that the summer is nigh at hand.

Try the Spirits

We may look for angels and receive their ministrations, but we are to try the spirits and prove them, for it is often the case that men make a mistake in regard to these things. God has so ordained that when He has communicated, no vision is to be taken but what you see by the seeing of the eye, or what you hear by the hearing of the ear. When you see a vision, pray for the interpretation; if you get not this, shut it up; there must be certainty in this matter. An open vision will manifest that which is more important. Lying spirits are going forth in the earth. There will be great manifestations of spirits, both false and true.

Angels Do Not Have Wings

Being born again, comes by the Spirit of God through ordinances. An angel of God never has wings. Some will say that they have seen a spirit; that he offered them his hand, but they did not touch it. This is a lie. First, it is contrary to the plan of God; a spirit cannot come but in glory; an angel has flesh and bones; we see not their glory. The devil may appear as an angel of light. Ask God to reveal it; if it be of the devil, he will flee from you; if of God, He will manifest Himself, or make it manifest. We may come to Jesus and ask Him; He will know all about it; if He comes to a little child, he will adapt himself to the language and capacity of a little child.

Not every spirit, or vision, or singing, is of God. The devil is an orator; he is powerful; he took our Savior on to a pinnacle of the Temple, and kept Him in the wilderness for forty days. The gift of discerning spirits will be given to the Presiding Elder. Pray for him that he may have this gift. Speak not in the gift of tongues without understanding it, or without interpretation. The devil can speak in tongues; the adversary will come with his work; he can tempt all classes; can speak in English or Dutch. Let no one speak in tongues unless he interpret, except by the consent of the one who is placed to preside; then he may discern or interpret, or another may. Let us seek for the glory of Abraham, Noah, Adam, the Apostles, who have communion with [knowledge of] these things, and then we shall be among that number when Christ comes. (July 2, 1839.) D. H. C. 3:383-392.

Saints Not to Escape Judgments

I explained concerning the coming of the Son of Man; also that it is a false idea that the Saints will escape all the judgments, whilst the wicked suffer; for all flesh is subject to suffer, and "the righteous shall hardly escape;" still many of the Saints will escape, for the just shall live by faith; yet many of the righteous shall fall a prey to disease, to pestilence, etc., by reason of the weakness of the flesh, and yet be saved in the Kingdom of God. So that it is an unhallowed principle to say that such and such have transgressed because they have been preyed upon by disease or death, for all flesh is subject to death; and the Savior has said, "Judge not, lest ye be judged." (September 29, 1839.) D. H. C. 4:11.

Letter of the Prophet to Elders Hyde and Page—Palestine Mission Considered

Nauvoo, Hancock County, Illinois.

May 14th, 1840

To Orson Hyde and John E. Page:

Dear Brethren: I am happy in being informed by your letter that your mission swells "larger and larger." It is a great and important mission, and one that is worthy those intelligences who surround the throne of Jehovah to be engaged in. Although it appears great at present, yet you have but just begun to realize the greatness, the extent and glory of the same. If there is anything calculated to interest the mind of the Saints, to awaken in them the finest sensibilities, and arouse them to enterprise and exertion, surely it is the great and precious promises made by our heavenly Father to the children of Abraham; and those engaged in seeking the outcasts of Israel, and the dispersed of Judah, cannot fail to enjoy the Spirit of the Lord and have the choicest blessings of heaven rest upon them in copious effusions.

A Blessing to the Covenant People

Brethren, you are in the pathway to eternal fame, and immortal glory; and inasmuch as you feel interested for the covenant people of the Lord, the God of their fathers shall bless you. Do not be discouraged on account of the greatness of the work; only be humble and faithful, and then you can say, "What art thou, O great mountain! before Zerubbabel shalt thou be brought down." He who scattered Israel has promised to gather them; therefore inasmuch as you are to be instrumental in this great work, He will endow you with power, wisdom, might and intelligence, and every qualification necessary; while your minds will expand wider and wider, until you can circumscribe the earth and the heavens, reach forth into eternity, and contemplate the mighty acts of Jehovah in all their variety and glory.

The Publication of Books

In answer to your inquiries respecting the translation and publication of the Book of Mormon, hymn book, history of the

Church, etc., I would say that I entirely approve of the same, and give my consent, with the exception of the hymn book, as a new edition, containing a greater variety of hymns, will be shortly published or printed in this place, which I think will be a standard work. As soon as it is printed, you shall have some sent to you, which you may get translated, and printed into any language you please.

Should we not be able to send some to you, and there should be a great call for hymn books where you may be, then I should have no objection to your publishing the present one. Were you to publish the Book of Mormon, Doctrine and Covenants, or hymn book, I desire the copyright of the same to be secured in my name.

With respect to publishing any other work, either original, or those which have been published before, you will be governed by circumstances; if you think necessary to do so, I shall have no objection whatever. It will be well to study plainness and simplicity in whatever you publish, "for my soul delighteth in plainness."

The Duty of Seventies

I feel much pleased with the spirit of your letter—and be assured, dear brethren, of my hearty cooperation, and my prayers for your welfare and success. In answer to your inquiry in a former letter, relative to the duty of the Seventies in regulating churches, etc., I say that the duties of the Seventies are more particularly to preach the Gospel, and build up churches, rather than regulate them, that a High Priest may take charge of them. If a High Priest should be remiss in his duty, and should lead, or suffer the Church to be led astray, depart from the ordinances of the Lord, then it is the duty of one of the Seventies, acting under the special direction of the Twelve, being duly commissioned by them with their delegated authority, to go to the Church, and if agreeable to a majority of the members of said Church, to proceed to regulate and put in order the same; otherwise, he can have no authority to act. D. H. C. 4:128-129.   JOSEPH SMITH, JUN.

Trials Before High Council

Saturday, July 11, 1840.—The High Council met at my office, when I taught them principles relating to their duty as a Council, and that they might be guided by the same in future, I ordered it to be recorded as follows: "That the Council should try no case without both parties being present, or having had an opportunity to be present; neither should they hear one person's complaint before his case is brought up for trial; neither should they suffer the character of any one to be exposed before the High Council without the person being present and ready to defend him or herself; that the minds of the councilors be not prejudiced for or against any one whose case they may possibly have to act upon." (July 11, 1840.) D. H. C. 4:154.

The Prophet's Letter to William W. Phelps, Welcoming Him Back into the Church

Nauvoo, Hancock County, Illinois,
July 22, 1840.

Dear Brother Phelps. — I must say that it is with no ordinary feelings I endeavor to write a few lines to you in answer to yours of the 29th ultimo; at the same time I am rejoiced at the privilege granted me.

You may in some measure realize what my feelings, as well as Elder Rigdon's and Brother Hyrum's were, when we read your letter—truly our hearts were melted into tenderness and compassion when we ascertained your resolves. I can assure you I feel a disposition to act on your case in a manner that will meet the approbation of Jehovah, (whose servant I am), and agreeable to the principles of truth and righteousness which have been revealed; and inasmuch as long-suffering, patience, and mercy have ever characterized the dealings of our heavenly Father towards the humble and penitent, I feel disposed to copy the example, cherish the same principles, and by so doing be a savior of my fellow men.

It is true, that we have suffered much in consequence of your behavior—the cup of gall, already full enough for mortals to drink, was indeed filled to overflowing when you turned against us. One with whom we had oft taken sweet counsel together, and enjoyed many refreshing seasons from the Lord— "had it been an enemy, we could have borne it. In the day that thou stoodest on the other side, in the day when strangers carried away captive his forces, and foreigners entered into his gates, and cast lots upon Far West, even thou wast as one of them; but thou shouldst not have looked on the day of thy brother, in the day that he became a stranger, neither shouldst thou have spoken proudly in the day of distress."

However, the cup has been drunk, the will of our Father has been done, and we are yet alive, for which we thank the Lord. And having been delivered from the hands of wicked men by the mercy of our God, we say it is your privilege to be delivered from the powers of the adversary, be brought into the liberty of God's dear children, and again take your stand among the Saints of the Most High, and by diligence, humility, and love unfeigned, commend yourself to our God, and your God, and to the Church of Jesus Christ.

Believing your confession to be real, and your repentance genuine, I shall be happy once again to give you the right hand of fellowship, and rejoice over the returning prodigal.

Your letter was read to the Saints last Sunday, and an expression of their feeling was taken, when it was unanimously Resolved, That W. W. Phelps should be received into fellowship.

> "Come on, dear brother, since the war is past,
> For friends at first, are friends again at last."

Yours as ever,

JOSEPH SMITH, JUN.,

—D. H. C. 4:162-164.

REMARKS ON PRIESTHOOD

At the Conference, October, 1840

The Melchizedek Priesthood Holds All Authority

In order to investigate the subject of the Priesthood, so important to this, as well as every succeeding generation, I shall proceed to trace the subject as far as I possibly can from the Old and New Testaments.

There are two Priesthoods spoken of in the Scriptures, viz., the Melchizedek and the Aaronic or Levitical. Although there are two Priesthoods, yet the Melchizedek Priesthood comprehends the Aaronic or Levitical Priesthood, and is the grand head, and holds the highest authority which pertains to the priesthood, and the keys of the Kingdom of God in all ages of the world to the latest posterity on the earth; and is the channel through which all knowledge, doctrine, the plan of salvation and every important matter is revealed from heaven.

Its institution was prior to "the foundation of this earth, or the morning stars sang together, or the Sons of God shouted for joy," and is the highest and holiest Priesthood, and is after the order of the Son of God, and all other Priesthoods are only parts, ramifications, powers and blessings belonging to the same, and are held, controlled, and directed by it. It is the channel through which the Almighty commenced revealing His glory at the beginning of the creation of this earth, and through which He has continued to reveal Himself to the children of men to the present time, and through which He will make known His purposes to the end of time.

Adam the First Man

Commencing with Adam, who was the first man,[1] who is spoken of in Daniel as being the "Ancient of Days," or in other words, the first and oldest of all, the great, grand progenitor of whom it is said in another place he is Michael, because he was the first and father of all, not only by progeny, but the first to hold the spiritual blessings, to whom was made known the plan of ordinances for the salvation of his posterity unto the end, and to whom Christ was first revealed, and through whom Christ has been revealed from heaven, and will continue to be revealed from henceforth. Adam holds the keys of the dispensation of the fullness of times; i.e., the dispensation of all the times have been and will be revealed through him from the beginning to Christ, and from Christ to the end of the dispen-

---

[1] The doctrine here taught by the Prophet that Adam was the first man, and because of that fact was named the "Ancient of Days," the "oldest of all," because he is the grand progenitor of the earth, is confirmed in several passages of scripture. In the D. and C. 84:16, the Lord says in speaking of the authority of Priesthood: "And from Enoch to Abel, who was slain by the conspiracy of his brother, who received the priesthood by the commandments of God, by the hand of his father Adam, who was the first man." Again in the Book of Moses, 1:34: "And the first man of all men, have I called Adam, which is many." (i.e. that is the name means *many*, because he is the father of all.) In the same record (Moses 3:7) we also read: "And I, the Lord God, formed man from the dust of the ground, and breathed into his nostrils the breath of life; and man became a living soul, the first flesh upon the earth, the first man also." In the Prophet Joseph Smith's revision of the Scriptures where the genealogy of our Lord is given in Luke (v. 45) we find the following: "And of Enos, and of Seth, and of Adam, who was formed of God, and the first man upon the earth."

sations that are to be revealed. "Having made known unto us the mystery of His will, according to His good pleasure which He hath purposed in Himself; that in the dispensation of the fullness of times He might gather together in one all things in Christ, both which are in heaven, and which are on earth; even in Him." (Ephesians 1:9-10.)

Ordinances Always the Same

Now the purpose in Himself in the winding up scene of the last dispensation is that all things pertaining to that dispensation should be conducted precisely in accordance with the preceding dispensations.

And again, God purposed in Himself that there should not be an eternal fullness until every dispensation should be fulfilled and gathered together in one, and that all things whatsoever, that should be gathered together in one in those dispensations unto the same fullness and eternal glory, should be in Christ Jesus; therefore He set the ordinances to be the same forever and ever, and set Adam to watch over them, to reveal them from heaven to man, or to send angels to reveal them. "Are they not all ministering spirits, sent forth to minister for them who shall be heirs of salvation?" (Hebrews 1:14.)

These angels are under the direction of Michael or Adam, who acts under the direction of the Lord. From the above quotation we learn that Paul perfectly understood the purposes of God in relation to His connection with man, and that glorious and perfect order which He established in Himself, whereby he sent forth power, revelations, and glory.

Adam Received Commandments from God

God will not acknowledge that which He has not called, ordained, and chosen. In the beginning God called Adam by His own voice. "And the Lord called unto Adam and said unto him, Where art thou? And he said, I heard thy voice in the garden, and I was afraid because I was naked, and hid myself." (See Genesis 3:9-10.) Adam received commandments and instructions from God: this was the order from the beginning.

That he received revelations, commandments and ordinances at the beginning is beyond the power of controversy;

else how did they begin to offer sacrifices to God in an acceptable manner? And if they offered sacrifices they must be authorized by ordination. We read in Genesis 4:4, that Abel brought the firstlings of the flock and the fat thereof, and the Lord had respect to Abel and to his offering. And, again, "By faith Abel offered unto God a more excellent sacrifice than Cain, by which he obtained witness that he was righteous, God testifying of his gifts; and by it he being dead, yet speaketh." (Hebrews 11:4.) How doth he yet speak? Why he magnified the Priesthood which was conferred upon him, and died a righteous man, and therefore has become an angel of God by receiving his body from the dead, holding still the keys of his dispensation; and was sent down from heaven unto Paul to minister consoling words, and to commit unto him a knowledge of the mysteries of godliness.

And if this was not the case, I would ask, how did Paul know so much about Abel, and why should he talk about his speaking after he was dead? Hence, that he spoke after he was dead must be by being sent down out of heaven to administer.

Adam Holds the Keys of Presidency

This, then, is the nature of the Priesthood; every man holding the Presidency of his dispensation, and one man holding the Presidency of them all, even Adam; and Adam receiving his Presidency and authority from the Lord, but cannot receive a fullness until Christ shall present the Kingdom to the Father, which shall be at the end of the last dispensation.

Cain Cursed for Unrighteousness

The power, glory and blessings of the Priesthood could not continue with those who received ordination only as their righteousness continued; for Cain also being authorized to offer sacrifice, but not offering it in righteousness, was cursed. It signifies, then, that the ordinances must be kept in the very way God has appointed; otherwise their Priesthood will prove a cursing instead of a blessing.

The Mission of Enoch

If Cain had fulfilled the law of righteousness as did Enoch, he could have walked with God all the days of his life, and never failed of a blessing. "And Enoch walked with God after he begat Methuselah 300 years, and begat sons and daughters, and all the days of Enoch were 365 years; and Enoch walked with God, and he was not, for God took him." (Genesis 5:22-23.) Now this Enoch God reserved unto Himself, that he should not die at that time, and appointed unto him a ministry unto terrestrial bodies, of whom there has been but little revealed. He is reserved also unto the presidency of a dispensation, and more shall be said of him and terrestrial bodies in another treatise. He is a ministering angel, to minister to those who shall be heirs of salvation, and appeared unto Jude as Abel did unto Paul; therefore Jude spoke of him (14, 15 verses). And Enoch, the seventh from Adam, revealed these sayings: "Behold, the Lord cometh with ten thousand of His Saints."

Paul was also acquainted with this character, and received instructions from him. "By faith Enoch was translated, that he should not see death, and was not found, because God had translated him; for before his translation he had this testimony, that he pleased God; but without faith, it is impossible to please Him, for he that cometh to God must believe that He is, and that He is a revealer to those who diligently seek Him." (Hebrews 11:5-6.)

The Doctrine of Translation

Now the doctrine of translation is a power which belongs to this Priesthood. There are many things which belong to the powers of the Priesthood and the keys thereof, that have been kept hid from before the foundation of the world; they are hid from the wise and prudent to be revealed in the last times.

Many have supposed that the doctrine of translation was a doctrine whereby men were taken immediately into the presence of God, and into an eternal fullness, but this is a mistaken idea. Their place of habitation is that of the terrestrial order, and a place prepared for such characters He held in reserve to be ministering angels unto many planets, and who as yet have not entered into so great a fullness as those who are resurrected from the dead. "Others were tortured, not accepting deliverance, that they might obtain a better resurrection." (See Hebrews 11:35.)

Now it was evident that there was a better resurrection,

or else God would not have revealed it unto Paul. Wherein then, can it be said a better resurrection. This distinction is made between the doctrine of the actual resurrection and translation: translation obtains deliverance from the tortures and sufferings of the body, but their existence will prolong as to the labors and toils of the ministry, before they can enter into so great a rest and glory.

On the other hand, those who were tortured, not accepting deliverance, received an immediate rest from their labors. "And I heard a voice from heaven, saying, Blessed are the dead who die in the Lord, for from henceforth they do rest from their labors and their works do follow them." (See Revelation 14:13.)

They rest from their labors for a long time, and yet their work is held in reserve for them, that they are permitted to do the same work, after they receive a resurrection for their bodies. But we shall leave this subject and the subject of the terrestrial bodies for another time, in order to treat upon them more fully.

The Keys of Priesthood

The next great, grand Patriarch [after Enoch] who held the keys of the Priesthood was Lamech. "And Lamech lived one hundred and eighty-two years and begat a son, and he called his name Noah, saying, this same shall comfort us concerning our work and the toil of our hands because of the ground which the Lord has cursed." (See Genesis 5:28-29.) The Priesthood continued from Lamech to Noah: "And God said unto Noah, The end of all flesh is before me, for the earth is filled with violence through them and behold I will destroy them with the earth." (Genesis 6:13.)

Thus we behold the keys of this Priesthood consisted in obtaining the voice of Jehovah that He talked with him [Noah] in a familiar and friendly manner, that He continued to him the keys, the covenants, the power and the glory, with which He blessed Adam at the beginning; and the offering of sacrifice, which also shall be continued at the last time; for all the ordinances and duties that ever have been required by the Priesthood, under the directions and commandments of the Almighty in any of the dispensations, shall all be had in the last dispensation, therefore all things had under the authority of the Priesthood at any former period, shall be had again, bringing to pass the restoration spoken of by the mouth of all the Holy Prophets; then shall the sons of Levi offer an acceptable offering to the Lord. "And he shall sit as a refiner and purifier of silver; and he shall purify the sons of Levi, and purge them as gold and silver, that they may offer unto the Lord." (See Malachi 3:3.)

Sacrifice to Be Part of Restoration

It will be necessary here to make a few observations on the doctrine set forth in the above quotation, and it is generally supposed that sacrifice was entirely done away when the Great Sacrifice [i.e.,] the sacrifice of the Lord Jesus was offered up, and that there will be no necessity for the ordinance of sacrifice in future; but those who assert this are certainly not acquainted with the duties, privileges and authority of the Priesthood, or with the Prophets.

The offering of sacrifice has ever been connected and forms a part of the duties of the Priesthood. It began with the Priesthood, and will be continued until after the coming of Christ, from generation to generation. We frequently have mention made of the offering of sacrifice by the servants of the Most High in ancient days, prior to the law of Moses; which ordinances will be continued when the Priesthood is restored with all its authority, power and blessings.

The Mission of Elijah

Elijah was the last Prophet that held the keys of the Priesthood, and who will, before the last dispensation, restore the authority and deliver the keys of the Priesthood, in order that all the ordinances may be attended to in righteousness. It is true that the Savior had authority and power to bestow this blessing; but the sons of Levi were too prejudiced. "And I will send Elijah the Prophet before the great and terrible day of the Lord," etc., etc. Why send Elijah? Because he holds the keys of the authority to administer in all the ordinances of the Priesthood; and without the authority is given, the ordinances could not be administered in righteousness.

It is a very prevalent opinion that the sacrifices which were offered were entirely consumed. This was not the case; if you read Leviticus 2:2-3, you will observe that the priests took a part as a memorial and offered it up before the Lord, while the remainder was kept for the maintenance of the priests; so that the offerings and sacrifices are not all consumed upon the altar—but the blood is sprinkled, and the fat and certain other portions are consumed.

All Ordinances Restored

These sacrifices, as well as every ordinance belonging to the Priesthood, will, when the Temple of the Lord shall be built, and the sons of Levi be purified, be fully restored and attended to in all their powers, ramifications, and blessings. This ever did and ever will exist when the powers of the Melchizedek Priesthood are sufficiently manifest; else how can the restitution of all things spoken of by the Holy Prophets be brought to pass. It is not to be understood that the law of Moses will be established again with all its rites and variety of ceremonies; this has never been spoken of by the prophets; but those things which existed prior to Moses' day, namely, sacrifice, will be continued.

It may be asked by some, what necessity for sacrifice, since the Great Sacrifice was offered? In answer to which, if repentance, baptism, and faith existed prior to the days of Christ, what necessity for them since that time? The Priesthood has descended in a regular line from father to son, through their succeeding generations. (See Book of Doctrine and Covenants.) (October 5, 1840.) D. H. C. 4:207-212.

An Epistle of the Prophet to the Twelve

To the Traveling High Council and Elders of the Church of Jesus Christ of Latter-day Saints in Great Britain:

Beloved Brethren.—May grace, mercy, and peace rest upon you from God the Father and the Lord Jesus Christ. Having several communications lying before me from my brethren the Twelve, some of which ere this have merited a reply, but from the multiplicity of business which necessarily engages my attention, I have delayed communicating with you to the present time.

Be assured, beloved brethren, that I am no disinterested observer of the things which are transpiring on the face of the whole earth; and amidst the general movements which are in progress, none is of more importance than the glorious work in which you are now engaged; consequently I feel some anxiety on your account, that you may by your virtue, faith, diligence and charity commend yourselves to one another, to the Church of Christ, and to your Father who is in heaven; by whose grace you have been called to so holy a calling; and be enabled to perform the great and responsible duties which rest upon you. And I can assure you, that from the information I have received, I feel satisfied that you have not been remiss in your duty; but that your diligence and faithfulness have been such as must secure you the smiles of that God whose servant you are, and also the good will of the Saints throughout the world.

The Gospel in England

The spread of the Gospel throughout England is certainly pleasing; the contemplation of which cannot but afford feelings of no ordinary kind, in the bosom of those who have borne the heat and burden of the day; and who were its firm supporters and strenuous advocates in infancy, while surrounded with circumstances the most unpropitious, and its destruction threatened on all hands; like the gallant bark that has braved the storm unhurt, spreads her canvas to the breeze, and nobly cuts her way through the yielding wave, more conscious than ever of the strength of her timbers, and the experience and capability of her captain, pilot, and crew.

It is likewise very satisfactory to my mind, that there has been such a good understanding between you, and that the Saints have so cheerfully hearkened to counsel, and vied with each other in this labor of love, and in the promotion of truth and righteousness. This is as it should be in the Church of Jesus Christ; unity is strength. "How pleasing it is for brethren to dwell together in unity!" Let the Saints of the Most High ever cultivate this principle, and the most glorious blessings must result, not only to them individually, but to the whole Church—the order of the kingdom will be maintained, its officers respected, and its requirements readily and cheerfully obeyed.

Love a Characteristic of Deity

Love is one of the chief characteristics of Deity, and ought to be manifested by those who aspire to be the sons of God. A man filled with the love of God, is not content with blessing his family alone, but ranges through the whole world, anxious to bless the whole human race. This has been your feeling, and caused you to forego the pleasures of home, that you might be a blessing to others, who are candidates for immortality, but strangers to truth; and for so doing, I pray that heaven's choicest blessings may rest upon you.

Being requested to give my advice respecting the propriety of your returning in the spring, I will do so willingly. I have reflected on the subject some time, and am of the opinion that it would be wisdom in you to make preparations to leave the scene of your labors in the spring. Having carried the testimony to that land, and numbers having received it, the leaven can now spread without your being obliged to stay.

Another thing—there have been whisperings of the Spirit that there will be some agitations, excitements, and trouble in the land in which you are now laboring. I would therefore say, in the meantime be diligent: organize the churches, and let everyone stand in his proper place, so that those who cannot come with you in the spring, may not be left as sheep without a shepherd.

A Place of Gathering

I would likewise observe, that inasmuch as this place has been appointed for the gathering of the Saints, it is necessary that it should be attended to in the order that the Lord intends it should. To this end I would say, that as there are great numbers of the Saints in England who are extremely poor, and not accustomed to the farming business, who must have certain preparations made for them before they can support themselves in this country, therefore to prevent confusion and disappointment when they arrive here, let those men who are accustomed to make machinery, and those who can command capital, though it be small, come here as soon as convenient, and put up machinery, and make such other preparations as may be necessary, so that when the poor come on, they may have employment to come to. This place has advantages for manufacturing and commercial purposes, which but very few can boast of; and the establishing of cotton factories, foundries, potteries, etc., would be the means of bringing in wealth, and raising it to a very important elevation.

I need not occupy more space on this subject, as its reasonableness must be obvious to every mind.

Printing of Books

In my former epistle I told you my mind respecting the printing of the Book of Mormon, hymn book, etc. I have been favored by receiving a hymn book from you, and as far as I have examined it, I highly approve of it, and think it to be a very valuable collection. I am informed that the Book of Mormon is likewise printed, which I am glad to hear, and should be pleased to hear that it was printed in all the different languages of the earth. You can use your own pleasure respecting the printing of the Doctrine and Covenants. If there is a great demand for it, I have no objections, but would rather encourage it.

I can say, that as far as I have been made acquainted with your movements, I am perfectly satisfied that they have been in wisdom; and I have no doubt but that the Spirit of the Lord has directed you, and this proves to my mind that you have been humble, and your desires have been for the salvation of your fellow men, and not for your own aggrandizement, and selfish interests. As long as the Saints manifest such a disposition, their counsels will be approved of, and their exertions crowned with success.

There are many things of much importance, on which you ask counsel, but which I think you will be perfectly able to decide upon, as you are more conversant with the peculiar circumstances than I am; and I feel great confidence in your united wisdom; therefore you will excuse me for not entering into detail. If I should see anything that is wrong, I would take the privilege of making known my mind to you, and pointing out the evil.

If Elder Parley P. Pratt should wish to remain in England some time longer than the rest of the Twelve, he will feel himself at liberty to do so, as his family are with him, consequently his circumstances are somewhat different from the rest; and likewise it is necessary that someone should remain who is conversant with the rules and regulations of the Church, and continue the paper which is published. Consequently, taking all these things into consideration, I would not press it upon Brother Pratt to return in the spring.

The Saints Prospering

I am happy to inform you that we are prospering in this place, and that the Saints are more healthy than formerly; and from the decrease of sickness this season, when compared with the last, I am led to the conclusion that this must eventually become a healthy place.   There are at present about 3,000 inhabitants in Nauvoo, and numbers are flocking in daily. Several stakes have been set off in different parts of the country, which are in prosperous circumstances.

Provisions are much lower than when you left.   Flour is about $4 per barrel.   Corn and potatoes about 25 cents per bushel; and other things in proportion.   There has been a very plentiful harvest throughout the Union.

The Temple

You will observe, by the Times and Seasons, that we are about building a temple for the worship of our God in this place.   Preparations are now making; every tenth day is devoted by the brethren for quarrying rock, etc.   We have secured one of the most lovely situations for it in this region of country.   It is expected to be considerably larger than the one in Kirtland, and on a more magnificent scale, and which will undoubtedly attract the attention of the great men of the earth.

We have a bill before the legislature for the incorporation of the city of Nauvoo, and for the establishment of a seminary of learning, and other purposes, which I expect will pass in a short time.

Death of Patriarch Joseph Smith

You will also receive intelligence of the death of my father; which event, although painful to the family and to the Church generally, yet the sealing testimony of the truth of the work of the Lord was indeed satisfactory.   Brother Hyrum succeeds him as Patriarch of the Church, according to his last directions and benedictions.

Several persons of eminence and distinction in society have joined the Church and become obedient to the faith; and I am happy to inform you that the work is spreading very fast upon this continent.   Some of the brethren are now in New Orleans.

and we expect a large gathering from the south. I have had the pleasure of welcoming about one hundred brethren who came with Brother Turley; the remainder I am informed stayed in Kirtland, not having means to get any further. I think that those who came here this fall, did not take the best possible route, or the least expensive. Most of the brethren have obtained employment of one kind or another, and appear tolerably well contented, and seem disposed to hearken to counsel.

Spread of the Gospel

Brothers Robinson and Smith lately had a letter from Elders Kimball, Smith and Woodruff, which gave us information of the commencement of the work of the Lord in the city of London, which I was glad to hear. I am likewise informed that Elders have gone to Australia and to the East Indies. I feel desirous that every providential opening of the kind should be filled, and that you should, prior to your leaving England, send the Gospel into as many parts as you possibly can.

Beloved brethren, you must be aware in some measure of my feelings, when I contemplate the great work which is now rolling on, and the relationship which I sustain to it, while it is extending to distant lands, and thousands are embracing it. I realize in some measure my responsibility, and the need I have of support from above, and wisdom from on high, that I may be able to teach this people, which have now become a great people, the principles of righteousness, and lead them agreeably to the will of Heaven; so that they may be perfected, and prepared to meet the Lord Jesus Christ when He shall appear in great glory. Can I rely on your prayers to our heavenly Father on my behalf, and on all the prayers of all my brethren and sisters in England, (whom having not seen, yet I love), that I may be enabled to escape every stratagem of Satan, surmount every difficulty, and bring this people to the enjoyment of those blessings which are reserved for the righteous? I ask this at your hands in the name of the Lord Jesus Christ.

Let the Saints remember that great things depend on their individual exertion, and that they are called to be co-workers with us and the Holy Spirit in accomplishing the great work of the last days; and in consideration of the extent, the blessings and glories of the same, let every selfish feeling be not only buried, but annihilated; and let love to God and man predominate, and reign triumphant in every mind, that their hearts may become like unto Enoch's of old, and comprehend all things, present, past and future, and come behind in no gift, waiting for the coming of the Lord Jesus Christ.

Saints to Live unto God

The work in which we are unitedly engaged is one of no ordinary kind. The enemies we have to contend against are subtle and well skilled in maneuvering; it behooves us to be on the alert to concentrate our energies, and that the best feelings should exist in our midst; and then, by the help of the Almighty, we shall go on from victory to victory, and from conquest to conquest; our evil passions will be subdued, our prejudices depart; we shall find no room in our bosoms for hatred; vice will hide its deformed head, and we shall stand approved in the sight of Heaven, and be acknowledged the sons of God.

Let us realize that we are not to live to ourselves, but to God; by so doing the greatest blessings will rest upon us both in time and in eternity.

Baptism for the Dead

I presume the doctrine of "baptism for the dead" has ere this reached your ears, and may have raised some inquiries in your minds respecting the same. I cannot in this letter give you all the information you may desire on the subject; but aside from knowledge independent of the Bible, I would say that it was certainly practiced by the ancient churches; and St. Paul endeavors to prove the doctrine of the resurrection from the same, and says, "Else what shall they do which are baptized for the dead, if the dead rise not at all? Why are they then baptized for the dead?"

I first mentioned the doctrine in public when preaching the funeral sermon of Brother Seymour Brunson: and have since then given general instructions in the Church on the subject. The Saints have the privilege of being baptized for those of their relatives who are dead, whom they believe would have embraced the Gospel, if they had been privileged with hearing it, and who have received the Gospel in the spirit, through the instrumentality of those who have been commissioned to preach to them while in prison.

Without enlarging on the subject, you will undoubtedly see its consistency and reasonableness; and it presents the Gospel of Christ in probably a more enlarged scale than some have imagined it. But as the performance of this rite is more particularly confined to this place, it will not be necessary to enter into particulars; at the same time I always feel glad to give all the information in my power, but my space will not allow me to do it.

We had a letter from Elder Hyde, a few days ago, who is in New Jersey, and is expecting to leave for England as soon as Elder Page reaches him. He requested to know if converted Jews are to go to Jerusalem or to come to Zion. I therefore wish you to inform him that converted Jews must come here.

Give my kind love to all the brethren and sisters, and tell them I should have been pleased to come over to England to see them, but I am afraid that I shall be under the necessity of remaining here for some time; therefore I give them a pressing invitation to come and see me.

I remain, dear brethren, yours affectionately,

JOSEPH SMITH.

(Oct. 19, 1840.) D. H. C. 4:226-232.

Description of Paul

Given by the Prophet Joseph, January 5, 1841, at the organization of a school of instruction: "He is about five feet high; very dark hair; dark complexion; dark skin; large Roman nose; sharp face; small black eyes, penetrating as eternity; round shoulders; a whining voice, except when elevated, and then it almost resembled the roaring of a lion. He was a good orator, active and diligent, always employing himself in doing good to his fellow man."

Different Degrees of the Priesthood of Melchizedek

"Answer to the question, Was the Priesthood of Melchizedek taken away when Moses died? All Priesthood is Melchizedek, but there are different portions or degrees of it. That portion which brought Moses to speak with God face to face was taken away; but that which brought the ministry of angels remained.   All the prophets had the Melchizedek Priesthood and were ordained by God himself."

Elements Are Eternal

The elements are eternal.   That which has a beginning will surely have an end; take a ring, it is without beginning or end— cut it for a beginning place and at the same time you have an ending place.

A key: Every principle proceeding from God is eternal and any principle which is not eternal is of the devil.   The sun has no beginning or end; the rays which proceed from himself have no bounds, consequently are eternal.

So it is with God.   If the soul of man had a beginning it will surely have an end.   In the translation "without form and void" it should be read, empty and desolate.   The word created should be formed, or organized.

Observation on the Sectarian God

"That which is without body, parts and passions is nothing. There is no other God in heaven but that God who has flesh and bones.   John 5:26.   As the Father hath life in himself, even so hath he given to the Son to have life in himself.   God the Father took life unto himself precisely as Jesus did."

"The first step in salvation of man is the laws of eternal and self-existent principles.   Spirits are eternal.   At the first organization in heaven we were all present, and saw the Savior chosen and appointed and the plan of salvation made, and we sanctioned it.

"We came to this earth that we might have a body and present it pure before God in the celestial kingdom.   The great principle of happiness consists in having a body.   The devil has no body, and herein is his punishment.   He is pleased when he can obtain the tabernacle of man, and when cast out by the Savior he asked to go into the herd of swine, showing that he would prefer a swine's body to having none.

"All beings who have bodies have power over those who have not.   The devil has no power over us only as we permit him.   The moment we revolt at anything which comes from God, the devil takes power.   This earth will be rolled back into the presence of God, and crowned with celestial glory."

EXCERPTS FROM A PROCLAMATION OF THE FIRST PRESIDENCY TO THE SAINTS SCATTERED ABOAD

* * *

Nauvoo

The name of our City (Nauvoo) is of Hebrew origin, and signifies a beautiful situation, or place, carrying with it, also, the idea of rest; and is truly descriptive of the most delightful location. It is situated on the east bank of the Mississippi River, at the head of the Des Moines Rapids, in Hancock County, bounded on the east by an extensive prairie of surpassing beauty, and on the north, west and south, by the Mississippi. This place has been objected to by some on account of the sickness which has prevailed in the summer months, but * * * all the eastern and southern portions of the City of Nauvoo, are as healthful as any other portions of the western country, to acclimatized citizens. * * *

The population of the city is increasing with unparalleled rapidity, numbering more than 3,000 inhabitants. Every facility is afforded, in the city and adjacent country, in Hancock County, for the successful prosecution of the mechanical arts and the pleasing pursuits of agriculture. The waters of the Mississippi can be successfully used for manufacturing purposes to almost an unlimited extent.—D. H. C. 4:268.

* * *

The Temple

The Temple of the Lord is in process of erection here, where the Saints will come to worship the God of their fathers, according to the order of His house and the powers of the Holy Priesthood, and will be so constructed as to enable all the functions of the Priesthood to be duly exercised, and where instructions from the Most High will be received, and from this place go forth to distant lands. Let us then concentrate all our powers, under the provisions of our *magna charta* granted by the Illinois legislature, at the "City of Nauvoo" and surrounding country, and strive to emulate the action of the ancient covenant fathers and patriarchs, in those things which are of such vast importance to this and every succeeding generation.— D. H. C. 4:269.

* * *

The Gathering of Saints

The greatest temporal and spiritual blessings which always come from faithfulness and concerted effort, never attended individual exertion or enterprise. The history of all past ages abundantly attests this fact. In addition to all temporal blessings, there is no other way for the Saints to be saved in these last days, [than by the gathering] as the concurrent testimony of all the holy prophets clearly proves, for it is written—"They shall come from the east, and be gathered from the west; the north shall give up, and the south shall keep not back." "The sons of God shall be gathered from afar, and his daughters from the ends of the earth."

It is also the concurrent testimony of all the prophets, that this gathering together of all the Saints, must take place before the Lord comes to "take vengeance upon the ungodly," and "to be glorified and admired by all those who obey the Gospel." The fiftieth Psalm, from the first to the fifth verse inclusive, describes the glory and majesty of that event. (Jan. 8, 1841.) D. H. C. 4:272.

Order of the Priesthood in Temple Building

The following instruction was given at the time of the laying of the corner stones of the Nauvoo Temple, April 6, 1841.

If the strict order of the Priesthood were carried out in the building of Temples, the first stone would be laid at the south-east corner, by the First Presidency of the Church. The south-west corner should be laid next. The third, or north-west corner next; and the fourth, or north-east corner last. The First Presidency should lay the south-east corner stone and dictate who are the proper persons to lay the other corner stones.

If a Temple is built at a distance, and the First Presidency are not present, then the Quorum of the Twelve Apostles are the persons to dictate the order for that Temple; and in the absence of the Twelve Apostles, then the Presidency of the Stake will lay the south-east corner stone; the Melchizedek Priesthood laying the corner stones on the east side of the Temple, and the Lesser Priesthood those on the west side.— D. H. C. 4:331.

Report of the First Presidency at the April Conference, 1841

The Presidency of the Church of Jesus Christ of Latter-day Saints, feel great pleasure in assembling with the Saints at another general conference, under circumstances so auspicious and cheering; and with grateful hearts to Almighty God for His providential regard, they cordially unite with the Saints, on this occasion, in ascribing honor, glory, and blessing to His Holy name.

It is with unfeigned pleasure that they have to make known the steady and rapid increase of the Church in this state, the United States, and Europe. The anxiety to become acquainted with the principles of the Gospel, on every hand is intense, and the cry of "come over and help us," is reaching the Elders on the wings of every wind; while thousands who have heard the Gospel have become obedient thereto, and are rejoicing in its gifts and blessings. Prejudice, with its attendant train of evil, is giving way before the force of truth, whose benign rays are penetrating the nations afar off.

Missionary Reports Satisfactory

The reports from the Twelve Apostles in Europe are very satisfactory, and state that the work continues to progress with unparalleled rapidity, and that the harvest is truly great. In the Eastern States the faithful laborers are successful, and many are flocking to the standard of truth. Nor is the South keeping back. Churches have been raised up in the Southern and Western States, and a very pressing invitation has been received from New Orleans, for some of the Elders to visit that city; which has been complied with. In our own state and immediate neighborhood, many are avowing their attachment to the principles of our holy religion, and have become obedient to the faith.

Peace and prosperity attend us; and we have favor in the sight of God and virtuous men. The time was, when we were looked upon as deceivers, and that "Mormonism" would soon pass away, come to nought, and be forgotten. But the time has gone by when it is looked upon as a transient matter, or a bubble on the wave, and it is now taking a deep hold in the hearts and affections of all those, who are noble-minded enough to lay aside the prejudice of education, and investigate the subject with candor and honesty. The truth, like the sturdy oak, has stood unhurt amid the contending elements, which have beat upon it with tremendous force. The floods have rolled, wave after wave, in quick succession, and have not swallowed it up. "They have lifted up their voice, O Lord; the floods have lifted up their voice; but the Lord of Hosts is mightier than the mighty waves of the sea"; nor have the flames of persecution, with all the influence of mobs, been able to destroy it; but like Moses' bush, it has stood unconsumed, and now at this moment presents an important spectacle both to men and angels. Where can we turn our eyes to behold such another? We contemplate a people who have embraced a system of religion, unpopular, and the adherence to which has brought upon them repeated persecutions. A people who, for their love for God, and attachment to His cause, have suffered hunger, nakedness, perils, and almost every privation. A people who, for the sake of their religion, have had to mourn the premature death of parents, husbands, wives, and children. A people, who have preferred death to slavery and hypocrisy, and have honorably maintained their characters, and stood firm and immovable, in times that have tried men's souls. Stand fast, ye Saints of God, hold on a little while longer, and the storm of life will be past, and you will be rewarded by that God whose servants you are, and who will duly appreciate all your toils and afflictions for Christ's sake and the Gospel's. Your names will be handed down to posterity as Saints of God and virtuous men.

A Prayer for Continued Peace

But we hope that those scenes of blood will never more occur, but that many, very many, such scenes as the present will be witnessed by the Saints, and that in the Temple, the foundation of which has been so happily laid, will the Saints of the Most High continue to congregate from year to year in peace and safety.

From the kind and generous feelings, manifested by the citizens of this state, since our sojourn among them, we may continue to expect the enjoyment of all the blessings of civil and religious liberty, guaranteed by the Constitution. The citizens of Illinois have done themselves honor, in throwing the mantle of the Constitution over a persecuted and afflicted people; and have given evident proof that they are not only in the enjoyment of the privileges of freemen themselves, but also that they willingly and cheerfully extend that invaluable blessing to others, and that they freely award to faithfulness and virtue their due.

The proceedings of the legislature, in regard to the citizens of this place, have been marked with philanthropy and benevolence; and they have laid us under great and lasting obligations, in granting us the several liberal charters we now enjoy, and by which we hope to prosper until our city becomes the most splendid, our University the most learned, and our Legion the most effective of any in the Union.

Impoverished Saints

In consequence of the impoverished condition of the Saints, the buildings which are in course of erection do not progress as fast as could be desired; but from the interest which is generally manifested by the Saints at large, we hope to accomplish much by a combination of effort, and a concentration of action, and erect the Temple and other public buildings, which we so much need for our mutual instruction and the education of our children.

From the reports which have been received, we may expect a large emigration this season. The proclamation which was sent, some time ago, to the churches abroad, has been responded to, and great numbers are making preparations to come and locate themselves in this city and vicinity.

From what we now witness, we are led to look forward with pleasing anticipation to the future, and soon expect to see the thousands of Israel flocking to this region in obedience to the heavenly command; numerous inhabitants—Saints— thickly studding the flowery and wide-spread prairies of Illinois; temples for the worship of our God erecting in various parts, and great peace resting upon Israel.

We would call the attention of the Saints more particularly to the building of the Temple, for on its speedy erection great blessings depend. The zeal which is manifested by the Saints in this city is, indeed, praiseworthy, and, we hope will be imitated by the Saints in the various stakes and branches of the Church, and that those who cannot contribute labor will bring their gold and their silver, their brass and their iron, with the pine tree, and box tree, to beautify the same.

We are glad to hear of the organization of the different quorums in this city, and hope that their organization will be attended to in every stake and branch of the Church, for the Almighty is a lover of order and good government.

From the faith and enterprise of the Saints generally, we feel greatly encouraged and cheerfully attend to the important duties devolving upon us, knowing that we not only have the approval of Heaven, but also that our efforts for the establishment of Zion and the spread of truth, are cheerfully seconded by the thousands of Israel.

In conclusion we would say, brethren, be faithful, let your love and moderation be known unto all men; be patient, be mindful to observe all the commandments of your Heavenly Father, and the God of all grace shall bless you. Even so. Amen.—D. H. C. 4:336-339.

JOSEPH SMITH, President,
ROBERT B. THOMPSON, Clerk.

* * *

The Prophet's Discourse on Gospel Principles

At 10 o'clock a.m. [May 16, 1841], a large concourse of the Saints assembled on the meeting ground, and were addressed by President Joseph Smith, who spoke at considerable length.

The Doctrine of Agency

He commenced his observations by remarking that the kindness of our Heavenly Father called for our heartfelt gratitude. He then observed that Satan was generally blamed for the evils which we did, but if he was the cause of all our wickedness, men could not be condemned. The devil could not compel mankind to do evil; all was voluntary. Those who resisted the Spirit of God, would be liable to be led into temptation, and then the association of heaven would be withdrawn from those who refused to be made partakers of such great glory. God would not exert any compulsory means, and the devil could not; and such ideas as were entertained [on these subjects] by many were absurd. The creature was made subject to vanity, not willingly, but Christ subjected the same in hope— all are subjected to vanity while they travel through the crooked paths and difficulties which surround them. Where is the man that is free from vanity? None ever were perfect but Jesus;

and why was He perfect? Because He was the Son of God, and had the fullness of the Spirit, and greater power than any man. But notwithstanding their vanity, men look forward with hope (because they are "subjected in hope") to the time of their deliverance.

The First Principles

The speaker then made some observations on the first principles of the Gospel, observing, that many of the Saints who had come from different states and nations had only a very superficial knowledge of these principles, not having heard them fully investigated.

He then briefly stated the principles of faith, repentance, and baptism for the remission of sins, these were believed by some of the righteous societies of the day, but the doctrine of laying on of hands for the gift of the Holy Ghost was discarded by them.

The speaker then referred to the 6th chapter of Hebrews, 1st and 2nd verses, "Not laying again the foundation of repentance from dead works," &c., but of the doctrine of baptisms, laying on of hands, the resurrection, and eternal judgment, &c. That the doctrine of eternal judgment was perfectly understood by the Apostles, is evident from several passages of Scripture. Peter preached repentance and baptism for the remission of sins to the Jews who had been led to acts of violence and blood by their leaders; but to the rulers he said, "I wot that through ignorance ye did it, as did also your rulers." "Repent ye therefore, and be converted, that your sins may be blotted out, when the times of refreshing (redemption) shall come from the presence of the Lord, and He shall send Jesus Christ, which before was preached unto you," &c. The time of redemption here had reference to the time when Christ should come; then, and not till then, would their sins be blotted out. Why? Because they were murderers, and no murderer hath eternal life. Even David must wait for those times of refreshing, before he can come forth and his sins be blotted out. For Peter, speaking of him says, "David hath not yet ascended into heaven, for his sepulchre is with us to this day." His remains were then in the tomb. Now, we read that many bodies of the Saints arose at Christ's resurrection, probably all the Saints, but it seems that David did not. Why? Because he had been a murderer. If the ministers of religion had a proper understanding of the doctrine of eternal judgment, they would not be found attending the man who forfeited his life to the injured laws of his country, by shedding innocent blood; for such characters cannot be forgiven, until they have paid the last farthing. The prayers of all the ministers in the world can never close the gates of hell against a murderer.

The Doctrine of Election

He then spoke on the subject of election, and read the 9th chapter of Romans, from which it was evident that the election there spoken of was pertaining to the flesh, and had reference to the seed of Abraham, according to the promise God made to Abraham, saying, "In thee, and in thy seed, all the families of the earth shall be blessed." To them belonged the adoption and the covenants, &c. Paul said, when he saw their unbelief, "I wish myself accursed"—according to the flesh—not according to the spirit. Why did God say to Pharaoh, "For this cause have I raised thee up"? Because Pharaoh was a fit instrument—a wicked man, and had committed acts of cruelty of the most atrocious nature. The election of the promised seed still continues, and in the last day, they shall have the Priesthood restored unto them, and they shall be the "saviors on Mount Zion," the ministers of our God; if it were not for the remnant which was left, then might men now be as Sodom and Gomorrah. The whole of the chapter had reference to the Priesthood and the house of Israel; and unconditional election of individuals to eternal life was not taught by the Apostles. God did elect or predestinate, that all those who would be saved, should be saved in Christ Jesus, and through obedience to the Gospel; but He passes over no man's sins, but visits them with correction, and if His children will not repent of their sins He will discard them.

This is an imperfect sketch of a very interesting discourse, which occupied more than two hours in delivery, and was listened to with marked attention, by the vast assembly present. (May 16, 1841.) D. H. C. 4:358-360.

Three Independent Principles

May 16, 1841. There are three independent principles; the Spirit of God, the spirit of man, and the spirit of the devil. All men have power to resist the devil.

They who have tabernacles, have power over those who have not. The doctrine of eternal judgment; Acts 2:41. Peter preached, Repent, and be baptized in the name of Jesus Christ, for the remission of sins, &c.; but in Acts 3:19 he says, Repent, and be converted, that your sins may be blotted out when the times of redemption shall come, and he shall send Jesus, &c.

The Three Personages

Everlasting covenant was made between three personages before the organization of this earth, and relates to their dispensation of things to men on the earth; these personages, according to Abraham's record, are called God the first, the Creator; God the second, the Redeemer; and God the third, the witness or Testator.—MSS.

The Twelve Next to the First Presidency

President Joseph Smith now arriving, proceeded to state to the conference at considerable length, the object of their present meeting, and, in addition to what President Young had stated in the morning, said that the time had come when the Twelve should be called upon to stand in their place next to the First Presidency, and attend to the settling of immigrants and the business of the Church at the stakes, and assist to bear off the kingdom victoriously to the nations, and as they had been faithful, and had borne the burden in the heat of the day, that it was right that they should have an opportunity of providing something for themselves and families, and at the same time relieve him, so that he might attend to the business of translating.

Moved, seconded and carried, that the conference approve of the instructions of President Smith in relation to the Twelve, and that they proceed accordingly to attend to the duties of their office. (Aug. 16, 1841.) D. H. C. 4:403.

Trust in God When Sick

Sunday, Sept. 5, 1841. I preached to a large congregation at the stand, on the science and practice of medicine, desiring to persuade the Saints to trust in God when sick, and not in an arm of flesh, and live by faith and not by medicine, or poison; and when they were sick, and had called for the Elders to pray for them, and they were not healed, to use herbs and mild food. —D. H. C. 4:414.

ITEMS OF INSTRUCTION

Baptism for the Dead

President Joseph Smith, by request of the Twelve Apostles, gave instructions on the doctrine of baptism for the dead, which were listened to with intense interest by the large assembly. He presented baptism for the dead as the only way that men can appear as saviors on Mount Zion.

The proclamation of the first principles of the Gospel was a means of salvation to men individually; and it was the truth, not men, that saved them; but men, by actively engaging in rites of salvation substitutionally became instrumental in bringing multitudes of their kindred into the kingdom of God.

Angels and Ministering Spirits

He explained the difference between an angel and a ministering spirit; the one a resurrected or translated body, with its spirit ministering to embodied spirits—the other a disembodied spirit, visiting and ministering to disembodied spirits. Jesus Christ became a ministering spirit (while His body was lying in the sepulchre) to the spirits in prison, to fulfill an important part of His mission, without which He could not have perfected His work, or entered into His rest.   After His resurrection He appeared as an angel to His disciples.

Translated bodies cannot enter into rest until they have undergone a change equivalent to death.   Translated bodies are designed for future missions.

The angel that appeared to John on the Isle of Patmos was a translated or resurrected body [i.e. personage].   Jesus Christ went in body after His resurrection, to minister to resurrected bodies.   There has been a chain of authority and power from Adam down to the present time.

The best way to obtain truth and wisdom is not to ask it from books, but to go to God in prayer, and obtain divine teaching.   It is no more incredible that God should *save* the dead, than that he should *raise* the dead.

Pardoning Mercy an Eternal Principle

There is never a time when the spirit is too old to approach God.   All are within the reach of pardoning mercy, who have not committed the unpardonable sin, which hath no forgiveness, neither in this world, nor in the world to come. There is a way to release the spirits of the dead; that is by the power and authority of the Priesthood—by binding and loosing on earth. This doctrine appears glorious, inasmuch as it exhibits the greatness of divine compassion and benevolence in the extent of the plan of human salvation.

This glorious truth is well calculated to enlarge the understanding, and to sustain the soul under troubles, difficulties and distresses. For illustration, suppose the case of two men, brothers, equally intelligent, learned, virtuous and lovely, walking in uprightness and in all good conscience, so far as they have been able to discern duty from the muddy stream of tradition, or from the blotted page of the book of nature.

One dies and is buried, having never heard the Gospel of reconciliation; to the other the message of salvation is sent, he hears and embraces it, and is made the heir of eternal life. Shall the one become the partaker of glory and the other be consigned to hopeless perdition? Is there no chance for his escape? Sectarianism answers "none." Such an idea is worse than atheism. The truth shall break down and dash in pieces all such bigoted Pharisaism; the sects shall be sifted, the honest in heart brought out, and their priests left in the midst of their corruption.

Sectarian Baptism

Many objections are urged against the Latter-day Saints for not admitting the validity of sectarian baptism, and for withholding fellowship from sectarian churches. Yet to do otherwise would be like putting new wine into old bottles, and putting old wine into new bottles. What! new revelations in the old churches? New revelations would knock out the bottom of their bottomless pit. New wine into old bottles! The bottles burst and the wine runs out! What! Sadducees in the new church! Old wine in new leathern bottles will leak through the pores and escape. So the Sadducee saints mock at authority, kick out of the traces, and run to the mountains of perdition, leaving the long echo of their braying behind them.

He then referred to the [lack of] charity of the sects, in denouncing all who disagree with them in opinion, and in joining in persecuting the Saints, who believe that even such may be saved, in this world and in the world to come (murderers and apostates excepted).

Salvation for the Dead

This doctrine presents in a clear light the wisdom and mercy of God in preparing an ordinance for the salvation of the dead, being baptized by proxy, their names recorded in heaven and they judged according to the deeds done in the body. This doctrine was the burden of the scriptures. Those Saints who neglect it in behalf of their deceased relatives, do it at the peril of their own salvation. The dispensation of the fullness of times will bring to light the things that have been revealed in all former dispensations; also other things that have not been before revealed. He shall send Elijah, the Prophet, &c., and restore all things in Christ.

President Joseph Smith then announced: "There shall be no more baptisms for the dead, until the ordinance can be attended to in the Lord's House; and the Church shall not hold another General Conference, until they can meet in said house. For thus saith the Lord!"² (Oct. 3, 1841.) D. H. C. 4:424-426.

Do Not Accuse the Brethren

I charged the Saints not to follow the example of the adversary in accusing the brethren, and said, "If you do not accuse each other, God will not accuse you. If you have no accuser you will enter heaven, and if you will follow the revelations and instructions which God gives you through me, I will take you into heaven as my back load. If you will not accuse me, I will not accuse you. If you will throw a cloak of charity over my sins, I will over yours—for charity covereth a multitude of sins. What many people call sin is not sin; I do many things to break down superstition, and I will break it down"; I referred to the curse of Ham for laughing at Noah, while in his wine, but doing no harm. Noah was a righteous man, and yet he drank wine and became intoxicated; the Lord did not forsake him in consequence thereof, for he retained all the power of his Priesthood, and when he was accused by Canaan,

---

²The reason for the commandment from the Lord discontinuing baptism for the dead in the Mississippi River is found in the fact that the font in the Nauvoo Temple had been prepared for these ordinances. It was only in the days of poverty and when there was no font in a Temple, that the Lord granted baptism for the dead outside of his holy house. November 8, 1841, the font in the Nauvoo Temple was dedicated and from that time forth until the exodus baptism for the dead in the Temple in Nauvoo was performed.

he cursed him by the Priesthood which he held, and the Lord had respect to his word, and the Priesthood which he held, notwithstanding he was drunk, and the curse remains upon the posterity of Canaan until the present day. (November 7, 1841.) D. H. C. 4:445-446.

Perfection of the Book of Mormon

Sunday, 28.—I spent the day in the council with the Twelve Apostles at the house of President Young, conversing with them upon a variety of subjects. Brother Joseph Fielding was present, having been absent four years on a mission to England. I told the brethren that the Book of Mormon was the most correct of any book on earth, and the keystone of our religion, and a man would get nearer to God by abiding by its precepts, than by any other book. (November 28, 1841.) D. H. C. 4:461.

IMPORTANT INSTRUCTIONS

Value of Chastisement

President Joseph arose and said: "Brother Kimball has given you a true explanation of the parable," and then read the parable of the vine and its branches, and explained it, and said, "If we keep the commandments of God, we should bring forth fruit and be the friends of God, and know what our Lord did.

"Some people say I am a fallen Prophet, because I do not bring forth more of the word of the Lord, Why do I not do it? Are we able to receive it? No! Not one in this room. He then chastened the congregation for their wickedness and unbelief, 'for whom the Lord loveth he chasteneth, and scourgeth every son and daughter whom he receiveth,' and if we do not receive chastisements then we are bastards and not sons."

On the subject of revelation, he said, a man would command his son to dig potatoes and saddle his horse, but before he had done either he would tell him to do something else. This is all considered right; but as soon as the Lord gives a commandment and revokes that decree and commands something else, then the Prophet is considered fallen. Because we will not receive chastisement at the hands of the Prophets and Apostles, the Lord chastiseth us with sickness and death. Let not any man publish his own righteousness, for others can see that for him; sooner let him confess his sins, and then he will be forgiven, and he will bring forth more fruit. When a corrupt man is chastised he gets angry and will not endure it. The reason we do not have the secrets of the Lord revealed unto us, is because we do not keep them but reveal them; we do not keep our own secrets, but reveal our difficulties to the world, even to our enemies, then how would we keep the secrets of the Lord? I can keep a secret till Doomsday. What greater love hath any man than that he lay down his life for his friend; then why not fight for our friend until we die? (December 19, 1841.) D. H. C. 4:478-479.

The Gift of Tongues

Sunday, December 26, 1841.—The public meeting of the Saints was at my house this evening, and after Patriarch Hyrum Smith and Elder Brigham Young had spoken on the principles of faith, and the gifts of the Spirit, I read the 13th chapter of First Corinthians, also a part of the 14th chapter, and remarked that the gift of tongues was necessary in the Church; but that if Satan could not speak in tongues, he could not tempt a Dutchman, or any other nation, but the English, for he can tempt the Englishman, for he has tempted me, and I am an Englishman; but the gift of tongues by the power of the Holy Ghost in the Church, is for the benefit of the servants of God to preach to unbelievers, as on the day of Pentecost. When devout men from every nation shall assemble to hear the things of God, let the Elders preach to them in their own mother tongue, whether it is German, French, Spanish or Irish, or any other, and let those interpret who understand the language spoken, in their own mother tongue, and this is what the Apostle meant in First Corinthians 14:27. (December 26, 1841.) D. H. C. 4:485-486.

Announcement Respecting Work on the Temple

To the Brethren in Nauvoo City: Greeting.— It is highly important for the forwarding of the Temple, that an equal distribution of labor should be made in relation to time; as a superabundance of hands one week, and none the next, tends to retard the progress of the work; therefore every brother is requested to be particular to labor on the day set apart for the same, in his ward; and to remember that he that sows sparingly, shall also reap sparingly, so that if the brethren want a plentiful harvest, they will do well to be at the place of labor in good season in the morning, bringing all necessary tools, according to their occupation, and those who have teams bring them also, unless otherwise advised by the Temple Committee. Should any one be detained from his labor by unavoidable circumstances on the day appointed, let him labor the next day, or the first day possible.

N. B.—The captains of the respective wards are particularly requested to be at the place of labor on their respective days, and keep an accurate account of each man's work, and be ready to exhibit a list of the same when called for.

The heart of the Trustee is daily made to rejoice in the good feelings of the brethren, made manifest in their exertion to carry forward the work of the Lord, and rear His Temple; and it is hoped that neither planting, sowing, or reaping will hereafter be made to interfere with the regulations hinted at above.

JOSEPH SMITH,
Trustee in Trust.
(February 21, 1842.) D. H. C. 4:517.

The Prophet's Sermon on Life and Death; the Resurrection and the Salvation of Children

President Smith read the 14th chapter of Revelation, and said—We have again the warning voice sounded in our midst, which shows the uncertainty of human life; and in my leisure moments I have meditated upon the subject, and asked the question, why it is that infants, innocent children, are taken away from us, especially those that seem to be the most intelligent and interesting. The strongest reasons that present themselves to my mind are these: This world is a very wicked world; and it is a proverb that the "world grows weaker and wiser"; if that is the case, the world grows more wicked and corrupt. In the earlier ages of the world a righteous man, and a man of God and of intelligence, had a better chance to do good, to be believed and received than at the present day; but in these days such a man is much opposed and persecuted by most of the inhabitants of the earth, and he has much sorrow to pass through here. The Lord takes many away even in infancy, that they may escape the envy of man, and the sorrows and evils of this present world; they were too pure, too lovely, to live on earth; therefore, if rightly considered, instead of mourning we have reason to rejoice as they are delivered from evil, and we shall soon have them again.

Do Not Procrastinate Repentance

What chance is there for infidelity when we are parting with our friends almost daily? None at all. The infidel will grasp at every straw for help until death stares him in the face, and then his infidelity takes its flight, for the realities of the eternal world are resting upon him in mighty power; and when every earthly support and prop fails him, he then sensibly feels the eternal truths of the immortality of the soul. We should take warning and not wait for the death-bed to repent, as we see the infant taken away by death, so may the youth and middle-aged, as well as the infant be suddenly called into eternity. Let this, then, prove as a warning to all not to procrastinate repentance, or wait till a death-bed, for it is the will of God that man should repent and serve Him in health, and in the strength and power of his mind, in order to secure his blessing, and not wait until he is called to die.

Redemption of Little Children

The doctrine of baptizing children, or sprinkling them, or they must welter in hell, is a doctrine not true, not supported in Holy Writ, and is not consistent with the character of God. All children are redeemed by the blood of Jesus Christ, and the moment that children leave this world, they are taken to the bosom of Abraham. The only difference between the old and young dying is, one lives longer in heaven and eternal light and glory than the other, and is freed a little sooner from this miserable wicked world. Notwithstanding all this glory, we for a moment lose sight of it, and mourn the loss, but we do not mourn as those without hope.

Decrees Fixed and Immovable

My intention was to have spoken on the subject of baptism, but having a case of death before us, I thought proper to refer to that subject. I will now, however, say a few words upon baptism, as I intended.

God has made certain decrees which are fixed and immovable; for instance, God set the sun, the moon, and the stars in the heavens, and gave them their laws, conditions and bounds, which they cannot pass, except by His commandments; they all move in perfect harmony in their sphere and order, and are as lights, wonders and signs unto us. The sea also has its bounds which it cannot pass. God has set many signs on the earth, as well as in the heavens; for instance, the oak of the forest, the fruit of the tree, the herb of the field, all bear a sign that seed hath been planted there; for it is a decree of the Lord that every tree, plant, and herb bearing seed should bring forth of its kind, and cannot come forth after any other law or principle.[3] Upon the same principle do I contend that baptism is a sign ordained of God, for the believer in Christ to take upon himself in order to enter into the kingdom of God, "for except ye are born of water and of the Spirit ye cannot enter into the Kingdom of God," said the Savior. It is a sign and a commandment which God has set for man to enter into His kingdom. Those who seek to enter in any other way will seek in vain; for God will not receive them, neither will the angels acknowledge their works as accepted, for they have not obeyed the ordinances, nor attended to the signs which God ordained for the salvation of man, to prepare him for, and give him a title to, a celestial glory; and God had decreed that all who will not obey His voice shall not escape the damnation of hell. What is the damnation of hell? To go with that society who have not obeyed His commands.

Baptism and the Gift of the Holy Ghost

Baptism is a sign to God, to angels, and to heaven that we do the will of God, and there is no other way beneath the heavens whereby God hath ordained for man to come to Him to be saved, and enter into the Kingdom of God, except faith in Jesus Christ, repentance, and baptism for the remission of sins, and any other course is in vain; then you have the promise of the gift of the Holy Ghost.

What is the sign of the healing of the sick? The laying on of hands is the sign or way marked out by James, and the custom of the ancient Saints as ordered by the Lord, and we

---

[3]This very positive statement by the Prophet, that every tree, plant, and herb, and evidently every other creature, cannot produce except after its kind, is in harmony not only with the scriptures, but also with all known facts in the world.

cannot obtain the blessings by pursuing any other course except the way marked out by the Lord. What if we should
attempt to get the gift of the Holy Ghost through any other
means except the signs or way which God hath appointed—
would we obtain it? Certainly not; all other means would fail.
The Lord says do so and so, and I will bless you.

Key Words of the Priesthood

There are certain key words and signs belonging to the
Priesthood which must be observed in order to obtain the
blessing. The sign of Peter was to repent and be baptized for
the remission of sins, with the promise of the gift of the Holy
Ghost; and in no other way is the gift of the Holy Ghost
obtained.

Difference Between the Holy Ghost and the Gift
of the Holy Ghost

There is a difference between the Holy Ghost and the gift
of the Holy Ghost. Cornelius received the Holy Ghost before
he was baptized, which was the convincing power of God unto
him of the truth of the Gospel, but he could not receive the
gift of the Holy Ghost until after he was baptized. Had he
not taken this sign or ordinance upon him, the Holy Ghost
which convinced him of the truth of God, would have left him.
Until he obeyed these ordinances and received the gift of the
Holy Ghost, by the laying on of hands, according to the order
of God, he could not have healed the sick or commanded an
evil spirit to come out of a man, and it obey him; for the spirits
might say unto him, as they did to the sons of Sceva: "Paul we
know and Jesus we know, but who are ye?" It mattereth not
whether we live long or short on the earth after we come to
a knowledge of these principles and obey them unto the end.
I know that all men will be damned if they do not come in the
way which He hath opened, and this is the way marked out by
the word of the Lord.

The Universal Resurrection

As concerning the resurrection, I will merely say that all
men will come from the grave as they lie down, whether old
or young; there will not be "added unto their stature one cubit,"
neither taken from it; all will be raised by the power of God,

having spirit in their bodies, and not blood. Children will be enthroned in the presence of God and the Lamb with bodies of the same stature[4] that they had on earth, having been redeemed by the blood of the Lamb; they will there enjoy the fullness of that light, glory and intelligence, which is prepared in the celestial kingdom. "Blessed are the dead who die in the Lord, for they rest from their labors and their works do follow them."

The speaker, before closing, called upon the assembly before him to humble themselves in faith before God, and in mighty prayer and fasting to call upon the name of the Lord, until the elements were purified over our heads, and the earth sanctified under our feet, that the inhabitants of this city may escape the power of disease and pestilence, and the destroyer that rideth upon the face of the earth, and that the Holy Spirit of God may rest upon this vast multitude.

Baptisms Performed

At the close of the meeting, President Smith said he should attend to the ordinance of baptism in the river, near his house, at two o'clock, and at the appointed hour, the bank of the Mississippi was lined with a multitude of people, and President Joseph Smith went into the river and baptized eighty persons for the remission of their sins, and what added joy to the scene was, that the first person baptized was M. L. D. Wasson, a nephew of Mrs. Emma Smith—the first of her kindred that has embraced the fullness of the Gospel.

At the close of this interesting scene, the administrator lifted up his hands towards heaven, and implored the blessing of God to rest upon the people; and truly the Spirit of God did rest upon the multitude, to the joy and consolation of our hearts.

---

[4]In the *Improvement Era* for June, 1904, President Joseph F. Smith in an editorial on the Resurrection said:

"The body will come forth as it is laid to rest, for there is no growth or development in the grave. As it is laid down, so will it arise, and changes to perfection will come by the law of restitution. But the spirit will continue to expand and develop, and the body, after the resurrection will develop to the full stature of man."

This may be accepted as the doctrine of the Church in respect to the resurrection of children and their future development to the full stature of men and women; and it is alike conformable to that which will be regarded as both reasonable and desirable.

After baptism, the congregation again repaired to the grove, near the Temple, to attend to the ordinance of confirmation, and, notwithstanding President Smith had spoken in the open air to the people, and stood in the water and baptized about eighty persons, about fifty of those baptized received their confirmation under his hands in the after part of the day. While this was progressing, great numbers were being baptized in the font for the dead. (March 20, 1842.) D. H. C. 4:553-557.

Synopsis of the Prophet's Sermon on Baptism for the Dead

This was an interesting day. A large assembly met in the grove near the Temple. Brother Amasa Lyman addressed the people in a very interesting manner. He was followed by Joseph, the Seer, who made some highly edifying and instructive remarks concerning baptism for the dead. He said the Bible supported the doctrine, quoting I Cor. 15:29: "Else what shall they do which are baptized for the dead, if the dead rise not at all, why are they then baptized for the dead?" If there is one word of the Lord that supports the doctrine of baptism for the dead, it is enough to establish it as a true doctrine. Again; if we can, by the authority of the Priesthood of the Son of God, baptize a man in the name of the Father, of the Son, and of the Holy Ghost, for the remission of sins, it is just as much our privilege to act as an agent, and be baptized for the remission of sins for and in behalf of our dead kindred, who have not heard the Gospel, or the fullness of it. (March 27, 1842.) D. H. C. 4:568-569.

Synopsis of the Prophet's Remarks to the Female Relief Society

President Joseph Smith arose. Spoke of the organization of the Female Relief Society; said he was deeply interested, that it might be built up to the Most High in an acceptable manner; that its rules must be observed; that none should be received into it but those who were worthy; proposed a close examination of every candidate; that the society was growing too fast. It should grow up by degrees, should commence with a few individuals, thus have a select society of the virtuous, and those who would walk circumspectly; commended them for their zeal, but said sometimes their zeal was not according to knowledge. One principal object of the institution was to purge out iniquity; said they must be extremely careful in all their examinations, or the consequences would be serious.

All difficulties which might and would cross our way must be surmounted. Though the soul be tried, the heart faint, and the hands hang down, we must not retrace our steps; there must be decision of character, aside from sympathy. When instructed, we must obey that voice, observe the laws of the Kingdom of God, that the blessings of heaven may rest down upon us. All must act in concert, or nothing can be done, and should move according to the ancient Priesthood; hence the Saints should be a select people, separate from all the evils of the world—choice, virtuous, and holy. The Lord was going to make of the Church of Jesus Christ a kingdom of Priests, a holy people, a chosen generation, as in Enoch's day, having all the gifts as illustrated to the Church in Paul's epistles and teachings to the churches in his day—that it is the privilege of each member to live long and enjoy health. He then blessed the Saints. (March 30, 1842.) D. H. C. 4:570.

"Try the Spirits"
The Prophet's Editorial in the Times and Seasons

Recent occurrences that have transpired amongst us render it an imperative duty devolving upon me to say something in relation to the spirits by which men are actuated.

It is evident from the Apostles' writings, that many false spirits existed in their day, and had "gone forth into the world," and that it needed intelligence which God alone could impart to detect false spirits, and to prove what spirits were of God. The world in general have been grossly ignorant in regard to this one thing, and why should they be otherwise—for "the things of God knoweth no man, but the Spirit of God."

The Egyptians were not able to discover the difference between the miracles of Moses and those of the magicians until they came to be tested together; and if Moses had not appeared in their midst, they would unquestionably have thought that the miracles of the magicians were performed through the mighty power of God, for they were great miracles that were performed by them—a supernatural agency was developed, and great power manifested.

*   *   *

It would have been equally as difficult for us to tell by what spirit the Apostles prophesied, or by what power the Apostles spoke and worked miracles. Who could have told whether the power of Simon, the sorcerer, was of God or of the devil?

There always did, in every age, seem to be a lack of intelligence pertaining to this subject. Spirits of all kinds have been manifested, in every age, and almost among all people. If we go among the pagans, they have their spirits; the Mohammedans, the Jews, the Christians, the Indians—all have their spirits, all have a supernatural agency, and all contend that their spirits are of God. Who shall solve the mystery? "Try the spirits," says John, but who is to do it? The learned, the eloquent, the philosopher, the sage, the divine—all are ignorant. The heathens will boast of their gods, and of the great things that have been unfolded by their oracles. The Mussulman will boast of his Koran, and of the divine communications that his progenitors have received. The Jews have had numerous instances, both ancient and modern, among them of men who have professed to be inspired, and sent to bring about great events, and the Christian world has not been slow in making up the number.

Ignorance of the Nature of Spirits

"Try the spirits," but what by? Are we to try them by the creeds of men? What preposterous folly—what sheer ignorance—what madness! Try the motions and actions of an eternal being (for I contend that all spirits are such) by a thing that was conceived in ignorance, and brought forth in folly—a cobweb of yesterday! Angels would hide their faces, and devils would be ashamed and insulted, and would say, "Paul we know, and Jesus we know, but who are ye?" Let each man of society make a creed and try evil spirits by it, and the devil would shake his sides; it is all that he would ask—all that he would desire. Yet many of them do this, and hence "many spirits are abroad in the world."

One great evil is, that men are ignorant of the nature of spirits; their power, laws, government, intelligence, etc., and imagine that when there is anything like power, revelation, or vision manifested, that it must be of God. Hence the Methodists, Presbyterians, and others frequently possess a spirit that will cause them to lie down, and during its operation, animation is frequently entirely suspended; they consider it to be the power of God, and a glorious manifestation from God—a manifestation of what? Is there any intelligence communicated? Are the curtains of heaven withdrawn, or the purposes of God developed? Have they seen and conversed with an angel—or have the glories of futurity burst upon their view? No! but their body has been inanimate, the operation of their spirit suspended, and all the intelligence that can be obtained from them when they arise, is a shout of "glory," or "hallelujah," or some incoherent expression; but they have had "the power."

The Shaker will whirl around on his heel, impelled by a supernatural agency or spirit, and think that he is governed by the Spirit of God; and the Jumper will jump and enter into all kinds of extravagances. A Primitive Methodist will shout under the influence of that spirit, until he will rend the heavens with his cries; while the Quakers (or Friends) moved as they think, by the Spirit of God, will sit still and say nothing. Is God the author of all this? If not of all of it, which does He recognize? Surely, such a heterogeneous mass of confusion never can enter into the kingdom of heaven.

Discerning of Spirits by Power of Priesthood

Every one of these professes to be competent to try his neighbor's spirit, but no one can try his own, and what is the reason? Because they have not a key to unlock, no rule wherewith to measure, and no criterion whereby they can test it. Could any one tell the length, breadth or height of a building without a rule? Test the quality of metals without a criterion, or point out the movements of the planetary systems, without a knowledge of astronomy? Certainly not; and if such ignorance as this is manifested about a spirit of this kind, who can describe an angel of light? If Satan should appear as one in glory, who can tell his color, his signs, his appearance, his glory, or what is the manner of his manifestation? Who can detect the spirit of the French prophets with their revelations and their visions, and power of manifestations? Or who can point out the spirit of the Irvingites, with their apostles and prophets, and visions and tongues, and interpretations, etc. Or who can drag into daylight and develop the hidden mysteries of the false spirits that so frequently are made manifest among the Latter-day Saints? We answer that no man can do this without the Priesthood, and having a knowledge of the laws by which spirits are governed; for as no man knows the things of God, but by the Spirit of God, so no man knows the spirit of the devil, and his power and influence, but by possessing intelligence which is more than human, and having unfolded through the medium of the Priesthood the mysterious operations of his devices; without knowing the angelic form, the sanctified look and gesture, and the zeal that is frequently manifested by him for the glory of God, together with the prophetic spirit, the gracious influence, the godly appearance, and the holy garb, which are so characteristic of his proceedings and his mysterious windings.

A man must have the discerning of spirits before he can drag into daylight this hellish influence and unfold it unto the world in all its soul-destroying, diabolical, and horrid colors; for nothing is a greater injury to the children of men than to be under the influence of a false spirit when they think they have the Spirit of God. Thousands have felt the influence of its terrible power and baneful effects. Long pilgrimages have been undertaken, penances endured, and pain, misery and ruin have followed in their train; nations have been convulsed, kingdoms overthrown, provinces laid waste, and blood, carnage and desolation are habiliments in which it has been clothed.

*   *   *

The Spirit of God the Spirit of Knowledge

As we have noticed before, the great difficulty lies in the ignorance of the nature of spirits, of the laws by which they are governed, and the signs by which they may be known; if it requires the Spirit of God to know the things of God; and the spirit of the devil can only be unmasked through that medium, then it follows as a natural consequence that unless some person or persons have a communication, or revelation from God, unfolding to them the operation of the spirit, they must eternally remain ignorant of these principles; for I contend that if one man cannot understand these things but by the Spirit of God, ten thousand men cannot; it is alike out of the reach of the wisdom of the learned, the tongue of the eloquent, the power of the mighty. And we shall at last have to come to this conclusion, whatever we may think of revelation, that without it we can neither know nor understand anything of God, or the devil; and however unwilling the world may be to acknowledge this principle, it is evident from the multifarious creeds and notions concerning this matter that they understand nothing of this principle, and it is equally as plain that without a divine communication they must remain in ignorance. The world always mistook false prophets for true ones, and those that were sent of God, they considered to be false prophets, and hence they killed, stoned, punished and imprisoned the true prophets, and these had to hide themselves "in deserts and dens, and caves of the earth," and though the most honorable men of the earth, they banished them from their society as vagabonds, whilst they cherished, honored and supported knaves, vagabonds, hypocrites, impostors, and the basest of men.

The Gift of Discernment of Spirits

A man must have the discerning of spirits, as we before stated, to understand these things, and how is he to obtain this gift if there are no gifts of the Spirit? And how can these gifts be obtained without revelation? "Christ ascended into heaven, and gave gifts to men; and He gave some Apostles, and some Prophets, and some Evangelists, and some Pastors and Teachers." And how were Apostles, Prophets, Pastors, Teachers and Evangelists chosen? By prophecy (revelation) and by laying on of hands—by a divine communication, and a divinely appointed ordinance—through the medium of the Priesthood, organized according to the order of God, by divine appointment. The Apostles in ancient times held the keys of this Priesthood—of the mysteries of the Kingdom of God, and consequently were enabled to unlock and unravel all things pertaining to the government of the Church, the welfare of society, the future destiny of men, and the agency, power and influence of spirits; for they could control them at pleasure, bid them depart in the name of Jesus, and detect their mischievous and mysterious operations when trying to palm themselves upon the Church in a religious garb, and militate against the interest of the Church and spread of truth. We read that they "cast out devils in the name of Jesus," and when a woman possessing the spirit of divination, cried before Paul and Silas, "these are the servants of the Most High God that show unto us the way of salvation," they detected the spirit. And although she spake favorably of them, Paul commanded the spirit to come out of her, and saved themselves from the opprobrium that might have been heaped upon their heads, through an alliance with her, in the development of her wicked principles, which they certainly would have been charged with, if they had not rebuked the evil spirit.

The Gift Held by the Prophets

A power similar to this existed through the medium of the Priesthood in different ages. Moses could detect the magician's power, and show that he [himself] was God's servant—he knew when he was upon the mountain (through revelation) that Israel was engaged in idolatry; he could develop the sin of Korah, Dathan and Abiram, detect witches and wizards in their proceedings, and point out the true prophets of the Lord. Joshua knew how to detect the man who had stolen the wedge of gold and the Babylonish garment. Michaiah could point out the false spirit by which the four hundred prophets were governed; and if his advice had been taken, many lives would have been spared, ((II Chronicles 18) Elijah, Elisha, Isaiah, Jeremiah, Ezekiel, and many other prophets possessed this power. Our Savior, the Apostles, and even the members of the Church were endowed with this gift, for, says Paul, (I Corinthians 12), "To one is given the gift of tongues, to another the interpretation of tongues, to another the working of miracles, to another prophecy, to another the discerning of spirits." All these proceeded from the same Spirit of God, and were the gifts of God. The Ephesian church were enabled by this principle, "to try those that said they were apostles, and were not, and found them liars." (Revelation 2:2.)

Difference Between Body and Spirit

In tracing the thing to the foundation, and looking at it philosophically, we shall find a very material difference between the body and the spirit; the body is supposed to be organized matter, and the spirit, by many, is thought to be immaterial, without substance. With this latter statement we should beg leave to differ, and state the spirit is a substance; that it is material, but that it is more pure, elastic and refined matter than the body; that it existed before the body, can exist in the body; and will exist separate from the body, when the body will be mouldering in the dust; and will in the resurrection, be again united with it.

Spirits Eternal

Without attempting to describe this mysterious connection, and the laws that govern the body and the spirit of man, their relationship to each other, and the design of God in relation to the human body and spirit, I would just remark, that the spirits of men are eternal, that they are governed by the same Priesthood that Abraham, Melchizedek, and the Apostles were: that they are organized according to that Priesthood which is everlasting, "without beginning of days or end of years,"—that they all move in their respective spheres, and are governed by the law of God; that when they appear upon the earth they are in a probationary state, and are preparing, if righteous, for a future and greater glory; that the spirits of good men cannot interfere with the wicked beyond their prescribed bounds, for Michael, the Archangel, dared not bring a railing accusation against the devil, but said, "The Lord rebuke thee, Satan."

Wicked Spirits Restricted in Power

It would seem also, that wicked spirits have their bounds, limits, and laws by which they are governed or controlled, and know their future destiny; hence, those that were in the maniac said to our Savior, "Art thou come to torment us before the time," and when Satan presented himself before the Lord, among the sons of God, he said that he came "from going to and fro in the earth, and from wandering up and down in it;" and he is emphatically called the prince of the power of the air; and, it is very evident that they possess a power that none but those who have the Priesthood can control, as we have before adverted to, in the case of the sons of Sceva.

Having said so much upon the general principles, without referring to the peculiar situation, power, and influence of the magicians of Egypt, the wizards and witches of the Jews, the oracles of the heathen, their necromancers, soothsayers, and astrologers, the maniacs or those possessed of devils in the Apostles' days, we will notice, and try to detect (so far as we have the Scriptures for our aid) some few instances of the development of false spirits in more modern times, and in this our day.

False Prophets

The "French Prophets" were possessed of a spirit that deceived; they existed in Vivaris and Dauphany, in great numbers in the year 1688; there were many boys and girls from seven to twenty-five; they had strange fits, as in tremblings and faintings, which made them stretch out their legs and arms, as in a swoon; they remained awhile in trances, and coming out of them, uttered all that came in their mouths. [see Buck's Theological Dictionary]

Now God never had any prophets that acted in this way; there was nothing indecorous in the proceeding of the Lord's prophets in any age; neither had the apostles nor prophets in the apostles' day anything of this kind. Paul says, "Ye may all prophesy, one by one; and if anything be revealed to another let the first hold his peace, for the spirit of the prophets is subject to the prophets;" but here we find that the prophets are subject to the spirit, and falling down, have twitchings, tumblings, and faintings through the influence of that spirit, being entirely under its control. Paul says, "Let everything be done decently and in order," but here we find the greatest disorder and indecency in the conduct of both men and women, as above described. The same rule would apply to the fallings, twitchings, swoonings, shaking, and trances of many of our modern revivalists.

Johanna Southcott professed to be a prophetess, and wrote a book of prophecies in 1804, she became the founder of a people that are still extant. She was to bring forth, in a place appointed, a son, that was to be the Messiah, which thing has failed. Independent of this, however, where do we read of a woman that was the founder of a church, in the word of God? Paul told the women in his day, "To keep silence in the church, and that if they wished to know anything to ask their husbands at home;" he would not suffer a woman "to rule, or to usurp authority in the church;" but here we find a woman the founder of a church, the revelator and guide, the Alpha and Omega, contrary to all acknowledged rule, principle, and order.

Jemimah Wilkinson was another prophetess that figured largely in America, in the last century. She stated that she was taken sick and died, and that her soul went to heaven, where it still continues. Soon after, her body was reanimated with the spirit and power of Christ, upon which she set up as a public teacher, and declared that she had an immediate revelation. Now the Scriptures positively assert that "Christ is the firstfruit, afterwards those that are Christ's at His coming, then cometh the end." But Jemimah, according to her testimony, died, and rose again before the time mentioned in the Scriptures. The idea of her soul being in heaven while her body was [living] on earth, is also preposterous. When God breathed into man's nostrils, he became a living soul, before that he did not live, and when that was taken away his body died; and so did our Savior when the spirit left the body, nor did His body live until His spirit returned in the power of His resurrection. But Mrs. Wilkinson's soul [life] was in heaven, and her body without the soul [or life] on earth, living [without the soul, or] without life!

Irvingites

The Irvingites are a people that have counterfeited the truth, perhaps the nearest of any of our modern sectarians. They commenced about ten years ago in the city of London, in England; they have churches formed in various parts of England and Scotland, and some few in Upper Canada. Mr. Irving, their founder, was a learned and talented minister of the Church of Scotland, he was a great logician, and a powerful orator, but withal wild and enthusiastic in his views. Moving in the higher circles, and possessing talent and zeal, placed him in a situation to become a conspicuous character, and to raise up a society similar to that which is called after his name.

The Irvingites have apostles, prophets, pastors, teachers, evangelists, and angels. They profess to have the gift of tongues, and the interpretation of tongues, and, in some few instances, to have the gift of healing.

The first prophetic spirit that was manifested was in some Misses Campbell that Mr. Irving met with, while on a journey in Scotland; they had [what is termed among their sect] "utterances," which were evidently of a supernatural agency. Mr. Irving, falling into the common error of considering all supernatural manifestations to be of God, took them to London with him, and introduced them into his church.

They were there honored as the prophetesses of God, and when they spoke, Mr. Irving or any of his ministers had to keep silence. They were peculiarly wrought upon before the congregation, and had strange utterances, uttered with an unnatural. shrill voice, and with thrilling intonations they frequently made use of a few broken, unconnected sentences, that were ambiguous, incoherent, and incomprehensible; at other times they were more clearly understood. They would frequently cry out, "There is iniquity! There is iniquity!" And Mr. Irving has been led, under the influence of this charge, to fall down upon his knees before the public congregation, and to confess his sin, not knowing whether he had sinned, nor wherein, nor whether the thing referred to him or somebody else. During these operations, the bodies of the persons speaking were powerfully wrought upon, their countenances were distorted, they had frequent twitchings in their hands, and the whole system was powerfully convulsed at intervals: they sometimes, however, (it is supposed) spoke in correct tongues, and had true interpretations.

Under the influence of this spirit the church was organized by these women; apostles, prophets, etc., were soon called, and a systematic order of things introduced, as above mentioned. A Mr. Baxter (afterwards one of their principal prophets) upon going into one of their meetings, says, "I saw a power manifested, and thought that was the power of God, and asked that it might fall upon me, and it did so, and I began to prophesy." Eight or nine years ago they had about sixty preachers going through the streets of London, testifying that London was to be the place where the "two witnesses" spoken of by John, were to prophesy; that (they) the church and the spirit were the witnesses, and that at the end of three years and a half there was to be an earthquake and great destruction, and our Savior was to come. Their apostles were collected together at the appointed time watching the event, but Jesus did not come, and the prophecy was then ambiguously explained away. They frequently had signs given them by the spirit to prove to them that what was manifested to them should take place. Mr. Baxter related an impression that he had concerning a child. It was manifested to him that he should visit the child, and lay hands upon it, and that it should be healed; and to prove to him that this was of God, he should meet his brother in a certain place, who should speak unto him certain words. His brother addressed him precisely in the way and manner that the manifestation designated. The sign took place, but when he laid his hands upon the child it did not recover. I cannot vouch for the authority of the last statement, as Mr. Baxter at that time had left the Irvingites, but it is in accord-

ance with many of their proceedings, and the thing never ha
been attempted to be denied.

All This Is Wrong

It may be asked, where is there anything in all this that
is wrong?

First. The church was organized by women, and God
placed in the Church (first apostles, secondarily prophets,) and
not first women; but Mr. Irving placed in his church first women
(secondarily apostles,) and the church was founded and organized by them. A woman has no right to found or organize a
church—God never sent them to do it.

Second. Those women would speak in the midst of a
meeting, and rebuke Mr. Irving or any of the church. Now
the Scripture positively says, "Thou shalt not rebuke an Elder,
but entreat him as a father;" not only this, but they frequently
accused the brethren, thus placing themselves in the seat of
Satan, who is emphatically called "the accuser of the brethren."

Third. Mr. Baxter received the spirit on asking for it,
without attending to the ordinances, and began to prophesy,
whereas the scriptural way of attaining the gift of the Holy
Ghost is by baptism, and by laying on of hands.

Fourth. As we have stated in regard to others, the spirit
of the prophets is subject to the prophets; but those prophets
were subject to the spirits, the spirits controlling their bodies
at pleasure.

But it may be asked how Mr. Baxter could get a sign from
a second person? To this we would answer, that Mr. Baxter's
brother was under the influence of the same spirit as himself,
and being subject to that spirit he could be easily made to
speak to Mr. Baxter whatever the spirit should dictate; but
there was not power in the spirit to heal the child.

Satan May Give Manifestations in Tongues

Again it may be asked, how it was that they could speak
in tongues if they were of the devil. We would answer that
they could be made to speak in another tongue, as well as their
own, as they were under the control of that spirit, and the
devil can tempt the Hottentot, the Turk, the Jew, or any other
nation; and if these men were under the influence of his spirit,

they of course could speak Hebrew, Latin, Greek, Italian, Dutch, or any other language that the devil knew.

Some will say, "try the spirits" by the word. "Every spirit that confesseth that Jesus Christ is come in the flesh is of God, and every spirit that confesseth not that Jesus Christ is come in the flesh is not of God." 1 John 4:2, 3. One of the Irvingites once quoted this passage whilst under the influence of a spirit, and then said, "I confess that Jesus Christ is come in the flesh." And yet these prophecies failed, their Messiah did not come; and the great things spoken of by them have fallen to the ground. What is the matter here? Did not the Apostle speak the truth? Certainly he did—but he spoke to a people who were under the penalty of death, the moment they embraced Christianity; and no one without a knowledge of the fact would confess it, and expose themselves to death, and this was consequently given as a criterion to the church or churches to which John wrote. But the devil on a certain occasion cried out, "I know thee, who thou art, the Holy One of God!" Here was a frank acknowledgment under other circumstances that "Jesus had come in the flesh." On another occasion the devil said, "Paul we know, and Jesus we know"—of course, "come in the flesh." No man nor sect of men without the regular constituted authorities, the Priesthood and discerning of spirits, can tell true from false spirits. This power they possessed in the Apostles' day, but it has departed from the world for ages.

False Spirits in the Church

The Church of Jesus Christ of Latter-day Saints has also had its false spirits; and as it is made up of all those different sects professing every variety of opinion, and having been under the influence of so many kinds of spirits, it is not to be wondered at if there should be found among us false spirits.

Soon after the Gospel was established in Kirtland, and during the absence of the authorities of the Church, many false spirits were introduced, many strange visions were seen, and wild, enthusiastic notions were entertained; men ran out of doors under the influence of this spirit, and some of them got upon the stumps of trees and shouted, and all kinds of extravagances were entered into by them; one man pursued a ball that he said he saw flying in the air, until he came to a precipice, when he jumped into the top of a tree, which saved his life;

and many ridiculous things were entered into, calculated to bring disgrace upon the Church of God, to cause the Spirit of God to be withdrawn, and to uproot and destroy those glorious principles which had been developed for the salvation of the human family. But when the authorities returned, the spirit was made manifest, those members that were exercised with it were tried for their fellowship, and those that would not repent and forsake it were cut off.

At a subsequent period a Shaker spirit was on the point of being introduced, and at another time the Methodist and Presbyterian falling down power, but the spirit was rebuked and put down, and those who would not submit to rule and good order were disfellowshiped. We have also had brethren and sisters who have had the gift of tongues falsely; they would speak in a muttering, unnatural voice, and their bodies be distorted like the Irvingites before alluded to; whereas, there is nothing unnatural in the Spirit of God. A circumstance of this kind took place in Upper Canada, but was rebuked by the presiding Elder; another, a woman near the same place, professed to have the discerning of spirits, and began to accuse another sister of things that she was not guilty of, which she said she knew was so by the spirit, but was afterwards proven to be false; she placed herself in the capacity of the accuser of the brethren," and no person through the discerning of spirits can bring a charge against another, they must be proven guilty by positive evidence, or they stand clear.

There have also been ministering angels in the Church which were of Satan appearing as an angel of light. A sister in the state of New York had a vision, who said it was told her that if she would go to a certain place in the woods, an angel would appear to her. She went at the appointed time, and saw a glorious personage descending, arrayed in white, with sandy colored hair; he commenced and told her to fear God, and said that her husband was called to do great things, but that he must not go more than one hundred miles from home, or he would not return; whereas God had called him to go to the ends of the earth, and he has since been more than one thousand miles from home, and is yet alive. Many true things were spoken by this personage, and many things that were false. How, it may be asked, was this known to be a bad angel? By the color of his hair; that is one of the signs that he can be known by, and by his contradicting a former revelation.

We have also had brethren and sisters who have written revelations, and who have started forward to lead this Church. Such was a young boy in Kirtland, Isaac Russell, of Missouri, and Gladden Bishop, and Oliver Olney of Nauvoo. The boy is now living with his parents who have submitted to the laws of the Church. Mr. Russell stayed in Far West, from whence he was to go to the Rocky Mountains, led by three Nephites; but the Nephites never came, and his friends forsook him, all but some of the blood relations, who have since been nearly destroyed by the mob. Mr. Bishop was tried by the High Council, his papers examined, condemned and burned, and he cut off the Church. He acknowledged the justice of the decision, and said "that he now saw his error, for if he had been governed by the revelations given before, he might have known that no man was to write revelations for the Church, but Joseph Smith," and begged to be prayed for, and forgiven by the brethren. Mr. Olney has also been tried by the High Council and disfellowshiped, because he would not have his writings tested by the word of God; evidently proving that he loves darkness rather than light, because his deeds are evil. (April 1, 1842.) D. H. C. 4:571-581.

Remarks of the Prophet at the Funeral of Ephraim Marks

The Saints in Nauvoo assembled at the house of President Marks, at an early hour in the morning, to pay their last respects to the body of Ephraim Marks, son of President William Marks, who died on the evening of the 7th. A large procession formed and walked to the Grove, where a numerous congregation had assembled. President Joseph Smith spoke upon the occasion with much feeling and interest. Among his remarks he said, "It is a very solemn and awful time. I never felt more solemn; it calls to mind the death of my oldest brother, Alvin, who died in New York, and my youngest brother, Don Carlos Smith, who died in Nauvoo. It has been hard for me to live on earth and see these young men upon whom we have leaned for support and comfort taken from us in the midst of their youth. Yes, it has been hard to be reconciled to these things. I have sometimes thought that I should have felt more reconciled to have been called away myself if it had been the will of God; yet I know we ought to be still and know it is of God, and be reconciled to His will; all is right. It will be but a short time before we shall all in like manner be called; it may be the case with me as well as you. Some have supposed that Brother Joseph could not die; but this is a mistake: it is true there have been times when I have had the promise of my life to accomplish such and such things, but, having now accomplished those things, I have not at present any lease of my life, I am as liable to die as other men.

I can say in my heart, that I have not done anything against Ephraim Marks that I am sorry for, and I would ask any of his companions if they have done anything against him that they are sorry for, or that they would not like to meet and answer for at the bar of God, if so, let it prove as a warning to all to deal justly before God, and with all mankind, then we shall be clear in the day of judgment.

When we lose a near and dear friend, upon whom we have set our hearts, it should be a caution unto us not to set our affections too firmly upon others, knowing that they may in like manner be taken from us. Our affections should be placed upon God and His work, more intensely than upon our fellow beings. (April 9, 1842.) D. H. C. 4:587.

Synopsis of Remarks of the Prophet—Reproof of all Wickedness

Joseph the Seer arose in the power of God; reproved and rebuked wickedness before the people, in the name of the Lord God. He wished to say a few words to suit the condition of the general mass, and then said: I shall speak with authority of the Priesthood in the name of the Lord God, which shall prove a savor of life unto life, or of death unto death. Notwithstanding this congregation profess to be Saints, yet I stand in the midst of all [kinds of] characters and classes of men. If you wish to go where God is, you must be like God, or possess the principles which God possesses, for if we are not drawing towards God in principle, we are going from Him and drawing towards the devil. Yes, I am standing in the midst of all kinds of people.

Search your hearts, and see if you are like God. I have searched mine, and feel to repent of all my sins.

Men Are Saved Through Obedience to Knowledge

We have thieves among us, adulterers, liars, hypocrites. If God should speak from heaven, he would command you not to steal, not to commit adultery, not to covet, nor deceive, but be faithful over a few things. As far as we degenerate from God, we descend to the devil and lose knowledge, and without knowledge we cannot be saved, and while our hearts are filled with evil, and we are studying evil, there is no room in our hearts for good, or studying good. Is not God good? Then you be good; if He is faithful, then you be faithful. Add to your faith virtue, to virtue knowledge, and seek for every good thing.

The Church must be cleansed, and I proclaim against all iniquity. A man is saved no faster than he gets knowledge, for if he does not get knowledge, he will be brought into captivity by some evil power in the other world, as evil spirits will have more knowledge, and consequently more power than many men who are on the earth. Hence it needs revelation to assist us, and give us knowledge of the things of God.

What is the reason that the Priests of the day do not get revelation? They ask only to consume it upon their lusts. Their hearts are corrupt, and they cloak their iniquity by saying there are no more revelations. But if any revelations are given of God, they are universally opposed by the priests and Christendom at large; for they reveal their wickedness and abominations. (April 10, 1842.) D. H. C. 4:588.

Baptism for the Dead

The great designs of God in relation to the salvation of the human family, are very little understood by the professedly wise and intelligent generation in which we live. Various and conflicting are the opinions of men concerning the plan of salvation, the requisitions of the Almighty, the necessary preparations for heaven, the state and condition of departed spirits, and the happiness or misery that is consequent upon the practice of righteousness and iniquity according to their several notions of virtue and vice.

The Mussulman condemns the heathen, the Jew, and the Christian, and the whole world of mankind that reject his Koran, as infidels, and consigns the whole of them to perdition.

The Jew believes that the whole world that rejects his faith and are not circumcised, are Gentile dogs, and will be damned. The heathen is equally as tenacious about his principles, and the Christian consigns all to perdition who cannot bow to his creed, and submit to his *ipse dixit*.

Justice of the Great Lawgiver

But while one portion of the human race is judging and condemning the other without mercy, the Great Parent of the universe looks upon the whole of the human family with a fatherly care and paternal regard; He views them as His off-spring, and without any of those contracted feelings that influence the children of men, causes "His sun to rise on the evil and on the good, and sendeth rain on the just and on the unjust." He holds the reins of judgment in His hands; He is a wise Lawgiver, and will judge all men, not according to the narrow, contracted notions of men, but, "according to the deeds done in the body whether they be good or evil," or whether these deeds were done in England, America, Spain, Turkey, or India. He will judge them, "not according to what they have not, but according to what they have," those who have lived without law, will be judged without law, and those who have a law, will be judged by that law. We need not doubt the wisdom and intelligence of the Great Jehovah; He will award judgment or mercy to all nations according to their several deserts, their means of obtaining intelligence, the laws by which they are governed, the facilities afforded them of obtaining correct information, and His inscrutable designs in relation to the human family; and when the designs of God shall be made manifest, and the curtain of futurity be withdrawn, we shall all of us eventually have to confess that the Judge of all the earth has done right.

Christ Preached to Spirits in Prison

The situation of the Christian nations after death, is a subject that has called forth all the wisdom and talent of the philosopher and the divine, and it is an opinion which is generally received, that the destiny of man is irretrievably fixed at his death, and that he is made either eternally happy, or eternally miserable; that if a man dies without a knowledge of God, he must be eternally damned, without any mitigation of his punishment, alleviation of his pain, or the most latent hope of a deliverance while endless ages shall roll along. However orthodox this principle may be, we shall find that it is at variance with the testimony of Holy Writ, for our Savior says, that all manner of sin and blasphemy shall be forgiven men wherewith they shall blaspheme; but the blasphemy against the Holy Ghost shall not be forgiven, neither in this world, nor in the world to come, evidently showing that there are sins which may be forgiven in the world to come, although the sin of blasphemy [against the Holy Ghost] cannot be forgiven. Peter, also, in speaking concerning our Savior, says, that "He went and preached unto the spirits in prison, which sometimes were disobedient, when once the long-suffering of God waited in the days of Noah" (I Peter iii:19, 20). Here then we have an account of our Savior preaching to the spirits in prison, to spirits that had been imprisoned from the days of Noah; and what did He preach to them? That they were to stay there? Certainly not! Let His own declaration testify. "He hath sent me to heal the broken-hearted, to preach deliverance to the captives, and recovering of sight to the blind, to set at liberty them that are bruised." (Luke iv:18.) Isaiah has it—"To bring out the prisoners from the prison, and them that sit in darkness from the prison house." (Isaiah xlii:7.) It is very evident from this that He not only went to preach to them, but to deliver, or bring them out of the prison house. Isaiah, in testifying concerning the calamities that will overtake the inhabitants of the earth, says, "The earth shall reel to and fro like a drunkard, and shall be removed like a cottage; and the transgression thereof shall be heavy upon it; and it shall fall and not rise again. And it shall come to pass in that day, that the Lord shall punish the host of the high ones that are on high, and the kings of the earth upon the earth. And they shall be gathered together, as prisoners are gathered in the pit, and shall be shut up in the prison, and after many days shall they be visited." Thus we find that God will deal with all the human family equally, and that as the antediluvians had their day of visitation, so will those characters referred to by Isaiah, have their time of visitation and deliverance; after having been many days in prison.

Plan of Salvation Before the World Was

The great Jehovah contemplated the whole of the events connected with the earth, pertaining to the plan of salvation, before it rolled into existence, or ever "the morning stars sang together" for joy; the past, the present, and the future were and are, with Him, one eternal "now;" He knew of the fall of Adam, the iniquities of the antediluvians, of the depth of iniquity that would be connected with the human family, their weakness and strength, their power and glory, apostasies, their crimes, their righteousness and iniquity; He comprehended the fall of man, and his redemption; He knew the plan of salvation and pointed it out; He was acquainted with the situation of all nations and with their destiny; He ordered all things according to the council of His own will; He knows the situation of both the living and the dead, and has made ample provision for their redemption, according to their several circumstances, and the laws of the kingdom of God, whether in this world, or in the world to come.

False Doctrines in the World

The idea that some men form of the justice, judgment, and mercy of God, is too foolish for an intelligent man to think of: for instance, it is common for many of our orthodox preachers to suppose that if a man is not what they call converted, if he dies in that state he must remain eternally in hell without any hope. Infinite years in torment must he spend, and never, never, never have an end; and yet this eternal misery is made frequently to rest upon the merest casualty. The breaking of a shoe-string, the tearing of a coat of those officiating, or the peculiar location in which a person lives, may be the means, indirectly of his damnation, or the cause of his not being saved. I will suppose a case which is not extraordinary: Two men, who have been equally wicked, who have neglected religion, are both of them taken sick at the same time; one of them has the good fortune to be visited by a praying man, and he gets converted a few minutes before he dies; the other sends for three different praying men, a tailor, a shoemaker, and a tinman; the tinman has a handle to solder to a can, the tailor has a buttonhole to work on some coat that he needed in a hurry, and the shoemaker has a patch to put on somebody's boot;

they none of them can go in time, the man dies, and goes to hell: one of these is exalted to Abraham's bosom, he sits down in the presence of God and enjoys eternal, uninterrupted happiness, while the other, equally as good as he, sinks to eternal damnation, irretrievable misery and hopeless despair, because a man had a boot to mend, the button-hole of a coat to work, or a handle to solder on to a saucepan.

Plans of Jehovah Just

The plans of Jehovah are not so unjust, the statements of holy writ so visionary, nor the plan of salvation for the human family so incompatible with common sense; at such proceedings God would frown with indignance, angels would hide their heads in shame, and every virtuous, intelligent man would recoil.

If human laws award to each man his deserts, and punish all delinquents according to their several crimes, surely the Lord will not be more cruel than man, for He is a wise legislator, and His laws are more equitable, His enactments more just, and His decisions more perfect than those of man; and as man judges his fellow man by law, and punishes him according to the penalty of the law, so does God of heaven judge "according to the deeds done in the body." To say that the heathens would be damned because they did not believe the Gospel would be preposterous, and to say that the Jews would all be damned that do not believe in Jesus would be equally absurd; for "how can they believe on him of whom they have not heard, and how can they hear without a preacher, and how can he preach except he be sent;" consequently neither Jew nor heathen can be culpable for rejecting the conflicting opinions of sectarianism, nor for rejecting any testimony but that which is sent of God, for as the preacher cannot preach except he be sent, so the hearer cannot believe without he hear a "sent" preacher, and cannot be condemned for what he has not heard, and being without law, will have to be judged without law.

What of the Fathers?

When speaking about the blessings pertaining to the Gospel, and the consequences connected with disobedience to the requirements, we are frequently asked the question, what has become of our fathers? Will they all be damned for not obeying the Gospel, when they never heard it? Certainly not. But they will possess the same privilege that we here enjoy, through the medium of the everlasting Priesthood, which not only administers on earth, but also in heaven, and the wise dispensations of the great Jehovah; hence those characters referred to by Isaiah will be visited by the Priesthood, and come out of their prison upon the same principle as those who were disobedient in the days of Noah were visited by our Savior [who possessed the everlasting Melchizedek Priesthood] and had the Gospel preached to them by Him in prison; and in order that they might fulfill all the requisitions of God, living friends were baptized for their dead friends, and thus fulfilled the requirement of God, which says, "Except a man be born of water and of the Spirit, he cannot enter into the kingdom of God," they were baptized of course, not for themselves, but for their dead.

Chrysostum says that the Marcionites practiced baptism for their dead. "After a catechumen was dead, they had a living man under the bed of the deceased; then coming to the dead man, they asked him whether he would receive baptism, and he making no answer, the other answered for him, and said that he would be baptized in his stead; and so they baptized the living for the dead." The church of course at that time was degenerate, and the particular form might be incorrect, but the thing is sufficiently plain in the Scriptures, hence Paul, in speaking of the doctrine, says, "Else what shall they do which are baptized for the dead, if the dead rise not at all? Why are they then baptized for the dead?" (I Cor. xv:29.)

Responsibility of the Jews

Hence it was that so great a responsibility rested upon the generation in which our Savior lived, for, says he, "That upon you may come all the righteous blood shed upon the earth, from the blood of righteous Abel unto the blood of Zacharias, son of Barachias, whom ye slew between the temple and the altar. Verily I say unto you, all these things shall come upon this generation." (Matthew xxiii:35, 36.) Hence as they possessed greater privileges than any other generation, not only pertaining to themselves, but to their dead, their sin was greater, as they not only neglected their own salvation but that of their progenitors, and hence their blood was required at their hands:

Saviors on Mount Zion

And now as the great purposes of God are hastening to their accomplishment, and the things spoken of in the Prophets are fulfilling, as the kingdom of God is established on the earth, and the ancient order of things restored, the Lord has manifested to us this day and privilege, and we are commanded to be baptized for our dead, thus fulfilling the words of Obadiah, when speaking of the glory of the latter-day: "And saviors shall come up on Mount Zion to judge the remnant of Esau, and the kingdom shall be the Lord's." A view of these things reconciles the Scriptures of truth, justifies the ways of God to man, places the human family upon an equal footing, and harmonizes with every principle of righteousness, justice and truth. We will conclude with the words of Peter: "For the time past of our life may suffice us to have wrought the will of the Gentiles." "For, for this cause was the Gospel preached also to them that are dead, that they might be judged according to men in the flesh, but live according to God in the Spirit." (April 15, 1842.) D. H. C. 4:595-599.

REMARKS OF THE PROPHET TO THE RELIEF SOCIETY

All Offices in Church Honorable

President Smith arose and called the attention of the meeting to the 12th chapter of Corinthians—"Now concerning spiritual gifts, I would not have you ignorant." Said that the passage in the third verse, which reads, "No man can say that Jesus is the Lord, but by the Holy Ghost," should be translated "no man can know that Jesus is the Lord, but by the Holy Ghost." He continued to read the chapter, and give instructions respecting the different offices, and the necessity of every individual acting in the sphere allotted him or her, and filling the several offices to which they are appointed. He spoke of the disposition of many men to consider the lower offices in the Church dishonorable, and to look with jealous eyes upon the standing of others who are called to preside over them; that it was the folly and nonsense of the human heart for a person to be aspiring to other stations than those to which they are appointed of God for them to occupy; that it was better for individuals to magnify their respective calling, and wait patiently till God shall say to them, "come up higher."

He said the reason of these remarks being made was, that some little foolish things were circulating in the society, against some sisters not doing right in laying hands on the sick. Said that if the people had common sympathies they would rejoice that the sick could be healed; that the time had not been before that these things could be in their proper order; that the Church is not fully organized, in its proper order, and cannot be, until the Temple is completed, where places will be provided for the administration of the ordinances of the Priesthood.

Gifts of the Gospel

President Smith continued the subject, by quoting the commission given to the ancient Apostles in Mark, 16th chapter, 15th, 16th, 17th, 18th verses, "Go ye into all the world, and preach the Gospel to every creature. He that believeth and is baptized shall be saved; but he that believeth not shall be damned. And these signs shall follow them that believe: In my name shall they cast out devils; they shall speak with new tongues; they shall take up serpents; and if they drink any deadly thing, it shall not hurt them; they shall lay hands on the sick, and they shall recover."

No matter who believeth, these signs, such as healing the sick, casting out devils, etc., should follow all that believe, whether male or female. He asked the Society if they could not see by this sweeping promise, that wherein they are ordained, if it is the privilege of those set apart to administer in that authority, which is conferred on them; and if the sisters should have faith to heal the sick, let all hold their tongues, and let everything roll on.

He said, if God has appointed him, and chosen him as an instrument to lead the Church, why not let him lead it through? Why stand in the way when he is appointed to do a thing? Who knows the mind of God? Does He not reveal things differently from what we expect? He remarked that he was continually rising, although he had everything bearing him down, standing in his way, and opposing; notwithstanding all this opposition, he always comes out right in the end.

Respecting females administering for the healing of the sick, he further remarked, there could be no evil in it, if God gave His sanction by healing; that there could be no more sin in any female laying hands on and praying for the sick, than in wetting the face with water; it is no sin for anybody to administer that has faith, or if the sick have faith to be healed by their administration.

He reproved those that were disposed to find fault with the management of the concerns of the Church, saying God had called him to lead the Church, and he would lead it right; those that undertake to interfere will be ashamed when their own folly is made manifest; that he calculates to organize the Church in its proper order as soon as the Temple is completed.

Aspiring Men

President Smith continued by speaking of the difficulties he had to surmount ever since the commencement of the work, in consequence of aspiring men. "Great big Elders," as he called them, who caused him much trouble; to whom he had taught the things of the kingdom in private councils, they would then go forth into the world and proclaim the things he had taught them, as their own revelations; said the same aspiring disposition will be in this Society, and must be guarded against; that every person should stand, and act in the place appointed, and thus sanctify the Society and get it pure.   He said he had been trampled under foot by aspiring Elders, for all were infected with that spirit; for instance, John E. Page and others had been aspiring; they could not be exalted, but must run away as though the care and authority of the Church were vested with them.   He said he had a subtle devil to deal with, and could only curb him by being humble.

The Prophet's Intimation of His Death

As he had this opportunity, he was going to instruct the ladies of this Society, and point out the way for them to conduct themselves, that they might act according to the will of God; that he did not know that he should have many opportunities of teaching them, as they were going to be left to themselves; they would not long have him to instruct them; that the Church would not have his instructions long, and the world would not be troubled with him a great while, and would not have his teachings [in person].

He spoke of delivering the keys of the Priesthood to the Church, and said that the faithful members of the Relief Society should receive them with their husbands, that the Saints whose integrity has been tried and proved faithful, might know how to ask the Lord and receive an answer; for according to his prayers, God had appointed him elsewhere.

He exhorted the sisters always to concentrate their faith and prayers for, and place confidence in their husbands, whom God has appointed for them to honor, and in those faithful men whom God has placed at the head of the Church to lead His people; that we should arm and sustain them with our prayers; for the keys of the kingdom are about to be given to them, that they may be able to detect everything false; as well as to all the Elders who shall prove their integrity in due season.

Corruption Not to Be Condoned

He said if one member becomes corrupt, and you know it, you must immediately put it away, or it will either injure or destroy the whole body. The sympathies of the heads of the Church have induced them to bear a long time with those who were corrupt until they are obliged to cut them off, lest all become contaminated; you must put down iniquity, and by your good examples, stimulate the Elders to good works; if you do right, there is no danger of your going too fast.

He said he did not care how fast we run in the path of virtue; resist evil, and there is no danger; God, men, and angels will not condemn those that resist everything that is evil, and devils cannot; as well might the devil seek to dethrone Jehovah, as overthrow an innocent soul that resists everything which is evil.

This is a charitable Society, and according to your natures; it is natural for females to have feelings of charity and benevolence. You are now placed in a situation in which you can act according to those sympathies which God has planted in your bosoms.

To Dwell with God, the Soul Must Be Pure

If you live up to these principles, how great and glorious will be your reward in the celestial kingdom! If you live up to your privileges, the angels cannot be restrained from being your associates. Females, if they are pure and innocent, can come in the presence of God; for what is more pleasing to God than innocence; you must be innocent, or you cannot come up before God; if we would come before God, we must keep ourselves pure, as He is pure.

The Devil's Power to Deceive

The devil has great power to deceive; he will so transform things as to make one gape at those who are doing the will of God. You need not be teasing your husbands because of their deeds, but let the weight of your innocence, kindness and affection be felt, which is more mighty than a millstone hung about the neck; not war, not jangle, not contradiction, or dispute, but meekness, love, purity—these are the things that should magnify you in the eyes of all good men. Achan [see Joshua vii] must be brought to light, iniquity must be purged out from the midst of the Saints; then the veil will be rent, and the blessings of heaven will flow down—they will roll down like the Mississippi river.

If this Society listen to the counsel of the Almighty, through the heads of the Church, they shall have power to command queens in their midst.

I now deliver it as a prophecy, if the inhabitants of this state, with the people of the surrounding country, will turn unto the Lord with all their hearts, ten years will not roll around before the kings and queens of the earth will come unto Zion, and pay their respects to the leaders of this people; they shall come with their millions, and shall contribute of their abundance for the relief of the poor, and the building up and beautifying of Zion.

After this instruction, you will be responsible for your own sins; it is a desirable honor that you should so walk before our heavenly Father as to save yourselves; we are all responsible to God for the manner we improve the light and wisdom given by our Lord to enable us to save ourselves.

Beware of Self-Righteousness

President Smith continued reading from the above-mentioned chapter, and to give instructions respecting the order of God, as established in the Church, saying everyone should aspire only to magnify his own office and calling.

He then commenced reading the 13th chapter—"Though I speak with the tongues of men and angels, and have not charity, I am become as sounding brass, or a tinkling cymbal;" and said, don't be limited in your views with regard to your neighbor's virtue, but beware of self-righteousness, and be limited in the estimate of your own virtues, and not think yourselves more righteous than others; you must enlarge your souls towards each other, if you would do like Jesus, and carry your fellow-creatures to Abraham's bosom. He said he had manifested long-suffering, forbearance and patience towards the Church, and also to his enemies; and we must bear with each other's failings, as an indulgent parent bears with the foibles of his children.

President Smith then read the 2nd verse—"Though I have the gift of prophecy, and understand all mysteries, and all knowledge; and though I have all faith, so that I could remove mountains, and have not charity, I am nothing." He then said, though a man should become mighty, do great things, overturn mountains, perform mighty works, and should then turn from his high station to do evil, to eat and drink with the drunken, all his former deeds would not save him, but he would go to destruction! As you increase in innocence and virtue, as you increase in goodness, let your hearts expand, let them be enlarged towards others; you must be long-suffering, and bear with the faults and errors of mankind.

How precious are the souls of men! The female part of the community are apt to be contracted in their views. You must not be contracted, but you must be liberal in your feelings. Let this Society teach women how to behave towards their husbands, to treat them with mildness and affection. When a man is borne down with trouble, when he is perplexed with care and difficulty, if he can meet a smile instead of an argument or a murmur—if he can meet with mildness, it will calm down his soul and soothe his feelings; when the mind is going to despair, it needs a solace of affection and kindness.

Instruction Through the Priesthood

You will receive instructions through the order of the Priesthood which God has established, through the medium of those appointed to lead, guide and direct the affairs of the Church in this last dispensation; and I now turn the key in your behalf in the name of the Lord, and this Society shall rejoice, and knowledge and intelligence shall flow down from this time henceforth; this is the beginning of better days to the poor and needy, who shall be made to rejoice and pour forth blessings on your heads.

When you go home, never give a cross or unkind word to your husbands, but let kindness, charity and love crown your works henceforward; don't envy the finery and fleeting show of sinners, for they are in a miserable situation; but as far as you can, have mercy on them, for in a short time God will destroy them, if they will not repent and turn unto him.

Let your labors be mostly confined to those around you, in the circle of your own acquaintance, as far as knowledge is concerned, it may extend to all the world; but your administering should be confined to the circle of your immediate acquaintance, and more especially to the members of the Relief Society. Those ordained to preside over and lead you, are authorized to appoint the different officers, as the circumstances shall require.

The Gift of Tongues

If you have a matter to reveal, let it be in your own tongue; do not indulge too much in the exercise of the gift of tongues, or the devil will take advantage of the innocent and unwary. You may speak in tongues for your own comfort, but I lay this down for a rule, that if anything is taught by the gift of tongues, it is not to be received for doctrine.

President Smith then gave instruction respecting the propriety of females administering to the sick by the prayer of faith, the laying on of hands, or the anointing with oil; and said it was according to revelation that the sick should be nursed with herbs and mild food, and not by the hand of an enemy. Who are better qualified to administer than our faithful and zealous sisters, whose hearts are full of faith, tenderness, sympathy and compassion. No one. Said he was never placed in similar circumstances before, and never had given the same instruction; and closed his instructions by expressing his heartfelt satisfaction in improving this opportunity.

The Spirit of the Lord was poured out in a very powerful manner, never to be forgotten by those present on this interesting occasion. (April 28, 1842.) D. H. C. 4:602-607.

THE TEMPLE

Diligence of the Saints in Building the Temple

This noble edifice is progressing with great rapidity; strenuous exertions are being made on every hand to facilitate its erection, and materials of all kinds are in a great state of forwardness, and by next fall we expect to see the building enclosed; if not the top stone raised with "shouting of grace—grace unto it." There have been frequently, during the winter, as many as one hundred hands quarrying rock, while at the same time multitudes of others have been engaged in hauling, and in other kinds of labor.

A company was formed last fall to go up to the pine country to purchase mills, and prepare and saw lumber for the Temple and the Nauvoo House, and the reports from them are very favorable: another company has started, this last week, to take their place and to relieve those that are already there: on their return they are to bring a very large raft of lumber, for the use of the above-named houses.

While the busy multitudes have thus been engaged in their several vocations performing their daily labor, and working one-tenth of their time, others have not been less forward in bringing in their tithings and consecrations for the same great object. Never since the foundation of this Church was laid, have we seen manifested a greater willingness to comply with the requisitions of Jehovah, a more ardent desire to do the will of God, more strenuous exertions used, or greater sacrifices made than there have been since the Lord said, "Let the Temple be built by the tithing of my people." It seemed as though the spirit of enterprise, philanthropy and obedience rested simultaneously upon old and young, and brethren and sisters, boys and girls, and even strangers, who were not in the Church, united with an unprecedented liberality in the accomplishment of this great work; nor could the widow, in many instances, be prevented, out of her scanty pittance from throwing in her two mites.

We feel at this time to tender to all, old and young, both in the Church and out of it, our unfeigned thanks for their unprecedented liberality, kindness, diligence, and obedience which they have so opportunely manifested on the present occasion. Not that we are personally or individually benefitted in a pecuniary point of view, but when the brethren, as in this instance, show a unity of purpose and design, and all put their shoulder to the wheel, our care, labor, toil and anxiety is materially diminished, our yoke is made easy and our burden is light.

The Cause of God a Common Cause

The cause of God is one common cause, in which the Saints are alike all interested; we are all members of the one common body, and all partake of the same spirit, and are baptized into one baptism and possess alike the same glorious hope. The advancement of the cause of God and the building up of Zion is as much one man's business as another's. The only difference is, that one is called to fulfill one duty, and another another duty; "but if one member suffers, all the members suffer with it, and if one member is honored all the rest rejoice with it, and the eye cannot say to the ear, I have no need of thee, nor the head to the foot, I have no need of thee;" party feelings, separate interests, exclusive designs should be lost sight of in the one common cause, in the interest of the whole.

All Things to Be Gathered in One

The building up of Zion is a cause that has interested the people of God in every age; it is a theme upon which prophets, priests and kings have dwelt with peculiar delight; they have looked forward with joyful anticipation to the day in which we live; and fired with heavenly and joyful anticipations they have sung and written and prophesied of this our day; but they died without the sight; we are the favored people that God has made choice of to bring about the Latter-day glory; it is left for us to see, participate in and help to roll forward the Latter-day glory, "the dispensation of the fulness of times, when God will gather together all things that are in heaven, and all things that are upon the earth," "even in one," when the Saints of God will be gathered in one from every nation, and kindred, and people, and tongue, when the Jews will be gathered together into one, the wicked will also be gathered together to be destroyed, as spoken of by the prophets; the Spirit of God will also dwell with His people, and be withdrawn from the rest of the nations, and all things whether in heaven or on earth will be in one, even in Christ. The heavenly Priesthood will unite with the earthly, to bring about those great purposes; and whilst we are thus united in one common cause, to roll forth the kingdom of God, the heavenly Priesthood are not idle spectators, the Spirit of God will be showered down from above, and it will dwell in our midst. The blessings of the Most High will rest upon our tabernacles, and our name will be handed down to future ages; our children will rise up and call us blessed; and generations yet unborn will dwell with peculiar delight upon the scenes that we have passed through, the privations that we have endured; the untiring zeal that we have manifested; the all but insurmountable difficulties that we have overcome in laying the foundation of a work that brought about the glory and blessing which they will realize; a work that God and angels have contemplated with delight for generations past; that fired the souls of the ancient patriarchs and prophets; a work that is destined to bring about the destruction of the powers of darkness, the renovation of the earth, the glory of God, and the salvation of the human family. (May 2, 1842.) D. H. C. 4:608-610.

A Catacomb of Mummies Found in Kentucky

Had Mr. Ash in his researches consulted the Book of Mormon his problem would have been solved, and he would have found no difficulty in accounting for the mummies being found in the above mentioned case. The Book of Mormon gives an account of a number of the descendants of Israel coming to this continent; and it is well known that the art of embalming was known among the Hebrews, as well as among the Egyptians, although, perhaps, not so generally among the former, as among the latter people; and their method of embalming also might be different from that of the Egyptians. Jacob and Joseph were no doubt embalmed in the manner of the Egyptians, as they died in that country. (Gen. 50:2, 3, 26.) When our Savior was crucfied his hasty burial obliged them only to wrap his body in linen with a hundred pounds of myrrh, aloes, and similar spices, (part of the ingredients of embalming) given by Nicodemus for that purpose; but Mary and other holy women had prepared ointment and spices for embalming it. (Matt. xxvii:59; Luke xxiii:56; John xix:39, 40.)

This art was no doubt transmitted from Jerusalem to this continent, by the before mentioned emigrants, which accounts for the finding of the mummies, and at the same time is another strong evidence of the authenticity of the Book of Mormon. (May 2, 1842.) T. & S. 3:781-782.

SECTION FIVE
1842 – 1843

SECTION FIVE

Highest Order of Priesthood Revealed

Wednesday, 4.—I spent the day in the upper part of the store, that is in my private office * * * in council with General James Adams, of Springfield, Patriarch Hyrum Smith, Bishops Newel K. Whitney and George Miller, and President Brigham Young and Elders Heber C. Kimball and Willard Richards, instructing them in the principles and order of the Priesthood, attending to washings, anointings, endowments and the communication of keys pertaining to the Aaronic Priesthood, and so on to the highest order of the Melchizedek Priesthood, setting forth the order pertaining to the Ancient of Days, and all those plans and principles by which any one is enabled to secure the fullness of those blessings which have been prepared for the Church of the Firstborn, and come up and abide in the presence of the Eloheim in the eternal worlds. In this council was instituted the ancient order of things for the first time in these last days. And the communications I made to this council were of things spiritual, and to be received only by the spiritual minded: and there was nothing made known to these men but what will be made known to all the Saints of the last days, so soon as they are prepared to receive, and a proper place is prepared to communicate them, even to the weakest of the Saints; therefore let the Saints be diligent in building the Temple, and all houses which they have been, or shall hereafter be, commanded of God to build; and wait their time with patience in all meekness, faith, perseverance unto the end, knowing assuredly that all these things referred to in this council are always governed by the principle of revelation. (May 4, 1842.) D. H. C. 5:1-2.

ADDRESS OF THE PROPHET TO THE RELIEF SOCIETY

Beware of Excessive Zeal

President Joseph Smith read the 14th chapter of Ezekiel—said the Lord had declared by the Prophet, that the people should each one stand for himself, and depend on no man or men in that state of corruption of the Jewish church—that right-eous persons could only deliver their own souls—applied it to the present state of the Church of Jesus Christ of Latter-day Saints—said if the people departed from the Lord, they must fall—that they were depending on the Prophet, hence were darkened in their minds, in consequence of neglecting the duties devolving upon themselves, envious towards the inno-cent, while they afflict the virtuous with their shafts of envy.

There is another error which opens a door for the adver-sary to enter. As females possess refined feelings and sensi-tiveness, they are also subject to overmuch zeal, which must ever prove dangerous, and cause them to be rigid in a religious capacity—[they] should be armed with mercy, notwithstanding the iniquity among us.

The Spirit of Forgiveness

Said he had been instrumental in bringing iniquity to light —it was a melancholy thought and awful that so many should place themselves under the condemnation of the devil, and going to perdition. With deep feeling he said that they are fellow mortals, we loved them once, shall we not encourage them to reformation? We have not yet forgiven them seventy times seven, as our Savior directed; perhaps we have not for-given them once. There is now a day of salvation to such as repent and reform;—and they who repent not should be cast out from this society; yet we should woo them to return to God, lest they escape not the damnation of hell! Where there is a mountain top, there is also a valley—we should act in all things on a proper medium to every immortal spirit. Notwithstanding the unworthy are among us, the virtuous should not, from self-importance, grieve and oppress needlessly, those unfortunate ones—even these should be encouraged to hereafter live to be honored by this society, who are the best portions of the community. Said he had two things to recom-mend to the members of this society, to put a double watch over the tongue; no organized body can exist without this at all. All organized bodies have their peculiar evils, weaknesses and difficulties, the object is to make those not so good reform and return to the path of virtue that they may be numbered with the good, and even hold the keys of power, which will influence to virtue and goodness—should chasten and reprove, and keep it all in silence, not even mention them again; then you will be established in power, virtue, and holiness, and the wrath of God will be turned away.

Guard the Tongue

I have one request to make of the President and members of the society, that you search yourselves—the tongue is an unruly member—hold your tongues about things of no moment—a little tale will set the world on fire. At this time, the truth on the guilty should not be told openly, strange as this may seem, yet this is a policy. We must use precaution in bringing sinners to justice, lest in exposing these heinous sins we draw the indignation of a Gentile world upon us (and, to their imagination, justly too). It is necessary to hold an influence in the world, and thus spare ourselves an extermination; and also accomplish our end in spreading the Gospel, or holiness, in the earth. If we were brought to desolation, the disobedient would find no help. There are some who are obedient, yet men cannot steady the ark—my arm cannot do it—God must steady it. To the iniquitous show yourselves merciful.

I am advised by some of the heads of the Church to tell the Relief Society to be virtuous, but to save the Church from desolation and the sword; beware, be still, be prudent, repent, reform, but do it in a way not to destroy all around you. I do not want to cloak iniquity—all things contrary to the will of God, should be cast from us, but don't do more hurt than good, with your tongues—be pure in heart. Jesus designs to save the people out of their sins. Said Jesus, "Ye shall do the work, which ye see me do." These are the grand key-words for the society to act upon. If I were not in your midst to aid and counsel you, the devil would overcome you. I want the innocent to go free—rather spare ten iniquitous among you, than condemn one innocent one. "Fret not thyself because of evildoers." God will see to it. (May 26, 1842.) D. H. C. 5:19-21.

MINUTES OF MEETING OF THE FEMALE RELIEF SOCIETY, AT THE GROVE, NAUVOO, JUNE 9, 1842
(Reported by Miss E. R. Snow)

The Principal of Mercy

President Joseph Smith opened the meeting by prayer, and then addressed the congregation on the design of the institution. Said it is no matter how fast the society increases, if all the members are virtuous; that we must be as particular with regard to the character of members now, as when the society was first started; that sometimes persons wish to crowd themselves into a society of this kind when they do not intend to pursue the ways of purity and righteousness, as if the society would be a shelter to them in their iniquity.

He said that henseforth no person shall be admitted, but by presenting regular petitions, signed by two or three members in good standing in the society, and whoever comes in must be of good report.

* * *

Said he was going to preach mercy. Suppose that Jesus Christ and holy angels should object to us on frivolous things, what would become of us? We must be merciful to one another, and overlook small things.

* * *

Christ said he came to call sinners to repentance, to save them. Christ was condemned by the self-righteous Jews because He took sinners into His society; He took them upon the principle that they repented of their sins. It is the object of this society to reform persons, not to take those that are corrupt and foster them in their wickedness; but if they repent, we are bound to take them, and by kindness sanctify and cleanse them from all unrighteousness by our influence in watching over them. Nothing will have such influence over people as the fear of being disfellowshiped by so goodly a society as this. * * *

Nothing is so much calculated to lead people to forsake sin as to take them by the hand, and watch over them with tenderness. When persons manifest the least kindness and love to me, O what power it has over my mind, while the opposite course has a tendency to harrow up all the harsh feelings and depress the human mind.

Satan Retards the Human Mind

It is one evidence that men are unacquainted with the principles of godliness to behold the contraction of affectionate feelings and lack of charity in the world. The power and glory of godliness is spread out on a broad principle to throw out the mantle of charity. God does not look on sin with allowance, but when men have sinned, there must be allowance made for them.

All the religious world is boasting of righteousness: it is the doctrine of the devil to retard the human mind, and hinder our progress, by filling us with self-righteousness. The nearer we get to our heavenly Father, the more we are disposed to look with compassion on perishing souls; we feel that we want to take them upon our shoulders, and cast their sins behind our backs. My talk is intended for all this society; if you would have God have mercy on you, have mercy on one another.

* * *

Men Cannot Be Compelled into Kingdom

He then made a promise in the name of the Lord, saying that that soul who has righteousness enough to ask God in the secret place for life, every day of their lives, shall live to three score years and ten. We must walk uprightly all the day long. How glorious are the principles of righteousness! We are full of selfishness; the devil flatters us that we are very righteous, when we are feeding on the faults of others. We can only live by worshiping our God; all must do it for themselves; none can do it for another. How mild the Savior dealt with Peter, saying, "When thou art converted, strengthen thy brethren." At another time, He said to him, "Lovest thou me?" and having received Peter's reply, He said, "Feed my sheep." If the sisters loved the Lord, let them feed the sheep, and not destroy them. How oft have wise men and women sought to dictate Brother Joseph by saying, "O, if I were Brother Joseph I would do this and that;" but if they were in Brother Joseph's shoes they would find that men or women could not be compelled into the kingdom of God, but must be dealt with in long-suffering, and at last we shall save them. The way to keep all the Saints together, and keep the work rolling, is to wait with all long-suffering, till God shall bring such characters to justice. There should be no license for sin, but mercy should go hand in hand with reproof.

Sisters of the society, shall there be strife among you? I will not have it. You must repent, and get the love of God. Away with self-righteousness! The best measure or principle to bring the poor to repentance is to administer to their wants.

The Ladies' Relief Society is not only to relieve the poor, but to save souls.

President Smith then said that he would give a lot of land to the society by deeding to the treasurer, that the society may build houses for the poor. He also said he would give a house, frame not finished, and that Brother Cahoon will move it on to the aforesaid lot, and the society can pay him by giving orders on the store; that it was a good plan to set those to work who are owing widows, and thus make an offset, &c.— D. H. C. 5:23-25.

The Gift of the Holy Ghost

An Editorial in the "Times and Seasons," by the Prophet

Various and conflicting are the opinions of men in regard to the gift of the Holy Ghost. Some people have been in the habit of calling every supernatural manifestation the effects of the Spirit of God, whilst there are others that think there is no manifestation connected with it at all; and that it is nothing but a mere impulse of the mind, or an inward feeling, impression, or secret testimony or evidence, which men possess, and that there is no such a thing as an outward manifestation.

It is not to be wondered at that men should be ignorant, in a great measure, of the principles of salvation, and more especially of the nature, office, power, influence, gifts, and blessings of the gift of the Holy Ghost, when we consider that the human family have been enveloped in gross darkness and ignorance for many centuries past, without revelation, or any just criterion [by which] to arrive at a knowledge of the things of God, which can only be known by the Spirit of God. Hence it not infrequently occurs, that when the Elders of this Church preach to the inhabitants of the world, that if they obey the Gospel they shall receive the gift of the Holy Ghost, that the people expect to see some wonderful manifestation, some great display of power, or some extraordinary miracle performed; and it is often the case that young members of this Church for want of better information, carry along with them their old notions of things, and sometimes fall into egregious errors. We have lately had some information concerning a few members that are in this dilemma, and for their information make a few remarks upon the subject.

Gifts of the Spirit

We believe in the gift of the Holy Ghost being enjoyed now, as much as it was in the Apostles' days; we believe that it [the gift of the Holy Ghost] is necessary to make and to organize the Priesthood, that no man can be called to fill any office in the ministry without it; we also believe in prophecy, in tongues, in visions, and in revelations, in gifts, and in healings; and that these things cannot be enjoyed without the gift of the Holy Ghost. We believe that the holy men of old spake as they were moved by the Holy Ghost, and that holy men in these days speak by the same principle; we believe in its being a comforter and a witness bearer, that it brings things past to our remembrance, leads us into all truth, and shows us of things to come; we believe that "no man can know that Jesus is the Christ, but by the Holy Ghost." We believe in it [this gift of the Holy Ghost] in all its fullness, and power, and greatness, and glory; but whilst we do this, we believe in it rationally, consistently, and scripturally, and not according to the wild vagaries, foolish notions and traditions of men.

* * *

Diversity of Gifts

We believe that the Holy Ghost is imparted by the laying on of hands of those in authority, and that the gift of tongues, and also the gift of prophecy are gifts of the Spirit, and are obtained through that medium; but then to say that men always prophesied and spoke in tongues when they had the imposition of hands, would be to state that which is untrue, contrary to the practice of the Apostles, and at variance with holy writ; for Paul says, "To one is given the gift of tongues, to another the gift of prophecy, and to another the gift of healing;" and again: "Do all prophesy? do all speak with tongues? do all interpret?" evidently showing that all did not possess these several gifts; but that one received one gift, and another received another gift—all did not prophesy, all did not speak in tongues, all did not work miracles; but all did receive the gift of the Holy Ghost; sometimes they spake in tongues and prophesied in the Apostles' days, and sometimes they did not. The same is the case with us also in our administrations, while more frequently there is no manifestation at all, that is visible to the surrounding multitude; this will appear plain when we consult the writings of the Apostles, and notice their proceedings in relation to this matter. Paul, in 1st Cor. xii, says, "Now concerning spiritual gifts, brethren, I would not have you ignorant;" it is evident from this, that some of them were ignorant in relation to these matters, or they would not need instruction.

The Gift of Prophecy

Again in chapter xiv, he says, "Follow after charity and desire spiritual gifts, but rather that ye may prophesy." It is very evident from these Scriptures that many of them had not spiritual gifts, for if they had spiritual gifts where was the necessity of Paul telling them to follow after them, and it is as evident that they did not all receive those gifts by the imposition of the hands; for they as a Church had been baptized and confirmed by the laying on of hands—and yet to a Church of this kind, under the immediate inspection and superintendency of the Apostles, it was necessary for Paul to say, "Follow after charity, and desire spiritual gifts, but rather that ye may prophesy," evidently showing that those gifts were in the Church, but not enjoyed by all in their outward manifestations.

But suppose the gifts of the Spirit were immediately, upon the imposition of hands, enjoyed by all, in all their fulness and power, the skeptic would still be as far from receiving any testimony except upon a mere casualty as before, for all the gifts of the Spirit are not visible to the natural vision, or understanding of man; indeed very few of them are. We read that "Christ ascended into heaven and gave gifts unto men; and He gave some Apostles, and some Prophets, and some Evangelists, and some Pastors and Teachers." (Eph. iv).

The Church a Compact Body

The Church is a compact body composed of different members, and is strictly analogous to the human system, and Paul, after speaking of the different gifts, says, "Now ye are the body of Christ and members in particular; and God hath set some in the Church, first Apostles, secondarily Prophets, thirdly Teachers, after that miracles, then gifts of healing, helps, governments, diversities of tongues. Are all Teachers? Are all workers of miracles? Do all speak with tongues? Do all interpret?" It is evident that they do not; yet are they all members of one body. All members of the natural body are not the eye, the ear, the head or the hand—yet the eye cannot say to the ear, I have no need of thee, nor the head to the foot, I have no need of thee; they are all so many component parts in the perfect machine—the one body; and if one member suffer, the whole of the members suffer with it; and if one member rejoice, all the rest are honored with it.

These, then, are all gifts; they come from God; they are of God; they are all the gifts of the Holy Ghost; they are what Christ ascended into heaven to impart; and yet how few of them could be known by the generality of men. Peter and John were Apostles, yet the Jewish court scourged them as impostors. Paul was both an Apostle and prophet, yet they stoned him and put him into prison. The people knew nothing about it, although he had in his possession the gift of the Holy Ghost. Our Savior was "anointed with the oil of gladness above his fellows," yet so far from the people knowing Him, they said He was Beelzebub and crucified Him as an impostor. Who could point out a Pastor, a Teacher, or an Evangelist by their appearance, yet had they the gift of the Holy Ghost?

The World Cannot Know the Gifts of the Spirit

But to come to the other members of the Church, and examine the gifts as spoken of by Paul, and we shall find that the world can in general know nothing about them, and that there is but one or two that could be immediately known, if they were all poured out immediately upon the imposition of hands. In I Cor. xii, Paul says, "There are diversities of gifts yet the same spirit, and there are differences of administrations but the same Lord; and there are diversities of operations, but it is the same God which worketh all in all. But the manifestations of the Spirit is given unto every man to profit withal. For to one is given, by the Spirit, the Word of Wisdom, to another, the word of knowledge by the same Spirit; to another faith, by the same Spirit; to another the gifts of healing, by the same Spirit; to another the working of miracles; to another prophecy; to another the discerning of spirits; to another divers kinds of tongues; to another the interpretation of tongues. But all these worketh that one and the selfsame spirit, dividing to each man severally as he will."

The Things of God Known Only by the Spirit of God

There are several gifts mentioned here, yet which of them all could be known by an observer at the imposition of hands? The word of wisdom, and the word of knowledge, are as much gifts as any other, yet if a person possessed both of these gifts, or received them by the imposition of hands, who would know it? Another might receive the gift of faith, and they would be as ignorant of it. Or suppose a man had the gift of healing or power to work miracles, that would not then be known; it would require time and circumstances to call these gifts into operation. Suppose a man had the discerning of spirits, who would be the wiser of it? Or if he had the interpretation of tongues, unless someone spoke in an unknown tongue, he of course would have to be silent; there are only two gifts that could be made visible—the gift of tongues and the gift of prophecy. These are things that are the most talked about, and yet if a person spoke in an unknown tongue, according to Paul's testimony, he would be a barbarian to those present. They would say that it was gibberish; and if he prophesied they would call it nonsense. The gift of tongues is the smallest gift perhaps of the whole, and yet it is one that is the most sought after.

So that according to the testimony of Scripture and the manifestations of the Spirit in ancient days, very little could be known about it by the surrounding multitude, except on some extraordinary occasion, as on the day of Pentecost.

The greatest, the best, and the most useful gifts would be known nothing about by an observer. It is true that a man might prophesy, which is a great gift, and one that Paul told the people—the Church—to seek after and to covet, rather than to speak in tongues; but what does the world know about prophesying? Paul says that it "serveth only to those that believe." But does not the Scriptures say that they spake in tongues and prophesied? Yes; but who is it that writes these Scriptures? Not the men of the world or mere casual observers, but the Apostles—men who knew one gift from another, and of course were capable of writing about it; if we had the testimony of the Scribes and Pharisees concerning the outpouring of the Spirit on the day of Pentecost, they would have told us that it was no gift, but that the people were "drunken with new

wine," and we shall finally have to come to the same conclusion that Paul did—"No man knows the things of God but
by the Spirit of God;" for with the great revelations of Paul
when he was caught up into the third heaven and saw things
that were not lawful to utter, no man was apprised of it until
he mentioned it himself fourteen years after; and when John
had the curtains of heaven withdrawn, and by vision looked
through the dark vista of future ages, and contemplated events
that should transpire throughout every subsequent period of
time, until the final winding up scene—while he gazed upon
the glories of the eternal world, saw an innumerable company
of angels and heard the voice of God—it was in the Spirit,
on the Lord's day, unnoticed and unobserved by the world.

*   *   *

The Necessity of Prayer

The Lord cannot always be known by the thunder of His
voice, by the display of His glory or by the manifestation of
His power, and those that are the most anxious to see these
things, are the least prepared to meet them, and were the
Lord to manifest His powers as He did to the children of Israel,
such characters would be the first to say, "Let not the Lord
speak any more, lest we His people die."

We would say to the brethren, seek to know God in your
closets, call upon him in the fields. Follow the directions of
the Book of Mormon, and pray over, and for your families,
your cattle, your flocks, your herds, your corn, and all things
that you possess; ask the blessing of God upon all your labors,
and everything that you engage in. Be virtuous and pure;
be men of integrity and truth; keep the commandments of God;
and then you will be able more perfectly to understand the
difference between right and wrong—between the things of
God and the things of men; and your path will be like that of
the just, which shineth brighter and brighter unto the perfect
day.

The True Use of Tongues

Be not so curious about tongues, do not speak in tongues
except there be an interpreter present; the ultimate design of
tongues is to speak to foreigners, and if persons are very
anxious to display their intelligence, let them speak to such in

their own tongues. The gifts of God are all useful in their place, but when they are applied to that which God does not intend, they prove an injury, a snare and a curse instead of a blessing. We may some future time enter more fully into this subject, but shall let this suffice for the present. (June 15, 1842.) D. H. C. 5:26-32.

The Government of God

An Editorial by the Prophet on the Failure of Man-made Governments and the Right of God to Rule

The government of the Almighty has always been very dissimilar to the governments of men, whether we refer to His religious government, or to the government of nations. The government of God has always tended to promote peace, unity, harmony, strength, and happiness; while that of man has been productive of confusion, disorder, weakness, and misery.

Man's Government Brings Misery and Destruction

The greatest acts of the mighty men have been to depopulate nations and to overthrow kingdoms; and whilst they have exalted themselves and become glorious, it has been at the expense of the lives of the innocent, the blood of the oppressed, the moans of the widow, and the tears of the orphan.

Egypt, Babylon, Greece, Persia, Carthage, Rome—each was raised to dignity amidst the clash of arms and the din of war; and whilst their triumphant leaders led forth their victorious armies to glory and victory, their ears were saluted with the groans of the dying and the misery and distress of the human family; before them the earth was a paradise, and behind them a desolate wilderness; their kingdoms were founded in carnage and bloodshed, and sustained by oppression, tyranny, and despotism. The designs of God, on the other hand, have been to promote the universal good of the universal world; to establish peace and good will among men; to promote the principles of eternal truth; to bring about a state of things that shall unite man to his fellow man; cause the world to "beat their swords into plowshares, and their spears into pruning hooks," make the nations of the earth dwell in peace, and to bring about the millennial glory, when "the earth shall yield its increase, resume its paradisean glory, and become as the garden of the Lord."

Failure of the Governments of Men

The great and wise of ancient days have failed in all their attempts to promote eternal power, peace and happiness. Their nations have crumbled to pieces; their thrones have been cast down in their turn, and their cities, and their mightiest works of art have been annihilated; or their dilapidated towers, or time-worn monuments have left us but feeble traces of their former magnificence and ancient grandeur. They proclaim as with a voice of thunder, those imperishable truths—that man's strength is weakness, his wisdom is folly, his glory is his shame.

Monarchial, aristocratical, and republican governments of their various kinds and grades, have, in their turn, been raised to dignity, and prostrated in the dust. The plans of the greatest politicians, the wisest senators, and most profound statesmen have been exploded; and the proceedings of the greatest chieftains, the bravest generals, and the wisest kings have fallen to the ground. Nation has succeeded nation, and we have inherited nothing but their folly. History records their puerile plans, their short-lived glory, their feeble intellect and their ignoble deeds.

Has Man Increased in Intelligence?

Have we increased in knowledge or intelligence? Where is there a man that can step forth and alter the destiny of nations and promote the happiness of the world? Or where is there a kingdom or nation that can promote the universal happiness of its own subjects, or even their general well-being? Our nation, which possesses greater resources than any other, is rent, from center to circumference, with party strife, political intrigues, and sectional interest; our counselors are panic stricken, our legislators are astonished, and our senators are confounded, our merchants are paralyzed, our tradesmen are disheartened, our mechanics out of employ, our farmers distressed, and our poor crying for bread, our banks are broken, our credit ruined, and our states overwhelmed in debt, yet we are, and have been in peace.

Man Not Able to Govern Himself

What is the matter? Are we alone in this thing? Verily no. With all our evils we are better situated than any other nation. Let Egypt, Turkey, Spain, France, Italy, Portugal, Germany, England, China, or any other nation, speak, and tell the tale of their trouble, their perplexity, and distress, and we should find that their cup was full, and that they were preparing to drink the dregs of sorrow. England, that boasts of her literature, her science, commerce, &c., has her hands reeking with the blood of the innocent abroad, and she is saluted with the cries of the oppressed at home. Chartism, O'Connelism, and radicalism are gnawing her vitals at home; and Ireland, Scotland, Canada, and the east are threatening her destruction abroad. France is rent to the core, intrigue, treachery, and treason lurk in the dark, and murder, and assassination stalk forth at noonday. Turkey, once the dread of European nations, has been shorn of her strength, has dwindled into her dotage, and has been obliged to ask her allies to propose to her tributary terms of peace; and Russia and Egypt are each of them opening their jaws to devour her. Spain has been the theater of bloodshed, of misery and woe for years past. Syria is now convulsed with war and bloodshed. The great and powerful empire of China, which has for centuries resisted the attacks of barbarians, has become tributary to a foreign foe, her batteries thrown down, many of her cities destroyed, and her villages deserted. We might mention the Eastern Rajahs, the miseries and oppressions of the Irish; the convulsed state of Central America; the situation of Texas and Mexico; the state of Greece, Switzerland and Poland; nay, the world itself presents one great theater of misery, woe, and "distress of nations with perplexity." All, all, speak with a voice of thunder, that man is not able to govern himself, to legislate for himself, to protect himself, to promote his own good, nor the good of the world.

The Design of Jehovah

It has been the design of Jehovah, from the commencement of the world, and is His purpose now, to regulate the affairs of the world in His own time, to stand as a head of the universe, and take the reins of government in His own hand. When that is done, judgment will be administered in righteousness; anarchy and confusion will be destroyed, and "nations will learn war no more." It is for want of this great governing principle, that all this confusion has existed; "for it is not in man that walketh, to direct his steps;" this we have fully shown.

If there was anything great or good in the world, it came from God. The construction of the first vessel was given to Noah, by revelation. The design of the ark was given by God, "a pattern of heavenly things." The learning of the Egyptians, and their knowledge of astronomy was no doubt taught them by Abraham and Joseph, as their records testify, who received it from the Lord. The art of working in brass, silver, gold, and precious stones, was taught by revelation, in the wilderness. The architectural designs of the Temple at Jerusalem, together with its ornaments and beauty, were given of God. Wisdom to govern the house of Israel was given to Solomon, and the Judges of Israel; and if he had always been their king, and they subject to his mandate, and obedient to his laws, they would still have been a great and mighty people—the rulers of the universe, and the wonder of the world.

Government Established by God

If Nebuchadnezzar, or Darius, or Cyrus, or any other king possessed knowledge or power, it was from the same source, as the Scriptures abundantly testify. If, then, God puts up one, and sets down another at His pleasure, and made instruments of kings, unknown to themselves, to fulfill His prophecies, how much more was He able, if man would have been subject to His mandate, to regulate the affairs of this world, and promote peace and happiness among the human family!

The Lord has at various times commenced this kind of government, and tendered His services to the human family. He selected Enoch, whom He directed, and gave His law unto, and to the people who were with him; and when the world in general would not obey the commands of God, after walking with God, he translated Enoch and his church, and the Priesthood or government of heaven was taken away.

Abraham was guided in all his family affairs by the Lord; was conversed with by angels, and by the Lord; was told where to go, and when to stop; and prospered exceedingly in all that he put his hand unto; it was because he and his family obeyed the counsel of the Lord.

When Egypt was under the superintendence of Joseph it prospered, because he was taught of God; when they oppressed the Israelites, destruction came upon them. When the children of Israel were chosen with Moses at their head, they were to be a peculiar people, among whom God should place His name; their motto was: "The Lord is our lawgiver; the Lord is our Judge; the Lord is our King; and He shall reign over us." While in this state they might truly say, "Happy is that people, whose God is the Lord." Their government was a theocracy; they had God to make their laws, and men chosen by Him to administer them; He was their God, and they were His people. Moses received the word of the Lord from God Himself; he was the mouth of God to Aaron, and Aaron taught the people, in both civil and ecclesiastical affairs; they were both one, there was no distinction; so will it be when the purposes of God shall be accomplished: when "the Lord shall be King over the whole earth" and "Jerusalem His throne." "The law shall go forth from Zion, and the word of the Lord from Jerusalem."

Universal Peace to Come from God

This is the only thing that can bring about the "restitution of all things spoken of by all the holy Prophets since the world was"—"the dispensation of the fullness of times, when God shall gather together all things in one." Other attempts to promote universal peace and happiness in the human family have proved abortive; every effort has failed; every plan and design has fallen to the ground; it needs the wisdom of God, the intelligence of God, and the power of God to accomplish this. The world has had a fair trial for six thousand years; the Lord will try the seventh thousand Himself; "He whose right it is, will possess the kingdom, and reign until He has put all things under His feet;" iniquity will hide its hoary head, Satan will be bound, and the works of darkness destroyed; righteousness will be put to the line, and judgment to the plummet, and "he that fears the Lord will alone be exalted in that day." To bring about this state of things, there must of necessity be great confusion among the nations of the earth; "distress of nations with perplexity." Am I asked what is the cause of the present distress? I would answer, "Shall there be evil in a city and the Lord hath not done it?"

Earth Now Groaning Under Corruption

The earth is groaning under corruption, oppression, tyranny and bloodshed; and God is coming out of His hiding place, as He said He would do, to vex the nations of the earth. Daniel, in his vision, saw convulsion upon convulsion; he "beheld till the thrones were cast down, and the Ancient of Days did sit;" and one was brought before him like unto the Son of Man; and all nations, kindred, tongues, and peoples, did serve and obey Him. It is for us to be righteous, that we may be wise and understand; for none of the wicked shall understand; but the wise shall understand, and they that turn many to righteousness shall shine as the stars for ever and ever.

It Behooves Us to Be Wise

As a Church and a people it behooves us to be wise, and to seek to know the will of God, and then be willing to do it; for "blessed is he that heareth the word of the Lord, and keepeth it," say the Scriptures. 'Watch and pray always," says our Savior, "that ye may be accounted worthy to escape the things that are to come on the earth, and to stand before the Son of Man." If Enoch, Abraham, Moses, and the children of Israel, and all God's people were saved by keeping the commandments of God, we, if saved at all, shall be saved upon the same principle. As God governed Abraham, Isaac and Jacob as families, and the children of Israel as a nation; so we, as a Church, must be under His guidance if we are prospered, preserved and sustained. Our only confidence can be in God; our only wisdom obtained from Him; and He alone must be our protector and safeguard, spiritually and temporally, or we fall.

We have been chastened by the hand of God heretofore for not obeying His commands, although we never violated any human law, or transgressed any human precept; yet we have treated lightly His commands, and departed from His ordinances, and the Lord has chastened us sore, and we have felt His arm and kissed the rod; let us be wise in time to come and ever remember that "to obey is better than sacrifice, and to hearken than the fat of rams." The Lord has told us to build the Temple and the Nauvoo House; and that command is as binding upon us as any other; and that man who engages not in these things is as much a transgressor as though he broke any other commandment; he is not a doer of God's will, not a fulfiller of His laws.

The Saints Subject to Divine Counsel

In regard to the building up of Zion, it has to be done by the counsel of Jehovah, by the revelations of heaven; and we should feel to say, "If the Lord go not with us, carry us not up hence." We would say to the Saints that come here, we have laid the foundation for the gathering of God's people to this place, and they expect that when the Saints do come, they will be under the counsel that God has appointed. The Twelve are set apart to counsel the Saints pertaining to this matter; and we expect that those who come here will send before them their wise men according to revelation; or if not practicable, be subject to the counsel that God has given, or they cannot receive an inheritance among the Saints, or be considered as God's people, and they will be dealt with as transgressors of the laws of God. We are trying here to gird up our loins, and purge from our midst the workers of iniquity; and we hope that when our brethren arrive from abroad, they will assist us to roll forth this good work, and to accomplish this great design, that "Zion may be built up in righteousness; and all nations flock to her standard;" that as God's people, under His direction, and obedient to His law, we may grow up in righteousness and truth; that when His purposes shall be accomplished, we may receive an inheritance among those that are sanctified. (July 15, 1842.) D. H. C. 5:61-66.

Letter of the Prophet to Governor Carlin—Satisfied with the Governor's Attitude

Esteemed Sir:—Your favor of the 27th instant per Brevet Major-General Wilson Law is before me. I cannot let this opportunity pass without tendering to you my warmest thanks for the friendly treatment my lady as well as those with her received at your hands during the late visit, and also for the friendly feelings breathed forth in your letter. Your Excellency may be assured that they are duly appreciated by me, and shall be reciprocated.

I am perfectly satisfied with regard to the subject under consideration, and with your remarks. I shall consider myself and our citizens secure from harm under the broad canopy of the law under your administration. We look to you for protection in the event of any violence being used towards us, knowing that our innocence with regard to all the accusations in circulation will be duly evidenced before an enlightened public.

Any service we can do the state at any time will be cheerfully done, for our ambition is to be serviceable to our country.

With sentiments of respect and esteem, I remain your humble servant.

JOSEPH SMITH.

D. H. C. 5:83.

Prophecy That the Saints Would Be Driven to Rocky Mountains

Saturday, Aug. 6, 1842.—Passed over the river to Montrose, Iowa, in company with General Adams, Colonel Brewer, and others, and witnessed the installation of the officers of the Rising Sun Lodge Ancient York Masons, at Montrose, by General James Adams, Deputy Grand-Master of Illinois. While the Deputy Grand-Master was engaged in giving the requisite instructions to the Master-elect, I had a conversation with a number of brethren in the shade of the building on the subject of our persecutions in Missouri and the constant annoyance which has followed us since we were driven from that state. I prophesied that the Saints would continue to suffer much affliction and would be driven to the Rocky Mountains, many would apostatize, others would be put to death by our persecutors or lose their lives in consequence of exposure or disease, and some of you will live to go and assist in making settlements and build cities and see the Saints become a mighty people in the midst of the Rocky Mountains. (Aug. 6, 1842.) D. H. C. 5:85.

Happiness the Design of Existence

Happiness is the object and design of our existence; and will be the end thereof, if we pursue the path that leads to it; and this path is virtue, uprightness, faithfulness, holiness, and keeping all the commandments of God. But we cannot keep all the commandments without first knowing them, and we cannot expect to know all, or more than we now know unless we comply with or keep those we have already received. That which is wrong under one circumstance, may be, and often is, right under another.

God said, "Thou shalt not kill;" at another time He said, "Thou shalt utterly destroy." This is the principle on which the government of heaven is conducted—by revelation adapted to the circumstances in which the children of the kingdom are placed. Whatever God requires is right, no matter what it is, although we may not see the reason thereof till long after the events transpire. If we seek first the kingdom of God, all good things will be added. So with Solomon: first he asked wisdom, and God gave it him, and with it every desire of his heart, even things which might be considered abominable to all who understand the order of heaven only in part, but which in reality were right because God gave and sanctioned by special revelation.

A parent may whip a child, and justly, too, because he stole an apple; whereas if the child had asked for the apple, and the parent had given it, the child would have eaten it with a better appetite; there would have been no stripes; all the pleasure of the apple would have been secured, all the misery of stealing lost.

Every Gift from God Is Just

This principle will justly apply to all of God's dealings with His children. Everything that God gives us is lawful and right; and it is proper that we should enjoy His gifts and blessings whenever and wherever He is disposed to bestow; but if we should seize upon those same blessings and enjoyments without law, without revelation, without commandment, those blessings and enjoyments would prove cursings and vexations in the end, and we should have to lie down in sorrow and wailings of everlasting regret. But in obedience there is joy and peace unspotted, unalloyed; and as God has designed our happiness—and the happiness of all His creatures, he never has—He never will institute an ordinance or give a commandment to His people that is not calculated in its nature to promote that happiness which He has designed, and which will not end in the greatest amount of good and glory to those who become the recipients of his law and ordinances. Blessings offered, but rejected, are no longer blessings, but become like the talent hid in the earth by the wicked and slothful servant; the proffered good returns to the giver; the blessing is bestowed on those who will receive and occupy; for unto him that hath shall be given, and he shall have abundantly, but unto him that hath not or will not receive, shall be taken away that which he hath, or might have had.

> Be wise today; 'tis madness to defer;
> Next day the fatal precedent may plead.
> Thus on till wisdom is pushed out of time
> Into eternity.

Men Are Judged According to Their Deeds

Our heavenly Father is more liberal in His views, and boundless in His mercies and blessings, than we are ready to believe or receive; and, at the same time, is more terrible to the workers of iniquity, more awful in the executions of His punishments, and more ready to detect every false way, than we are apt to suppose Him to be. He will be inquired of by His children. He says, "Ask and ye shall receive, seek and ye shall find;" but, if you will take that which is not your own, or which I have not given you, you shall be rewarded according to your deeds; but no good thing will I withhold from them who walk uprightly before me, and do my will in all things— who will listen to my voice and to the voice of my servant whom I have sent; for I delight in those who seek diligently to know my precepts, and abide by the law of my kingdom; for all things shall be made known unto them in mine own due time, and in the end they shall have joy. (Aug. 27, 1842.) D. H. C. 5:134-136.

MINUTES OF THE FEMALE RELIEF SOCIETY'S MEETING—REMARKS OF THE PROPHET

The Church to Prevail Against All Evil Powers

President Joseph Smith arose and said, "I am happy and thankful for the privilege of being present on this occasion. Great exertions have been made on the part of our enemies to carry me to Missouri and destroy my life; but the Lord has hedged up their way, and they have not, as yet, accomplished their purpose. God has enabled me to keep out of their hands. I have warred a good warfare, insomuch as I have outgeneralled or whipped out all Bennett's corrupt host.

My feelings at the present time are that, inasmuch as the Lord Almighty has preserved me until today, He will continue to preserve me, by the united faith and prayers of the Saints, until I have fully accomplished my mission in this life, and so firmly established the dispensation of the fullness of the priesthood in the last days, that all the powers of earth and hell can never prevail against it.

This constant persecution reminds me of the words of the Savior, when He said to the Pharisees, "Go ye, and tell that fox, Behold, I cast out devils, and I do cures today and tomorrow, and the third day I shall be perfected." I suspect that my Heavenly Father has decreed that the Missourians shall not get me into their power; if they do, it will be because I do not keep out of their way.

I shall triumph over my enemies: I have begun to triumph over them at home, and I shall do it abroad. All those that rise up against me will surely feel the weight of their iniquity upon their own heads. Those that speak evil of me and the Saints are ignorant or abominable characters, and full of iniquity. All the fuss, and all the stir, and all the charges got up against me are like the jack-a-lantern, which cannot be found.

No Man Without Fault

Although I do wrong, I do not the wrongs that I am charged with doing; the wrong that I do is through the frailty of human nature, like other men. No man lives without fault. Do you think that even Jesus, if He were here, would be without fault in your eyes? His enemies said all manner of evil against Him—they all watched for iniquity in Him. How easy it was for Jesus to call out all the iniquity of the hearts of those whom He was among!

Most Injury Comes from Little Evils

The servants of the Lord are required to guard against those things that are calculated to do the most evil. The little foxes spoil the vines—little evils do the most injury to the Church. If you have evil feelings, and speak of them to one another, it has a tendency to do mischief. These things result in those evils which are calculated to cut the throats of the heads of the Church.

When I do the best I can—when I am accomplishing the greatest good, then the most evils and wicked surmisings are got up against me. I would to God that you would be wise. I now counsel you, that if you know anything calculated to disturb the peace or injure the feelings of your brother or sister, hold your tongues and the least harm will be done.

The Female Relief Society have taken a most active part in my welfare against my enemies, in petitioning to the governor in my behalf. These measures were all necessary. Do you not see that I foresaw what was coming, beforehand, by the spirit of prophecy? All these movements had an influence in my redemption from the hand of my enemies. If these measures had not been taken, more serious consequences would have resulted. I have come here to bless you. The Society have done well: their principles are to practice holiness. God loves you, and your prayers in my behalf shall avail much: let them not cease to ascend to God continually in my behalf.

Persistence of Wicked Men

The enemies of this people will never get weary of their persecution against the Church, until they are overcome. I expect they will array everything against me that is in their power to control, and that we shall have a long and tremendous warfare. He that will war the true Christian warfare against the corruptions of these last days will have wicked men and angels of devils, and all the infernal powers of darkness continually arrayed against him. When wicked and corrupt men oppose, it is a criterion to judge if a man is warring the Christian warfare. When all men speak evil of you falsely, blessed are ye. Shall a man be considered bad, when men speak evil of him? No. If a man stands and opposes the world of sin, he may expect to have all wicked and corrupt spirits arrayed against him. But it will be but a little season, and all these afflictions will be turned away from us, inasmuch as we are faithful, and are not overcome by these evils. By seeing the blessings of the endowment rolling on, and the kingdom increasing and spreading from sea to sea, we shall rejoice that we were not overcome by these foolish things.

Baptism for the Dead

A few very important things have been manifested to me in my absence respecting the doctrine of baptism for the dead, which I shall communicate to the Saints next Sabbath, if nothing should occur to prevent me.

★ ★ ★ ★

President Smith said, "I have one remark to make respecting the baptism for the dead to suffice for the time being, until I have opportunity to discuss the subject at greater length—all persons baptized for the dead must have a recorder present, that he may be an eyewitness to record and testify of the truth and validity of his record. It will be necessary, in the Grand Council, that these things be testified to by competent witnesses. Therefore let the recording and witnessing of baptisms for the dead be carefully attended to from this time forth. If there is any lack, it may be at the expense of our friends; they may not come forth."[1] (Aug. 31, 1842.) D. H. C. 5:139-141.

Persecution the Heritage of the Righteous

From an Editorial in the "Times and Seasons," by the Prophet

★ ★ ★ ★

Abel was slain for his righteousness, and how many more up to the flood is not of much consequence to us now. But if we believe in present revelation, as published in the "Times and Seasons" last spring, Abraham, the prophet of the Lord, was laid upon the iron bedstead for slaughter; and the book of Jasher, which has not been disproved as a bad author, says he was cast into the fire of the Chaldees. Moses, the man of God, who killed an Egyptian persecutor of the children of Israel, was driven from his country and kindred. Elijah had to flee his country, for they sought his life,—and he was fed by ravens. Daniel was cast into a den of lions: Micaiah was fed on the bread of affliction; and Jeremiah was cast into the filthy hole under the Temple; and did these afflictions come upon these prophets of the Lord on account of transgression? No! It was the iron hand of persecution—like the chains of Missouri! And mark—when these old prophets suffered, the vengeance of God, in due time, followed and left the wicked opposers of the Lord's anointed like Sodom and Gomorrah; like the Egyptians;

---

[1]See D. & C., Sections 127, 128.

like Jezebel, who was eaten by dogs; and like all Israel, which were led away captive, till the Lord had spent his fury upon them—even to this day.

Let us come into New Testament times—so many are ever praising the Lord and His apostles. We will commence with John the Baptist. When Herod's edict went forth to destroy the young children, John was about six months older than Jesus, and came under this hellish edict, and Zacharias caused his mother to take him into the mountains, where he was raised on locusts and wild honey. When his father refused to disclose his hiding place, and being the officiating high priest at the Temple that year, was slain by Herod's order, between the porch and the altar, as Jesus said. John's head was taken to Herod, the son of this infant murderer, in a charger—notwithstanding there was never a greater prophet born of a woman than him!

Jesus, the Son of God was crucified with his hands and feet nailed to the wood!

* * *

Saints Come Through Tribulation

It is a shame to the Saints to talk of chastisements, and transgressions, when all the Saints before them, prophets and apostles, have had to come up through great tribulation; whether a Herod, a Nero, or a Boggs, causes the affliction, or the blood to be shed, is all the same—these murderers will have their reward! and the saints theirs. How many have had to wander in sheep skins and goat skins, and live in caves and dens of the mountains, because the world was unworthy of their society! And was transgression or chastisement connected with their seclusion from the enjoyment of society? No! But remember, brethren, he that offends one of the least of the Saints, would be better off with a millstone tied to his neck and he and the stone plunged into the depth of the sea! Remember that he that gives a cup of cold water in the name of a disciple, to one of the saints in prison, or secluded from friends by reason of vexatious law suits, intended for persecution, shall in no wise lose his reward.

Never, while the spirit of liberty, or the virtue of a saint, hold communion in the flesh, let us hear of those who profess to be governed by the law of God, and make their garments

clean in the blood of the Lamb, shrinking from the assistance
of those who bear the ark of the Lord—in the hour of danger!

*   *   *

Baptism

Upon looking over the sacred pages of the Bible, searching
into the prophets and sayings of the apostles, we find no subject
so nearly connected with salvation, as that of baptism.   In the
first place, however, let us understand that the word baptize is
derived from the Greek verb "baptiso," and means to immerse
or overwhelm, and that sprinkle is from the Greek verb "ran-
tiso," and means to scatter on by particles; then we can treat
the subject as one inseparably connected with our eternal welfare; and always bear in mind that it is one of the only methods
by which we can obtain a remission of sins in this world, and be
prepared to enter into the joys of our Lord in the world to come.

As it is well known that various opinions govern a large
portion of the sectarian world as to this important ordinance of
the gospel, it may not be amiss to introduce the commissions
and commands of Jesus Himself on the subject.—He said to
the Twelve, or rather eleven at the time: Go ye therefore, and
teach all nations, baptizing them in the name of the Father, and
of the Son, and of the Holy Ghost; teaching them to observe
all things whatsoever I have commanded you: Thus it is recorded by Matthew.   In Mark we have these important words:
Go ye into all the world, and preach the gospel to every
creature.   He that believeth and is baptized shall be saved, and
he that believeth not shall be damned.   And to show how the
believers are to be known from the unbelievers, he continues
and says: And these signs shall follow them that believe: in
my name shall they cast out devils: they shall speak with new
tongues: they shall take up serpents: and if they drink any
deadly thing it shall not hurt them: they shall lay hands on the
sick and they shall recover.   And in Luke we find the finishing
clause like this,—that it was necessary that Christ should die
and rise the third day — that remission of sins should be
preached in his name among all nations, beginning at Jerusalem.
And ye are witnesses of these things.

Witnesses

We will now examine the witnesses.   As it will be recol-
lected, they were to wait at Jerusalem till they were endowed

with power from on high and then go and teach all nations whatsoever the Lord had commanded them.   As Peter held the keys of the kingdom, we will examine him first.

Now on the day of Pentecost, when there was a marvelous display of the gifts, according to the promise in Mark, many were pricked in the heart, and said unto Peter, and to the rest of the Apostles, Men and brethren what shall we do?   Peter said unto them: Repent, and be baptized every one of you in the name of Jesus Christ, for the remission of sins, and ye shall receive the gift of the Holy Ghost, etc.—Here one of the witnesses says in so many words, repent and be baptized. And we are of the opinion that Peter having been taught by the Lord, and commissioned by the Lord, and endowed by the Lord, would be about as correct a counselor, or ambassador as we or they could enquire of to know the right way to enter into the kingdom.

Again, Luke in his record of the Acts of the Apostles, says: And it came to pass, that while Apollos was at Corinth, Paul having passed through the upper coasts, came to Ephesus; and finding certain disciples, he said unto them, Have ye received the Holy Ghost since ye believed?   And they said unto him, We have not so much as heard whether there be any Holy Ghost.   And he said unto them, Unto what then were ye baptized?   And they said: unto John's baptism.   Then said Paul, John verily baptized with the baptism of repentance, saying unto the people, that they should believe on him which should come after him, that is on Christ Jesus.   When they heard this, they were baptized in the name of the Lord Jesus.—And when Paul had laid his hands upon them, the Holy Ghost came on them; and they spake with tongues, and prophesied.

From the above witnesses we are informed that baptism was the essential point on which they could receive the gift of the Holy Ghost.   It seems from the reasoning above that some sectarian Jew had been baptizing like John, but had forgotten to inform them that there was one to follow by the name of Jesus Christ, to baptize with fire and the Holy Ghost:— which showed these converts that their first baptism was illegal, and when they heard this they were gladly baptized, and after hands were laid on them, they received the gifts, according to promise, and spake with tongues and prophesied. * * * The Apostle says the Gospel is the power of God unto salvation unto them that believe; and also informs us that life and immortality were brought to light through the gospel; that the scripture, as Paul said to the Galatians, foreseeing that God would justify the heathen through faith, preached before the gospel unto Abraham: saying, In thee shall all nations be blessed.

Gospel Always the Same

Now taking it for granted that the scriptures say what they mean, and mean what they say, we have sufficient grounds to go on and prove from the Bible that the gospel has always been the same; the ordinances to fulfill its requirements, the same, and the officers to officiate, the same; and the signs and fruits resulting from the promises, the same: therefore, as Noah was a preacher of righteousness he must have been baptized and ordained to the priesthood by the laying on of the hands, etc. For no man taketh this honor unto himself except he be called of God as was Aaron, and Aaron was baptized in the cloud and in the sea, together with all Israel, as is related by the Apostle in Corinthians. This position or fact, is witnessed in this manner: the covenant of circumcision made with Abraham, and practiced steadily up to the departing of Israel out of Egypt, was abandoned in the wilderness, forty years— and renewed by Joshua after he passed over Jordan, and encamped at Gilgal, where he made sharp knives and circumcised the whole male portion of the church.

* * *

Man Must Be Born Again

Nicodemus came to Jesus by night, and said unto him, Rabbi, we know that thou art a teacher come from God: for no man can do these miracles that thou doest, except God be with him. Jesus answered and said unto him, Verily, verily, I say unto thee, Except a man be born again he cannot see the kingdom of God. Nicodemus saith unto him, How can a man be born when he is old? can he enter the second time into his mother's womb, and be born?—Jesus answered, Verily, verily, I say unto thee, Except a man be born of water, and of the Spirit, he cannot enter into the kingdom of God. This strong and positive answer of Jesus, as to water baptism, settles the question: If God is the same yesterday, today, and forever: it is no wonder He is so positive in the great declaration: He that believes and is baptized shall be saved, and he that believes not shall be damned!   There was no other name given under heaven, nor no other ordinance admitted, whereby men could be saved: No wonder the Apostle said, being "buried with him in baptism," ye shall rise from the dead! No wonder Paul had to arise and be baptized and wash away his sins: No wonder the angel told good old Cornelius that he must send for Peter to learn how to be saved: Peter could baptize, and angels could not, so long as there were legal officers in the flesh holding the keys of the kingdom, or the authority of the priesthood. There is one evidence still further on this point, and that is that Jesus himself when he appeared to Paul on his way to Damascus, did not inform him how he could be saved.   He had set in the church first Apostles, and secondly prophets, for the work of the ministry, perfecting of the saints, etc.; and as the grand rule of heaven was that nothing should ever be done on earth without revealing the secret to his servants the prophets, agreeably to Amos 3:7, so Paul could not learn so much from the Lord relative to his duty in the common salvation of man, as he could from one of Christ's ambassadors called with the same heavenly calling of the Lord, and endowed with the same power from on high—so that what they loosed on earth, should be loosed in heaven; and what they bound on earth should be bound in heaven: He, the Lord being a priest forever, after the order of Melchizedek, and the anointed Son of God, from before the foundation of the world, and they the begotten sons of Jesus through the gospel, to teach all nations—and lo I am with you always to the end of the world— that is—by the other comforter which the world cannot receive —for ye are the witnesses—having the testimony of Jesus which is the spirit of prophecy.

Necessity of Repentance

From what has already been introduced as testimony to prove that no man can be saved without baptism, it will be seen and acknowledged that if there was sin among men, re- pentance was as necessary at one time or age of the world as another—and that other foundation can no man lay than that is laid, which is Jesus Christ. If, then, Abel was a righteous man he had to become so by keeping the commandments; if

Enoch was righteous enough to come into the presence of God, and walk with him, he must have become so by keeping his commandments, and so of every righteous person, whether it was Noah, a preacher of righteousness; Abraham, the father of the faithful; Jacob, the prevailer with God; Moses, the man who wrote of Christ, and brought forth the law by command-ment, as a schoolmaster to bring men to Christ, or whether it was Jesus Christ himself, who had no need of repentance, having no sin, according to his solemn declaration to John:—now let me be baptized: for no man can enter the kingdom without obeying this ordinance: for thus it becometh us to fulfil ALL RIGHTEOUSNESS.   Surely, then, if it became John and Jesus Christ, the Savior, to fulfil all righteousness to be baptized—so surely, then, it will become every other person that seeks the kingdom of heaven to go and do likewise; for he is the door, and if any person climbs up any other way, the same is a thief and a robber!

Baptism Required in All Ages

In the former ages of the world, before the Saviour came in the flesh, "the saints" were baptized in the name of Jesus Christ to come, because there never was any other name whereby men could be saved; and after he came in the flesh and was crucified, then the saints were baptized in the name of Jesus Christ, crucified, risen from the dead and ascended into heaven, that they might be buried in baptism like him, and be raised in glory like him, that as there was but one Lord, one faith, one baptism, and one God and father of us all, even so there was but one door to the mansions of bliss.   Amen. (Sept. 1, 1842.)   T. & S. 3:902-905.

"FACTS ARE STUBBORN THINGS"

Greatness of the Jaredites and Nephites

From an extract from "Stephen's Incidents of Travel in Central America," it will be seen that the proof of the Nephites and Lamanites dwelling on this continent, according to the account in the Book of Mormon, is developing itself in a more satisfactory way than the most sanguine believer in that revela-tion could have anticipated.   It certainly affords us a gratifica-tion that the world of mankind does not enjoy, to give publicity to such important developments of the remains and ruins of those mighty people.

When we read in the Book of Mormon that Jared and his brother came on to this continent from the confusion and scattering at the Tower, and lived here more than a thousand years, and covered the whole continent from sea to sea, with towns and cities; and that Lehi went down by the Red Sea to the great Southern Ocean, and crossed over to this land, and landed a little south of the Isthmus of Darien, and improved the country according to the word of the Lord, as a branch of the house of Israel, and then read such a goodly traditionary account as the one below, we can not but think the Lord has a hand in bringing to pass his strange act, and proving the Book of Mormon true in the eyes of all the people. The extract below, comes as near the real fact, as the four Evangelists do to the crucifixion of Jesus.—Surely "facts are stubborn things." It will be as it ever has been, the world will prove Joseph Smith a true prophet by circumstantial evidence, in experiments, as they did Moses and Elijah. Now read Stephen's story:

"According to Fuentes, the chronicler of the kingdom of Guatemala, the kings of Quiche and Cachiquel were descended from the Toltecan Indians, who, when they came into this country, found it already inhabited by people of different nations. According to the manuscripts of Don Juan Torres, the grandson of the last king of the Quiches, which was in the possession of the lieutenant general appointed by Pedro de Alvarado, and which Fuentes says he obtained by means of Father Francis Vasques, the historian of the order of San Francis, the Toltecas themselves descended from the house of Israel, who were released by Moses from the tyranny of Pharaoh, and after crossing the Red Sea, fell into idolatry. To avoid the reproofs of Moses, or from fear of his inflicting upon them some chastisement, they separated from him and his brethren, and under the guidance of Tanub, their chief, passed from one continent to the other, to a place which they called the seven caverns, a part of the kingdom of Mexico, where they founded the celebrated city of Tula." (Sept. 15, 1842.) T. & S. 3:921-922.

Effects of Disobeying Counsel

About ten in the forenoon I rode up and viewed the Temple. I expressed my satisfaction at the arrangements, and was pleased with the progress made in the sacred edifice. After conversing with several of the brethren, and shaking hands with numbers who were very much rejoiced to see their Prophet again, I returned home; but soon afterwards went over to the store, where a number of brethren and sisters were assembled, who had arrived this morning from the neighborhood of New York, Long Island, &c. After Elders Taylor, Woodruff and Samuel Bennett had addressed the brethren and sisters, I spoke to them at considerable length, showing them the proper course to pursue, and how to act in regard to making purchases of land, &c.

I showed them that it was generally in consequence of the brethren disregarding or disobeying counsel that they became dissatisfied and murmured; and many when they arrived here, were dissatisfied with the conduct of some of the Saints, because everything was not done perfectly right, and they get angry, and thus the devil gets advantage over them to destroy them. I told them I was but a man, and they must not expect me to be perfect; if they expected perfection from me, I should expect it from them; but if they would bear with my infirmities and the infirmities of the brethren, I would likewise bear with their infirmities.

I told them it was likely I would have again to hide up in the woods, but they must not be discouraged, but build up the city, the Temple, &c. When my enemies take away my rights, I will bear it and keep out of the way; but if they take away your rights, I will fight for you. I blessed them and departed. (Oct. 29, 1842.) D. H. C. 5:181.

The Rule of Christ in the Millennium

While in conversation at Judge Adams' during the evening, I said, Christ and the resurrected Saints will reign over the earth during the thousand years. They will not probably dwell upon the earth, but will visit it when they please, or when it is necessary to govern it. There will be wicked[2] men on the

---

[2]The Prophet's statement that there will be wicked men on the earth during the Millennium has caused considerable confusion in the minds of many who have read in the Scripture in many places that when Christ comes the earth shall be cleansed from its wickedness, and that the wicked shall not stand, but shall be consumed. See D. and C. 5:18-19, 29:8-10, 101:23-25; Isaiah 24:1-3; Malachi 4:1. The evil-minded inhabitants, those "who love and make a lie" and are guilty of all manner of corruption, will be consumed

earth during the thousand years. The heathen nations who will not come up to worship will be visited with the judgments of God, and must eventually be destroyed from the earth. (Dec. 30, 1842.) D. H. C. 5:212.

What Constitutes a Prophet?

If any person should ask me if I were a prophet, I should not deny it, as that would give me the lie; for, according to John, the testimony of Jesus is the spirit of prophecy; therefore, if I profess to be a witness or teacher, and have not the spirit of prophecy, which is the testimony of Jesus, I must be a false witness; but if I be a true teacher and witness, I must possess the spirit of prophecy, and that constitutes a prophet; and any man who says he is a teacher or a preacher of righteousness, and denies the spirit of prophecy, is a liar, and the truth is not in him; and by this key false teachers and impostors may be detected. (Dec. 30, 1842.) D. H. C. 5:215-216.

Status of the Negro

At five went to Mr. Sollars' with Elders Hyde and Richards. Elder Hyde inquired the situation of the negro. I replied, they came into the world slaves, mentally and physically. Change their situation with the whites, and they would be like them. They have souls, and are subjects of salvation. Go into Cincinnati or any city, and find an educated negro, who rides in his carriage, and you will see a man who has risen by the powers of his own mind to his exalted state of respectability. The slaves in Washington are more refined than many in high places, and the black boys will take the shine off many of those they brush and wait on.

Elder Hyde remarked, "Put them on the level, and they will rise above me." I replied, if I raised you to be my equal, and then attempted to oppress you, would you not be indignant and try to rise above me, as did Oliver Cowdery, Peter Whit-

---

and pass away when Christ comes. In using the term "wicked men" in this instruction at the home of Judge Adams, the Prophet did so in the same sense in which the Lord uses it in the eighty-fourth section of the Doctrine and Covenants, 49-53. The Lord in this scripture speaks of those who have not received the Gospel as being under the bondage of sin, and hence "wicked." However, many of these people are honorable, clean living men, but they have not embraced the Gospel. The inhabitants of the terrestrial order will remain on the earth during the Millennium, and this class are without the Gospel ordinances. See D. and C. 76:73-76.

mer, and many others, who said I was a fallen Prophet, and they were capable of leading the people, although I never attempted to oppress them, but had always been lifting them up? Had I anything to do with the negro, I would confine them by strict law to their own species, and put them on a national equalization.

Necessity of Faith

Because faith is wanting, the fruits are. No man since the world was had faith without having something along with it. The ancients quenched the violence of fire, escaped the edge of the sword, women received their dead, etc. By faith the worlds were made. A man who has none of the gifts has no faith; and he deceives himself, if he supposes he has. Faith has been wanting, not only among the heathen, but in professed Christendom also, so that tongues, healings, prophecy, and prophets and apostles, and all the gifts and blessings have been wanting.

Some of the company thought I was not a very meek Prophet; so I told them: "I am meek and lowly in heart," and will personify Jesus for a moment, to illustrate the principle, and cried out with a loud voice, "Woe unto you, ye doctors; woe unto you, ye lawyers; woe unto you, ye scribes, Pharisees, and hypocrites!" But you cannot find the place where I ever went that I found fault with their food, their drink, their house, their lodgings; no, never; and this is what is meant by the meekness and lowliness of Jesus.

False Reports

Mr. Sollars stated that James Mullone, of Springfield, told him as follows:—"I have been to Nauvoo, and seen Joe Smith, the Prophet: he had a gray horse, and I asked him where he got it; and Joe said, "You see that white cloud." "Yes." "Well, as it came along, I got the horse from that cloud." This is a fair specimen of the ten thousand foolish lies circulated by this generation to bring the truth and its advocates into disrepute.

What is it that inspires professors of Christianity generally with a hope of salvation? It is that smooth, sophisticated influence of the devil, by which he deceives the whole world. But, said Mr. Sollars, "May I not repent and be baptized, and not pay any attention to dreams, visions, and other gifts of the

Spirit?" I replied: "Suppose I am traveling and am hungry, and meet with a man and tell him I am hungry, and he tells me to go yonder, there is a house of entertainment, go and knock, and you must conform to all the rules of the house, or you cannot satisfy your hunger; knock, call for food, sit down and eat;—and I go and knock, and ask for food, and sit down to the table, but do not eat, shall I satisfy my hunger? No. I must eat. The gifts are the food; and the graces of the Spirit are the gifts of the Spirit. When I first commenced this work and had got two or three individuals to believe, I went about thirty miles with Oliver Cowdery, to see them. We had only one horse between us. When we arrived, a mob of about one hundred men came upon us before we had time to eat, and chased us all night; and we arrived back again a little after daylight, having traveled about sixty miles in all, and without food. I have often traveled all night to see the brethren; and, when traveling to preach the Gospel among strangers, have frequently been turned away without food." (Jan. 2, 1843.) D. H. C. 5:217-219.

The Kingdom of God

Some say the kingdom of God was not set up on the earth until the day of Pentecost, and that John did not preach the baptism of repentance for the remission of sins. But I say, in the name of the Lord, that the kingdom of God was set up on the earth from the days of Adam to the present time, whenever there has been a righteous man on earth unto whom God revealed His word and gave power and authority to administer in His name. And where there is a priest of God— a minister who has power and authority from God to administer in the ordinances of the gospel and officiate in the priesthood of God—there is the kingdom of God. And, in consequence of rejecting the Gospel of Jesus Christ and the Prophets whom God hath sent, the judgments of God have rested upon people, cities, and nations, in various ages of the world, which was the case with the cities of Sodom and Gomorrah, that were destroyed for rejecting the Prophets.

Where the Kingdom of God is Not, There is No Salvation

Now I will give my testimony. I care not for man. I speak boldly and faithfully and with authority. How is it with the kingdom of God? Where did the kingdom of God begin? Where there is no kingdom of God there is no salvation. What constitutes the kingdom of God? Where there is a prophet, a priest, or a righteous man unto whom God gives His oracles, there is the kingdom of God; and where the oracles of God are not, there the kingdom of God is not.

In these remarks, I have no allusion to the kingdoms of the earth. We will keep the laws of the land; we do not speak against them; we never have, and we can hardly make mention of the state of Missouri, of our persecutions there, but what the cry goes forth that we are guilty of larceny, burglary, arson, treason, murder, &c., &c., which is false. We speak of the kingdom of God on the earth, not the kingdoms of men.

Need of Revelation

The plea of many in this day is, that we have no right to receive revelations; but if we do not get revelations, we do not have the oracles of God; and if they have not the oracles of God, they are not the people of God. But say you, What will become of the world, or the various professors of religion who do not believe in revelation and the oracles of God as continued to His Church in all ages of the world, when He has a people on earth? I tell you, in the name of Jesus Christ, they will be damned; and when you get into the eternal world, you will find it will be so, they cannot escape the damnation of hell.

John Held Keys of Aaronic Priesthood

As touching the Gospel and baptism that John preached, I would say that John came preaching the Gospel for the remission of sins; he had his authority from God, and the oracles of God were with him, and the kingdom of God for a season seemed to rest with John alone. The Lord promised Zacharias that he should have a son who was a descendant of Aaron, the Lord having promised that the priesthood should continue with Aaron and his seed throughout their generations. Let no man take this honor upon himself, except he be called of God, as was Aaron; and Aaron received his call by revelation. An angel of God also appeared unto Zacharias while in the Temple, and told him that he should have a son, whose name should be John, and he should be filled with the Holy

Ghost. Zacharias was a priest of God, and officiating in the Temple, and John was a priest after his father, and held the keys of the Aaronic Priesthood, and was called of God to preach the Gospel of the kingdom of God. The Jews, as a nation, having departed from the law of God and the Gospel of the Lord, prepared the way for transferring it to the Gentiles.

But, says one, the kingdom of God could not be set up in the days of John, for John said the kingdom was at hand. But I would ask if it could be any nearer to them than to be in the hands of John. The people need not wait for the days of Pentecost to find the kingdom of God, for John had it with him, and he came forth from the wilderness crying out, "Repent ye, for the kingdom of heaven is nigh at hand," as much as to say, "Out here I have got the kingdom of God, and you can get it, and I am coming after you; and if you don't receive it, you will be damned;" and the scriptures represent that all Jerusalem went out unto John's baptism. There was a legal administrator, and those that were baptized were subjects for a king; and also the laws and oracles of God were there; therefore the kingdom of God was there; for no man could have better authority to administer than John; and our Savior submitted to that authority Himself, by being baptized by John; therefore the kingdom of God was set up on the earth, even in the days of John.

The Kingdom and Its Fruits

There is a difference between the kingdom of God and the fruits and blessings that flow from the kingdom; because there were more miracles, gifts, visions, healings, tongues, &c., in the days of Jesus Christ and His apostles, and on the day of Pentecost, than under John's administration, it does not prove by any means that John had not the kingdom of God, any more than it would that a woman had not a milkpan because she had not a pan of milk, for while the pan might be compared to the kingdom, the milk might be compared to the blessings of the kingdom.

John was a priest after the order of Aaron, and had the keys of that priesthood, and came forth preaching repentance and baptism for the remission of sins, but at the same time cries out, "There cometh one mightier than I after me, the latchet of whose shoes I am not worthy to stoop down and unloose," and Christ came according to the words of John, and He was greater than John, because He held the keys of the Melchizedek Priesthood and kingdom of God, and had before revealed the priesthood of Moses, yet Christ was baptized by John to fulfill all righteousness; and Jesus in His teaching says, "Upon this rock I will build my Church, and the gates of hell shall not prevail against it." What rock? Revelation.

Again he says, "Except a man be born of water and of the Spirit, he cannot enter into the kingdom of God;" and, "heaven and earth shall pass away, but my words shall not pass away." If a man is born of water and of the Spirit, he can get into the kingdom of God. It is evident the kingdom of God was on the earth, and John prepared subjects for the kingdom, by preaching the Gospel to them and baptizing them, and he prepared the way before the Savior, or came as a forerunner, and prepared subjects for the preaching of Christ; and Christ preached through Jerusalem on the same ground where John had preached; and when the apostles were raised up, they worked in Jerusalem, and Jesus commanded them to tarry there until they were endowed with power from on high. Had they not work to do in Jerusalem? They did work, and prepared a people for the Pentecost. The kingdom of God was with them before the day of Pentecost, as well as afterwards; and it was also with John, and he preached the same Gospel and baptism that Jesus and the apostles preached after him. The endowment was to prepare the disciples for their missions unto the world.

Divine Authority Necessary to Make Ordinances Valid

Whenever men can find out the will of God and find an administrator legally authorized from God, there is the kingdom of God; but where these are not, the kingdom of God is not. All the ordinances, systems, and administrations on the earth are of no use to the children of men, unless they are ordained and authorized of God; for nothing will save a man but a legal administrator; for none others will be acknowledged either by God or angels.

I know what I say; I understand my mission and business. God Almighty is my shield; and what can man do if God is my friend? I shall not be sacrificed until my time comes; then I shall be offered freely. All flesh is as grass, and a governor is no better than other men; when he dies he is but a bag of dust. I thank God for preserving me from my enemies; I have no enemies but for the truth's sake. I have no desire but to do all men good. I feel to pray for all men. We don't ask any people to throw away any good they have got; we only ask them to come and get more. What if all the world should embrace this Gospel? They would then see eye to eye, and the blessings of God would be poured out upon the people, which is the desire of my whole soul. Amen. (Jan. 22, 1843.) D. H. C. 5:256-259.

Politics

To the Editor of The Wasp:—

Dear Sir: I have, of late, had repeated solicitations to have something to do in relation to the political farce about dividing the county; but as my feelings revolt at the idea of having anything to do with politics, I have declined in every instance in having anything to do on the subject. I think it would be well for politicians to regulate their own affairs. I wish to be let alone, that I may attend strictly to the spiritual welfare of the church.

Please insert the above and oblige.

JOSEPH SMITH.

Nauvoo, Jan. 23, 1843.—The Wasp, Jan. 28, 1843, page 3.

The Greatness and Mission of John the Baptist

The question arose from the saying of Jesus—"Among those that are born of women there is not a greater prophet than John the Baptist; but he that is least in the kingdom of God is greater than he." How is it that John was considered one of the greatest prophets? His miracles could not have constituted his greatness.

First. He was entrusted with a divine mission of preparing the way before the face of the Lord. Whoever had such a trust committed to him before or since? No man.

Secondly. He was entrusted with the important mission, and it was required at his hands, to baptize the Son of Man. Whoever had the honor of doing that? Whoever had so great a privilege and glory? Whoever led the Son of God into the waters of baptism, and had the privilege of beholding the Holy Ghost descend in the form of a dove, or rather in the *sign* of the dove, in witness of that administration? The sign of the dove was instituted before the creation of the world, a witness for the Holy Ghost, and the devil cannot come in the sign of a dove. The Holy Ghost is a personage, and is in the form of a personage. It does not confine itself to the *form* of the dove, but in *sign* of the dove. The Holy Ghost cannot be transformed into a dove; but the sign of a dove was given to John to signify the truth of the deed, as the dove is an emblem or token of truth and innocence.

Thirdly. John, at that time, was the only legal administrator in the affairs of the kingdom there was then on the earth, and holding the keys of power. The Jews had to obey his instructions or be damned, by their own law; and Christ Himself fulfilled all righteousness in becoming obedient to the law which he had given to Moses on the mount, and thereby magnified it and made it honorable, instead of destroying it. The son of Zacharias wrested the keys, the kingdom, the power, the glory from the Jews, by the holy anointing and decree of heaven, and these three reasons constitute him the greatest prophet born of a woman.

Christ Considered Least in the Kingdom by Jews

Second question:—How was the least in the kingdom of heaven greater than he?

In reply I asked—Whom did Jesus have reference to as being the least? Jesus was looked upon as having the least claim in God's kingdom, and [seemingly] was least entitled to their credulity as a prophet; as though He had said—"He that is considered the least among you is greater than John—that is I myself."

The Parables of Jesus and the Interpretation of the Scriptures

In reference to the prodigal son, I said it was a subject I had never dwelt upon; that it was understood by many to be one of the intricate subjects of the scriptures; and even the Elders of this Church have preached largely upon it, without having any rule of interpretation. What is the rule of interpretation? Just no interpretation at all. Understand it precisely as it reads. I have a key by which I understand the scriptures. I enquire, what was the question which drew out the answer, or caused Jesus to utter the parable? It is not national; it does not refer to Abraham, Israel or the Gentiles, in a national capacity, as some suppose. To ascertain its meaning, we must dig up the root and ascertain what it was that drew the saying out of Jesus.

While Jesus was teaching the people, all the publicans and sinners drew near to hear Him; "and the Pharisees and scribes murmured, saying: This man receiveth sinners, and eateth with them." This is the keyword which unlocks the parable of the prodigal son. It was given to answer the murmurings and questions of the Sadducees and Pharisees, who were querying, finding fault, and saying, "How is it that this man as great as He pretends to be, eats with publicans and sinners?" Jesus was not put to it so, but He could have found something to illustrate His subject, if He had designed it for a nation or nations; but He did not. It was for men in an individual capacity; and all straining on this point is a bubble. "This man receiveth sinners and eateth with them."

And he spake this parable unto them—"What man of you, having an hundred sheep, if he lose one of them doth not leave the ninety-and-nine in the wilderness, and go after that which is lost, until he find it? And when he hath found it, he layeth it on his shoulders, rejoicing. And when he cometh home, he calleth together his friends and neighbors, saying unto them, Rejoice with me; for I have found my sheep which was lost. I say unto you, that likewise joy shall be in heaven over one sinner that repenteth, more than over ninety-and-nine just persons which need no repentance." The hundred sheep represent one hundred Sadducees and Pharisees, as though Jesus had said, "If you Sadducees and Pharisees are in the sheepfold, I have no mission for you; I am sent to look up sheep that are lost; and when I have found them, I will back them up and make joy in heaven." This represents hunting after a few individuals, or one poor publican, which the Pharisees and Sadducees despised.

He also gave them the parable of the woman and her ten pieces of silver, and how she lost one, and searching diligently, found it again, which gave more joy among the friends and neighbors than the nine which were not lost; like I say unto you, there is joy in the presence of the angels of God over one sinner that repenteth, more than over ninety-and-nine just persons that are so righteous; they will be damned anyhow; you cannot save them. (Jan. 29, 1843.) D. H. C. 5:260-262.

Scriptural Correction

"The Spirit maketh intercession for us with groanings which cannot be uttered." It would be better thus: "The Spirit maketh intercession for us with striving which cannot be expressed." (Feb. 2, 1843.) D. H. C. 5:264.

The Calling of a Prophet

Wednesday, Feb. 8.—This morning I read German and visited with a brother and sister from Michigan, who thought that "a prophet is always a prophet;" but I told them that a prophet was a prophet only when he was acting as such.— D. H. C. 5:265.

The Sign Seeker

When I was preaching in Philadelphia, a Quaker called out for a sign. I told him to be still. After the sermon, he again asked for a sign. I told the congregation the man was an adulterer; that a wicked and adulterous generation seeketh after a sign; and that the Lord had said to me in a revelation, that any man who wanted a sign was an adulterous person. "It is true," cried one, "for I caught him in the very act," which the man afterwards confessed when he was baptized. (Feb. 9, 1843.) D. H. C. 5:268.

Views of the Prophet on Constitutional Powers

Situated as we are, with a flood of immigration constantly pouring in upon us, I consider that it is not only prudential, but absolutely necessary to protect the inhabitants of this city from being imposed upon by a spurious currency. Many of our eastern and old country friends are altogether unacquainted with the situation of the banks in this region of country; and as they generally bring specie with them, they are perpetually in danger of being gulled by speculators. Besides there is so much uncertainty in the solvency of the best of banks, that I think it much safer to go upon the hard money system altogether. I have examined the Constitution upon this subject and find my doubts removed. The Constitution is not a law, but it empowers the people to make laws. For instance, the Constitution governs the land of Iowa, but it is not a law for the people. The Constitution tells us what shall not be a lawful tender. Art. I, Section 10 declares that nothing else except gold and silver shall be lawful tender, this not saying that gold and silver shall be lawful tender. It only provides that the states may make a law to make gold and silver lawful tender. I know of no state in the Union that has passed such a law; and I am sure that Illinois has not. The legislature has ceded up to us the privilege of enacting such laws as are not inconsistent with the Constitution of the United States and the state of Illinois; and we stand in the same relation to the state as the state does to the Union. The clause referred to in the Constitution is for the legislature—it is not a law for the people. The different states, and even Congress itself, have passed many laws diametrically contrary to the Constitution of the United States.

The state of Illinois has passed a stay law making property a lawful tender for the payment of debts; and if we have no law on the subject we must be governed by it. Shall we be such fools as to be governed by its laws, which are unconstitutional? No! We will make a law for gold and silver; and then the state law ceases and we can collect our debts. Powers not delegated to the states or reserved from the states are constitutional. The Constitution acknowledges that the people have all power not reserved to itself. I am a lawyer; I am a big lawyer and comprehend heaven, earth and hell, to bring forth knowledge that shall cover up all lawyers, doctors and other big bodies. This is the doctrine of the Constitution, so help me God. The Constitution is not law to us, but it makes provision for us whereby we can make laws. Where it provides that no one shall be hindered from worshiping God according to his own conscience, is a law. No legislature can enact a law to prohibit it. The Constitution provides to regulate bodies of men and not individuals. (Feb. 25, 1843.) D. H. C. 5:289-290.

The "Sign" of the Son of Man

Sir:—Among the many signs of the times and other strange things which are continually agitating the minds of men, I notice a small speculation in the *Chicago Express,* upon the certificate of one Hyrum Redding, of Ogle county, Illinois, stating that he has seen the sign of the Son of Man as foretold in the 24th chapter of Matthew.

The slanderous allusion of a "seraglio" like the Grand Turk, which the editor applies to me, he may take to himself, for, "out of the abundance of the heart the mouth speaketh." Every honest man who has visited the city of Nauvoo since it existed, can bear record of better things, and place me in the front ranks of those who are known to do good for the sake of goodness, and show all liars, hypocrites and abominable creatures that, while vice sinks them down to darkness and woe, virtue exalts me and the Saints to light and immortality.

The editor, as well as some others, "thinks that Joe Smith has his match at last," because Mr. Redding thinks that he has seen the sign of the Son of Man. But I shall use my right, and declare that, notwithstanding Mr. Redding may have seen a wonderful appearance in the clouds one morning about sunrise (which is nothing very uncommon in the winter season) he has not seen the sign of the Son of Man, as foretold by Jesus; neither has any man, nor will any man, until after the sun shall have been darkened and the moon bathed in blood; for the Lord hath not shown me any such sign; and as the prophet saith, so it must be—"Surely the Lord God will do nothing, but He revealeth His secret unto His servants the prophets." (See Amos 3:7.)   Therefore, hear this, O earth: The Lord will not come to reign over the righteous, in this world, in 1843, nor until everything for the Bridegroom is ready,

Yours respectfully,
JOSEPH SMITH.

(Feb. 28, 1843.)   D. H. C. 5:290-291.

Battle of Gog and Magog

The battle of Gog and Magog will be after the millennium. The remnant of all the nations that fight against Jerusalem were commanded to go up to Jerusalem to worship in the millennium. (March 4, 1843.)   D. H. C. 5:298.

Giving Blessings a Tax on Strength

Elder Jedediah M. Grant enquired of me the cause of my turning pale and losing strength last night while blessing children.   I told him that I saw that Lucifer would exert his influence to destroy the children that I was blessing, and I strove with all the faith and spirit that I had to seal upon them a blessing that would secure their lives upon the earth; and so much virtue went out of me into the children, that I became weak, from which I have not yet recovered; and I referred to the case of the woman touching the hem of the garment of Jesus. (Luke, 8th chapter.)   The virtue here referred to is the spirit of life; and a man who exercises great faith in administering to the sick, blessing little children, or confirming, is liable to become weakened. (March 14, 1843.) D. H. C. 5:303.

SECTION SIX
1843 – 1844

SECTION SIX

---◆---

A Prophecy

I prophesied, in the name of the Lord Jesus Christ, that Orrin Porter Rockwell would get away honorably from the Missourians. (March 15, 1843.) D. H. C. 5:305.

Proclamation

To the Citizens of Nauvoo:

Whereas it appears, by the republication of the foregoing proceedings and declaration, that I have not altered my views on the subject of stealing: And

Whereas it is reported that there now exists a band of desperadoes, bound by oaths of secrecy, under severe penalties in case any member of the combination divulges their plans of stealing and conveying properties from station to station, up and down the Mississippi and other routes: And

Whereas it is reported that the fear of the execution of the pains and penalties of their secret oath on their persons prevents some members of said secret association (who have, through falsehood and deceit, been drawn into their snares) from divulging the same to the legally constituted authorities of the land:

Know ye, therefore, that I, Joseph Smith, mayor of the city of Nauvoo, will grant and insure protection against all personal mob violence to each and every citizen of this city who will freely and voluntarily come before me and truly make known the names of all such abominable characters as are engaged in said secret combination for stealing, or are accessory thereto, in any manner. And I would respectfully solicit the co-operation of all ministers of justice in this and the neighboring states to ferret out a band of thievish outlaws from our midst. Given under my hand at Nauvoo City, this 25th day of March, A.D., 1843.

JOSEPH SMITH,
Mayor of said City.

—D. H. C. 5:310.

THE PROPHET ON THE SECOND COMING OF CHRIST

Remarks at the Conference of the Church

The question has been asked, can a person not belonging to the Church bring a member before the high council for trial? I answer, No. If I had not actually got into this work and been called of God, I would back out. But I cannot back out: I have no doubt of the truth. Were I going to prophesy, I would say the end [of the world] would not come in 1844, 5, or 6, or in forty years. There are those of the rising generation who shall not taste death till Christ comes.

I was once praying earnestly upon this subject, and a voice said unto me, "My son, if thou livest until thou art eighty-five years of age, thou shalt see the face of the Son of Man." I was left to draw my own conclusions concerning this; and I took the liberty to conclude that if I did live to that time, He would make His appearance. But I do not say whether He will make His appearance or I shall go where He is. I prophesy in the name of the Lord God, and let it be written—the Son of Man will not come in the clouds of heaven till I am eighty-five years old. Then read the 14th chapter of Revelation, 6th and 7th verses—"And I saw another angel fly in the midst of heaven, having the everlasting gospel to preach unto them that dwell on the earth, and to every nation, and kindred, and tongue, and people, saying with a loud voice, Fear God and give glory to Him, for the hour of His judgment is come." And Hosea, 6th chapter, After two days, etc.,—2,520 years; which brings it to 1890. The coming of the Son of Man never will be—never can be till the judgments spoken of for this hour are poured out: which judgments are commenced. Paul says, "Ye are the children of the light, and not of the darkness, that that day should overtake you as a thief in the night." It is not the design of the Almighty to come upon the earth and crush it and grind it to powder, but he will reveal it to His servants the prophets.

Judah must return, Jerusalem must be rebuilt, and the temple, and water come out from under the temple, and the waters of the Dead Sea be healed. It will take some time to rebuild the walls of the city and the temple, &c.; and all this must be done before the Son of Man will make His appearance. There will be wars and rumors of wars, signs in the heavens above and on the earth beneath, the sun turned into darkness and the moon to blood, earthquakes in divers places, the seas heaving beyond their bounds; then will appear one grand sign of the Son of Man in heaven. But what will the world do? They will say it is a planet, a comet, etc. But the Son of man will come as the sign of the coming of the Son of Man, which will be as the light of the morning cometh out of the east. (April 6, 1843.) D. H. C. 5:336-337.

On Leaving Meetings Near the Close

President Joseph Smith stated that the business of the conference had closed, and the remainder would be devoted to instruction. It is an insult to a meeting for persons to leave just before its close. If they must go out, let them go half an hour before. No gentlemen will go out of a meeting just at closing. (April 7, 1843.) D. H. C. 5:338-339.

THE PROPHET EXPOUNDS THE SCRIPTURES

The Beasts of John's Revelation

The subject I intend to speak upon this morning is one that I have seldom touched upon since I commenced my ministry in the Church. It is a subject of great speculation, as well amongst the elders of this Church, as among the divines of the day: it is in relation to the beasts spoken of by John the Revelator. I have seldom spoken from the revelations; but as my subject is a constant source of speculation amongst the elders, causing a division of sentiment and opinion in relation to it, I now do it in order that division and differences of opinion may be done away with, and not that correct knowledge on the subject is so much needed at the present time.

It is not very essential for the elders to have knowledge in relation to the meaning of beasts, and heads and horns, and other figures made use of in the revelations; still, it may be necessary, to prevent contention and division and do away with suspense. If we get puffed up by thinking that we have much knowledge, we are apt to get a contentious spirit, and correct knowledge is necessary to cast out that spirit.

The Punishment of Suspense

The evil of being puffed up with correct (though useless) knowledge is not so great as the evil of contention. Knowledge does away with darkness, suspense and doubt; for these cannot exist where knowledge is.

There is no pain so awful as that of suspense. This is the punishment of the wicked; their doubt, anxiety and suspense cause weeping, wailing and gnashing of teeth.

In knowledge there is power. God has more power than all other beings, because he has greater knowledge; and hence he knows how to subject all other beings to Him. He has power over all.

I will endeavor to instruct you in relation to the meaning of the beasts and figures spoken of. I should not have called up the subject had it not been for this circumstance. Elder Pelatiah Brown, one of the wisest old heads we have among us, and whom I now see before me, has been preaching concerning the beast which was full of eyes before and behind; and for this he was hauled up for trial before the High Council.

* * * *

The High Council undertook to censure and correct Elder Brown, because of his teachings in relation to the beasts. Whether they actually corrected him or not, I am a little doubtful, but don't care. Father Brown came to me to know what he should do about it. The subject particularly referred to was the four beasts and four-and-twenty elders mentioned in Rev. 5:8—"And when he had taken the book, the four beasts and four-and-twenty elders fell down before the Lamb, having every one of them harps, and golden vials full of odors, which are the prayers of saints."

Father Brown has been to work and confounded all Christendom by making out that the four beasts represented the different kingdoms of God on the earth. The wise men of the day could not do anything with him, and why should we find fault? Anything to whip sectarianism, to put down priestcraft, and bring the human family to a knowledge of the truth. A club is better than no weapon for a poor man to fight with.

Father Brown did whip sectarianism, and so far so good; but I could not help laughing at the idea of God making use of the figure of a beast to represent His kingdom on the earth, consisting of men, when He could as well have used a far more noble and consistent figure. What! the Lord made use of the figure of a creature of the brute creation to represent that which is much more noble, glorious, and important—the glories and majesty of His kingdom? By taking a lesser figure to repre-sent a greater, you missed it that time, old gentleman; but the sectarians did not know enough to detect you.

When God made use of the figure of a beast in visions to the prophets He did it to represent those kingdoms which had degenerated and become corrupt, savage and beast-like in their dispositions, even the degenerate kingdoms of the wicked world; but He never made use of the figure of a beast nor any of the brute kind to represent His kingdom.

Daniel's Vision of Beasts

Daniel says (ch. 7, v. 16) when he saw the vision of the four beasts, "I came near unto one of them that stood by, and asked him the truth of all this," the angel interpreted the vision to Daniel; but we find, by the interpretation that the figures of beasts had no allusion to the kingdom of God. You there see that the beasts are spoken of to represent the kingdoms of the world, the inhabitants whereof were beastly and abominable characters; they were murderers, corrupt, carnivorous, and brutal in their dispositions. The lion, the bear, the leopard, and the ten-horned beast represented the kingdoms of the world, says Daniel; for I refer to the prophets to qualify my observations which I make, so that the young elders who know so much, may not rise up like a flock of hornets and sting me. I want to keep out of such a wasp-nest.

John's Vision of Futurity

There is a grand difference and distinction between the visions and figures spoken of by the ancient prophets, and those spoken of in the revelations of John. The things which John saw had no allusion to the scenes of the days of Adam, Enoch, Abraham or Jesus, only so far as is plainly represented by John, and clearly set forth by him. John saw that only which was lying in futurity and which was shortly to come to pass. See Rev. i:1-3, which is a key to the whole subject: "The reve-lation of Jesus Christ, which God gave unto Him, to show unto his servants things which must shortly come to pass; and He sent and signified it by His angel unto His servant John: who bare record of the word of God, and of the testimony of Jesus Christ, and of all things that he saw. Blessed is he that readeth, and they that hear the words of his prophecy and keep those

things that are written therein: for the time is at hand." Also
Rev. iv:1. "After this I looked, and, behold, a door was opened
in heaven; and the first voice which I heard was as it were of
a trumpet talking with me; which said, Come up hither, and I
will show thee things which must be hereafter."

The four beasts and twenty-four elders were out of every
nation; for they sang a new song, saying, "Thou art worthy
to take the book, and to open the seal thereof: for thou wast
slain, and hast redeemed us to God by thy blood out of every
kindred, and tongue, and people, and nation." (See Rev. 5:9.)
It would be great stuffing to crowd all nations into four beasts
and twenty-four elders.

Now, I make this declaration, that those things which
John saw in heaven had no allusion to anything that had been
on the earth previous to that time, because they were the
representation of "things which must shortly come to pass,"
and not of what has already transpired. John saw beasts that
had to do with things on the earth, but not in past ages. The
beasts which John saw had to devour the inhabitants of the
earth in days to come. "And I saw when the Lamb opened one of
the seals; and I heard, as it were the noise of thunder, one of
the four beasts saying, Come and see. And I saw, and beheld
a white horse: and he that sat on him had a bow; and a crown
was given unto him: and he went forth conquering, and to
conquer. And when he had opened the second seal, I heard
the second beast say, Come and see. And there went out
another horse that was red: and power was given to him that
sat thereon to take peace from the earth, and that they should
kill one another; and there was given unto him a great sword."
(Rev. 6:1, 2, 3, 4.) The book of Revelation is one of the plainest books God ever caused to be written.

The revelations do not give us to understand anything of
the past in relation to the kingdom of God. What John saw
and speaks of were things which he saw in heaven; those which
Daniel saw were on and pertaining to the earth.

Exceptions to Bible Translations

I am now going to take exceptions to the present translation of the Bible in relation to these matters. Our latitude and
longitude can be determined in the original Hebrew with far
greater accuracy than in the English version. There is a

grand distinction between the actual meaning of the prophets and the present translation. The prophets do not declare that they saw a beast or beasts, but that they saw the *image* or *figure* of a beast. Daniel did not see an actual bear or a lion, but the images or figures of those beasts. The translation should have been rendered "image" instead of "beast," in every instance where beasts are mentioned by the prophets. But John saw the actual beast in heaven, showing to John that beasts did actually exist there, and not to represent figures of things on the earth. When the prophets speak of seeing beasts in their visions, they mean that they saw the images, they being types to represent certain things. At the same time they received the interpretation as to what those images or types were designed to represent.

I make this broad declaration, that whenever God gives a vision of an image, or beast, or figure of any kind, He always holds Himself responsible to give a revelation or interpretation of the meaning thereof, otherwise we are not responsible or accountable for our belief in it. Don't be afraid of being damned for not knowing the meaning of a vision or figure, if God has not given a revelation or interpretation of the subject.

John saw curious looking beasts in heaven; he saw every creature that was in heaven,—all the beasts, fowls and fish in heaven,—actually there, giving glory to God. How do you prove it? (See Rev. 5:13.) "And every creature which is in heaven, and on the earth, and under the earth, and such as are in the sea, and all that are in them, heard I saying, Blessing, and honor, and glory, and power, be unto Him that sitteth upon the throne, and unto the Lamb for ever and ever."

Varied Creatures in Heaven

I suppose John saw beings there of a thousand forms, that had been saved from ten thousand times ten thousand earths like this,—strange beasts of which we have no conception: all might be seen in heaven. The grand secret was to show John what there was in heaven. John learned that God glorified Himself by saving all that His hands had made, whether beasts, fowls, fishes or men; and He will glorify Himself with them.

Says one, "I cannot believe in the salvation of beasts." Any man who would tell you that this could not be, would tell you that the revelations are not true. John heard the words of the beasts giving glory to God, and understood them. God who made the beasts could understand every language spoken by them. The four beasts were four of the most noble animals that had filled the measure of their creation, and had been saved from other worlds, because they were perfect: they were like angels in their sphere. We are not told where they came from, and I do not know; but they were seen and heard by John praising and glorifying God.

The popular religionists of the day tell us, forsooth, that the beasts spoken of in the Revelation represent kingdoms. Very well, on the same principle we can say that the twenty-four elders spoken of represent beasts; for they are all spoken of at the same time, and are represented as all uniting in the same acts of praise and devotion.

This learned interpretation is all as flat as a pancake! "What do you use such vulgar expressions for, being a prophet?" Because the old women understand it—they make pancakes. Deacon Homespun said the earth was flat as a pancake, and ridiculed the science which proved to the contrary. The whole argument is flat, and I don't know of anything better to represent it. The world is full of technicalities and misrepresentation, which I calculate to overthrow, and speak of things as they actually exist.

Again, there is no revelation to prove that things do not exist in heaven as I have set forth, nor yet to show that the beasts meant anything but beasts; and we never can comprehend the things of God and of heaven, but by revelation. We may spiritualize and express opinions to all eternity; but that is no authority.

Elders to Preach Repentance and Let Mysteries Alone

Oh, ye elders of Israel, hearken to my voice; and when you are sent into the world to preach, tell those things you are sent to tell; preach and cry aloud, "Repent ye, for the kingdom of heaven is at hand; repent and believe the Gospel." Declare the first principles, and let mysteries alone, lest ye be overthrown. Never meddle with the visions of beasts and subjects you do not understand. Elder Brown, when you go to Palmyra, say nothing about the four beasts, but preach those things the Lord has told you to preach about—repentance and baptism for the remission of sins.

He then read Rev. 13:1-8. John says, "And I saw one of his heads as it were wounded to death; and his deadly wound was healed; and all the world wondered after the beast." Some spiritualizers say the beast that received the wound was Nebuchadnezzar, some Constantine, some Mohammed, and others the Roman Catholic Church; but we will look at what John saw in relation to this beast. Now for the wasp's nest. The translators have used the term "dragon" for devil. Now it was a beast that John saw in heaven, and he was then speaking of "things which must shortly come to pass;" and consequently the beast that John saw could not be Nebuchadnezzar. The beast John saw was an actual beast, and an actual intelligent being gives him his power, and his seat, and great authority. It was not to represent a beast in heaven: it was an angel in heaven who has power in the last days to do a work.

"All the world wondered after the beast," Nebuchadnezzar and Constantine the Great not excepted. And if the beast was all the world, how could the world wonder after the beast? It must have been a wonderful beast to cause all human beings to wonder after it; and I will venture to say that when God allows the old devil to give power to the beast to destroy the inhabitants of the earth, all will wonder. Verse 4 reads, "And they worshiped the dragon which gave power unto the beast; and they worshiped the beast, saying, Who is like unto the beast? Who is able to make war with him?"

Some say it means the kingdom of the world. One thing is sure, it does not mean the kingdom of the Saints. Suppose we admit that it means the kingdoms of the world, what propriety would there be in saying, Who is able to make war with my great big self? If these spiritualized interpretations are true, the book contradicts itself in almost every verse. But they are not true.

There is a mistranslation of the word dragon in the second verse. The original word signifies the devil, and not dragon, as translated. In chapter 12, verse 9, it reads, "That old serpent, called the devil," and it ought to be translated devil in this case, and not dragon. It is sometimes translated Apollyon. Everything that we have not a key-word to, we will take it as it reads. The beasts which John saw and speaks of being in heaven, were actually living in heaven, and were actually to have power given to them over the inhabitants of the earth, precisely according to the plain reading of the revelations. I give this as a key to the elders of Israel. The independent beast is a beast that dwells in heaven, abstract [apart] from the human family. The beast that rose up out of the sea should be translated the image of a beast, as I have referred to it in Daniel's vision.

I have said more than I ever did before, except once at Ramus, and then up starts the little fellow (Charles Thompson) and stuffed me like a cock-turkey with the prophecies of Daniel, and crammed it down my throat with his finger. (April 8, 1843.) (D. H. C. 5:339-345.

REMARKS OF THE PROPHET ON THE DEATH OF LORENZO D. BARNES

The Resurrection

Almost all who have fallen in these last days in the Church have fallen in a strange land. This is a strange land to those who have come from a distance. We should cultivate sympathy for the afflicted among us. If there is a place on earth where men should cultivate the spirit and pour in the oil and wine in the bosoms of the afflicted, it is in this place; and this spirit is manifest here; and although a stranger and afflicted when he arrives, he finds a brother and a friend ready to administer to his necessities.

I would esteem it one of the greatest blessings, if I am to be afflicted in this world, to have my lot cast where I can find brothers and friends all around me. But this is not the thing I referred to: it is to have the privilege of having our dead buried on the land where God has appointed to gather His Saints together, and where there will be none but Saints, where they may have the privilege of laying their bodies where the Son of Man will make His appearance, and where they may hear the sound of the trump that shall call them forth to behold Him, that in the morn of the resurrection they may come forth in a body, and come up out of their graves and strike hands immediately in eternal glory and felicity, rather than be scattered thousands of miles apart. There is something good and sacred to me in this thing. The place where a man is buried is sacred to me. This subject is made mention of in the Book of Mormon and other scriptures. Even to the aborigines of this land, the burying places of their fathers are more sacred than anything else.

When I heard of the death of our beloved Brother Barnes, it would not have affected me so much, if I had the opportunity of burying him in the land of Zion.

I believe those who have buried their friends here, their condition is enviable. Look at Jacob and Joseph in Egypt, how they required their friends to bury them in the tomb of their fathers. See the expense which attended the embalming and the going up of the great company to the burial.

It has always been considered a great calamity not to obtain an honorable burial: and one of the greatest curses the ancient prophets could put on any man, was that he should go without a burial.

I have said, Father, I desire to die here among the Saints. But if this is not Thy will, and I go hence and die, wilt Thou find some kind friend to bring my body back, and gather my friends who have fallen in foreign lands, and bring them up hither, that we may all lie together.

I will tell you what I want. If tomorrow I shall be called to lie in yonder tomb, in the morning of the resurrection let me strike hands with my father, and cry, "My father," and he will say, "My son, my son," as soon as the rock rends and before we come out of our graves.

And may we contemplate these things so? Yes, if we learn how to live and how to die. When we lie down we contemplate how we may rise in the morning; and it is pleasing for friends to lie down together, locked in the arms of love, to sleep and wake in each other's embrace and renew their conversation.

The Righteous to Have Joy in the Resurrection

Would you think it strange if I relate what I have seen in vision in relation to this interesting theme? Those who have died in Jesus Christ may expect to enter into all that fruition of joy when they come forth, which they possessed or anticipated here.

So plain was the vision, that I actually saw men, before they had ascended from the tomb, as though they were getting up slowly. They took each other by the hand and said to each other, "My father, my son, my mother, my daughter, my brother, my sister." And when the voice calls for the dead to arise, suppose I am laid by the side of my father, what would be the first joy of my heart? To meet my father, my mother, my brother, my sister; and when they are by my side, I embrace them and they me.

It is my meditation all the day, and more than my meat and drink, to know how I shall make the Saints of God comprehend the visions that roll like an overflowing surge before my mind.

* * *

All your losses will be made up to you in the resurrection, provided you continue faithful. By the vision of the Almighty I have seen it.

More painful to me are the thoughts of annihilation than death. If I have no expectation of seeing my father, mother, brothers, sisters and friends again, my heart would burst in a moment, and I should go down to my grave.

The expectation of seeing my friends in the morning of the resurrection cheers my soul and makes me bear up against the evils of life. It is like their taking a long journey, and on their return we meet them with increased joy.

God has revealed His Son from the heavens and the doctrine of the resurrection also; and we have a knowledge that those we bury here God will bring up again, clothed upon and quickened by the Spirit of the great God; and what mattereth it whether we lay them down, or we lay down with them when we can keep them no longer? Let these truths sink down in our hearts, that we may even here begin to enjoy that which shall be in full hereafter.

Hosanna, hosanna, hosanna to Almighty God, that rays of light begin to burst forth upon us even now. I cannot find words in which to express myself. I am not learned, but I have as good feelings as any man.

O that I had the language of the archangel to express my feelings once to my friends! But I never expect to in this life. When others rejoice, I rejoice; when they mourn, I mourn.

To Marcellus Bates let me administer comfort. You shall soon have the company of your companion in a world of glory, and the friends of Brother Barnes and all the Saints who are mourning. This has been a warning voice to us all to be sober and diligent and lay aside mirth, vanity and folly, and to be prepared to die tomorrow.

* * *

President Joseph Smith said: "As president of this house, I

forbid any man leaving just as we are going to close the meeting. He is no gentleman who will do it. I don't care who does it, even if it were the king of England. I forbid it. (April 16, 1843.) D. H. C. 5:360-363.

Salvation Through Knowledge

It is not wisdom that we should have all knowledge at once presented before us; but that we should have a little at a time; then we can comprehend it. President Smith then read the 2nd Epistle of Peter, 1st chapter, 16th to last verses, and dwelt upon the 19th verse with some remarks.

Add to your faith knowledge, etc. The principle of knowledge is the principle of salvation. This principle can be comprehended by the faithful and diligent; and every one that does not obtain knowledge sufficient to be saved will be condemned. The principle of salvation is given us through the knowledge of Jesus Christ.

Salvation Is to Triumph over Enemies

Salvation is nothing more nor less than to triumph over all our enemies and put them under our feet. And when we have power to put all enemies under our feet in this world, and a knowledge to triumph over all evil spirits in the world to come, then we are saved, as in the case of Jesus, who was to reign until He had put all enemies under His feet, and the last enemy was death.

No Salvation Without a Tabernacle

Perhaps there are principles here that few men have thought of. No person can have this salvation except through a tabernacle.

Now, in this world, mankind are naturally selfish, ambitious and striving to excel one above another; yet some are willing to build up others as well as themselves. So in the other world there are a variety of spirits. Some seek to excel. And this was the case with Lucifer when he fell. He sought for things which were unlawful. Hence he was sent down, and it is said he drew many away with him; and the greatness of his punishment is that he shall not have a tabernacle. This is his punishment. So the devil, thinking to thwart the decree of God, by going up and down in the earth, seeking whom he may destroy—any person that he can find that will yield to him, he will bind him, and take possession of the body and reign there, glorying in it mightily, not caring that he had got merely a stolen body; and by and by some one having authority will come along and cast him out and restore the tabernacle to its rightful owner. The devil steals a tabernacle because he has not one of his own: but if he steals one, he is always liable to be turned out of doors.

Calling and Election

Now, there is some grand secret here, and keys to unlock the subject. Notwithstanding the apostle exhorts them to add to their faith, virtue, knowledge, temperance, etc., yet he exhorts them to make their calling and election sure. And though they had heard an audible voice from heaven bearing testimony that Jesus was the Son of God, yet he says we have a more sure word of prophecy, whereunto ye do well that ye take heed as unto a light shining in a dark place. Now, wherein could they have a more sure word of prophecy than to hear the voice of God saying, This is my beloved Son.

Now for the secret and grand key. Though they might hear the voice of God and know that Jesus was the Son of God, this would be no evidence that their election and calling was made sure, that they had part with Christ, and were joint heirs with Him. They then would want that more sure word of prophecy, that they were sealed in the heavens and had the promise of eternal life in the kingdom of God. Then, having this promise sealed unto them, it was an anchor to the soul, sure and steadfast. Though the thunders might roll and lightnings flash, and earthquakes bellow, and war gather thick around, yet this hope and knowledge would support the soul in every hour of trial, trouble and tribulation. Then knowledge through our Lord and Savior Jesus Christ is the grand key that unlocks the glories and mysteries of the kingdom of heaven.

Compare this principle once with Christendom at the present day, and where are they, with all their boasted religion, piety and sacredness while at the same time they are crying out against prophets, apostles, angels, revelations, prophesying and visions, etc. Why, they are just ripening for the damnation of hell. They will be damned, for they reject the most glorious principle of the Gospel of Jesus Christ and treat with disdain and trample under foot the key that unlocks the heavens and puts in our possession the glories of the celestial world. Yes, I say, such will be damned, with all their professed godliness. Then I would exhort you to go on and continue to call upon God until you make your calling and election sure for yourselves, by obtaining this more sure word of prophecy, and wait patiently for the promise until you obtain it, etc.

*   *   *

The Value of Aged Men in Counsel

The way to get along in any important matter is to gather unto yourselves wise men, experienced and aged men, to assist in council in all times of trouble. Handsome men are not apt to be wise and strong-minded men; but the strength of a strong-minded man will generally create coarse features, like the rough, strong bough of the oak. You will always discover in the first glance of a man, in the outlines of his features some--thing of his mind.

*   *   *

A man can bear a heavy burthen by practice and continuing to increase it. The inhabitants of this continent anciently were so constituted, and were so determined and persevering, either in righteousness or wickedness, that God visited them immediately either with great judgments or blessings. But the present generation, if they were going to battle, if they got any assistance from God, they would have to obtain it by faith. (May 14, 1843.) D. H. C. 5:387-390.

Meaning of Word Mormon

To the Editor of the *Times & Seasons:*

Sir:—Through the medium of your paper, I wish to correct an error among men that profess to be learned, liberal and wise; and I do it the more cheerfully, because I hope sober-thinking and sound-reasoning people will sooner listen to the voice of truth, than be led astray by the vain pretensions of the self-wise. The error I speak of, is the definition of the word "Mormon." It has been stated that this word was derived from the Greek word "mormo." This is not the case. There was no Greek or Latin upon the plates from which I, through the grace of God, translated the Book of Mormon. Let the language of that book speak for itself. On the 523d page, of the fourth edition, it reads: "And now behold we have written this record according to our knowledge in the characters, which are called among us the "Reformed Egyptian," being handed down and altered by us, according to our manner of speech; and if our plates had been sufficiently large, we should have written in Hebrew: but the Hebrew hath been altered by us, also; and if we could have written in Hebrew, behold ye would have had no imperfection in our record, but the Lord knoweth the things which we have written, and also, that none other people knoweth our language; therefore he hath prepared means for the interpretation thereof."

Here then the subject is put to silence, for "none other people knoweth our language," therefore the Lord, and not man, had to interpret, after the people were all dead. And as Paul said, "the world by wisdom know not God," so the world by speculation are destitute of revelation; and as God in his superior wisdom, has always given his Saints, wherever he had any on the earth, the same spirit, and that spirit, as John says, is the true spirit of prophecy, which is the testimony of Jesus, I may safely say that the word Mormon stands independent of the learning and wisdom of this generation.—Before I give a definition, however, to the word, let me say that the Bible in its widest sense, means good; for the Savior says according to the gospel of John, "I am the good shepherd;" and it will not be beyond the common use of terms, to say that good is among the most important in use, and though known by various names in different languages, still its meaning is the same, and is ever in opposition to "bad." We say from the Saxon, "good"; the Dane, "god"; the Goth, "goda"; the German, "gut"; the Dutch, "goed"; the Latin, "bonus"; the Greek, "kalos"; the Hebrew, "tob"; and the "Egyptian, "mon." Hence, with the addition of "more," or the contraction, "mor," we have the word "mormon"; which means, literally, "more good."

Yours,

JOSEPH SMITH.

(May 15, 1843.) T. & S. 4:194.

Remarks of the Prophet at Ramus—Importance of the Eternity of the Marriage Covenant

Except a man and his wife enter into an everlasting covenant and be married for eternity, while in this probation, by the power and authority of the Holy Priesthood, they will cease to increase when they die; that is, they will not have any children after the resurrection. But those who are married by the power and authority of the priesthood in this life, and continue without committing the sin against the Holy Ghost. will continue to increase and have children in the celestial glory. The unpardonable sin is to shed innocent blood, or be accessory thereto. All other sins will be visited with judgment in the flesh, and the spirit being delivered to the buffetings of Satan until the day of the Lord Jesus.

The way I know in whom to confide—God tells me in whom I may place confidence.

The Celestial Glory

In the celestial glory there are three heavens or degrees; and in order to obtain the highest, a man must enter into this order of the priesthood [meaning the new and everlasting covenant of marriage]; and if he does not, he cannot obtain it. He may enter into the other, but that is the end of his kingdom: he cannot have an increase." (May 16, 1843.) D. H. C. 5:391-2.

Salvation and Sure Word of Prophecy

Salvation means a man's being placed beyond the power of all his enemies.

The more sure word of prophecy means a man's knowing that he is sealed up unto eternal life by revelation and the spirit of prophecy, through the power of the holy priesthood. It is impossible for a man to be saved in ignorance.

Paul saw the third heavens, and I more. Peter penned the most sublime language of any of the apostles. (May 17, 1843.) D. H. C. 5:392.

God Breathed into Adam His Spirit

The 7th verse of 2nd chapter of Genesis ought to read— God breathed into Adam his spirit [i.e. Adam's spirit] or breath of life; but when the word "ruach" applies to Eve, it should be translated lives.

Eternal Duration of Matter

Speaking of eternal duration of matter, I said:

There is no such thing as immaterial matter. All spirit is

matter, but is more fine or pure, and can only be discerned by purer eyes. We cannot see it, but when our bodies are purified, we shall see that it is all matter. (May 17, 1843.) D. H. C. 5:392-3.

The Prophecy on the Head of Stephen A. Douglas

The following brief account of the Prophet's visit with Judge Douglas while at Carthage is from the journal of William Clayton, who was present. For the fulfilment of this prophecy the reader is referred to the comments in the *Documentary History of the Church*, 5:395-398.

Dined with Judge Stephen A. Douglas, who is presiding at court. After dinner Judge Douglas requested President Joseph to give him a history of the Missouri persecutions, which he did in a very minute manner, for about three hours. He also gave a relation of his journey to Washington City, and his application in behalf of the Saints to Mr. Van Buren, the President of the United States, for redress and Mr. Van Buren's pusillanimous reply, "Gentlemen, your cause is just, but I can do nothing for you;" and the cold, unfeeling manner in which he was treated by most of the senators and representatives in relation to the subject, Clay saying, "You had better go to Oregon," and Calhoun shaking his head solemnly, saying, "It's a nice question—a critical question, but it will not do to agitate it."

The judge listened with the greatest attention and spoke warmly in deprecation of the conduct of Governor Boggs and the authorities of Missouri, who had taken part in the extermination, and said that any people that would do as the mobs of Missouri had done ought to be brought to judgment: they ought to be punished.

President Smith, in concluding his remarks, said that if the government, which received into its coffers the money of citizens for its public lands, while its officials are rolling in luxury at the expense of its public treasury, cannot protect such citizens in their lives and property, it is an old granny anyhow; and I prophesy in the name of the Lord God of Israel, unless the United States redress the wrongs committed upon the Saints in the state of Missouri and punish the crimes committed by her officers that in a few years the government will be utterly overthrown and wasted, and there will not be so much as a potsherd left, for their wickedness in permitting the murder of men, women and children, and the wholesale plunder and extermination of thousands of her citizens to go unpunished, thereby perpetrating a foul and corroding blot upon the fair fame of this great republic, the very thought of which would have caused the high-minded and patriotic framers of the Constitution of the United States to hide their faces with shame. Judge, you will aspire to the presidency of the United States; and if ever you turn your hand against me or the Latter-day Saints, you will feel the weight of the hand of the Almighty upon you; and you will live to see and know that I have testified the truth to you; for the conversation of this day will stick to you through life.

He [Judge Douglas] appeared very friendly, and acknowledged the truth and propriety of President Smith's remarks. (May 18, 1843.) D. H. C. 5:393-394.

The Prophet's Discourse from II Peter, First Chapter— Reproof of Self-Righteousness

I do not know when I shall have the privilege of speaking in a house large enough to convene the people. I find my lungs are failing with continual preaching in the open air to large assemblies.

I do not think there have been many good men on the earth since the days of Adam; but there was one good man and his name was Jesus. Many persons think a prophet must be a great deal better than anybody else. Suppose I would condescend—yes, I will call it condescend, to be a great deal better than any of you, I would be raised up to the highest heaven; and who should I have to accompany me?

I love that man better who swears a stream as long as my arm yet deals justice to his neighbors and mercifully deals his substance to the poor, than the long, smooth-faced hypocrite.

I do not want you to think that I am very righteous, for I am not, God judges men according to the use they make of the light which He gives them.

"We have a more sure word of prophecy, whereunto you do well to take heed, as unto a light that shineth in a dark place. We were eyewitnesses of his majesty and heard the voice of his excellent glory." And what could be more sure? When He was transfigured on the mount, what could be more sure to them? Divines have been quarreling for ages about the meaning of this.

The Prophet's Characterization of Himself

I am like a huge, rough stone rolling down from a high mountain; and the only polishing I get is when some corner gets rubbed off by coming in contact with something else, striking with accelerated force against religious bigotry, priest-craft, lawyer-craft, doctor-craft, lying editors, suborned judges and jurors, and the authority of perjured executives, backed by mobs, blasphemers, licentious and corrupt men and women— all hell knocking off a corner here and a corner there. Thus I will become a smooth and polished shaft in the quiver of the Almighty, who will give me dominion over all and every one of them, when their refuge of lies shall fail, and their hiding place shall be destroyed, while these smooth-polished stones with which I come in contact become marred.

The Secrets of Peter's Writings

There are three grand secrets lying in this chapter, [II Peter i.] which no man can dig out, unless by the light of revelation, and which unlocks the whole chapter as the things that are written are only hints of things which existed in the prophet's mind, which are not written concerning eternal glory.

I am going to take up this subject by virtue of the knowl-edge of God in me, which I have received from heaven. The opinions of men, so far as I am concerned, are to me as the crackling of thorns under the pot, or the whistling of the wind. I break the ground; I lead the way like Columbus when he was invited to a banquet where he was assigned the most honorable place at the table, and served with the ceremonials which were observed towards sovereigns. A shallow courtier present, who was meanly jealous of him, abruptly asked him whether he thought that in case he had not discovered the Indies, there were not other men in Spain who would have been capable of the enterprise? Columbus made no reply, but took an egg and invited the company to make it stand on end. They all at-tempted it, but in vain; whereupon he struck it upon the table so as to break one end, and left it standing on the broken part, illustrating that when he had once shown the way to the new world nothing was easier than to follow it.

Things Unlawful to Utter

Paul ascended into the third heavens, and he could understand the three principal rounds of Jacob's ladder—the telestial, the terrestrial, and the celestial glories or kingdoms, where Paul saw and heard things which were not lawful for him to utter. I could explain a hundred fold more than I ever have of the glories of the kingdoms manifested to me in the vision, were I permitted, and were the people prepared to receive them.

The Lord deals with this people as a tender parent with a child, communicating light and intelligence and the knowledge of his ways as they can bear it. The inhabitants of the earth are asleep; they know not the day of their visitation. The Lord hath set the bow in the cloud for a sign that while it shall be seen, seed time and harvest, summer and winter shall not fail; but when it shall disappear, woe to that generation, for behold the end cometh quickly.

Calling and Election to Be Made Sure

Contend earnestly for the like precious faith with the Apostle Peter, "and add to your faith virtue," knowledge, temperance, patience, godliness, brotherly kindness, charity; "for if these things be in you, and abound, they make you that ye shall neither be barren nor unfruitful in the knowledge of our Lord Jesus Christ." Another point, after having all these qualifications, he lays this injunction upon the people "to make your calling and election sure." He is emphatic upon this subject—after adding all this virtue, knowledge, etc., "Make your calling and election sure." What is the secret—the starting point? "According as His divine power hath given unto us all things that pertain unto life and godliness." How did he obtain all things? Through the knowledge of Him who hath called him. There could not anything be given, pertaining to life and godliness, without knowledge. Woe! woe! woe to Christendom!—especially the divines and priests if this be true.

Salvation is for a man to be saved from all his enemies; for until a man can triumph over death, he is not saved. A knowledge of the priesthood alone will do this.

The Devil's Punishment

The spirits in the eternal world are like the spirits in this world. When those have come into this world and received

tabernacles, then died and again have risen and received glorified bodies, they will have an ascendency over the spirits who
have received no bodies, or kept not their first estate, like the
devil. The punishment of the devil was that he should not have
a habitation like men. The devil's retaliation is, he comes into
this world, binds up men's bodies, and occupies them himself.
When the authorities come along, they eject him from a stolen
habitation.

The design of the great God in sending us into this world,
and organizing us to prepare us for the eternal worlds, I shall
keep in my own bosom at present.

We have no claim in our eternal compact, in relation to
eternal things, unless our actions and contracts and all things
tend to this. But after all this, you have got to make your
calling and election sure. If this injunction would lie largely
on those to whom it was spoken, how much more those of the
present generation!

1st key: Knowledge is the power of salvation. 2nd key:
Make your calling and election sure. 3rd key: It is one thing
to be on the mount and hear the excellent voice, etc., and
another to hear the voice declare to you, You have a part and
lot in that kingdom. (May 21, 1843.) D. H. C. 5:401-403.

The Prophet on Forming Temperance Societies

Dear Brother:—In answer to yours of May 4th, concerning the Latter-day Saints forming a temperance society,
we would say, as Paul said—"Be not unequally yoked with
unbelievers, but contend for the faith once delivered to the
Saints"; and as Peter advises, so say we,

"Add to your knowledge, temperance." As Paul said he
had to become all things to all men, that he might thereby save
some, so must the elders of the last days do; and, being sent
out to preach the Gospel and warn the world of the judgments
to come, we are sure, when they teach as directed by the Spirit,
according to the revelations of Jesus Christ, that they will
preach the truth and prosper without complaint. Thus we have
no new commandment to give, but admonish elders and members
to live by every word that proceedeth forth from the mouth
of God, lest they come short of the glory that is reserved for
the faithful. (May 22, 1843.) D. H. C. 5:404.

Righteous Judgments

Brother Joseph then addressed the Twelve, and said that in all our counsels, especially while on trial of any one, we should see and observe all things appertaining to the subject, and discern the spirit by which either party was governed. We should be in a situation to understand every spirit and judge righteous judgment and not be asleep. We should keep order and not let the council be imposed upon by unruly conduct. The Saints need not think because I am familiar with them and am playful and cheerful, that I am ignorant of what is going on. Iniquity of any kind cannot be sustained in the Church, and it will not fare well where I am; for I am determined while I do lead the Church, to lead it right. (May 27, 1843.) D. H. C. 5:411.

Testimony Concerning Brigham Young and H. C. Kimball

Of the Twelve Apostles chosen in Kirtland, and ordained under the hands of Oliver Cowdery, David Whitmer and myself, there have been but two but what have lifted their heel against me—namely Brigham Young and Heber C. Kimball. (May 28, 1843.) D. H. C. 5:412.

The Purpose of the Gathering of Israel

A large assembly of the Saints met at the Temple stand. Hymn by the choir. Prayer by Elder Parley P. Pratt, and singing.

President Joseph Smith remarked—"I am a rough stone. The sound of the hammer and chisel was never heard on me until the Lord took me in hand. I desire the learning and wisdom of heaven alone. I have not the least idea, if Christ should come to the earth and preach such rough things as He preached to the Jews, but that this generation would reject Him for being so rough."

He then took for his text the 37th verse of 23rd chapter of Matthew—"O Jerusalem, Jerusalem, thou that killest the prophets and stonest them which are sent unto thee; how often would I have gathered thy children together, even as a hen gathereth her chickens under her wings, and ye would not."

This subject was presented to me since I came to the stand. What was the object of gathering the Jews, or the people of

God in any age of the world? I can never find much to say in expounding a text. A man never has half so much fuss to unlock a door, if he has a key, as though he had not, and had to cut it open with his jack-knife.

The main object was to build unto the Lord a house whereby He could reveal unto His people the ordinances of His house and the glories of His kingdom, and teach the people the way of salvation; for there are certain ordinances and principles that, when they are taught and practiced, must be done in a place or house built for that purpose.

Principles of the Gospel Never Change

It was the design of the councils of heaven before the world was, that the principles and laws of the priesthood should be predicated upon the gathering of the people in every age of the world. Jesus did everything to gather the people, and they would not be gathered, and He therefore poured out curses upon them. Ordinances instituted in the heavens before the foundation of the world, in the priesthood, for the salvation of men, are not to be altered or changed. All must be saved on the same principles.

Salvation for the Dead

It is for the same purpose that God gathers together His people in the last days, to build unto the Lord a house to prepare them for the ordinances and endowments, washings and anointings, etc. One of the ordinances of the house of the Lord is baptism for the dead. God decreed before the foundation of the world that that ordinance should be administered in a font prepared for that purpose in the house of the Lord. "This is only your opinion, sir," says the sectarian. * * *

If a man gets a fullness of the priesthood of God he has to get it in the same way that Jesus Christ obtained it, and that was by keeping all the commandments and obeying all the ordinances of the house of the Lord.

Where there is no change of priesthood, there is no change of ordinances, says Paul. If God has not changed the ordinances and the priesthood, howl, ye sectarians! If he has, when and where has He revealed it? Have ye turned revelators? Then why deny revelation?

Many men will say, "I will never forsake you, but will stand by you at all times." But the moment you teach them some of the mysteries of the kingdom of God that are retained in the heavens and are to be revealed to the children of men when they are prepared for them they will be the first to stone you and put you to death. It was this same principle that crucified the Lord Jesus Christ, and will cause the people to kill the prophets in this generation.

Many things are insoluble to the children of men in the last days: for instance, that God should raise the dead, and forgetting that things have been hid from before the foundation of the world, which are to be revealed to babes in the last days.

Some Men "Too Wise to Be Taught"

There are a great many wise men and women too in our midst who are too wise to be taught; therefore they must die in their ignorance, and in the resurrection they will find their mistake. Many seal up the door of heaven by saying, So far God may reveal and I will believe.

All men who become heirs of God and joint heirs with Jesus Christ will have to receive the fulness of the ordinances of his kingdom; and those who will not receive all the ordinances will come short of the fullness of that glory, if they do not lose the whole.

Paradise

I will say something about the spirits in prison. There has been much said by modern divines about the words of Jesus (when on the cross) to the thief, saying, "This day shalt thou be with me in paradise." King James' translators make it out to say paradise. But what is paradise? It is a modern word: it does not answer at all to the original word that Jesus made use of. Find the original of the word paradise. You may as easily find a needle in a haymow. Here is a chance for battle, ye learned men. There is nothing in the original word in Greek from which this was taken that signifies paradise; but it was—This day thou shalt be with me in the world of spirits: then I will teach you all about it and answer your inquiries. And Peter says he went and preached to the world of spirits (spirits in prison, I Peter, 3rd chap. 19th verse), so that they who would receive it could have it answered by proxy by those who live on the earth, etc.

Baptism for the Dead Taught in New Testament

The doctrine of baptism for the dead is clearly shown in the New Testament; and if the doctrine is not good, then throw the New Testament away; but if it is the word of God, then let the doctrine be acknowledged; and it was the reason why Jesus said unto the Jews, "How oft would I have gathered thy children together, even as a hen gathereth her chickens under her wings, and ye would not!"—that they might attend to the ordinances of baptism for the dead as well as other ordinances of the priesthood, and receive revelations from heaven, and be perfected in the things of the kingdom of God—but they would not. This was the case on the day of Pentecost: those blessings were poured out on the disciples on that occasion. God ordained that He would save the dead, and would do it by gathering His people together.

The World of Spirits

It always has been when a man was sent of God with the priesthood and he began to preach the fullness of the gospel, that he was thrust out by his friends, who are already to butcher him if he teach things which they imagine to be wrong; and Jesus was crucified upon this principle.

I will now turn linguist. There are many things in the Bible which do not, as they now stand, accord with the revelations of the Holy Ghost to me.

I will criticise a little further. There has been much said about the word hell, and the sectarian world have preached much about it, describing it to be a burning lake of fire and brimstone. But what is hell? It is another modern term, and is taken from hades. I'll hunt after hades as Pat did for the woodchuck.

Hades, the Greek, or Sheol, the Hebrew, these two significations mean a world of spirits. Hades, Sheol, paradise, spirits in prison, are all one: it is a world of spirits.

The righteous and the wicked all go to the same world of spirits until the resurrection. "I do not think so," says one. If you will go to my house any time, I will take my lexicon and prove it to you.

The great misery of departed spirits in the world of spirits, where they go after death, is to know that they come short of the glory that others enjoy and that they might have enjoyed themselves, and they are their own accusers. "But," says one, "I believe in one universal heaven and hell, where all go, and are all alike, and equally miserable or equally happy."

What! where all are huddled together—the honorable, virtuous, and murderers, and whoremongers, when it is written that they shall be judged according to the deeds done in the body? But St. Paul informs us of three glories and three heavens. He knew a man that was caught up to the third heavens. Now, if the doctrine of the sectarian world, that there is but one heaven, is true, Paul, what do you tell that lie for, and say there are three? Jesus said unto His disciples, "In my Father's house are many mansions, if it were not so, I would have told you. I go to prepare a place for you, and I will come and receive you to myself, that where I am ye may be also."

Men of God Endowed with Wisdom

Any man may believe that Jesus Christ is the Son of God, and be happy in that belief, and yet not obey his commandments, and at last be cut down for disobedience to the Lord's righteous requirements.

A man of God should be endowed with wisdom, knowledge, and understanding, in order to teach and lead the people of God. The sectarian priests are blind, and they lead the blind, and they will all fall into the ditch together. They build with hay, wood, and stubble, on the old revelations, without the true priesthood or spirit of revelation. If I had time, I would dig into hell, hades, sheol, and tell what exists there.

The Doctrine of the Godhead

There is much said about God and the Godhead. The scriptures say there are Gods many and Lords many, but to us there is but one living and true God, and the heaven of heavens could not contain him; for he took the liberty to go into other heavens. The teachers of the day say that the Father is God, the Son is God, and the Holy Ghost is God, and they are all in one body and one God. Jesus prayed that those that the Father had given him out of the world might be made one in them, as they were one [one in spirit, in mind, in purpose]. If I were to testify that the Christian world were wrong on this point, my testimony would be true.

Peter and Stephen testify that they saw the Son of Man standing on the right hand of God. Any person that had seen the heavens opened knows that there are three personages in the heavens who hold the keys of power, and one presides over all.

If any man attempts to refute what I am about to say, after I have made it plain, let him beware.

The Son Does What the Father Did

As the Father hath power in Himself, so hath the Son power in Himself, to lay down His life and take it again, so He has a body of His own. The Son doeth what He hath seen the Father do: then the Father hath some day laid down His life and taken it again; so He has a body of His own; each one will be in His own body; and yet the sectarian world believe the body of the Son is identical with the Father's.

Gods have an ascendency over the angels, who are ministering servants. In the resurrection, some are raised to be angels, others are raised to become Gods.

These things are revealed in the most holy places in a Temple prepared for that purpose. Many of the sects cry out, "Oh, I have the testimony of Jesus; I have the spirit of God; but away with Joe Smith; he says he is a prophet; but there are to be no prophets or revelators in the last days." Stop, sir! The Revelator says that the testimony of Jesus is the spirit of prophecy; so by your own mouth you are condemned. But to the text. Why gather the people together in this place? For the same purpose that Jesus wanted to gather the Jews—to receive the ordinances, the blessings, and glories that God has in store for His Saints.

I will now ask this assembly and all the Saints if you will now build this house and receive the ordinances and blessings which God has in store for you; or will you not build unto the Lord this house, and let Him pass by and bestow these blessings upon another people? I pause for a reply. (June 11, 1843.) D. H. C. 5:423-427.

The Cause of the Prophet's Success—Love for His Fellow-Man

Joseph remarked that all was well between him and the heavens; that he had no enmity against any one; and as the prayer of Jesus, or his pattern, so prayed Joseph—Father, forgive me my trespasses as I forgive those who trespass against me, for I freely forgive all men. If we would secure and cultivate the love of others, we must love others, even our enemies as well as friends.

Sectarian priests cry out concerning me, and ask, "Why is it this babbler gains so many followers, and retains them?" I answer, It is because I possess the principle of love. All I can offer the world is a good heart and a good hand.

The Saints can testify whether I am willing to lay down my life for my brethren. If it has been demonstrated that I have been willing to die for a "Mormon," I am bold to declare before Heaven that I am just as ready to die in defending the rights of a Presbyterian, a Baptist, or a good man of any other denomination; for the same principle which would trample upon the rights of the Latter-day Saints would trample upon the rights of the Roman Catholics, or of any other denomination who may be unpopular and too weak to defend themselves.

Love of Liberty

It is a love of liberty which inspires my soul—civil and religious liberty to the whole of the human race. Love of liberty was diffused into my soul by my grandfathers while they dandled me on their knees; and shall I want friends? No.

The inquiry is frequently made of me, "Wherein do you differ from others in your religious views?" In reality and essence we do not differ so far in our religious views, but that we could all drink into one principle of love. One of the grand fundamental principles of "Mormonism" is to receive truth, let it come from whence it may.

We believe in the Great Elohim who sits enthroned in yonder heavens. So do the Presbyterians. If a skilful mechanic, in taking a welding heat, uses borax, alum, etc., and succeeds in welding together iron or steel more perfectly than any other mechanic, is he not deserving of praise? And if by the principles of truth I succeed in uniting men of all denominations in the bonds of love, shall I not have attained a good object?

If I esteem mankind to be in error, shall I bear them down? No. I will lift them up, and in their own way too, if I cannot persuade them my way is better; and I will not seek to compel any man to believe as I do, only by the force of reasoning, for truth will cut its own way. Do you believe in Jesus Christ and the Gospel of salvation which he revealed? So do I. Christians should cease wrangling and contending with each other, and cultivate the principles of union and friendship in their midst; and they will do it before the millennium can be ushered in and Christ takes possession of His kingdom.

"Do you believe in the baptism of infants?" asks the Presbyterian. No. "Why?" Because it is nowhere written in the Bible. Circumcision is not baptism, neither was baptism instituted in the place of circumcision. Baptism is for remission of sins. Children have no sins. Jesus blessed them and said, "Do what you have seen me do." Children are all made alive in Christ, and those of riper years through faith and repentance.

So far we are agreed with other Christian denominations. They all preach faith and repentance. The gospel requires baptism by immersion for the remission of sins, which is the meaning of the word in the original language—namely, to bury or immerse.

Necessity of Ordinances

We ask the sects, Do you believe this? They answer, No. I believe in being converted. I believe in this tenaciously. So did the Apostle Peter and the disciples of Jesus. But I further believe in the gift of the Holy Ghost by the laying on of hands. Evidence by Peter's preaching on the day of Pentecost, Acts 2:38. You might as well baptize a bag of sand as a man, if not done in view of the remission of sins and getting of the Holy Ghost. Baptism by water is but half a baptism, and is good for nothing without the other half—that is, the baptism of the Holy Ghost.

The Savior says, "Except a man be born of water and of the Spirit, he cannot enter into the kingdom of God." "Though we or an angel from heaven, preach any other gospel unto you than that which we have preached unto you, let him be accursed," according to Galatians 1:8. (July 9, 1843.) D. H. C. 5:498-500.

Discourse—Burden of the Prophet's Ministry—Friendship

I commence my remarks by reading this text—Luke xvi:16: "The law and the prophets were until John: since that time the kingdom of God is preached, and every man presseth into it."

I do not know that I shall be able to preach much; but,

with the faith of the Saints, may say something instructive. It has gone abroad that I proclaimed myself no longer a prophet. I said it last Sabbath ironically: I supposed you would all understand. It was not that I would renounce the idea of being a prophet, but that I had no disposition to proclaim myself such. But I do say that I bear the testimony of Jesus, which is the spirit of prophecy.

There is no greater love than this, that a man lay down his life for his friends. I discover hundreds and thousands of my brethren ready to sacrifice their lives for me.

The burdens which roll upon me are very great. My persecutors allow me no rest, and I find that in the midst of business and care the spirit is willing, but the flesh is weak. Although I was called of my Heavenly Father to lay the foundation of this great work and kingdom in this dispensation, and testify of His revealed will to scattered Israel, I am subject to like passions as other men, like the prophets of olden times.

Notwithstanding my weaknesses, I am under the necessity of bearing the infirmities of others, who, when they get into difficulty, hang on to me tenaciously to get them out, and wish me to cover their faults. On the other hand, the same characters, when they discover a weakness in Brother Joseph, endeavor to blast his reputation, and publish it to all the world, and thereby aid my enemies in destroying the Saints. Although the law is given through me to the Church, I cannot be borne with a moment by such men. They are ready to destroy me for the least foible, and publish my imaginary failings from Dan to Beersheba, though they are too ignorant of the things of God, which have been revealed to me, to judge of my actions, motives or conduct, in any correct manner whatever.

The only principle upon which they judge me is by comparing my acts with the foolish traditions of their fathers and nonsensical teachings of hireling priests, whose object and aim were to keep the people in ignorance for the sake of filthy lucre; or as the prophet says, to feed themselves, not the flock. Men often come to me with their troubles, and seek my will, crying, Oh, Brother Joseph, help me! help me! But when I am in trouble few of them sympathize with me or extend to me relief. I believe in a principle of reciprocity, if we do live in a devilish and wicked world where men busy themselves in watching for iniquity, and lay snares for those who reprove in the gate.

Loyalty to Friends

I see no faults in the Church, and therefore let me be resurrected with the Saints, whether I ascend to heaven or descend to hell, or go to any other place. And if we go to hell, we will turn the devils out of doors and make a heaven of it. Where this people are, there is good society. What do we care where we are, if the society be good? I don't care what a man's character is; if he's my friend—a true friend, I will be a friend to him, and preach the Gospel of salvation to him, and give him good counsel, helping him out of his difficulties.

Friendship is one of the grand fundamental principles of "Mormonism"; [it is designed] to revolutionize and civilize the world, and cause wars and contentions to cease and men to become friends and brothers. Even the wolf and the lamb shall dwell together; the leopard shall lie down with the kid, the calf, the young lion and the fatling; and a little child shall lead them; the bear and the cow shall lie down together, and the sucking child shall play on the hole of the asp, and the weaned child shall play on the cockatrice's den; and they shall not hurt or destroy in all my holy mountain, saith the Lord of hosts. (Isaiah.)

Love Begets Love

It is a time-honored adage that love begets love. Let us pour forth love—show forth our kindness unto all mankind, and the Lord will reward us with everlasting increase; cast our bread upon the waters and we shall receive it after many days, increased to a hundredfold. Friendship is like Brother Turley in his blacksmith shop welding iron to iron; it unites the human family with its happy influence.

I do not dwell upon your faults, and you shall not upon mine. Charity, which is love, covereth a multitude of sins, and I have often covered up all the faults among you; but the prettiest thing is to have no faults at all. We should cultivate a meek, quiet and peaceable spirit.

Have the Presbyterians any truth? Yes. Have the Baptists, Methodists, etc., any truth? Yes. They all have a little truth mixed with error. We should gather all the good and true principles in the world and treasure them up, or we shall not come out true "Mormons."

Last Monday morning certain brethren came to me and said they could hardly consent to receive Hyrum as a prophet, and for me to resign. But I told them, "I only said it to try your faith; and it is strange, brethren, that you have been in the Church so long, and not yet understand the Melchizedek Priesthood."

* * *

It is contrary to Governor Ford's oath of office, to send a man to Missouri, where he is proscribed in his religious opinions; for he is sworn to support the Constitution of the United States and also of this State, and these constitutions guarantee religious as well as civil liberty to all religious societies whatever. (July 23, 1843.) D. H. C. 5:516-518.

Proverbs of the Prophet Joseph Smith—1843

1st. Never exact of a friend in adversity what you would require in prosperity.

2nd. If a man prove himself to be honest in his deal, and an enemy come upon him wickedly, through fraud or false pretences and because he is stronger than he, maketh him his prisoner and spoil him with his goods, never say unto that man in the day of his adversity, pay me what thou owest, for if thou doest it, thou addest a deeper wound, and condemnation shall come upon thee and thy riches shall be justified in the days of thine adversity if they mock at thee.

3rd. Never afflict thy soul for what an enemy hath put it out of thy power to do, if thy desires are ever so just.

4th. Let thy hand never fail to hand out that that thou owest while it is yet within thy grasp to do so, but when thy stock fails, say to thy heart, be strong, and to thine anxieties cease, for man, what is he; he is but dung upon the earth and although he demand of thee the cattle of a thousand hills, he cannot possess himself of his own life. God made him and thee and gave all things in common.

5th. There is one thing under the sun which I have learned and that is that the righteousness of man is sin because it exacteth over much; nevertheless, the righteousness of God is just, because it exacteth nothing at all, but sendeth the rain on the just and the unjust, seed time and harvest, for all of which man is ungrateful. (1843.) MSS. Historian's Office.

Excerpts from a Sermon by President Joseph Smith

July 23rd, 1843.

Last Monday morning certain men came to me and said: "Brother Joseph, Hyrum is no prophet—he can't lead the church; you must lead the church. If you resign, all things will go wrong; you must not resign; if you do the church will be scattered." I felt curious and said: "Have we not learned the Priesthood after the order of Melchizedek, which includes both Prophets, Priests and Kings: see Rev. 1 Chap., 6th v., and I will advance your Prophet to a Priest, and then to a King—not to the Kingdoms of this earth, but of the Most High God. See Rev. 5 Chap., 10th v. — 'Thou hast made us unto our God, Kings and Priests, and we shall reign on the earth.'"

If I should be exalted would there not be a great many of my enemies disappointed in Missouri, when they wake up and find themselves in hell, see what they might have obtained, and realize what they have lost by not listening to my voice, and obeying my instructions?

Matth. 5 Chap., 17 and 18 v.—"Think not that I am come to destroy the law, or the prophets; I am not come to destroy but to fulfil. For verily I say unto you, till heaven and earth pass, one jot or one tittle shall in no wise pass from the law till all be fulfilled."

And again, Matth. 11 Chap., 12 and 13 v.—"And from the days of John the Baptist, until now, the Kingdom of Heaven suffereth violence, and the violent take it by force. For all the prophets and the law prophesied until John." John held the Aaronic Priesthood and was a legal administrator, and the forerunner of Christ, and came to prepare the way before him.

Christ was the head of the Church, the chief corner stone, the spiritual rock upon which the church was built, and the gates of hell shall not prevail against it. He built up the Kingdom, chose Apostles, and ordained them to the Melchizedek Priesthood, giving them power to administer in the ordinances of the Gospel. John was a priest after the order of Aaron before Christ.

See Exodus 30 Chap. 30 and 31 v.—"And thou shalt anoint Aaron and his sons, and consecrate them, that they may minister unto me in the priest's office. And thou shalt speak unto the children of Israel, saying, This shall be an holy anointing oil unto me throughout your generations." Also Exodus 40 Chap., 15 v.—"And thou shalt anoint them as thou didst anoint their father (Aaron) that they may minister unto me in the priest's office; for their anointing shall surely be an everlasting Priesthood throughout their generations."

Here is a little of law which must be fulfilled. The Levitical Priesthood is forever hereditary—fixed on the head of Aaron and his sons forever, and was in active operation down to Zacharias the father of John. Zacharias would have had no child had not God given him a son. He sent his angel to declare unto Zacharias that his wife Elizabeth should bear him a son, whose name was to be called John.

The keys of the Aaronic Priesthood were committed unto him, and he was as the voice of one crying in the wilderness saying: "Prepare ye the way of the Lord and make his paths straight."

The Kingdom of heaven suffereth violence, etc.

The kingdom of heaven continueth in authority until John.

The authority taketh it by absolute power.

John having the power took the Kingdom by authority.

How have you obtained all this great knowledge? By the gift of the Holy Ghost.

Wrested the Kingdom from the Jews.

Of these stony Gentiles—these dogs—to raise up children unto Abraham.

The Savior said unto John, I must be baptized by you. Why so? To fulfil all righteousness. John refuses at first, but afterwards obeyed by administering the ordinance of baptism unto him, Jesus having no other legal administrator to apply to.

There is no salvation between the two lids of the Bible without a legal administrator. Jesus was then the legal administrator, and ordained His Apostles.—MSS. Historian's Office.

The Prophet's Remarks at the Funeral of Judge Higbee

Brethren and Sisters, you will find these words in II Peter iii:10, 11:—"But the day of the Lord will come as a thief in the night; in the which the heavens shall pass away with a great noise, and the elements shall melt with fervent heat, the earth also and the works that are therein shall be burned up.

Seeing then that all these things shall be dissolved, what manner of persons ought ye to be in all holy conversation and godliness."

I am not like other men. My mind is continually occupied with the business of the day, and I have to depend entirely upon the living God for every thing I say on such occasions as these.

The great thing for us to know is to comprehend what God did institute before the foundation of the world. Who knows it? It is the constitutional disposition of mankind to set up stakes and set bounds to the works and ways of the Almighty.

* * *

But I will give you a more painful thought. Suppose you have an idea of a resurrection, etc., and yet know nothing at all of the Gospel, nor comprehend one principle of the order of heaven, but find yourselves disappointed—yes, at last find yourselves disappointed in every hope or anticipation, when the decision goes forth from the lips of the Almighty. Would not this be a greater disappointment—a more painful thought than annihilation?

Had I inspiration, revelation, and lungs to communicate what my soul has contemplated in times past, there is not a soul in this congregation but would go to their homes and shut their mouths in everlasting silence on religion till they had learned something.

Why be so certain that you comprehend the things of God, when all things with you are so uncertain. You are welcome to all the knowledge and intelligence I can impart to you. I do not grudge the world all the religion they have got: they are welcome to all the knowledge they possess.

The sound saluted my ears—"Ye are come unto Mount Zion, and unto the city of the living God, the heavenly Jerusalem, and to an innumerable company of angels, to the general assembly and church of the firstborn, which are written in heaven, and to God the Judge of all, and to the spirits of just men made perfect, and to Jesus the Mediator of the new covenant" (Hebrew xii:22, 23, 24). What would it profit us to come unto the spirits of the just men, but to learn and come up to the standard of their knowledge?

Where has Judge Higbee gone?

Covenants of the Fathers Revealed

Who is there that would not give all his goods to feed the poor, and pour out his gold and silver to the four winds, to go where Judge Higbee has gone?

That which hath been hid from before the foundation of the world is revealed to babes and sucklings in the last days.

The world is reserved unto burning in the last days. He shall send Elijah the prophet, and he shall reveal the covenants of the fathers in relation to the children, and the covenants of the children in relation to the fathers.

Four destroying angels holding power over the four quarters of the earth until the servants of God are sealed in their foreheads, which signifies sealing the blessing upon their heads, meaning the everlasting covenant, thereby making their calling and election sure. When a seal is put upon the father and mother, it secures their posterity, so that they cannot be lost, but will be saved by virtue of the covenant of their father and mother.

To the mourners I would say—Do as the husband and the father would instruct you, and you shall be reunited.

The speaker continued to teach the doctrine of election and the sealing powers and principles, and spoke of the doctrine of election with the seed of Abraham, and the sealing of blessings upon his posterity, and the sealing of the fathers and children, according to the declarations of the prophets. He then spoke of Judge Higbee in the world of spirits, and the blessings which he would obtain, and of the kind spirit and disposition of Judge Higbee while living; none of which was reported. (Aug. 13, 1843.) D. H. C. 5:529-531.

The Priesthood

President Smith read the 7th Chap. Hebrews and said: Salem is designed for a Hebrew term. It should be Shiloam, which signifies righteousness and peace: as it is, it is nothing— neither Hebrew, Greek, Latin, French, nor any other language.

I say to all those who are disposed to set up stakes for the Almighty, You will come short of the glory of God.

To become a joint heir of the heirship of the Son, one must put away all his false traditions.

* * *

If I have sinned, I have sinned outwardly; but surely I have contemplated the things of God.

Respecting the Melchizedek Priesthood, the sectarians never professed to have it; consequently they never could save any one, and would all be damned together. There was an Episcopal priest who said he had the priesthood of Aaron, but had not the priesthood of Melchizedek: and I bear testimony that I never have found the man who claimed the Priesthood of Melchizedek. The power of the Melchizedek Priesthood is to have the power of "endless lives"; for the everlasting covenant cannot be broken.

The law was given under Aaron for the purpose of pouring out judgments and destructions.

* * *

Three Grand Orders

There are three grand orders of priesthood referred to here.

1st. The King of Shiloam (Salem) had power and authority over that of Abraham, holding the key and the power of endless life. Angels desire to look into it, but they have set up too many stakes. God cursed the children of Israel because they would not receive the last law from Moses.

The sacrifice required of Abraham in the offering up of Isaac, shows that if a man would attain to the keys of the kingdom of an endless life; he must sacrifice all things. When God offers a blessing or knowledge to a man, and he refuses to receive it, he will be damned. The Israelites prayed that God would speak to Moses and not to them; in consequence of which he cursed them with a carnal law.

What was the power of Melchizedek? 'Twas not the Priesthood of Aaron which administers in outward ordinances, and the offering of sacrifices. Those holding the fulness of the Melchizedek Priesthood are kings and priests of the Most High God, holding the keys of power and blessings. In fact, that Priesthood is a perfect law of theocracy, and stands as God to give laws to the people, administering endless lives to the sons and daughters of Adam.

Abraham says to Melchizedek, I believe all that thou hast taught me concerning the priesthood and the coming of the

Son of Man; so Melchizedek ordained Abraham and sent him away. Abraham rejoiced, saying, Now I have a priesthood.

The Mission of Elijah

Salvation could not come to the world without the mediation of Jesus Christ.

How shall God come to the rescue of this generation? He will send Elijah the prophet. The law revealed to Moses in Horeb never was revealed to the children of Israel as a nation. Elijah shall reveal the covenants to seal the hearts of the fathers to the children, and the children to the fathers.

The anointing and sealing is to be called, elected and made sure.

"Without father, without mother, without descent, having neither beginning of days nor end of life, but made like unto the Son of God, abideth a priest continually." The Melchizedek Priesthood holds the right from the eternal God, and not by descent from father and mother; and that priesthood is as eternal as God Himself, having neither beginning of days nor end of life.

The 2nd Priesthood is Patriarchal authority. Go to and finish the temple, and God will fill it with power, and you will then receive more knowledge concerning this priesthood.

The 3rd is what is called the Levitical Priesthood, consisting of priests to administer in outward ordinances, made without an oath; but the Priesthood of Melchizedek is by an oath and covenant.

The Holy Ghost is God's messenger to administer in all those priesthoods.

Jesus Christ is the heir of this Kingdom—the Only Begotten of the Father according to the flesh, and holds the keys over all this world.

Men have to suffer that they may come upon Mount Zion and be exalted above the heavens.

I know a man that has been caught up to the third heavens, and can say, with Paul, that we have seen and heard things that are not lawful to utter. (Aug. 27, 1843.) D.H.C. 5:554-556.

Instructions Respecting Plurality of Wives

In the afternoon, rode to the prairie to show some of the brethren some land. Evening, at home, and walked up and down the streets with my scribe. Gave instructions to try those persons who were preaching, teaching, or practicing the doctrine of plurality of wives; for, according to the law, I hold the keys of this power in the last days; for there is never but one on earth at a time on whom the power and its keys are conferred; *and I have constantly said no man shall have but one wife at a time, unless the Lord directs otherwise.* (Oct. 5, 1843.) D. H. C. 6:46.

THE PROPHET'S REMARKS ON THE DEMISE OF JAMES ADAMS

How Salvation Is Acquired

All men know that they must die. And it is important that we should understand the reasons and causes of our exposure to the vicissitudes of life and of death, and the designs and purposes of God in our coming into the world, our sufferings here, and our departure hence. What is the object of our coming into existence, then dying and falling away, to be here no more? It is but reasonable to suppose that God would reveal something in reference to the matter, and it is a subject we ought to study more than any other. We ought to study it day and night, for the world is ignorant in reference to their true condition and relation. If we have any claim on our Heavenly Father for anything, it is for knowledge on this important subject. Could we read and comprehend all that has been written from the days of Adam, on the relation of man to God and angels in a future state, we should know very little about it. Reading the experience of others, or the revelation given to *them,* can never give *us* a comprehensive view of our condition and true relation to God. Knowledge of these things can only be obtained by experience through the ordinances of God set forth for that purpose. Could you gaze into heaven five minutes, you would know more than you would by reading all that ever was written on the subject.

We are only capable of comprehending that certain things exist, which we may acquire by certain fixed principles. If men would acquire salvation, they have got to be subject, before they leave this world, to certain rules and principles, which were fixed by an unalterable decree before the world was.

The disappointment of hopes and expectations at the resurrection would be indescribably dreadful.

Angels and Spirits

The organization of the spiritual and heavenly worlds, and of spiritual and heavenly beings, was agreeable to the most perfect order and harmony: their limits and bounds were fixed irrevocably, and voluntarily subscribed to in their heavenly estate by themselves, and were by our first parents subscribed to upon the earth.   Hence the importance of embracing and subscribing to principles of eternal truth by all men upon the earth that expect eternal life.

I assure the Saints that truth, in reference to these matters, can and may be known through the revelations of God in the way of His ordinances, and in answer to prayer. The Hebrew Church "came unto the spirits of just men made perfect, and unto an innumerable company of angels, unto God the Father of all, and to Jesus Christ the Mediator of the new covenant." What did they learn by coming to the spirits of just men made perfect? Is it written? No. What they learned has not been and could not have been written. What object was gained by this communication with the spirits of the just? It was the established order of the kingdom of God: The keys of power and knowledge were with them to communicate to the Saints. Hence the importance of understanding the distinction between the spirits of the just and angels.

Spirits can only be revealed in flaming fire and glory. Angels have advanced further, their light and glory being tabernacled; and hence they appear in bodily shape.   The spirits of just men are made ministering servants to those who are sealed unto life eternal, and it is through them that the sealing power comes down.

Patriarch Adams is now one of the spirits of the just men made perfect; and, if revealed now, must be revealed in fire; and the glory could not be endured. Jesus showed Himself to His disciples, and they thought it was His spirit, and they were afraid to approach His spirit. Angels have advanced higher in knowledge and power than spirits.

Concerning Brother James Adams, it should appear strange that so good and so great a man was hated. The deceased ought never to have had an enemy. But so it was. Wherever light shone, it stirred up darkness. Truth and error, good and evil cannot be reconciled. Judge Adams had some enemies, but such a man ought not to have had one. I saw him first at Springfield, when on my way from Missouri to Washington. He sought me out when a stranger, took me to his home, encouraged and cheered me, and gave me money. He has been a most intimate friend. I anointed him to the patriarchal power —to receive the keys of knowledge and power, by revelation to himself. He has had revelations concerning his departure, and has gone to a more important work. When men are prepared, they are better off to go hence. Brother Adams has gone to open up a more effectual door for the dead. The spirits of the just are exalted to a greater and more glorious work; hence they are blessed in their departure to the world of spirits. Enveloped in flaming fire, they are not far from us, and know and understand our thoughts, feelings, and motions, and are often pained therewith.

Flesh and blood cannot go there; but flesh and bones, quickened by the Spirit of God, can.

If we would be sober and watch in fasting and prayer, God would turn away sickness from our midst.

Hasten the work in the Temple, renew your exertions to forward all the work of the last days, and walk before the Lord in soberness and righteousness. Let the Elders and Saints do away with lightmindedness, and be sober. (Oct. 9, 1843.) D. H. C. 6:50-52.

The Prophet on the Constitution of the United States and the Bible—Temporal Economics

It is one of the first principles of my life, and one that I have cultivated from my childhood, having been taught it by my father, to allow every one the liberty of conscience. I am the greatest advocate of the Constitution of the United States there is on the earth. In my feelings I am always ready to die for the protection of the weak and oppressed in their just rights. The only fault I find with the Constitution is, it is not broad enough to cover the whole ground.

Although it provides that all men shall enjoy religious freedom, yet it does not provide the manner by which that freedom can be preserved, nor for the punishment of Government officers who refuse to protect the people in their religious

rights, or punish those mobs, states, or communities who interfere with the rights of the people on account of their religion.
Its sentiments are good, but it provides no means of enforcing
them. It has but this one fault. Under its provision, a man
or a people who are able to protect themselves can get along
well enough; but those who have the misfortune to be weak
or unpopular are left to the merciless rage of popular fury.

The Constitution should contain a provision that every
officer of the Government who should neglect or refuse to
extend the protection guaranteed in the Constitution should be
subject to capital punishment; and then the president of the
United States would not say, "*Your cause is just, but I can
do nothing for you,*" a governor issue exterminating orders,
or judges say, "The men ought to have the protection of law,
but it won't please the mob; the men must die, anyhow, to
satisfy the clamor of the rabble; they must be hung, or Missouri
be damned to all eternity." Executive writs could be issued
when they ought to be, and not be made instruments of cruelty
to oppress the innocent, and persecute men whose religion is
unpopular.

The Creeds of Men

I cannot believe in any of the creeds of the different
denominations, because they all have some things in them I
cannot subscribe to, though all of them have some truth. I
want to come up into the presence of God, and learn all things;
but the creeds set up stakes, and say, "Hitherto shalt thou
come, and no further"; which I cannot subscribe to.

Errors in the Bible

I believe the Bible as it read when it came from the pen
of the original writers. Ignorant translators, careless transcrib-
ers, or designing and corrupt priests have committed many
errors. As it read, Gen. vi:6, "It repented the Lord that he
had made man on the earth"; also, Num. xxiii:19, "God is
not a man, that he should lie; neither the Son of man, that he
should repent"; which I do not believe. But it ought to read,
"It repented *Noah* that God made man." This I believe, and
then the other quotation stands fair. If any man will prove
to me, by one passage of Holy Writ, one item I believe to be
false, I will renounce and disclaim it as far as I promulgated
it.

The first principles of the Gospel, as I believe, are, faith, repentance, baptism for the remission of sins, with the promise of the Holy Ghost.

Look at Heb. vi:1 contradictions—"Therefore leaving the principles of the doctrine of Christ, let us go on unto perfection." If a man leaves the principles of the doctrine of Christ, how can he be saved in the principles? This is a contradiction. I don't believe it. I will render it as it should be—"Therefore not leaving the principles of the doctrine of Christ, let us go on unto perfection, not laying again the foundation of repentance from dead works, and of faith toward God, of the doctrine of baptisms, and of laying on of hands, and of resurrection of the dead, and of eternal judgment."

The Kingdom of God

It is one thing to see the kingdom of God, and another thing to enter into it. We must have a change of heart to see the kingdom of God, and subscribe the articles of adoption to enter therein.

No man can receive the Holy Ghost without receiving revelations. The Holy Ghost is a revelator.

Punishments Await this Generation

I prophesy, in the name of the Lord God of Israel, anguish and wrath and tribulation and the withdrawing of the Spirit of God from the earth await this generation, until they are visited with utter desolation. This generation is as corrupt as the generation of the Jews that crucified Christ; and if He were here to-day, and should preach the same doctrine He did then, they would put Him to death. I defy all the world to destroy the work of God; and I prophesy they never will have power to kill me till my work is accomplished, and I am ready to die.   * * *

Temporal Economy—Care of the Poor

The temporal economy of this people should be to establish and encourage manufactures, and not to take usury for their money. I do not want to bind the poor here to starve. Go out into the country and into the neighboring cities, and get food, and gird up your loins, and be sober. When you get food, return, if you have a mind to.

Some say it is better to give to the poor than build the Temple. The building of the Temple has sustained the poor who were driven from Missouri, and kept them from starving; and it has been the best means for this object which could be devised.

Oh, all ye rich men of the Latter-day Saints from abroad, I would invite you to bring up some of your money—your gold, your silver, and your precious things, and give to the Temple. We want iron, steel, spades, and quarrying and mechanical tools.

It would be a good plan to get up a forge to manufacture iron, and bring in raw materials of every variety, and erect manufacturing establishments of all kinds, and surround the rapids with mills and machinery.

I never stole the value of a pin's head, or a picayune in my life; and when you are hungry don't steal. Come to me, and I will feed you.

The secret of Masonry is to keep a secret. It is good economy to entertain strangers—to entertain sectarians. Come up to Nauvoo, ye sectarian priests of the everlasting Gospel, as they call it, and you shall have my pulpit all day.

Woe to ye rich men, who refuse to give to the poor, and then come and ask me for bread. Away with all your meanness, and be liberal. We need purging, purifying and cleansing. You that have little faith in your Elders when you are sick, get some little simple remedy in the first stages. If you send for a doctor at all, send in the first stages.

All ye doctors who are fools, not well read, and do not understand the human constitution, stop your practice. And all ye lawyers who have no business, only as you hatch it up, would to God you would go to work or run away! (Oct. 15, 1843.) D. H. C. 6:56-59.

Discourse: The Sealing Power in the Priesthood

There are many people assembled here to-day, and throughout the city, and from various parts of the world, who say that they have received to a certainty a portion of the knowledge from God, by revelation, in the way that He has ordained and pointed out.

I shall take the broad ground, then, that we have received

a portion of knowledge from God by immediate revelation, and from the same source we can receive all knowledge.

The Sending of Elijah

What shall I talk about to-day? I know what Brother Cahoon wants me to speak about. He wants me to speak about the coming of Elijah in the last days. I can see it in his eye. I will speak upon that subject then.

The Bible says, "I will send you Elijah the Prophet before the coming of the great and dreadful day of the Lord; and he shall turn the heart of the fathers to the children, and the heart of the children to the fathers, lest I come and smite the earth with a curse."

Now, the word *turn* here should be translated *bind,* or seal. But what is the object of this important mission? or how is it to be fulfilled? The keys are to be delivered, the spirit of Elijah is to come, the Gospel to be established, the Saints of God gathered, Zion built up, and the Saints to come up as saviors on Mount Zion.

But how are they to become saviors on Mount Zion? By building their temples, erecting their baptismal fonts, and going forth and receiving all the ordinances, baptisms, confirmations, washings, anointings, ordinations and sealing powers upon their heads, in behalf of all their progenitors who are dead, and redeem them that they may come forth in the first resurrection and be exalted to thrones of glory with them; and herein is the chain that binds the hearts of the fathers to the children, and the children to the fathers, which fulfills the mission of Elijah. And I would to God that this temple was now done, that we might go into it, and go to work and improve our time, and make use of the seals while they are on earth.

Saints Have Not Much Time

The Saints have not too much time to save and redeem their dead, and gather together their living relatives, that they may be saved also, before the earth will be smitten, and the consumption decreed falls upon the world.

I would advise all the Saints to go with their might and gather together all their living relatives to this place, that they may be sealed and saved, that they may be prepared against the day that the destroying angel goes forth; and if the whole

Church should go to with all their might to save their dead, seal their posterity, and gather their living friends, and spend none of their time in behalf of the world, they would hardly get through before night would come, when no man can work; and my only trouble at the present time is concerning ourselves, that the Saints *will be divided, broken up, and scattered,* before we get our salvation secure; for there are so many fools in the world for the devil to operate upon, it gives him the advantage oftentimes.

All Ordinances Necessary

The question is frequently asked, "Can we not be saved without going through with all those ordinances? I would answer, No, not the fulness of salvation. Jesus said, There are many mansions in my Father's house, and I will go and prepare a place for you. *House* here named should have been translated kingdom; and any person who is exalted to the highest mansion has to abide a celestial law, and the whole law too.

But there has been a great difficulty in getting anything into the heads of this generation. It has been like splitting hemlock knots with a corn-dodger for a wedge, and a pumpkin for a beetle. Even the Saints are slow to understand.

Unwillingness of Saints to Learn

I have tried for a number of years to get the minds of the Saints prepared to receive the things of God; but we frequently see some of them, after suffering all they have for the work of God, will fly to pieces like glass as soon as anything comes that is contrary to their traditions: they cannot stand the fire at all. How many will be able to abide a celestial law, and go through and receive their exaltation, I am unable to say, as many are called, but few are chosen. (Jan. 20, 1844.) D. H. C. 6:183-185.

Views of the Prophet on His Candidacy for President of the United States

I would not have suffered my name to have been used by my friends on anywise as President of the United States, or candidate for that office, if I and my friends could have had the privilege of enjoying our religious and civil rights as Amer-

ican citizens, even those rights which the Constitution guarantees unto all her citizens alike. But this as a people we have
been denied from the beginning. Persecution has rolled upon
our heads from time to time, from portions of the United States,
like peals of thunder, because of our religion; and no portion
of the Government as yet has stepped forward for our relief.
And in view of these things, I feel it to be my right and privilege
to obtain what influence and power I can, lawfully, in the United
States, for the protection of injured innocence; and if I lose
my life in a good cause I am willing to be sacrificed on the altar
of virtue, righteousness and truth, in maintaining the laws and
Constitution of the United States, if need be, for the general
good of mankind. (Feb. 8, 1844.) D. H. C. 6:210-211.

Western Movement for the Church Contemplated

I instructed the Twelve Apostles to send out a delegation
and investigate the locations of California and Oregon, and hunt
out a good location, where we can remove to after the temple
is completed, and where we can build a city in a day, and
have a government of our own, get up into the mountains,
where the devil cannot dig us out, and live in a healthful climate,
where we can live as old as we have a mind to. (Feb. 20, 1844.)
D. H. C. 6:222.

To Gain Salvation the Laws of God Must Be Obeyed

I * * * spoke to the people, showing them that to get
salvation we must not only do some things, but everything
which God has commanded. Men may preach and practice
everything except those things which God commands us to do,
and will be damned at last. We may tithe mint and rue,
and all manner of herbs, and still not obey the commandments of God. The object with me is to obey and teach
others to obey God in just what He tells us to do. It mattereth
not whether the principle is popular or unpopular, I will always
maintain a true principle, even if I stand alone in it. (Feb. 21,
1844.) D. H. C. 6:223.

The Western Exploring Equipment

Met with the Twelve in the assembly room concerning the
Oregon and California Exploring Expedition; Hyrum and Sidney present. I told them I wanted an exploration of all that

mountain country. Perhaps it would be best to go direct to Santa Fe. "Send twenty-five men: let them preach the Gospel wherever they go. Let that man go that can raise $500, a good horse and mule, a double-barrel gun, one-barrel rifle, and the other smooth bore, a saddle and bridle, a pair of revolving pistols, bowie-knife, and a good sabre. Appoint a leader, and let them beat up for volunteers. I want every man that goes to be a king and a priest. When he gets on the mountains, he may want to talk with his God; when with the savage nations have power to govern, &c. If we don't get volunteers, wait till after the election." (Feb. 23, 1844.) D. H. C. 6:224.

A Prophecy of Deliverance of the Saints

I gave some important instructions, and prophesied that within five years we should be out of the power of our old enemies, whether they were apostates or of the world; and told the brethren to record it, that when it comes to pass they need not say they had forgotten the saying. (Feb. 25, 1844.) D. H. C. 6:225.

The Worthy to Receive Endowments

In relation to those who give in property for the temple. We want them to bring it to the proper source, and to be careful into whose hands it comes, that it may be entered into the Church books, so that those whose names are found in the Church books shall have the first claim to receive their endowments in the temple. I intend to keep the door at the dedication myself, and not a man shall pass who has not paid his bonus.

Remarks on Political Matters

As to politics, I care but little about the presidential chair. I would not give half as much for the office of President of the United States as I would for the one I now hold as Lieutenant-General of the Nauvoo Legion.

We have as good a right to make a political party to gain power to defend ourselves, as for demagogues to make use of our religion to get power to destroy us. In other words, as the world has used the power of government to oppress and persecute us, it is right for us to use it for the protection of our rights. We will whip the mob by getting up a candidate for President.

When I get hold of the Eastern papers, and see how popular I am, I am afraid myself that I shall be elected; but if I should be, I would not say, *"Your cause is just, but I can do nothing for you."*

What I have said in my views in relation to the annexation of Texas is with some unpopular; the people are opposed to it. Some of the Anti-Mormons are good fellows. I say it, however, in anticipation that they will repent. They object to Texas on account of slavery. Why, it is the very reason she ought to be received, so that we may watch over them; for, of the two evils, we should reject the greatest.

Governor Houston of Texas, says—"If you refuse to receive us into the United States, we must go to the British Government for protection."

This would certainly be bad policy for this nation; the British are now throughout the whole country, trying to bribe all they can; and the first thing they would do, if they got possession, would be to set the negroes and the Indians to fight, and they would use us up. British officers are now running all over Texas to establish British influence in that country.

It will be more honorable for us to receive Texas and set the negroes free, and use the negroes and Indians against our foes. Don't let Texas go, lest our mothers and the daughters of the land should laugh us in the teeth; and if these things are not so, God never spoke by any Prophet since the world began.

How much better it is for the nation to bear a little expense than to have the Indians and British upon us and destroy us all. We should grasp all the territory we can. I know much that I do not tell. I have had bribes offered me, but I have rejected them.

The government will not receive any advice or counsel from me: they are self-sufficient. But they must go to hell and work out their own salvation with fear and trembling.

The South holds the balance of power. By annexing Texas, I can do away with this evil. As soon as Texas was annexed, I would liberate the slaves in two or three States, indemnifying their owners, and send the negroes to Texas, and from Texas to Mexico, where all colors are alike. And if that was not sufficient, I would call upon Canada, and annex it. (March 7, 1844.) D. H. C. 6:243-244.

Discourses of the Prophet—Elias, Elijah, Messiah

There is a difference between the spirit and office of Elias and Elijah. It is the spirit of Elias I wish first to speak of; and in order to come at the subject, I will bring some of the testimony from the Scripture and give my own.

In the first place, suffice it to say, I went into the woods to inquire of the Lord, by prayer, His will concerning me, and I saw an angel, and he laid his hands upon my head, and ordained me to a Priest after the order of Aaron, and to hold the keys of this Priesthood, which office was to preach repentance and baptism for the remission of sins, and also to baptize. But I was informed that this office did not extend to the laying on of hands for the giving of the Holy Ghost; that that office was a greater work, and was to be given afterward; but that my ordination was a preparatory work, or a going before, which was the spirit of Elias; for the spirit of Elias was a going before to prepare the way for the greater, which was the case with John the Baptist. He came crying through the wilderness, "Prepare ye the way of the Lord, make his paths straight." And they were informed, if they could receive it, it was the spirit of Elias; and John was very particular to tell the people, he was not that Light, but was sent to bear witness of that Light.

He told the people that his mission was to preach repentance and baptize with water; but it was He that should come after him that should baptize with fire and the Holy Ghost.

If he had been an impostor, he might have gone to work beyond his bounds, and undertook to have performed ordinances which did not belong to that office and calling, under the spirit of Elias.

Mission of Elias to Prepare the Way

The spirit of Elias is to prepare the way for a greater revelation of God, which is the Priesthood of Elias, or the Priesthood that Aaron was ordained unto. And when God sends a man into the world to prepare for a greater work, holding the keys of the power of Elias, it was called the doctrine of Elias, even from the early ages of the world.

John's mission was limited to preaching and baptizing; but what he did was legal; and when Jesus Christ came to any of John's disciples, He baptized them with fire and the Holy Ghost.

We find the Apostles endowed with greater power than John: their office was more under the spirit and power of Elijah than Elias.

In the case of Phillip when he went down to Samaria, when he was under the spirit of Elias, he baptized both men and women. When Peter and John heard of it, they went down and laid hands upon them, and they received the Holy Ghost. This shows the distinction between the two powers.

When Paul came to certain disciples, he asked if they had received the Holy Ghost? They said, No. Who baptized you, then? We were baptized unto John's baptism. No, you were not baptized unto John's baptism, or you would have been baptized by John. And so Paul went and baptized them, for he knew what the true doctrine was, and he knew that John had not baptized them. And these principles are strange to me, that men who have read the Scriptures of the New Testament are so far from it.

What I want to impress upon your minds is the difference of power in the different parts of the Priesthood, so that when any man comes among you, saying, "I have the spirit of Elias," you can know whether he be true or false; for any man that comes, having the spirit and power of Elias, he will not transcend his bounds.

John did not transcend his bounds, but faithfully performed that part belonging to his office; and every portion of the great building should be prepared right and assigned to its proper place; and it is necessary to know who holds the keys of power, and who does not, or we may be likely to be deceived.

That person who holds the keys of Elias hath a preparatory work. But if I spend much more time in conversing about the spirit of Elias, I shall not have time to do justice to the spirit and power of Elijah.

This is the Elias spoken of in the last days, and here is the rock upon which many split, thinking the time was past in the days of John and Christ, and no more to be. But the

spirit of Elias was revealed to me, and I know it is true; therefore I speak with boldness, for I know verily my doctrine is
true.

Mission of Elijah

Now for Elijah. The spirit, power, and calling of Elijah
is, that ye have power to hold the key of the revelations,
ordinances, oracles, powers and endowments of the fulness of
the Melchizedek Priesthood and of the kingdom of God on
the earth; and to receive, obtain, and perform all the ordinances
belonging to the kingdom of God, even unto the turning of the
hearts of the fathers unto the children, and the hearts of the
children unto the fathers, even those who are in heaven.

Malachi says, "I will send you Elijah the prophet before
the coming of the great and dreadful day of the Lord: and he
shall turn the hearts of the fathers to the children, and the heart
of the children to their fathers, lest I come and smite the earth
with a curse."

Now, what I am after is the knowledge of God, and I take
my own course to obtain it. What are we to understand by
this in the last days?

In the days of Noah, God destroyed the world by a flood,
and He has promised to destroy it by fire in the last days:
but before it should take place, Elijah should first come and
turn the hearts of the fathers to the children, &c.

Now comes the point. What is this office and work of
Elijah? It is one of the greatest and most important subjects
that God has revealed. He should send Elijah to seal the
children to the fathers, and the fathers to the children.

For the Living and the Dead

Now was this merely confined to the living, to settle difficulties with families on earth? By no means. It was a far
greater work. Elijah! what would you do if you were here?
Would you confine your work to the living alone? No: I would
refer you to the Scriptures, where the subject is manifest: that
is, without us, they could not be made perfect, nor we without
them; the fathers without the children, nor the children without
the fathers.

I wish you to understand this subject, for it is important;
and if you receive it, this is the spirit of Elijah, that we

redeem our dead, and connect ourselves with our fathers which are in heaven, and seal up our dead to come forth in the first resurrection; and here we want the power of Elijah to seal those who dwell on earth to those who dwell in heaven. This is the power of Elijah and the keys of the kingdom of Jehovah.

Sealing on Earth and in Heaven

Let us suppose a case. Suppose the great God who dwells in heaven should reveal himself to Father Cutler here, by the opening heavens, and tell him, I offer up a decree that whatsoever you seal on earth with your decree, I will seal it in heaven; you have the power then; can it be taken off? No. Then what you seal on earth, by the keys of Elijah, is sealed in heaven; and this is the power of Elijah, and this is the difference between the spirit and power of Elias and Elijah; for while the spirit of Elias is a forerunner, the power of Elijah is sufficient to make our calling and election sure; and the same doctrine, where we are exhorted to go on to perfection, not laying again the foundation of repentance from dead works, and of laying on of hands, resurrection of the dead, &c.

We cannot be perfect without the fathers, &c. We must have revelation from them, and we can see that the doctrine of revelation far transcends the doctrine of no revelation; for one truth revealed from heaven is worth all the sectarian notions in existence.

This spirit of Elijah was manifest in the days of the Apostles, in delivering certain ones to the buffetings of Satan, that they might be saved in the day of the Lord Jesus. They were sealed by the spirit of Elijah unto the damnation of hell until the day of the Lord, or revelation of Jesus Christ.

Here is the doctrine of election that the world has quarreled so much about; but they do not know anything about it.

Falling from Grace

The doctrine that the Presbyterians and Methodists have quarreled so much about—one in grace, always in grace, or falling away from grace, I will say a word about. They are both wrong. Truth takes a road between them both, for while the Presbyterian says: "Once in grace, you cannot fall"; the Methodist says: "You can have grace today, fall from it tomorrow, next day have grace again; and so follow on, changing continually." But the doctrine of the Scriptures and the spirit of Elijah would show them both false, and take a road between them both; for, according to the Scripture, if men have received the good word of God, and tasted of the powers of the world to come, if they shall fall away, it is impossible to renew them again, seeing they have crucified the Son of God afresh, and put Him to an open shame; so there is a possibility of falling away; you could not be renewed again, and the power of Elijah cannot seal against this sin, for this is a reserve made in the seals and power of the Priesthood.

I will make every doctrine plain that I present, and it shall stand upon a firm basis, and I am at the defiance of the world, for I will take shelter under the broad cover of the wings of the work in which I am engaged. It matters not to me if all hell boils over; I regard it only as I would the crackling of the thorns under a pot.

Murderers Have No Forgiveness

A murderer, for instance, one that sheds innocent blood, cannot have forgiveness. David sought repentance at the hand of God carefully with tears, for the murder of Uriah; but he could only get it through hell: he got a promise that his soul should not be left in hell.

Although David was a king, he never did obtain the spirit and power of Elijah and the fullness of the Priesthood; and the Priesthood that he received, and the throne and kingdom of David is to be taken from him and given to another by the name of David in the last days, raised up out of his lineage.

Peter referred to the same subject on the day of Pentecost, but the multitude did not get the endowment that Peter had; but several days after, the people asked, "What shall we do?" Peter says, "I would ye had done it ignorantly," speaking of crucifying the Lord &c. He did not say to them, "Repent and be baptized for the remission of your sins"; but he said, "Repent ye therefore, and be converted, that your sins may be blotted out, when the times of refreshing shall come from the presence of the Lord." (Acts iii:19.)

This is the case with murderers. They could not be baptized for the remission of sins, for they had shed innocent blood.

Again: The doctrine or sealing power of Elijah is as follows:—If you have power to seal on earth and in heaven, then we should be wise. The first thing you do, go and seal on earth your sons and daughters unto yourself, and yourself unto your fathers in eternal glory, and go ahead, and not go back, but use a little wisdom, and seal all you can, and when you get to heaven tell your Father that what you seal on earth should be sealed in heaven, according to his promise. I will walk through the gate of heaven and claim what I seal, and those that follow me and my counsel.

The Lord once told me that what I asked for I should have. I have been afraid to ask God to kill my enemies, lest some of them should, peradventure, repent.

I asked a short time since for the Lord to deliver me out of the hands of the Governor of Missouri, and if it needs must be to accomplish it, to take him away; and the next news that came pouring down from there was, that *Governor Reynolds had shot himself.* And I would now say, Beware, O earth, how you fight against the Saints of God and shed innocent blood; for in the days of Elijah, his enemies came upon him, and fire was called down from heaven and destroyed them.

Mission of Messiah

The spirit of Elias is first, Elijah second, and Messiah last. Elias is a forerunner to prepare the way, and the spirit and power of Elijah is to come after, holding the keys of power, building the Temple to the capstone, placing the seals of the Melchizedek Priesthood upon the house of Israel, and making all things ready; then Messiah comes to His Temple, which is last of all.

Messiah is above the spirit and power of Elijah, for He made the world, and was that spiritual rock unto Moses in the wilderness. Elijah was to come and prepare the way and build up the kingdom before the coming of the great day of the Lord, although the spirit of Elias might begin it.

I have asked of the Lord concerning His coming; and while asking the Lord, He gave a sign and said, "In the days of Noah I set a bow in the heavens as a sign and token that in any year that the bow should be seen the Lord would not come; but there should be seed time and harvest during that year: but whenever you see the bow withdrawn, it shall be a token that there shall be famine, pestilence, and great distress among the nations, and that the coming of the Messiah is not far distant.

But I will take the responsibility upon myself to prophesy in the name of the Lord, that Christ will not come this year, as Father Miller has prophesied, for we have seen the bow; and I also prophesy, in the name of the Lord, that Christ will not come in forty years; and if God ever spoke by my mouth, He will not come in that length of time. Brethren, when you go home, write it down, that it may be remembered.

Jesus Christ never did reveal to any man the precise time that He would come. Go and read the Scriptures, and you cannot find anything that specifies the exact hour He would come; and all that say so are false teachers.

There are some important things concerning the office of the Messiah in the organization of the world, which I will speak of hereafter. May God Almighty bless you and pour out His Spirit upon you, is the prayer of your unworthy servant. Amen. (March 10, 1844.) D. H. C. 6:249-254.

The Power of Truth

President Joseph Smith again arose and said—In relation to the power over the minds of mankind which I hold, I would say, It is in consequence of the power of truth in the doctrines which I have been an instrument in the hands of God of presenting unto them, and not because of any compulsion on my part. I wish to ask if ever I got any of it unfairly? if I have not reproved you in the gate? I ask, Did I ever exercise any compulsion over any man? Did I not give him the liberty of disbelieving any doctrine I have preached, if he saw fit? Why do not my enemies strike a blow at the doctrine? They cannot do it: it is truth, and I defy all men to upset it. I am the voice of one crying in the wilderness, "Repent ye of your sins and prepare the way for the coming of the Son of Man; for the kingdom of God has come unto you, and henceforth the ax is laid unto the root of the tree; and every tree that bringeth not forth good fruit, God Almighty * * * shall hew it down and cast it into the fire." (March 24, 1844.) D. H. C. 6:273.

"THE KING FOLLETT DISCOURSE"

The Being and Kind of Being God Is; The Immortality of the Intelligence of Man

By Joseph Smith the Prophet

President Joseph Smith delivered the following discourse before about twenty thousand Saints at the April conference of the Church, 1844, being the funeral sermon of Elder King Follett. Reported by Willard Richards, Wilford Woodruff, Thomas Bullock and William Clayton. This discourse was first published in the *Times and Seasons* of August 15, 1844:

Beloved Saints, I will call the attention of this congregation while I address you on the subject of the dead. The decease of our beloved brother, Elder King Follett, who was crushed in a well by the falling of a tub of rock, has more immediately led me to that subject. I have been requested to speak by his friends and relatives, but inasmuch as there are a great many in this congregation who live in this city as well as elsewhere, who have lost friends, I feel disposed to speak on the subject in general, and offer you my ideas, so far as I have ability, and so far as I shall be inspired by the Holy Spirit to dwell on this subject.

I want your prayers and faith that I may have the instruction of Almighty God and the gift of the Holy Ghost, so that I may set forth things that are true and which can be easily comprehended by you, and that the testimony may carry conviction to your hearts and minds of the truth of what I shall say. Pray that the Lord may strengthen my lungs, stay the winds, and let the prayers of the Saints to heaven appear, that they may enter into the ears of the Lord of Sabaoth, for the effectual prayers of the righteous avail much. There is strength here, and I verily believe that your prayers will be heard.

Before I enter fully into the investigation of the subject which is lying before me, I wish to pave the way and bring up the subject from the beginning, that you may understand it. I will make a few preliminaries, in order that you may understand the subject when I come to it. I do not intend to please your ears with superfluity of words or oratory, or with much learning; but I intend to edify you with the simple truths from heaven.

The Character of God

In the first place, I wish to go back to the beginning—to the morn of creation. There is the starting point for us to look to, in order to understand and be fully acquainted with the mind, purposes and decrees of the Great Elohim, who sits in yonder heavens as he did at the creation of this world. It is necessary for us to have an understanding of God himself in the beginning. If we start right, it is easy to go right all the time; but if we start wrong, we may go wrong, and it be a hard matter to get right.

There are but a very few beings in the world who understand rightly the character of God. The great majority of mankind do not comprehend anything, either that which is past, or that which is to come, as it respects their relationship to God. They do not know, neither do they understand the nature of that relationship; and consequently they know but little above the brute beast, or more than to eat, drink and sleep. This is all man knows about God or his existence, unless it is given by the inspiration of the Almighty.

If a man learns nothing more than to eat, drink and sleep, and does not comprehend any of the designs of God, the beast comprehends the same things. It eats, drinks, sleeps, and knows nothing more about God; yet it knows as much as we, unless we are able to comprehend by the inspiration of Almighty God. If men do not comprehend the character of God, they do not comprehend themselves. I want to go back to the beginning, and so lift your minds into a more lofty sphere and a more exalted understanding than what the human mind generally aspires to.

What Kind of Being Is God?

I want to ask this congregation, every man, woman and child, to answer the question in their own heart, what kind of a being God is? Ask yourselves; turn your thoughts into your hearts, and say if any of you have seen, heard, or communed with him. This is a question that may occupy your attention for a long time. I again repeat the question—What kind of a being is God? Does any man or woman know? Have any of you seen him, heard him, or communed with him? Here is the question that will, peradventure, from this time henceforth occupy your attention.   The Scriptures inform us that "This is life eternal that they might know thee, the only true God, and Jesus Christ whom thou hast sent."

If any man does not know God, and inquires what kind of a being he is,—if he will search diligently his own heart— if the declaration of Jesus and the apostles be true, he will realize that he has not eternal life; for there can be eternal life on no other principle.

My first object is to find out the character of the only wise and true God, and what kind of a being he is; and if I am so fortunate as to be the man to comprehend God, and explain or convey the principles to your hearts, so that the Spirit seals them upon you, then let every man and woman henceforth sit in silence, put their hands on their mouths, and never lift their hands or voices, or say anything against the man of God or the servants of God again.   But if I fail to do it, it becomes my duty to renounce all further pretensions to revelations and inspirations, or to be a prophet; and I should be like the rest of the world—a false teacher, be hailed as a friend, and no man would seek my life.   But if all religious teachers were honest enough to renounce their pretensions to godliness when their ignorance of the knowledge of God is made manifest, they will all be as badly off as I am, at any rate; and you might as well take the lives of other false teachers as that of mine, if I am false.   If any man is authorized to take away my life because he thinks and says I am a false teacher, then, upon the same principle, we should be justified in taking away the life of every false teacher, and where would be the end of blood?   And who would not be the sufferer?[1]

The Privilege of Religious Freedom

But meddle not with any man for his religion: and all governments ought to permit every man to enjoy his religion unmolested.   No man is authorized to take away life in consequence of difference of religion, which all laws and governments ought to tolerate and protect, right or wrong.   Every man has a natural, and, in our country, a constitutional right to be a false prophet, as well as a true prophet. If I show, verily, that

---

[1] These remarks will be better understood, if it is remembered that about this time the storms of a renewed persecution were bursting upon the Prophet, and his life was threatened upon every side.

I have the truth of God, and show that ninety-nine out of every hundred professing religious ministers are false teachers, having no authority, while they pretend to hold the keys of God's kingdom on earth, and was to kill them because they are false teachers, it would deluge the whole world with blood.

I will prove that the world is wrong, by showing what God is. I am going to enquire after God; for I want you all to know him, and to be familiar with him; and if I am bringing you to a knowledge of him, all persecutions against me ought to cease. You will then know that I am his servant; for I speak as one having authority.

God an Exalted Man

I will go back to the beginning before the world was, to show what kind of being God is. What sort of a being was God in the beginning? Open your ears and hear, all ye ends of the earth, for I am going to prove it to you by the Bible, and to tell you the designs of God in relation to the human race, and why He interferes with the affairs of man.

God himself was once as we are now, and is an exalted man, and sits enthroned in yonder heavens! That is the great secret. If the veil were rent today, and the great God who holds this world in its orbit, and who upholds all worlds and all things by his power, was to make himself visible,—I say, if you were to see him today, you would see him like a man in form— like yourselves in all the person, image, and very form as a man; for Adam was created in the very fashion, image and likeness of God, and received instruction from, and walked, talked and conversed with him, as one man talks and communes with another.

In order to understand the subject of the dead, for consolation of those who mourn for the loss of their friends, it is necessary we should understand the character and being of God and how he came to be so; for I am going to tell you how God came to be God. We have imagined and supposed that God was God from all eternity. I will refute that idea, and take away the veil, so that you may see.

These are incomprehensible ideas to some, but they are simple. *It is the first principle of the Gospel to know for a certainty the Character of God, and to know that we may converse with him as one man converses with another, and that he was once a man like us; yea, that God himself, the Father of us all, dwelt on an earth, the same as Jesus Christ himself did; and I will show it from the Bible.*

Power of the Father and the Son

I wish I was in a suitable place to tell it, and that I had the trump of an archangel, so that I could tell the story in such a manner that persecution would cease for ever. What did Jesus say? (Mark it, Elder Rigdon!) The Scriptures inform us that Jesus said, As the Father hath power in Himself, even so hath the Son power—to do what? Why, what the Father did. The answer is obvious—in a manner to lay down His body and take it up again. Jesus, what are you going to do? To lay down my life as my Father did, and take it up again. Do we believe it? If you do not believe it, you do not believe the Bible.[2] The Scriptures say it, and I defy all the learning and wisdom and all the combined powers of earth and hell together to refute it.

Here, then, is eternal life—to know the only wise and true God; and you have got to learn how to be Gods yourselves, and to be kings and priests to God, the same as all Gods have done before you,[3] namely, by going from one

---

[2]The argument here made by the Prophet is very much strengthened by the following passage: "The Son can do nothing of himself, but what he seeth the Father do; for what things soever he [the Father] doeth, these also doeth the Son likewise." (St. John 5:19).

[3]Perhaps no passage in the Prophet's discourse has given more offense than the one here noted, and yet men are coming to think and feel the truth of what he said. Henry Drummond, for instance (following the Prophet by half a century), in his really great work, *Natural Law in the Spiritual World*, in the chapter on Growth, wherein he points out the difference between the merely moral man and one whose life has been touched by the spiritual power of God, and so received something that the merely moral man has not received, says: "The end of salvation is perfection, the Christ-like mind, character and life. * * * Therefore the man who has within himself this great formative agent, Life [spiritual life] is nearer the end than the man who has morality alone. The latter can never reach perfection, the former *must*. For the life must develop out according to its type; and being a germ of the Christ-life, *it must unfold into a Christ.*" Joseph Smith's doctrine means no more than this.

Sir Oliver Lodge says much to the same effect in the following passage on "Christianity and Science" (Hibbert's Journal, April, 1906):

It is orthodox, therefore, to maintain that Christ's birth was miraculous and his death portentous, that he continued in existence otherwise than as we men continue, that his very body rose and ascended into heaven—whatever that collection of words may mean. But I suggest that such an attempt small degree to another, and from a small capacity to a great one; from grace to grace, from exaltation to exaltation, until you attain to the resurrection of the dead, and are able to dwell in everlasting burnings, and to sit in glory, as do those who sit enthroned in everlasting power. And I want you to know that God, in the last days, while certain individuals are proclaiming his name, is not trifling with you or me.

The Righteous to Dwell in Everlasting Burnings

These are the first principles of consolation. How consoling to the mourners when they are called to part with a husband, wife, father, mother, child, or dear relative, to know that, although the earthly tabernacle is laid down and dissolved, they shall rise again to dwell in everlasting burnings in immortal glory, not to sorrow, suffer, or die any more; but they shall be heirs of God and joint heirs with Jesus Christ. What is it? To inherit the same power, the same glory and the same exaltation, until you arrive at the station of a God, and ascend the throne of eternal power, the same as those who have gone before. What did Jesus do? Why; I do the things I saw my Father do when worlds came rolling into existence. My Father worked out his kingdom with fear and trembling, and I must do the same; and when I get my kingdom, I shall present it to my Father, so that he may obtain kingdom upon kingdom,

---

at exceptional glorification of his body is a pious heresy—a heresy which misses the truth lying open to our eyes. His humanity is to be recognized as real and ordinary and thorough and complete; not in middle life alone; but at birth, and at death and after death. Whatever happened to him may happen to any one of us, provided we attain the appropriate altitude; an altitude which, whether within our individual reach or not, is assuredly within reach of humanity. That is what he urged again and again. "Be born again." "Be ye perfect." "Ye are the sons of God." "My Father and your Father, my God and your God." The uniqueness of the ordinary humanity of Christ is the first and patent truth, masked only by well-meaning and reverent superstition. But the second truth is greater than that—without it the first would be meaningless and useless,—if man alone, what gain have we? The world is full of men. What the world wants is a God. Behold the God! —[That is, the God, Jesus Christ.]

The divinity of Jesus is the truth which now requires to be reperceived, to be illumined afresh by new knowledge, to be cleansed and revivified by the wholesome flood of scepticism which has poured over it: it can be freed now from all trace of grovelling superstition; and can be recognized freely and enthusiastically: the divinity of Jesus, and [the divinity] of all other noble and saintly souls, insofar as they, too, have been inflamed by a spark of Deity—insofar as they, too, can be recognized as manifestations of the Divine.—Notes by Elder B. H. Roberts.

and it will exalt him in glory. He will then take a higher exaltation, and I will take his place, and thereby become exalted myself. So that Jesus treads in the tracks of his Father, and inherits what God did before; and God is thus glorified and exalted in the salvation and exaltation of all his children. It is plain beyond disputation, and you thus learn some of the first principles of the Gospel, about which so much hath been said.

When you climb up a ladder, you must begin at the bottom, and ascend step by step, until you arrive at the top; and so it is with the principles of the Gospel—you must begin with the first, and go on until you learn all the principles of exaltation. But it will be a great while after you have passed through the veil before you will have learned them. It is not all to be comprehended in this world; it will be a great work to learn our salvation *and exaltation even beyond the grave.* I suppose I am not allowed to go into an investigation of anything that is not contained in the Bible. If I do, I think there are so many over-wise men here, that they would cry "treason" and put me to death. So I will go to the old Bible and turn commentator today.

Meaning of the Hebrew Scriptures

I shall comment on the very first Hebrew word in the Bible; I will make a comment on the very first sentence of the history of creation in the Bible—*Berosheit.* I want to analyze the word. *Baith*—in, by, through, and everything else. *Rosh*—the head. *Sheit*—grammatical termination. When the inspired man wrote it, he did not put the *baith* there. An old Jew without any authority added the word; he thought it too bad to begin to talk about the head! It read first, "The head one of the Gods brought forth the Gods." That is the true meaning of the words. *Baurau* signifies to bring forth. If you do not believe it, you do not believe the learned man of God. Learned men can teach you no more than what I have told you. *Thus the head God brought forth the Gods in the grand council.*

I will transpose and simplify it in the English language. Oh, ye lawyers, ye doctors, and ye priests, who have persecuted me, I want to let you know that the Holy Ghost knows something as well as you do. The head God called together the Gods and sat in grand council to bring forth the world. The grand councilors sat at the head in yonder heavens and contemplated the creation of the worlds which were created at the time.   When I say doctors and lawyers, I mean the doctors and lawyers of the Scriptures.   I have done so⁴ hitherto without explanation, to let the lawyers flutter and everybody laugh at them.   Some learned doctors might take a notion to say the Scriptures say thus and so; and we might believe the Scriptures; they are not to be altered.   But I am going to show you an error in them.

I have an old edition of the New Testament in the Latin, Hebrew, German and Greek languages.   I have been reading the German, and find it to be the most [nearly] correct translation, and to correspond nearest to the revelations which God has given to me for the last fourteen years.   It tells about Jacobus, the son of Zebedee.   It means Jacob.   In the English New Testament it is translated James.   Now, if Jacob had the keys, you might talk about James through all eternity and never get the keys.   In the 21st of the fourth chapter of Matthew, my old German edition gives the word Jacob instead of James.

The doctors (I mean doctors of law, not physic) say, "If you preach anything not according to the Bible, we will cry treason."   How can we escape the damnation of hell, except God be with us and reveal to us?   Men bind us with chains. The Latin says Jacobus, which means Jacob; the Hebrew says Jacob, the Greek says Jacob and the German says Jacob; here we have the testimony of four against one.   I thank God that I have got this old book; but I thank him more for the gift of the Holy Ghost.   I have got the oldest book in the world; but I [also] have the oldest book in my heart, even the gift of the Holy Ghost.   I have all the four Testaments.   Come here, ye learned men, and read, if you can.   I should not have introduced this testimony, were it not to back up the word *rosh*— the head, the Father of the Gods.   I should not have brought it up, only to show that I am right.

A Council of the Gods

In the beginning, the head of the Gods called a council of the Gods; and they came together and concocted a plan to create the world and people it.   When we begin to learn this

---

⁴i.e. Used the term "lawyer" without explanation hitherto.

way, we begin to learn the only true God, and what kind of a being we have got to worship. Having a knowledge of God, we begin to know how to approach him, and how to ask so as to receive an answer. When we understand the character of God, and know how to come to him, he begins to unfold the heavens to us, and to tell us all about it. When we are ready to come to him, he is ready to come to us.

Now, I ask all who hear me, why the learned men who are preaching salvation, say that God created the heavens and the earth out of nothing? The reason is, that they are unlearned in the things of God, and have not the gift of the Holy Ghost; they account it blasphemy in any one to contradict their idea. If you tell them that God made the world out of something, they will call you a fool. But I am learned, and know more than all the world put together. The Holy Ghost does, anyhow, and He is within me, and comprehends more than all the world: and I will associate myself with Him.

Meaning of the Word Create

You ask the learned doctors why they say the world was made out of nothing; and they will answer, "Doesn't the Bible say He *created* the world?" And they infer, from the word create, that it must have been made out of nothing. Now, the word create came from the word *baurau* which does not mean to create out of nothing; it means to organize; the same as a man would organize materials and build a ship.[5] Hence, we

---

[5] The view of the Prophet on this subject of creation is abundantly sustained by men of learning subsequent to his time. The Rev. Baden Powell, of Oxford University, for instance, writing for Kitto's *Cyclopaedia of Biblical Literature*, says: "The meaning of this word (create) has been commonly associated with the idea of 'making out of nothing.' But when we come to inquire more precisely into the subject, we can of course satisfy ourselves as to the meaning only from an examination of the original phrase." The learned professor then proceeds to say that three distinct Hebrew verbs are in different places employed with reference to the same divine act, and may be translated, respectively, "create," "make," "form or fashion." "Now," continues the Professor, "though each of these has its shade of distinction, yet the best critics understand them as so nearly synonymous that, at least in regard to the idea of making out of nothing, little or no foundation for that doctrine can be obtained from the first of these words." And, of course, if no foundation for the doctrine can be obtained from the first of these words— viz., the verb translated "create," then the chances are still less for there being any foundation for the doctrine of creation from nothing in the verb translated, "made," "formed," or "fashioned."

Professor Powell further says: "The idea of 'creation,' as meaning absoinfer that God had materials to organize the world out of chaos —chaotic matter, which is element, and in which dwells all the glory. Element had an existence from the time he had. The pure principles of element are principles which can never be

---

lutely 'making out of nothing,' or calling into existence that which did not exist before, in the strictest sense of the term, is not a doctrine of scripture; but it has been held by many on the grounds of natural theology, as enhancing the ideas we form of the divine power, and more especially since the contrary must imply the belief in the eternity and self-existence of matter."

Dr. William Smith's great dictionary of the Bible (Hackett edition, 1894) has no article on the term "create" or "creation," but in the article "earth" we have reference to the subject, and really an implied explanation as to why this work contains no treatise on "create" or "creation." "The act of creation itself, as recorded in the first chapter of Genesis, is a subject beyond and above the experience of man; human language, derived, as it originally was, from the sensible and material world, fails to find an adequate term to describe the act; for our word 'create' and the Hebrew *bara*, though most appropriate to express the idea of an original creation, are yet applicable and must necessarily be applicable to other modes of creation; nor does the addition of such expressions as 'out of things that were not,' or 'not from things which appear,' contribute much to the force of the declaration. The absence of a term which shall describe exclusively an original creation is a necessary infirmity of language; as the events occurred but once, the corresponding term must, in order to be adequate, have been coined for the occasion and reserved for it alone, which would have been impossible."

The philosophers with equal emphasis sustain the contention of the Prophet. Herbert Spencer, in his *First Principles,* (1860), said:

"There was once universally current, a notion that things could vanish into absolute nothing, or arise out of absolute nothing. * * * The current theology, in its teachings respecting the beginning and end of the world, is clearly pervaded by it. * * * The gradual accumulation of experiences, has tended slowly to reverse this conviction; until now, the doctrine that matter is indestructible has become a commonplace. All the apparent proofs that something can come of nothing, a wider knowledge has one by one cancelled. The comet that is suddenly discovered in the heavens and nightly waxes larger, is proved not to be a newly-created body, but a body that was until lately beyond the range of vision. The cloud which in the course of a few minutes forms in the sky, consists not of substance that has begun to be, but of substance that previously existed in a more diffused and transparent form. And similarly with a crystal or precipitate in relation to the fluid depositing it. Conversely, the seeming annihilations of matter turn out, on closer observation, to be only changes of state. It is found that the evaporated water, though it has become invisible, may be brought by condensation to its original shape. The discharged fowling-piece gives evidence that though the gunpowder has disappeared, there have appeared in place of it certain gases which, in assuming a larger volume, have caused the explosion."

Fiske follows Spencer, of course, and in his *Cosmic Philosophy* sums up the matter in these words. "It is now unconceivable that a particle of matter should either come into existence, or lapse into non-existence."

Robert Kennedy Duncan (1905), in his *New Knowledge* says: "Governing matter in all its varied forms, there is one great fundamental law which up to this time has been ironclad in its character. This law, known as the law of the conservation of mass, states that no particle of matter, however destroyed; they may be organized and re-organized, but not destroyed. They had no beginning, and can have no end.[6]

The Immortal Spirit

I have another subject to dwell upon, which is calculated to exalt man; but it is impossible for me to say much on this subject. I shall therefore just touch upon it, for time will not permit me to say all. It is associated with the subject of the resurrection of the dead,—namely, the soul—the mind of man— the immortal spirit.[7] Where did it come from? All learned men and doctors of divinity say that God created it in the beginning; but it is not so: the very idea lessens man in my estimation. I do not believe the doctrine; I know better. Hear it, all ye ends of the world; for God has told me so; and if you don't believe me, it will not make the truth without effect. I will make a man appear a fool before I get through; if he does not believe it. I am going to tell of things more noble.

We say that God himself is a self-existent being. Who told you so? It is correct enough; but how did it get into your heads? Who told you that man did not exist in like manner upon the same principles? Man does exist upon the same principles. God made a tabernacle and put a spirit into it, and

---

small, may be created or destroyed. All the king's horses and all the king's men cannot destroy a pin's head. We may smash that pin's head, dissolve it in acid, burn it in the electric furnace, employ, in a word, every annihilating agency, and yet that pin's head persists in being. Again, it is as uncreatable as it is indestructible. In other words, we cannot create something out of nothing. The material must be furnished for every existent article. The sum of matter in the universe is x pounds,—and, while it may be carried through a myriad of forms, when all is said and done, it is just—x pounds.— Note by Elder B. H. Roberts.

[6]"The elements are eternal, and spirit and element inseparably connected receive a fullness of joy. * * * The elements are the tabernacle of God; yea, man is the tabernacle of God, even temples." (D. and C. Sec. 93:33-35.)

[7]It appears to be very clear that the Prophet had in mind the *intelligence,* when he said "the soul—the mind of man—the immortal spirit," was not created or made, and he did not have reference to the spirit as a begotten child of God. It was the doctrine of the Prophet, and is of the Church, that the spirits of men are begotten sons and daughters of God. See the official statement of the First Presidency and the Council of the Twelve as published in the *Improvement Era,* August, 1916, under the caption, *The Father and The Son.* The passage in the Doctrine and Covenants on which this doctrine is based is found in Sec. 93:29-30, and is as follows: "Man was in the beginning with God. Intelligence, or the light of truth, was not created or made, neither indeed can be." See also the statements in following paragraphs.

it became a living soul. (Refers to the old Bible.) How does it read in the Hebrew? It does not say in the Hebrew that God created the spirit of man. It says "God made man out of the earth and put into him Adam's spirit, and so became a living body."

The mind or the intelligence which man possesses is co-equal[8] with God himself. I know that my testimony is true; hence, when I talk to these mourners, what have they lost? Their relatives and friends are only separated from their bodies for a short season: their spirits which existed with God have left the tabernacle of clay only for a little moment, as it were; and they now exist in a place where they converse together the same as we do on the earth.

I am dwelling on the immortality of the spirit of man. Is it logical to say that the intelligence of spirits is immortal, and yet that it had a beginning? The intelligence of spirits had no beginning, neither will it have an end. That is good logic. That which has a beginning may have an end. There never was a time when there were not spirits; for they are co-equal [co-eternal] with our Father in heaven.

---

[8]Undoubtedly the proper word here would be "co-eternal," not "co-equal." This illustrates the imperfection of the report made of the sermon. For surely the mind of man is not co-equal with God except in the matter of its eternity. It is the direct statement in the Book of Abraham—accepted by the Church as scripture—that there are differences in the intelligences that exist, that some are more intelligent than others; and that God is "more intelligent than them all" (Book of Abraham, Chapt. 3). I believe that this means more than that God is more intelligent than any other one of the intelligences. It means that he is more intelligent than all of the other intelligences combined. His intelligence is greater than that of the mass, and that has led me to say in the second Year Book of the Seventies:—"It is this fact doubtless which makes this One, 'more intelligent than them all'," God. He is the All-Wise One! The All-Powerful One! What he tells other Intelligences to do must be precisely the wisest, fittest thing that they could anywhere or anyhow learn—the thing which it will always behoove them, with right loyal thankfulness, and nothing doubting, to do. There goes with this, too, the thought that this All-Wise One will be the Unselfish One, the All-Loving One, the One who desires that which is highest, and best; not for himself alone, but for all: and that will be best for him too. His glory, his power, his joy will be enhanced by the uplifting of all, by enlarging them; by increasing their joy, power, and glory. And because this All Intelligent One is all this, and does all this, the other Intelligences worship him, submit their judgments and their will to his judgment and his will. He knows, and can do that which is best; and this submission of the mind to the Most Intelligent, Wisest—wiser than all—is worship. This is the whole meaning of the doctrine and the life of the Christ expressed in—"Father, not my will but Thy will, be done."—Note by Elder B. H. Roberts.

I want to reason more on the spirit of man; for I am dwelling on the body and spirit of man—on the subject of the dead. I take my ring from my finger and liken it unto the mind of man—the immortal part, because it has no beginning. Suppose you cut it in two; then it has a beginning and an end; but join it again, and it continues one eternal round. So with the spirit of man. As the Lord liveth, if it had a beginning, it will have an end. All the fools and learned and wise men from the beginning of creation, who say that the spirit of man had a beginning, prove that it must have an end; and if that doctrine is true, then the doctrine of annihilation would be true. But if I am right, I might with boldness proclaim from the house-tops that God never had the power to create the spirit of man at all. God himself could not create himself.

Intelligence is eternal and exists upon a self-existent principle. It is a spirit[9] from age to age, and there is no creation about it. All the minds and spirits that God ever sent into the world are susceptible of enlargement.

The Power to Advance in Knowledge

The first principles of man are self-existent with God. God himself, finding he was in the midst of spirits and glory, because he was more intelligent, saw proper to institute laws whereby the rest could have a privilege to advance like himself. The relationship we have with God places us in a situation to advance in knowledge. He has power to institute laws to instruct the weaker intelligences, that they may be exalted with himself, so that they might have one glory upon another, and all that knowledge, power, glory, and intelligence, which is requisite in order to save them in the world of spirits.[10]

---

[9]"A spirit from age to age"—not "spirit from age to age"; but "a spirit," that is, an entity, a person, an individual. This paragraph in the Prophet's remarks may well be taken as an interpretation of Doc. and Cov., Sec. 93:29.—Note by Elder B. H. Roberts.

[10]"Behold this is my work and my glory—to bring to pass the immortality and eternal life of man."—(The Lord to Moses, Book of Moses, chapt. 1:39; Pearl of Great Price)—that is, "to bring to pass the immortality and eternal life of man," as man. The passage has reference doubtless to man as composed of spirit and body—a proper "soul" (see Doc. and Cov. Sec. 88:15-16)—"For the spirit and the body is the soul of man; and the resurrection of the dead is the redemption of the soul." In other words, the "work" and the "glory" of God are achieved in bringing to pass the "immortality and eternal life of man," as man, in the eternal union of the spirit and body of man through the resurrection through the redemption of the soul. This

This is good doctrine. It tastes good. I can taste the principles of eternal life, and so can you. They are given to me by the revelations of Jesus Christ; and I know that when I tell you these words of eternal life as they are given to me, you taste them, and I know that you believe them. You say honey is sweet, and so do I. I can also taste the spirit of eternal life. I know it is good; and when I tell you of these things which were given me by inspiration of the Holy Spirit, you are bound to receive them as sweet, and rejoice more and more.

The Relation of Man to God

I want to talk more of the relation of man to God. I will open your eyes in relation to your dead. All things whatsoever God in his infinite wisdom has seen fit and proper to reveal to us, while we are dwelling in mortality, in regard to our mortal bodies, are revealed to us in the abstract, and independent of affinity of this mortal tabernacle, but are revealed to our spirits precisely as though we had no bodies at all; and those revelations which will save our spirits will save our bodies. God reveals them to us in view of no eternal dissolution of the body, or tabernacle. Hence the responsibility, the awful responsibility, that rests upon us in relation to our dead; for all the spirits who have not obeyed the Gospel in the flesh must either obey it in the spirit or be damned. Solemn thought!—dreadful thought! Is there nothing to be done?—no preparation—no salvation for our fathers and friends who have died without having had the opportunity to obey the decrees of the Son of Man? Would to God that I had forty days and nights in which to tell you all! I would let you know that I am not a "fallen prophet."[11]

---

brings into eternal union "spirit and element" declared by the word of God to be essential to a fulness of joy—"The elements are eternal, and spirit and element, inseparably connected, receive a fulness of joy; and when separated man cannot receive a fulness of joy" (Doc. and Cov., Sec. 93). Also, "Adam fell that men might be: and men are that they might have joy" (II Nephi 2:25). Indeed, the whole purpose of God in bringing to pass the earth life of man is to inure to the welfare and enlargement of man as urged in the teaching of the Prophet in the paragraph above. God affects man only to his advantage. See also Seventy's Year Book No. II, Lesson ii, note 6.—Note by Elder B. H. Roberts.

[11]Accusations were repeatedly being made about this time that President Smith was a fallen prophet. But when the mighty doctrines that in this discourse he is setting forth are taken into account, and the spiritual power with which he is delivering them is reckoned with, no more complete refuta-

Our Greatest Responsibility

What promises are made in relation to the subject of the salvation of the dead? and what kind of characters are those who can be saved, although their bodies are mouldering and decaying in the grave? When his commandments teach us, it is in view of eternity; for we are looked upon by God as though we were in eternity. God dwells in eternity, and does not view things as we do.

The greatest responsibility in this world that God has laid upon us is to seek after our dead. The Apostle says, "They without us cannot be made perfect;" (Hebrews 11:40) for it is necessary that the sealing power should be in our hands to seal our children and our dead for the fulness of the dispensation of times—a dispensation to meet the promises made by Jesus Christ before the foundation of the world for the salvation of man.

Now, I will speak of them. I will meet Paul half way. I say to you, Paul, you cannot be perfect without us. It is necessary that those who are going before and those who come after us should have salvation in common with us; and thus hath God made it obligatory upon man. Hence, God said, "I will send you Elijah the prophet before the coming of the great and dreadful day of the Lord; and he shall turn the heart of the fathers to the children, and the heart of the children to their fathers, lest I come and smite the earth with a curse." (Malachi 4:5-6.)

A Salvation for Men

I have a declaration to make as to the provisions which God hath made to suit the conditions of man—made from before the foundation of the world. What has Jesus said? All sin, and all blasphemies, and every transgression, except one, that man can be guilty of, may be forgiven; and there is a salvation for all men, either in this world or the world to come, who have not committed the unpardonable sin, there being a pro-

tion of his being a fallen prophet could be made. The Prophet lived his life in *crescendo*. From small beginnings, it rose in breadth and power as he neared its close. As a teacher he reached the climax of his career in this discourse. After it there was but one thing more he could do—seal his testimony with his blood. This he did less than three months later. Such is not the manner of life of false prophets.—Note by Elder B. H. Roberts.

vision either in this world or the world of spirits. Hence God hath made a provision that every spirit in the eternal world can be ferreted out and saved unless he has committed that unpardonable sin which cannot be remitted to him either in this world or the world of spirits. God has wrought out a salvation for all men, unless they have committed a certain sin; and every man who has a friend in the eternal world can save him, unless he has committed the unpardonable sin. And so you can see how far you can be a savior.

The Unpardonable Sin

A man cannot commit the unpardonable sin after the dissolution of the body, and there is a way possible for escape. Knowledge saves a man; and in the world of spirits no man can be exalted but by knowledge. So long as a man will not give heed to the commandments, he must abide without salvation. If a man has knowledge, he can be saved; although, if he has been guilty of great sins, he will be punished for them. But when he consents to obey the Gospel, whether here or in the world of spirits, he is saved.

A man is his own tormenter and his own condemner. Hence the saying, They shall go into the lake that burns with fire and brimstone. The torment of disappointment in the mind of man is as exquisite as a lake burning with fire and brimstone. I say, so is the torment of man.

I know the Scriptures and understand them. I said, no man can commit the unpardonable sin after the dissolution of the body, nor in this life, until he receives the Holy Ghost; but they must do it in this world. Hence the salvation of Jesus Christ was wrought out for all men, in order to triumph over the devil; for if it did not catch him in one place, it would in another; for he stood up as a Savior. All will suffer until they obey Christ himself.

The contention in heaven was—Jesus said there would be certain souls that would not be saved; and the devil said he could save them all, and laid his plans before the grand council, who gave their vote in favor of Jesus Christ. So the devil rose up in rebellion against God, and was cast down, with all who put up their heads for him. (Book of Moses—Pearl of Great Price, Chap. 4:1-4; Book of Abraham, Chap. 3:23-28.)

The Forgiveness of Sins

All sins shall be forgiven, except the sin against the Holy Ghost; for Jesus will save all except the sons of perdition. What must a man do to commit the unpardonable sin? He must receive the Holy Ghost, have the heavens opened unto him, and know God, and then sin against Him. After a man has sinned against the Holy Ghost, there is no repentance for him.[12] He has got to say that the sun does not shine while he sees it; he has got to deny Jesus Christ when the heavens have been opened unto him, and to deny the plan of salvation with his eyes open to the truth of it; and from that time he begins to be an enemy. This is the case with many apostates of the Church of Jesus Christ of Latter-day Saints.

When a man begins to be an enemy to this work, he hunts me, he seeks to kill me, and never ceases to thirst for my blood. He gets the spirit of the devil—the same spirit that they had who crucified the Lord of Life—the same spirit that sins against the Holy Ghost. You cannot save such persons; you cannot bring them to repentance; they make open war, like the devil, and awful is the consequence.

I advise all of you to be careful what you do, or you may by-and-by find out that you have been deceived. Stay yourselves; do not give way; don't make any hasty moves, you may be saved. If a spirit of bitterness is in you, don't be in haste. You may say, that man is a sinner. Well, if he repents, he shall be forgiven. Be cautious: await. When you find a spirit that wants bloodshed—murder, the same is not of God, but is of the devil. Out of the abundance of the heart of man the mouth speaketh.

"In My Father's House"

The best men bring forth the best works. The man who tells you words of life is the man who can save you. I warn you against all evil characters who sin against the Holy Ghost;

---

[12]"For it is impossible for those who were once enlightened, and have tasted of the heavenly gift, and were made partakers of the Holy Ghost, and have tasted the good word of God, and the powers of the world to come, if they shall fall away, to renew them again unto repentance; seeing they crucify to themselves the Son of God afresh, and put him to an open shame" (Heb. 6:4-6). Those who sin against the light and knowledge of the Holy Ghost may be said to crucify more than the body of our Lord, they crucify the Spirit.

for there is no redemption for them in this world nor in the world to come.

I could go back and trace every subject of interest concerning the relationship of man to God, if I had time. I can enter into the mysteries; I can enter largely into the eternal worlds; for Jesus said, "In my Father's house are many mansions; if it were not so, I would have told you. I go to prepare a place for you" (John 14:2). Paul says, "There is one glory of the sun, and another glory of the moon, and another glory of the stars; for one star differeth from another star in glory. So also is the resurrection of the dead" (1 Cor. 15:41). What have we to console us in relation to the dead? We have reason to have the greatest hope and consolations for our dead of any people on the earth; for we have seen them walk worthily in our midst, and seen them sink asleep in the arms of Jesus; and those who have died in the faith are now in the celestial kingdom of God. And hence is the glory of the sun.

Righteous Mourners Rejoice

You mourners have occasion to rejoice, speaking of the death of Elder King Follett; for your husband and father is gone to wait until the resurrection of the dead—until the perfection of the remainder; for at the resurrection your friend will rise in perfect felicity and go to celestial glory, while many must wait myriads of years before they can receive the like blessings; and your expectations and hopes are far above what man can conceive; for why has God revealed it to us?

I am authorized to say, by the authority of the Holy Ghost, that you have no occasion to fear; for he is gone to the home of the just. Don't mourn, don't weep. I know it by the testimony of the Holy Ghost that is within me; and you may wait for your friends to come forth to meet you in the morn of the celestial world.

Rejoice, O Israel! Your friends who have been murdered for the truth's sake in the persecutions shall triumph gloriously in the celestial world, while their murderers shall welter for ages in torment, even until they shall have paid the uttermost farthing. I say this for the benefit of strangers.

I have a father, brothers, children, and friends who have gone to a world of spirits. They are only absent for a moment. They are in the spirit, and we shall soon meet again. The time will soon arrive when the trumpet shall sound. When we depart, we shall hail our mothers, fathers, friends, and all whom we love, who have fallen asleep in Jesus. There will be no fear of mobs, persecutions, or malicious lawsuits and arrests; but it will be an eternity of felicity.[13]

* * *

Baptism

I will leave this subject here, and make a few remarks on the subject of baptism. The baptism of water, without the baptism of fire and the Holy Ghost attending it, is of no use; they are necessarily and inseparably connected. An individual must be born of water and the Spirit in order to get into the kingdom of God. In the German, the text bears me out the same as the revelations which I have given and taught for the last fourteen years on that subject. I have the testimony to put in their teeth. My testimony has been true all the time. You will find it in the declaration of John the Baptist. (Reads from the German.) John says, "I baptize you with water, but when Jesus comes, who has the power (or keys), he shall administer the baptism of fire and the Holy Ghost." Where is now all the sectarian world? And if this testimony is true, they are all damned as clearly as anathema can do it. I know the text is true. I call upon all you Germans who know that it is true to say, Aye. (Loud shouts of "Aye.")

Alexander Campbell, how are you going to save people with water alone? For John said his baptism was good for nothing without the baptism of Jesus Christ. 'Therefore, *not* leaving the principles of the doctrine of Christ, let us go on unto perfection; not laying again the foundation of repentance from dead works, and of faith toward God, of the doctrine of baptisms, and of laying on of hands, and of resurrection of the dead, and of eternal judgment. And this will we do, if God permit." (Heb. 6:1-3).

---

[13]The omitted paragraph indicated by the asterisks refers to the exaltation and power that will be wielded by children in the resurrection before attaining to the development of stature of men and women; but which developments will surely come to those who are raised from the dead as infants. It is quite evident that there was some imperfection in the report of the Prophet's remarks at this point, and hence the passage is omitted. Those who desire to investigate the matter more fully should consult the *Documentary History*, Vol. iv, pp. 556-7 and footnote. See also discourse of June 16, 1844, this volume.

There is one God, one Father, one Jesus, one hope of our calling, one baptism. * * * Many talk of baptism not being essential to salvation; but this kind of teaching would lay the foundation of their damnation. I have the truth, and am at the defiance of the world to contradict me, if they can.

I have now preached a little Latin, a little Hebrew, Greek, and German; and I have fulfilled all. I am not so big a fool as many have taken me to be. The Germans know that I read the German correctly.

A Call to Repentance

Hear it, all ye ends of the earth—all ye priests, all ye sinners, and all men. Repent! repent! Obey the Gospel. Turn to God; for your religion won't save you, and you will be damned. I do not say how long. There have been remarks made concerning all men being redeemed from hell; but I say that those who sin against the Holy Ghost cannot be forgiven in this world or in the world to come; they shall die the second death. Those who commit the unpardonable sin are doomed to *Gnolom*—to dwell in hell, worlds without end. As they concoct scenes of bloodshed in this world, so they shall rise to that resurrection which is as the lake of fire and brimstone. Some shall rise to the everlasting burnings of God; for God dwells in everlasting burnings, and some shall rise to the damnation of their own filthiness, which is as exquisite a torment as the lake of fire and brimstone.

I have intended my remarks for all, both rich and poor, bond and free, great and small. I have no enmity against any man. I love you all; but I hate some of your deeds. I am your best friend, and if persons miss their mark it is their own fault. If I reprove a man, and he hates me, he is a fool; for I love all men, especially these my brethren and sisters.

I rejoice in hearing the testimony of my aged friends. You don't know me; you never knew my heart. No man knows my history. I cannot tell it: I shall never undertake it. I don't blame any one for not believing my history. If I had not experienced what I have, I could not have believed it myself. I never did harm any man since I was born in the world. My voice is always for peace.

I cannot lie down until all my work is finished. I never

think any evil, nor do anything to the harm of my fellow-man. When I am called by the trump of the archangel and weighed in the balance, you will all know me then. I add no more. God bless you all. Amen. (April 7, 1844.) T. & S. Aug. 15, 1844.

President Joseph Smith's Remarks—The Whole of America Zion—April Conference, 1844

President Joseph Smith said:—It is just as impossible for me to continue the subject of yesterday as to raise the dead. My lungs are worn out. There is a time to all things, and I must wait. I will give it up, and leave the time to those who can make you hear, and I will continue the subject of my discourse some other time. I want to make a proclamation to the Elders. I wanted you to stay, in order that I might make this proclamation. You know very well that the Lord has led this Church by revelation. I have another revelation in relation to economy in the Church—a great, grand, and glorious revelation. I shall not be able to dwell as largely upon it now as at some other time; but I will give you the first principles. You know there has been great discussion in relation to Zion— where it is, and where the gathering of the dispensation is, and which I am now going to tell you. The prophets have spoken and written upon it; but I will make a proclamation that will cover a broader ground. *The whole of America is Zion itself from north to south, and is described by the Prophets, who declare that it is the Zion where the mountain of the Lord should be, and that it should be in the center of the land.* When Elders shall take up and examine the old prophecies in the Bible, they will see it.

Ordinances in the Temple

The declaration this morning is, that as soon as the Temple and baptismal font are prepared, we calculate to give the Elders of Israel their washings and anointings, and attend to those last and more impressive ordinances, without which we cannot obtain celestial thrones. But there must be a holy place prepared for that purpose. There was a proclamation made during the time that the foundation of the Temple was laid to that effect, and there are provisions made until the work is completed, so that men may receive their endowments and be made kings and priests unto the Most High God, having nothing to do with temporal things, but their whole time will be taken up with things pertaining to the house of God. These must, however, be a place built expressly for that purpose, and for men to be baptized for their dead. It must be built in this central place; for every man who wishes to save his father, mother, brothers, sisters and friends, must go through all the ordinances for each one of them separately, the same as for himself, from baptism to ordination, washing and anointings, and receive all the keys and powers of the Priesthood, the same as for himself.

Stakes of Zion

I have received instructions from the Lord that from henceforth wherever Elders of Israel shall build up churches and branches unto the Lord throughout the States, there shall be a stake of Zion. In the great cities, as Boston, New York, &c., there shall be stakes. It is a glorious proclamation, and I reserved it to the last, and designed it to be understood that this work shall commence after the washings, anointings and endowments have been performed here.

The Lord has an established law in relation to the matter: there must be a particular spot for the salvation of our dead. I verily believe there will be a place, and hence men who want to save their dead can come and bring their families, do their work by being baptized and attending to the other ordinances for their dead, and then may go back again to live and wait till they go to receive their reward. I shall leave my brethren to enlarge on this subject; it is my duty to teach the doctrine. I would teach it more fully—the spirit is willing but the flesh is weak. God is not willing to let me gratify you; but I must teach the Elders, and they should teach you. God made Aaron to be the mouthpiece for the children of Israel, and He will make me be god to you in His stead, and the Elders to be mouth for me; and if you don't like it, you must lump it. I have been giving Elder Adams instruction in some principles to speak to you, and if he makes a mistake, I will get up and correct him. (April 8, 1844.) D. H. C. 6:318-320.

President Joseph Smith's Address—Defense of His Prophetic Calling—Resurrection of the Dead—Fulness of Ordinances Necessary Both for the Living and Dead

The Savior has the words of eternal life. Nothing else can profit us. There is no salvation in believing an evil report against our neighbor. I advise all to go on to perfection, and search deeper and deeper into the mysteries of Godliness. A man can do nothing for himself unless God direct him in the right way; and the Priesthood is for that purpose.

The last time I spoke on this stand it was on the resurrection of the dead, when I promised to continue my remarks upon that subject. I still feel a desire to say something on this subject. Let us this very day begin anew, and now say, with all our hearts, we will forsake our sins and be righteous. I shall read the 24th chapter of Matthew, and give it a literal rendering and reading; and when it is rightly understood, it will be edifying.

I thought the very oddity of its rendering would be edifying anyhow—"And it will be preached, the Gospel of the kingdom, in the whole world, to a witness over all people: and then will the end come." I will now read it in German [which he did, and many Germans who were present said he translated it correctly].

Interpretation of Scripture

The Savior said when these tribulations should take place, it should be committed to a man who should be a witness over the whole world: the keys of knowledge, power and revelations should be revealed to a witness who should hold the testimony to the world. It has always been my province to dig up hidden mysteries—new things—for my hearers. Just at the time when some men think that I have no right to the keys of the Priesthood —just at that time I have the greatest right. The Germans are an exalted people. The old German translators are the most nearly correct—most honest of any of the translators; and therefore I get testimony to bear me out in the revelations that I have preached for the last fourteen years. The old German, Latin, Greek and Hebrew translations all say it is true: they cannot be impeached, and therefore I am in good company.

All the testimony is that the Lord in the last days would commit the keys of the Priesthood to a witness over all people.

Has the Gospel of the kingdom commenced in the last days? And will God take it from the man until He takes him Himself? I have read it precisely as the words flowed from the lips of Jesus Christ. John the Revelator saw an angel flying through the midst of heaven, having the everlasting Gospel to preach unto them that dwell on the earth.

The scripture is ready to be fulfilled when great wars, famines, pestilence, great distress, judgments, &c., are ready to be poured out on the inhabitants of the earth. John saw the angel having the holy Priesthood, who should preach the everlasting Gospel to all nations. God had an angel—a special messenger—ordained and prepared for that purpose in the last days. Woe, woe be to that man or set of men who lift up their hands against God and His witness in these last days: for they shall deceive almost the very chosen ones!

Eternal Judgment

My enemies say that I *have* been a true prophet. Why, I had rather be a fallen true prophet than a false prophet. When a man goes about prophesying, and commands men to obey his teachings, he must either be a true or false prophet. False prophets always arise to oppose the true prophets and they will prophesy so very near the truth that they will deceive almost the very chosen ones.

The doctrine of eternal judgments belongs to the first principles of the Gospel, in the last days. In relation to the kingdom of God, the devil always sets up his kingdom at the very same time in opposition to God. Every man who has a calling to minister to the inhabitants of the world was ordained to that very purpose in the Grand Council of heaven before this world was. I suppose I was ordained to this very office in that Grand Council. It is the testimony that I want that I am God's servant, and this people His people. The ancient prophets declared that in the last days the God of heaven should set up a kingdom which should never be destroyed, nor left to other people; and the very time that was calculated on, this people were struggling to bring it out. He that arms himself with gun, sword, or pistol, except in the defense of truth, will sometime be sorry for it. I never carry any weapon with me bigger than my penknife. When I was dragged before the cannon and muskets in Missouri, I was unarmed. God will always protect me until my mission is fulfilled.

I calculate to be one of the instruments of setting up the kingdom of Daniel by the word of the Lord, and I intend to lay a foundation that will revolutionize the whole world. I once offered my life to the Missouri mob as a sacrifice for my people, and here I am. It will not be by sword or gun that this kingdom will roll on: the power of truth is such that all nations will be under the necessity of obeying the Gospel. The prediction is that army will be against army: it may be that the Saints will have to beat their ploughs into swords, for it will not do for men to sit down patiently and see their children destroyed.

The Resurrection

My text is on the resurrection of the dead, which you will find in the 14th chapter of John—"In my Father's house are many mansions." It should be—"In my Father's kingdom are many kingdoms," in order that ye may be heirs of God and joint-heirs with me. I do not believe the Methodist doctrine of sending honest men and noble-minded men to hell, along with the murderer and the adulterer. They may hurl all their hell and fiery billows upon me, for they will roll off me as fast as they come on. But I have an order of things to save the poor fellows at any rate, and get them saved; for I will send men to preach to them in prison and save them if I can.

Salvation for the Dead

There are mansions for those who obey a celestial law, and there are other mansions for those who come short of the law every man in his own order. There is baptism for those to exercise who are alive, and baptism for the dead who die without the knowledge of the Gospel.

I am going on in my progress for eternal life. It is not only necessary that you should be baptized for your dead, but you will have to go through all the ordinances for them, the same as you have gone through to save yourselves. There will be 144,000 saviors on Mount Zion, and with them an innumerable host that no man can number. Oh! I beseech you to go forward, go forward and make your calling and your election sure; and if any man preach any other Gospel than that which I have preached, he shall be cursed; and some of you who now hear me shall see it, and know that I testify the truth concerning them.

The Resurrection Universal

In regard to the law of the Priesthood, there should be a place where all nations shall come up from time to time to receive their endowments; and the Lord has said this shall be the place for the baptisms for the dead. Every man that has been baptized and belongs to the kingdom has a right to be baptized for those who have gone before; and as soon as the law of the Gospel is obeyed here by their friends who act as proxy for them, the Lord has administrators there to set them free. A man may act as proxy for his own relatives; the ordinances of the Gospel which were laid out before the foundations of the world have thus been fulfilled by them, and we may be baptized for those whom we have much friendship for; but it must first be revealed to the man of God, lest we should run too far. "As in Adam all die, even so in Christ shall all be made alive;" all shall be raised from the dead. The Lamb of God hath brought to pass the resurrection, so that all shall rise from the dead.

God Almighty Himself dwells in eternal fire; flesh and blood cannot go there, for all corruption is devoured by the fire. "Our God is a consuming fire." When our flesh is quickened by the Spirit, there will be no blood in this tabernacle. Some dwell in higher glory than others.

Those who have done wrong always have that wrong gnawing them. Immortality dwells in everlasting burnings. I will from time to time reveal to you the subjects that are revealed by the Holy Ghost to me. All the lies that are now hatched up against me are of the devil, and the influence of the devil and his servants will be used against the kingdom of God. The servants of God teach nothing but principles of eternal life, by their works ye shall know them. A good man will speak good things and holy principles, and an evil man evil things. I feel, in the name of the Lord, to rebuke all such bad principles, liars, &c., and I warn all of you to look out whom you are going after. I exhort you to give heed to all the virtue and the teachings which I have given you. All men who are immortal dwell in everlasting burnings. You cannot go anywhere but where God can find you out. All men are born to die, and all men must rise; all must enter eternity.

In order for you to receive your children to yourselves you must have a promise—some ordinance; some blessing, in order to ascend above principalities, or else it may be an angel. They must rise just as they died; we can there hail our lovely infants with the same glory—the same loveliness in the celestial glory, where they all enjoy alike. They differ in stature, in size, the same glorious spirit gives them the likeness of glory and bloom; the old man with his silvery hairs will glory in bloom and beauty. No man can describe it to you—no man can write it.

When did I ever teach anything wrong from this stand? When was I ever confounded? I want to triumph in Israel before I depart hence and am no more seen. I never told you I was perfect; but there is no error in the revelations which I have taught. Must I, then, be thrown away as a thing of naught?

I enjoin for your consideration—add to your faith, virtue, love, &c. I say, in the name of the Lord, if these things are in you, you shall be fruitful. I testify that no man has power to reveal it but myself—things in heaven, in earth, and hell; and all shut your mouths for the future. I commend you all to God, that you may inherit all things; and may God add His blessing. Amen. (May 2, 1844.) D. H. C. 6:363-367.

The Prophet's Dreams on Conditions of Apostates at Nauvoo

In the evening I attended meeting in the Seventies' Hall. George J. Adams preached and I made some observations afterwards, and related a dream which I had a short time since. I thought I was riding out in my carriage, and my guardian angel was along with me. We went past the Temple and had not gone much further before we espied two large snakes so fast locked together that neither of them had any power. I inquired of my guide what I was to understand by that. He answered, "Those snakes represent Dr. Foster and Chauncey L. Higbee. They are your enemies and desire to destroy you; but you see they are so fast locked together that they have no power of themselves to hurt you." I then thought I was riding up Mulholland street, but my guardian angel was not along with me. On arriving at the prairie, I was overtaken and seized by William and Wilson Law and others, saying, "Ah, ah! we have got you at last! We will secure you and put you in a safe place!" and, without any ceremony dragged me out of my carriage, tied my hands behind me, and threw me into a deep, dry pit, where I remained in a perfectly helpless condition, and they went away. While struggling to get out, I heard Wilson Law screaming for help hard by. I managed to unloose myself so as to make a spring, when I caught hold of some grass which grew at the edge of the pit.

I looked out of the pit and saw Wilson Law at a little distance attacked by ferocious wild beasts, and heard him cry out, "Oh Brother Joseph, come and save me!" I replied, "I cannot, for you have put me into this deep pit." On looking out another way, I saw William Law with outstretched tongue, blue in the face, and the green poison forced out of his mouth, caused by the coiling of a large snake around his body. It had also grabbed him by the arm, a little above the elbow, ready to devour him. He cried out in the intensity of his agony, "Oh, Brother Joseph, Brother Joseph, come and save me, or I die!" I also replied to him, "I cannot, William; I would willingly, but you have tied me and put me in this pit, and I am powerless to help you or liberate myself." In a short time after my guide came and said aloud, "Joseph, Joseph, what are you doing there?" I replied, "My enemies fell upon me, bound me and threw me in." He then took me by the hand, and drew me out of the pit, set me free, and we went away rejoicing. (June 13. 1844.) D. H. C. 6:461-462.

Sermon by the Prophet—The Christian Godhead—Plurality of Gods

Meeting in the Grove, east of the Temple, June 16, 1844

* * *

President Joseph Smith read the 3rd chapter of Revelation, and took for his text 1st chapter, 6th verse—"And hath made us kings and priests unto God and His Father: to Him be glory and dominion forever and ever. Amen."

It is altogether correct in the translation. Now, you know that of late some malicious and corrupt men have sprung up and apostatized from the Church of Jesus Christ of Latter-day Saints, and they declare that the Prophet believes in a plurality of Gods, and, lo and behold! we have discovered a very great secret, they cry—"The Prophet says there are many Gods, and this proves that he has fallen."

It has been my intention for a long time to take up this subject and lay it clearly before the people, and show what my faith is in relation to this interesting matter. I have contemplated the saying of Jesus (Luke 17th chapter, 26th verse)— "And as it was in the days of Noah, so shall it be also in the days of the Son of Man." And if it does rain, I'll preach this doctrine, for the truth shall be preached.

Plurality of Gods

I will preach on the plurality of Gods. I have selected this text for that express purpose. I wish to declare I have always and in all congregations when I have preached on the subject of the Deity, it has been the plurality of Gods. It has been preached by the Elders for fifteen years.

I have always declared God to be a distinct personage, Jesus Christ a separate and distinct personage from God the Father, and that the Holy Ghost was a distinct personage and a Spirit: and these three constitute three distinct personages and three Gods. If this is in accordance with the New Testament, lo and behold! we have three Gods anyhow, and they are plural; and who can contradict it?

Our text says, "And hath made us kings and priests unto God and His Father." The Apostles have discovered that there were Gods above, for John says God was the Father of our Lord Jesus Christ. My object was to preach the scriptures, and preach the doctrine they contain, there being a God above, the Father of our Lord Jesus Christ. I am bold to declare I have taught all the strong doctrines publicly, and always teach stronger doctrines in public than in private.

John was one of the men, and apostles declare they were made kings and priests unto God, the Father of our Lord Jesus Christ. It reads just so in the Revelation, Hence the doctrine of a plurality of Gods is as prominent in the Bible as any other doctrine. It is all over the face of the Bible. It stands beyond the power of controversy. A wayfaring man, though a fool, need not err therein.

Paul says there are Gods many and Lords many. I want to set it forth in a plain and simple manner; but to us there is but one God— that is *pertaining to us;* and he is in all and through all. But if Joseph Smith says there are Gods many and Lords many, they cry, "Away with him! Crucify him! Crucify him!"

Mankind verily say that the Scriptures are with them. Search the Scriptures, for they testify of things that these apostates would gravely pronounce blasphemy. Paul, if Joseph Smith is a blasphemer, you are. I say there are Gods many and Lords many, but to us only one, and we are to be in subjection to that one, and no man can limit the bounds or the eternal existence of eternal time. Hath he beheld the eternal world, and is he authorized to say that there is only one God? He makes himself a fool if he thinks or says so, and there is an end of his career or progress in knowledge. He cannot obtain all knowledge, for he has sealed up the gate to it.

Scriptural Interpretation

Some say I do not interpret the Scripture the same as they do. They say it means the heathen's gods. Paul says there are Gods many and Lords many; and that makes a plurality of Gods, in spite of the whims of all men. Without a revelation, I am not going to give them the knowledge of the God of heaven. You know and I testify that Paul had no allusion to the heathen gods. I have it from God, and get over it if you can. I have a witness of the Holy Ghost, and a testimony that Paul had no allusion to the heathen gods in the text. I will show from the Hebrew Bible that I am correct, and the first word shows a plurality of Gods; and I want the apostates and learned men to come here and prove to the contrary, if they can. An unlearned boy must give you a little Hebrew. *Berosheit baurau Eloheim ait aushamayeen vehau auraits,* rendered by King James' translators, "In the beginning God created the heaven and the earth." I want to analyze the word *Berosheit. Rosh,* the head; *Sheit,* a grammatical termination; the *Baith* was not originally put there when the inspired man wrote it, but it has been since added by an old Jew. *Baurau* signifies to bring forth; *Eloheim* is from the word *Eloi,* God, in the singular number; and by adding the word *heim,* it renders it Gods. It read first, "In the beginning the head of the Gods brought forth the Gods," or, as others have translated it, "The head of the Gods called the Gods together." I want to show a little learning as well as other fools.   * * *

The head God organized the heavens and the earth. I defy all the world to refute me. In the beginning the heads of the Gods organized the heavens and the earth. Now the learned priests and the people rage, and the heathen imagine a vain thing. If we pursue the Hebrew text further, it reads, "The head one of the Gods said, Let us make a man in our own image." I once asked a learned Jew, "If the Hebrew language compels us to render all words ending in *heim* in the plural, why not render the first *Eloheim* plural?" He replied, "That is the rule with few exceptions; but in this case it would ruin the Bible." He acknowledged I was right. I came here to investigate these things precisely as I believe them. Hear and judge for yourselves; and if you go away satisfied, well and good.

In the very beginning the Bible shows there is a plurality of Gods beyond the power of refutation. It is a great subject I am dwelling on. The word *Eloheim* ought to be in the plural all the way through—Gods. The heads of the Gods appointed one God for us; and when you take [that] view of the subject, its sets one free to see all the beauty, holiness and perfection of the Gods. All I want is to get the simple, naked truth, and the whole truth.

Many men say there is one God; the Father, the Son and the Holy Ghost are only one God I say that is a strange God anyhow—three in one, and one in three! It is a curious organization. "Father, I pray not for the world, but I pray for them which thou hast given me." "Holy Father, keep through Thine own name those whom thou hast given me, that they may be one as we are." All are to be crammed into one God, according to sectarianism. It would make the biggest God in all the world. He would be a wonderfully big God—he would be a giant or a monster. I want to read the text to you myself—"I am agreed with the Father and the Father is agreed with me, and we are agreed as one." The Greek shows that it should be agreed. "Father, I pray for them which Thou hast given me out of the world, and not for those alone, but for them also which shall believe on me through their word, that they all may be agreed, as Thou, Father, are with me, and I with Thee, that they also may be agreed with us," and all come to dwell in unity, and in all the glory and everlasting burnings of the

Gods; and then we shall see as we are seen, and be as our God and He as His Father. I want to reason a little on this subject. I learned it by translating the papyrus which is now in my house.

Abraham's Reasoning

I learned a testimony concerning Abraham, and he reasoned concerning the God of heaven. "In order to do that," said he, "suppose we have two facts: that supposes another fact may exist—two men on the earth, one wiser than the other, would logically show that another who is wiser than the wisest may exist. Intelligences exist one above another, so that there is no end to them."

If Abraham reasoned thus—If Jesus Christ was the Son of God, and John discovered that God the Father of Jesus Christ had a Father, you may suppose that He had a Father also. Where was there ever a son without a father? And where was there ever a father without first being a son? Whenever did a tree or anything spring into existence without a progenitor? And everything comes in this way. Paul says that which is earthly is in the likeness of that which is heavenly, Hence if Jesus had a Father, can we not believe that *He* had a Father also? I despise the idea of being scared to death at such a doctrine, for the Bible is full of it.

I want you to pay particular attention to what I am saying. Jesus said that the Father wrought precisely in the same way as His Father had done before Him. As the Father had done before? He laid down His life, and took it up the same as His Father had done before. He did as He was sent, to lay down His life and take it up again; and then was committed unto Him the keys. I know it is good reasoning.

The Church Being Purged

I have reason to think that the Church is being purged. I saw Satan fall from heaven, and the way they ran was a caution. All these are wonders and marvels in our eyes in these last days. So long as men are under the law of God, they have no fears—they do not scare themselves.

I want to stick to my text, to show that when men open their lips against these truths they do not injure me, but injure themselves. To the law and to the testimony, for these principles are poured out all over the Scriptures. When things that are of the greatest importance are passed over by the weak-minded men without even a thought, I want to see truth in all its bearings and hug it to my bosom. I believe all that God ever revealed, and I never hear of a man being damned for believing too much; but they are damned for unbelief.

They found fault with Jesus Christ because He said He was the Son of God, and made Himself equal with God. They say of me, like they did of the Apostles of old, that I must be put down. What did Jesus say? "Is it not written in your law, I said, Ye are Gods? If He called them Gods unto whom the word of God came, and the Scriptures cannot be broken, say ye of Him whom the Father hath sanctified and sent into the world, Thou blasphemest; because I said I am the Son of God?" It was through Him that they drank of the spiritual rock. Of course He would take the honor to Himself. Jesus, if they were called Gods unto whom the word of God came, why should it be thought blasphemy that I should say I am the Son of God?

Eternal Glories

Go and read the vision in the Book of Covenants. There is clearly illustrated glory upon glory—one glory of the sun, another glory of the moon, and a glory of the stars; and as one star differeth from another star in glory, even so do they of the telestial world differ in glory, and every man who reigns in celestial glory is a God to his dominions. By the apostates admitting the testimony of the Doctrine and Covenants they damn themselves. Paul, what do you say? They impeached Paul and all went and left him. Paul had seven churches, and they drove him off from among them; and yet they cannot do it by me. I rejoice in that. My testimony is good.

Paul says, "There is one glory of the sun, and another glory of the moon, and another glory of the stars; for one star differeth from another star in glory. So also is the resurrection of the dead." They who obtain a glorious resurrection from the dead, are exalted far above principalities, powers, thrones, dominions and angels, and are expressly declared to be heirs of God and joint heirs with Jesus Christ, all having eternal power.

These Scriptures are a mixture of very strange doctrines

to the Christian world, who are blindly led by the blind. I will refer to another Scripture. "Now," says God, when He visited Moses in the bush, (Moses was a stammering sort of a boy like me) God said, "Thou shalt be a God unto the children of Israel." God said, "Thou shalt be a God unto Aaron, and he shall be thy spokesman." I believe those Gods that God reveals as Gods to be sons of God, and all can cry, "Abba, Father!" Sons of God who exalt themselves to be Gods, even from before the foundation of the world, and are the only Gods I have a reverence for.

John said he was a king. "And from Jesus Christ, who is the faithful witness, and the first begotten of the dead, and the Prince of the kings of the earth. Unto Him that loved us, and washed us from our sins in His own blood, and hath made us kings and priests unto God, and His Father; to him be glory and dominion forever and ever, Amen." Oh, Thou God who art King of kings and Lord of lords, the sectarian world, by their actions, declare, "We cannot believe Thee."

The old Catholic church traditions are worth more than all you have said. Here is a principle of logic that most men have no more sense than to adopt. I will illustrate it by an old apple tree. Here jumps off a branch and says, I am the true tree, and you are corrupt. If the whole tree is corrupt, are not its branches corrupt? If the Catholic religion is a false religion, how can any true religion come out of it? If the Catholic church is bad, how can any good thing come out of it? The character of the old churches have always been slandered by all apostates since the world began.

The Lord Will Not Acknowledge Traitors

I testify again, as the Lord lives, God never will acknowledge any traitors or apostates. Any man who will betray the Catholics will betray you; and if he will betray me, he will betray you. All men are liars who say they are of the true Church without the revelations of Jesus Christ and the Priesthood of Melchizedek, which is after the order of the Son of God.

It is in the order of heavenly things that God should always send a new dispensation into the world when men have apostatized from the truth and lost the priesthood, but when men come out and build upon other men's foundations, they do it on their own responsibility, without authority from God; and when the floods come and the winds blow, their foundations will be found to be sand, and their whole fabric will crumble to dust.

Did I build on any other man's foundation? I have got all the truth which the Christian world possessed, and an independent revelation in the bargain, and God will bear me off triumphant. I will drop this subject. I wish I could speak for three or four hours; but it is not expedient on account of the rain; I would still go on, and show you proof upon proofs; all the Bible is equal in support of this doctrine, one part as another. (June 16, 1844.) D. H. C. 6:473-479.

The Prophet Predicts His Death

The following items of history in relation to the surrender of the Prophet and Patriarch and their brutal martyrdom, are of such interest that they are included in this record. These brethren with a number of the leading Elders met at dusk, Saturday, June 22, 1844, in the Prophet's upper room. When they were assembled the Prophet presented to them a letter from Governor Ford which he read for the purpose of seeking the counsel of his brethren. At this point the narrative begins.

Joseph remarked: "There is no mercy here—no mercy here." Hyrum said, "No; just as sure as we fall into their hands we are dead men." Joseph replied, "Yes; what shall we do, Brother Hyrum?" He replied, "I don't know." All at once Joseph's countenance brightened up and he said, "The way is open. It is clear to my mind what to do. All they want is Hyrum and myself; then tell everybody to go about their business, and not to collect in groups, but to scatter about. There is no doubt they will come here and search for us. Let them search; they will not harm you in person or property, and not even a hair of your head. We will cross the river tonight, and go away to the West." He made a move to go out of the house to cross the river. When out of doors he told Butler and Hodge to take the *Maid of Iowa*, (in charge of Repsher) get it to the upper landing, and put his and Hyrum's families and effects upon her; then go down the Mississippi and up the Ohio River to Portsmouth, where they should hear from them. He then took Hodge by the hand and said, "Now, Brother Hodge, let what will come, don't deny the faith, and all will be well."

"I told Stephen Markham that if I and Hyrum were ever

taken again we should be massacred, or I was not a prophet of God. I want Hyrum to live to avenge my blood, but he is determined not to leave me."

* * *

Saturday, June 22, 1844, about 9 p.m. Hyrum came out of the Mansion and gave his hands to Reynolds Cahoon, at the same time saying, "A company of men are seeking to kill my brother Joseph, and the Lord has warned him to flee to the Rocky Mountains to save his life. Good-by, Brother Cahoon, we shall see you again." In a few minutes afterwards Joseph came from his family. His tears were flowing fast. He held a handkerchief to his face, and followed after Brother Hyrum without uttering a word.

Late that night the Prophet and Patriarch were taken across the river by Orrin P. Rockwell preparatory to their start towards the Rocky Mountains. Early the next morning other brethren joined them. That same morning a *posse* arrived in Nauvoo to arrest Joseph Smith, but they did not find him, but they did succeed in creating fear in the hearts of some of the timid. At one p.m. that day Orrin P. Rockwell, who had returned to Nauvoo, arrived with a letter from Emma Smith, requesting the Prophet to return to Nauvoo. The Prophet and Patriarch with Willard Richards were in a room where they had assembled provisions preparatory for their journey. Reynolds Cahoon informed the Prophet what the troops intended to do and urged upon him to give himself up, inasmuch as the Governor had pledged his faith and the faith of the state to protect him while he underwent a legal trial. The Prophet, however, knew that the word of the Governor was not to be received in good faith. At this point our narrative continues.

False Accusations

Reynolds Cahoon, Lorenzo D. Wasson and Hiram Kimball accused Joseph of cowardice for wishing to leave the people, adding that their property would be destroyed, and they left without house or home. Like the fable, when the wolves came the shepherd ran from the flock, and left the sheep to be devoured. To which Joseph replied: "If my life is of no value to my friends it is of none to myself."

Joseph said to Rockwell, "What shall I do?" Rockwell replied, "You are the oldest and ought to know best; and as you make your bed, I will lie with you." Joseph then turned to Hyrum, who was talking with Cahoon, and said, "Brother Hyrum, you are the oldest, what shall we do?" Hyrum said, "Let us go back and give ourselves up, and see the thing out." After studying a few moments, Joseph said, "If you go back I will go with you, but we shall be butchered." Hyrum said, "No, no; let us go back and put our trust in God, and we shall not be harmed. The Lord is in it. If we live or have to die, we will be reconciled to our fate." After a short pause Joseph told Cahoon to request Captain Daniel C. Davis to have his boat ready at half-past five to cross them over the river. (June 23, 1844.) D. H. C. 6:545-551

Letter: Joseph and Hyrum Smith to Governor Ford— Consenting to Go to Carthage

Bank of the River Mississippi,
Sunday, June 23rd, 1844, 2 p.m.

His Excellency Governor Ford:

Sir: I wrote you a long communication at 12 last night, expressive of my views of your Excellency's communication of yesterday. I thought your letter rather severe, but one of my friends has just come to me with an explanation from the captain of your *posse* which softened the subject matter of your communication, and gives us greater assurance of protection, and that your Excellency has succeeded in bringing in subjection the spirits which surround your Excellency to some extent. And I declare again the only objection I ever had or ever made on trial by my country at any time, was what I have made in my last letter—on account of assassins, and the reason I have to fear deathly consequences from their hands.

But from the explanation, I now offer to come to you at Carthage on the morrow, as early as shall be convenient for your *posse* to escort us into headquarters, provided we can have a fair trial, not be abused nor have my witnesses abused, and have all things done in due form of law, without partiality, and you may depend on my honor without the show of a great armed force to produce excitement in the minds of the timid.

We will meet your *posse*, if this letter is satisfactory, (if not, inform me) at or near the Mound, at or about two o'clock tomorrow afternoon, which will be as soon as we can get our witnesses and prepare for trial. We shall expect to take our witnesses with us, and not have to wait a subpoena or part at least, so as not to detain the proceedings, although we may want time for counsel.

We remain most respectfully, your Excellency's humble servants,

JOSEPH SMITH,
HYRUM SMITH.

(June 23, 1844.) D. H. C. 6:550.

The Start for Carthage

Joseph paused when they got to the Temple, and looked with admiration first on that, and then on the city, and remarked, "This is the loveliest place and the best people under the heavens; little do they know the trials that await them." As he passed out of the city, he called on Daniel H. Wells, Esq., who was unwell, and on parting he said, "Squire Wells, I wish you to cherish my memory, and not think me the worst man in the world either."

At ten minutes to 10 a.m. they arrived at Albert G. Fellows' farm, four miles west of Carthage, where they met Captain Dunn with a company of about sixty mounted militia, on seeing which Joseph said, "Do not be alarmed, brethren, for they cannot do more to you than the enemies of truth did to the ancient Saints—they can only kill the body." The company made a halt, when Joseph, Hyrum and several others went into Fellows' house with Captain Dunn, who presented an order from Governor Ford for all the state arms in possession of the Nauvoo Legion, which Joseph immediately countersigned.

Like a Lamb to the Slaughter

Henry G. Sherwood went up to Joseph and said, "Brother Joseph, shall I return to Nauvoo and regulate about getting the arms and get the receipts for them?" Joseph inquired if he was under arrest, or expected to be arrested. Sherwood answered "No," when Joseph directed him to return ahead of the company, gather the arms and do as well as he could in all things. Joseph then said to the company who were with him, "I am going like a lamb to the slaughter, but I am calm as a summer's morning. I have a conscience void of offense toward God and toward all men. If they take my life I shall die an innocent man, and my blood shall cry from the ground for vengeance, and it shall be said of me, 'He was murdered in cold blood!'" He then said to Father Sherwood, "Go, and God bless you." Sherwood then rode as swiftly as he could to Nauvoo. (June 24, 1844.) D. H. C. 6:554-555.

Joseph Smith to Governor Ford—Explaining His Return to Nauvoo

Four Miles West of Carthage Mound,
Hancock County, Illinois,
Monday, 10 o'clock.

His Excellency Governor Ford:

Dear Sir:—On my way to Carthage to answer your request this morning, I here met Captain Dunn, who has here made known to me your orders to surrender the state arms in possession of the Nauvoo Legion, which command I shall comply with; and that the same may be done properly and without trouble to the state, I shall return with Captain Dunn to Nauvoo, see that the arms are put into his possession, and shall then return to headquarters in his company, when I shall most cheerfully submit to any requisition of the Governor or our state.

With all due respect to your Excellency, I remain your obedient servant.

JOSEPH SMITH.

(June 24, 1844.) D. H. C. 6:556.

On the Way to Carthage

The company (about fifteen) then started again for Carthage, and when opposite to the Masonic Hall, Joseph said, "Boys, if I don't come back, take care of yourselves; I am going like a lamb to the slaughter." When they passed his farm he took a good look at it, and after they had passed it, he turned round several times to look again, at which some of the company made remarks, when Joseph said: "If some of you had got such a farm and knew you would not see it any more, you would want to take a good look at it for the last time." When they got to the edge of the woods near Nauvoo, they met A. C. Hodge returning from Carthage. He reported to Hyrum what he had heard in Carthage, told him what his feelings were and said, "Brother Hyrum, you are now clear, and if it was my duty to counsel you, I would say, do not go another foot, for they say they will kill you, if you go to Carthage," but as other persons gathered around, nothing further was said. (June 24, 1844.) D. H. C. 6:558.

The Prophet's Interview with Militia Officers

Several of the officers of the troops in Carthage, and other gentlemen, curious to see the Prophet, visited Joseph in his room. General Smith asked them if there was anything in his appearance that indicated he was the desperate character his enemies represented him to be; and he asked them to give him their honest opinion on the subject. The reply was, "No, sir, your appearance would indicate the very contrary, General Smith; but we cannot see what is in your heart, neither can we tell what are your intentions." To which Joseph replied, "Very true, gentlemen, you cannot see what is in my heart, and you are therefore unable to judge me or my intentions; but I can see what is in your hearts, and will tell you what I see. I can see that you thirst for blood, and nothing but my blood will satisfy you. It is not for crime of any description that I and my brethren are thus continually persecuted and harassed by our enemies, but there are other motives, and some of them I have expressed, so far as relates to myself; and inasmuch as you and the people thirst for blood, I prophesy, in the name of the Lord, that you shall witness scenes of blood and sorrow to your entire satisfaction. Your souls shall be perfectly satiated with blood, and many of you who are now present shall have an opportunity to face the cannon's mouth from sources you think not of; and those people that desire this great evil upon me and my brethren, shall be filled with regret and sorrow because of the scenes of desolation and distress that await them. They shall seek for peace, and shall not be able to find it. Gentlemen, you will find what I have told you to be true." (June 25, 1844.) D. H. C. 6:566.

Letter—Joseph Smith to Governor Ford—Soliciting an Interview

Carthage Jail, June 26, 1844,
Ten minutes past 8 a.m.

His Excellency Governor Ford:

Sir.—I would again solicit your Excellency for an interview having been much disappointed the past evening. I hope you will not deny me this privilege any longer than your public duties shall absolutely require.

We have been committed under a false mittimus, and

consequently the proceedings are illegal, and we desire the time may be hastened when all things shall be made right, and we relieved from this imprisonment.

Your servant,
JOSEPH SMITH.

P. S.—Please send an answer per bearer.
(June 26, 1844.) D. H. C. 6:575.

The Prophet's Premonition

At noon, June 26, 1844, Willard Richards, the recorder, made copies of orders from the Prophet to brethren in Nauvoo; while doing so—

—Joseph remarked, "I have had a good deal of anxiety about my safety since I left Nauvoo, which I never had before when I was under arrest. I could not help those feelings, and they have depressed me. Most of the forenoon was spent by Dan Jones and Col. Stephen Markham in hewing with a pen-knife a warped door to get it on the latch, thus preparing to fortify the place against any attack.

The Prophet, Patriarch, and their friends took turns preaching to the guards, several of whom were relieved before their time was out, because they admitted they were convinced of the innocence of the prisoners. They frequently admitted they had been imposed upon, and more than once it was heard, "Let us go home, boys, for I will not fight any longer against these men."

During the day Hyrum encouraged Joseph to think that the Lord, for His Church's sake, would release him from prison. Joseph replied, "Could my brother, Hyrum, but be liberated, it would not matter so much about me. Poor Rigdon, I am glad he is gone to Pittsburg out of the way; were he to preside he would lead the Church to destruction in less than five years." (June 26, 1844.) D. H. C. 6:592-593.

The Ill-Treatment of John Smith—5:30 p.m.

Patriarch John Smith came from Macedonia to jail to see his nephews, Joseph and Hyrum. The road was thronged with mobbers. Three of them snapped their guns at him, and he was threatened by many others who recognized him. The guard at the jail refused him admittance.

Joseph saw him through the prison window, and said to

the guard, "Let the old gentleman come in, he is my uncle." The guard replied they did not care who the hell he was uncle to, he should not go in.

Joseph replied, "You will not hinder so old and infirm a man as he is from coming in," and then said, "Come in, uncle;" on which, after searching him closely the guard let him pass into the jail, where he remained about an hour. He asked Joseph if he thought he should again get out of the hands of his enemies, when he replied, "My brother Hyrum thinks I shall. I wish you would tell the brethren in Macedonia that they can see by this, that it has not been safe for me to visit them; and tell Almon W. Babbitt I want him to come and assist me as an attorney at my expected trial tomorrow before Captain R. F. Smith. (June 26, 1844.) D. H. C. 6:597-598.

The Last Night in Jail

June 26, 1844, 9:15 p.m.—Elder John Taylor prayed. Willard Richards, John Taylor, John S. Fullmer, Stephen Markham and Dan Jones stayed with Joseph and Hyrum in the front room.

During the evening the Patriarch Hyrum Smith read and commented upon extracts from the Book of Mormon, on the imprisonment and deliverance of the servants of God for the Gospel's sake. Joseph bore a powerful testimony to the guards of the divine authenticity of the Book of Mormon, the restoration of the Gospel, the administration of angels, and that the kingdom of God was again established upon the earth, for the sake of which he was then incarcerated in that prison, and not because he had violated any law of God or man.

They retired to rest late. Joseph and Hyrum occupied the only bedstead in the room, while their friends lay side by side on the mattresses on the floor. Dr. Richards sat up writing until his last candle left him in the dark. The report of a gun fired close by caused Joseph to rise, leave the bed, and lay himself on the floor, having Dan Jones on his left, and John S. Fullmer on his right. Joseph laid out his right arm, and said to John S. Fullmer, "Lay your head on my arm for a pillow, Brother John;" and when all were quiet they conversed in a low tone about the prospects of their deliverance. Joseph gave expression to several presentiments that he had to die, and said, "I would like to see my family again," and "I would

to God that I could preach to the Saints in Nauvoo once more."
Fullmer tried to rally his spirits, saying he thought he would
often have that privilege, when Joseph thanked him for the
remark and good feelings expressed to him.

Soon after Dr. Richards retired to the bed which Joseph
had left, and when all were apparently fast asleep, Joseph
whispered to Dan Jones, "Are you afraid to die?" Dan said,
"Has that time come, think you? Engaged in such a cause I
do not think that death would have many terrors." Joseph
replied, "You will yet see Wales, and fulfill the mission appointed to you before you die." (June 26, 1844—midnight.)
D. H. C. 6:600-601.

Elder John Taylor's Account of Governor Ford's and President Smith's Interview

This account was written by John Taylor subsequent to the events here
portrayed.

———————

Governor.—General Smith, I believe you have given me a
general outline of the difficulties that have existed in the
country, in the documents forwarded to me by Dr. Bernhisel
and Mr. Taylor; but, unfortunately, there seems to be a dis-
crepancy between your statements and those of your enemies.
It is true that you are substantiated by evidence and affidavit,
but for such an extraordinary excitement as that which is now
in the country, there must be some cause, and I attribute the
last outbreak to the destruction of the *Expositor*, and to your
refusal to comply with the writ issued by Esq. Morrison. The
press in the United States is looked upon as the great bulwark
of American freedom, and its destruction in Nauvoo was represented and looked upon as a high-handed measure, and manifests to the people a disposition on your part to suppress the
liberty of speech and of the press; this, with your refusal to
comply with the requisition of a writ, I conceive to be the
principal cause of this difficulty, and you are, moreover, represented to me as turbulent and defiant of the laws and institutions of your country.

Gen. Smith.—Governor Ford, you, sir, as Governor of
this State, are aware of the prosecutions and persecutions that
I have endured. You know well that our course has been
peaceable and law-abiding, for I have furnished this State, ever

since our settlement here, with sufficient evidence of my pacific intentions, and those of the people with whom I am associated, by the endurance of every conceivable indignity and lawless outrage perpetrated upon me and upon this people since our settlement here, and you yourself know that I have kept you well posted in relation to all matters associated with the late difficulties. If you have not got some of my communications, it has not been my fault.

Agreeably to your orders, I assembled the Nauvoo Legion for the protection of Nauvoo and the surrounding country against an armed band of marauders, and ever since they have been mustered I have almost daily communicated with you in regard to all the leading events that have transpired; and whether in the capacity of mayor of the city, or lieutenant-general of the Nauvoo Legion, I have striven to preserve the peace and administer even-handed justice to all; but my motives are impugned, my acts are misconstrued, and I am grossly and wickedly misrepresented. I suppose I am indebted for my incarceration here to the oath of a worthless man that was arraigned before me and fined for abusing and maltreating his lame, helpless brother.

That I should be charged by you, sir, who know better, of acting contrary to law, is to me a matter of surprise. Was it the Mormons or our enemies who first commenced these difficulties? You know well it was not us; and when this turbulent, outrageous people commenced their insurrectionary movements, I made you acquainted with them, officially, asked your advice, and have followed strictly your counsel in every particular.

Who ordered out the Nauvoo Legion? I did, under your direction. For what purpose? To suppress these insurrectionary movements. It was at your instance, sir, that I issued a proclamation calling upon the Nauvoo Legion to be in readiness, at a moment's warning, to guard against the incursions of mobs, and gave an order to Jonathan Dunham, acting major-general, to that effect. Am I then to be charged for the acts of others; and because lawlessness and mobocracy abound, am I when carrying out your instructions, to be charged with not abiding the law? Why is it that I must be held accountable for other men's acts? If there is trouble in the country, neither I nor my people made it, and all that we have ever done, after much endurance on our part, is to maintain and uphold the Constitution and institutions of our country, and to protect an injured, innocent, and persecuted people against misrule and mob violence.

Concerning the destruction of the press to which you refer, men may differ somewhat in their opinions about it; but can it be supposed that after all the indignities to which we have been subjected outside, that this people could suffer a set of worthless vagabonds to come into our city, and right under our own eyes and protection, vilify and calumniate not only ourselves, but the character of our wives and daughters, as was impudently and unblushingly done in that infamous and filthy sheet? There is not a city in the United States that would have suffered such an indignity for twenty-four hours.

Our whole people were indignant, and loudly called upon our city authorities for redress of their grievances, which, if not attended to they themselves would have taken the matter into their own hands, and have summarily punished the audacious wretches, as they deserved.

The principles of equal rights that have been instilled into our bosoms from our cradles, as American citizens, forbid us submitting to every foul indignity, and succumbing and pandering to wretches so infamous as these. But, independent of this, the course that we pursued we considered to be strictly legal; for notwithstanding the insult we were anxious to be governed strictly by law, and therefore convened the City Council; and being desirous in our deliberations to abide law, summoned legal counsel to be present on the occasion.

Upon investigating the matter, we found that our City Charter gave us power to remove all nuisances; and, furthermore, upon consulting Blackstone upon what might be considered a nuisance, that distinguished lawyer, who is considered authority, I believe, in all our courts, states, among other things, that a libelous and filthy press may be considered a nuisance, and abated as such.

Here, then, one of the most eminent English barristers, whose works are considered standard with us, declares that a libelous press may be considered a nuisance; and our own charter, given us by the legislature of this State, gives us the power to remove nuisances; and by ordering that press abated as a nuisance, we conceived that we were acting strictly in accordance with law. We made that order in our corporate capacity, and the City Marshal carried it out. It is possible there may have been some better way, but I must confess that I could not see it.

In relation to the writ served upon us, we were willing to abide the consequences of our own acts, but were unwilling, in answering a writ of that kind, to submit to illegal exactions sought to be imposed upon us under the pretense of law, when we knew they were in open violation of it.

When that document was presented to me by Mr. Bettisworth, I offered, in the presence of more than 20 persons, to go to any other magistrate, either in our city or Appanoose, or any other place where we should be safe, but we all refused to put ourselves into the power of a mob.

What right had that constable to refuse our request? He had none according to law; for you know, Governor Ford, that the statute law in Illinois is, that the parties served with the writ shall go before him who issued it, or some other justice of the peace. Why, then, should we be dragged to Carthage, where the law does not compel us to go? Does not this look like many others of our prosecutions with which you are acquainted? And had we not a right to expect foul play?

This very act was a breach of law on his part—an assumption of power that did not belong to him, and an attempt, at least, to deprive us of our legal and constitutional rights and privileges. What could we do under the circumstances different from what we did do? We sued for, and obtained a writ of *habeas corpus* from the Municipal Court, by which we were delivered from the hands of Constable Bettisworth, and brought before and acquitted by the Municipal Court.

After our acquittal, in a conversation with Judge Thomas, although he considered the acts of the party illegal, he advised, that to satisfy the people, we had better go before another magistrate who was not in our Church.

In accordance with his advice we went before Esq. Wells, with whom you are well acquainted; both parties were present, witnesses were called on both sides, the case was fully investigated, and we were again dismissed.

And what is this intended desire to enforce the law, and these lying, base rumors put into circulation for, but to seek, through mob influence, under pretense of law, to make us submit to requisitions that are contrary to law, and subversive of every principle of justice?

And when you, sir, required us to come out here, we came, not because it was legal, but because you required it of us, and we were desirous of showing to you and to all men that we shrunk not from the most rigid investigation of our acts.

We certainly did expect other treatment than to be immured in a jail at the instance of these men, and I think, from your plighted faith, we had a right to, after disbanding our own forces, and putting ourselves entirely in your hands; and now, after having fulfilled my part, sir, as a man and an American citizen, I call upon you, Governor Ford, and think I have a right to do so, to deliver us from this place, and rescue us from this outrage that is sought to be practiced upon us by a set of infamous scoundrels.

Gov. Ford.—But you have placed men under arrest, detained men as prisoners, and given passes to others, some of which I have seen.

John P. Green, City Marshall.—Perhaps I can explain. Since these difficulties have commenced, you are aware that we have been placed under very peculiar circumstances, our city has been placed under a very rigid police guard; in addition to this, frequent guards have been placed outside the city to prevent any sudden surprise, and those guards have questioned suspected or suspicious persons as to their business.

To strangers, in some instances, passes have been given, to prevent difficulty in passing those guards. It is some of those passes that you have seen. No person, sir, has been imprisoned without a legal cause in our city.

Gov.—Why did you not give a more speedy answer to the *posse* that I sent out?

Gen. Smith.—We had matters of importance to consult upon. Your letter showed anything but an amicable spirit. We have suffered immensely in Missouri from mobs, in loss of property, imprisonment, and otherwise.

It took some time for us to weigh duly these matters. We could not decide upon the matters of such importance immediately, and your *posse* were too hasty in returning. We were consulting for a large people, and vast interests were at stake.

We had been outrageously imposed upon, and knew not

how far we could trust anyone; besides, a question necessarily arose, how shall we come? Your request was that we should come unarmed. It became a matter of serious importance to decide how far promises could be trusted, and how far we were safe from mob violence.

Geddes.—It certainly did look from all I have heard, from the general spirit of violence and mobocracy that here prevails, that it was not safe for you to come unprotected.

Gov.—I think that sufficient time was not allowed by the *posse* for you to consult and get ready. They were too hasty; but I suppose they found themselves bound by their orders. I think, too, there is a great deal of truth in what you say, and your reasoning is plausible; yet, I must beg leave to differ from you in relation to the acts of the City Council. That council, in my opinion, had no right to act in a legislative capacity, and in that of the judiciary.

They should have passed a law in relation to the matter, and then the Municipal Court, upon complaint, could have removed it; but for the City Council to take upon themselves the law-making and the execution of the laws, in my opinion, was wrong; besides, these men ought to have had a hearing before their property was destroyed; to destroy it without was an infringement of their rights; besides, it is so contrary to the feelings of the American people to interfere with the press.

And furthermore, I cannot but think that it would have been more judicious for you to have gone with Mr. Bettisworth to Carthage, notwithstanding the law did not require it. Concerning your being in jail, I am sorry for that, I wish it had been otherwise. I hope you will soon be released, but I cannot interfere.

Joseph Smith.—Governor Ford, allow me, sir, to bring one thing to your mind, that you seem to have overlooked. You state that you think it would have been better for us to have submitted to the requisition of Constable Bettisworth, and to have gone to Carthage.

Do you not know, sir, that that writ was served at the instance of an anti-Mormon mob, who had passed resolutions and published them to the effect that they would exterminate the Mormon leaders; and are you not informed that Captain Anderson was not only threatened when coming to Nauvoo, but had a gun fired at his boat by this said mob at Warsaw, when coming up to Nauvoo, and that this very thing was made use of as a means to get us into their hands, and we could not, without taking an armed force with us, go there without, according to their published declarations, going into the jaws of death?

To have taken a force would only have fanned the excitement, as they would have stated that we wanted to use intimidation, therefore we thought it the most judicious to avail ourselves of the protection of the law.

Gov.—I see, I see.

Joseph Smith.—Furthermore, in relation to the press, you say that you differ with me in opinion; be it so, the thing after all is a legal difficulty, and the courts I should judge competent to decide on the matter.

If our act was illegal, we are willing to meet it; and although I cannot see the distinction that you draw about the acts of the City Council, and what difference it could have made in point of fact, law, or justice, between the City Council's acting together or separate, or how much more legal it would have been for the Municipal Court, who were a part of the City Council, to act separate, instead of with the councilors.

Yet, if it is deemed that we did a wrong in destroying that press, we refuse not to pay for it. We are desirous to fulfill the law in every particular, and are responsible for our acts.

You say that the parties ought to have had a hearing. Had it been a civil suit, this of course would have been proper; but there was a flagrant violation of every principle of right, a nuisance, and it was abated on the same principle that any nuisance, stench, or putrified carcass would have been removed.

Our first step, therefore, was to stop the foul, noisome, filthy sheet, and then the next, in our opinion, would have been to have prosecuted the men for a breach of public decency.

And furthermore, again, let me say, Governor Ford, I shall look to you for our protection. I believe you are talking of going to Nauvoo; if you go, sir, I wish to go along. I refuse not to answer any law, but I do not consider myself safe here.

Gov.—I am in hopes that you will be acquitted; but if I go, I will certainly take you along. I do not, however, apprehend danger. I think you are perfectly safe, either here or anywhere else. I cannot, however, interfere with the law. I am placed in peculiar circumstances and seem to be blamed by all parties.

Joseph Smith.—Governor Ford, I ask nothing but what is legal. I have a right to expect protection at least from you; for, independent of law, you have pledged your faith, and that of the State, for my protection, and I wish to go to Nauvoo.

Gov.—And you shall have protection, General Smith. I did not make this promise without consulting my officers, who all pledged their honor to its fulfillment. I do not know that I shall go tomorrow to Nauvoo, but if I do, I will take you along. (June 26, 1844.) D. H. C. 6:579-585.

Letter: Joseph Smith to Emma Smith—Prophet's Instruction as to Reception of the Governor

Carthage Jail, June 27th, 1844.
20 minutes past eight a.m.

Dear Emma.—The Governor continues his courtesies, and permits us to see our friends. We hear this morning that the Governor will not go down with his troops today to Nauvoo, as we anticipated last evening; but if he does come down with his troops you will be protected; and I want you to tell Brother Dunham to instruct the people to stay at home and attend to their own business, and let there be no groups or gathering together, unless by permission of the Governor, they are called together to receive communications from the Governor, which would please our people, but let the Governor direct.

Brother Dunham of course will obey the orders of the government officers, and render them the assistance they require. There is no danger of any extermination order. Should there be a mutiny among the troops (which we do not anticipate, excitement is abating) a part will remain loyal and stand for the defense of the state and our rights.

There is one principle which is eternal; it is the duty of all men to protect their lives and the lives of the household, whenever necessity requires, and no power has a right to forbid it, should the last extreme arrive, but I anticipate no such extreme, but caution is the parent of safety.

JOSEPH SMITH.

P. S.—Dear Emma, I am very much resigned to my lot, knowing I am justified, and have done the best that could be done. Give my love to the children and all my friends, Mr. Brewer, and all who inquire after me: and as for treason, I know that I have not committed any, and they cannot prove anything of the kind, so you need not have any fears that anything can happen to us on that account. May God bless you all. Amen. (June 27, 1844.) D. H. C. 6:605.

Not Always Wise to Expose Evil

Thursday, a.m.—June 27, 1844.—

Said Joseph, "Our lives have already become jeopardized by revealing the wicked and bloodthirsty purposes of our enemies; and for the future we must cease to do so. All we have said about them is truth, but it is not always wise to relate all the truth. Even Jesus, the Son of God, had to refrain from doing so, and had to restrain His feelings many times for the safety of Himself and His followers, and had to conceal the righteous purposes of His heart in relation to many things pertaining to His Father's kingdom. When still a boy He had all the intelligence necessary to enable Him to rule and govern the kingdom of the Jews, and could reason with the wisest and most profound doctors of law and divinity, and make their theories and practice to appear like folly compared with the wisdom He possessed; but He was a boy only, and lacked physical strength even to defend His own person; and was subject to cold, to hunger and to death. So it is with the Church of Jesus Christ of Latter-day Saints; we have the revelation of Jesus, and the knowledge within us is sufficient to organize a righteous government upon the earth, and to give universal peace to all mankind, if they would receive it, but we lack the physical strength, as did our Savior when a child, to defend our principles, and we have of necessity to be afflicted, persecuted and smitten, and to bear it patiently until Jacob is of age, then he will take care of himself."

Wheelock took a list of witnesses' names that were wanted for the expected trial on Saturday. When the list was read over, a number of names were stricken out, among whom were Alpheus Cutler and Reynolds Cahoon, it being deemed by Brother Hyrum unnecessary for them to attend. Brother Joseph asked why they should not come. Hyrum answered, "They may be very good men, but they don't know enough to answer a question properly." Brother Joseph remarked, "That is sufficient reason."

The prisoners also sent many verbal messages to their families. They were so numerous that Dr. Richards proposed writing them all down, fearing Wheelock might forget, but Brother Hyrum fastened his eyes upon him, and with a look of penetration said, "Brother Wheelock will remember all that we tell him, and he will never forget the occurrences of this day."

The Prophet's Dream

Joseph related the following dream which he had last night:

I was back in Kirtland, Ohio, and thought I would take a walk out by myself, and view my old farm, which I found grown up with weeds and brambles, and altogether bearing evidence of neglect and want of culture. I went into the barn, which I found without floor or doors, with the weather-boarding off, and was altogether in keeping with the farm.

"While I viewed the desolation around me, and was contemplating how it might be recovered from the curse upon it, there came rushing into the barn a company of furious men, who commenced to pick a quarrel with me.

"The leader of the party ordered me to leave the barn and farm, stating it was none of mine, and that I must give up all hope of ever possessing it.

"I told him the farm was given me by the Church, and although I had not had any use of it for some time back, still I had not sold it, and according to righteous principles it belonged to me or the Church.

"He then grew furious and began to rail upon me, and threaten me, and said it never did belong to me nor to the Church.

"I then told him that I did not think it worth contending about, that I had no desire to live upon it in its present state, and if he thought he had a better right I would not quarrel with him about it but leave; but my assurance that I would not trouble him at present did not seem to satisfy him, as he seemed determined to quarrel with me, and threatened me with the destruction of my body.

"While he was thus engaged, pouring out his bitter words upon me, a rabble rushed in and nearly filled the barn, drew out their knives, and began to quarrel among themselves for the premises, and for a moment forgot me, at which time I took the opportunity to walk out of the barn about up to my ankles in mud.

"When I was a little distance from the barn, I heard them screeching and screaming in a very distressed manner, as it appeared they had engaged in a general fight with their knives. While they were thus engaged, the dream or vision ended."

Both Joseph and Hyrum bore a faithful testimony to the Latter-day work, and the coming forth of the Book of Mormon, and prophesied of the triumph of the Gospel over all the earth, exhorting the brethren present to faithfulness and persevering diligence in proclaiming the Gospel, building up the Temple, and performing all the duties connected with our holy religion.

Joseph dictated the following postscript to Emma:
Letter: Postscript.

P. S.—20 minutes to 10.—I just learn that the Governor is about to disband his troops, all but a guard to protect us and the peace, and come himself to Nauvoo and deliver a speech to the people. This is right as I suppose.

He afterwards wrote a few lines with his own hand, which were not copied. (June 27, 1844.) D. H. C. 6:608-611.

Letter: Joseph Smith to O. H. Browning—Engaging Browning as Legal Counsel

Carthage Jail, June 27th, 1844.

Lawyer Browning:—

Sir.—Myself and brother Hyrum are in jail on charge of treason, to come up for examination on Saturday morning, 29th inst., and we request your professional services at that time, on our defense, without fail.

Most respectfully your servant,

JOSEPH SMITH.

P. S.—There is no cause of action, for we have not been guilty of any crime, neither is there any just cause of suspicion against us; but certain circumstances make your attendance very necessary.

J. S.

—D. H. C. 6:613.

This account brings us up to the afternoon of the day of the martyrdom. At 1:30 p.m. on that day some of the visitors at the prison were forced to leave, and Joseph Smith, Hyrum

Smith, John Taylor and Willard Richards were left to themselves. At 3:15 after the change of guards, they, the guards, became more severe and threatening. About this time Elder Taylor sang—*A Poor Wayfaring Man of Grief*. When he finished the song the Prophet requested him to sing it again, which he did, reluctantly, as he did not feel like singing. At 4 p.m. Hyrum did some reading to his fellow prisoners. The guard was again changed, only eight men being stationed at the jail, the main body of the Carthage Greys were in camp a quarter of a mile distant, on the public square. At 5 p.m. the jailor, Mr. Stigall, suggested that the brethren return to the cell where they would be safer. The Prophet turned to Dr. Richards and said, "If we go into the cell, will you go in with us?" The Doctor replied, "Brother Joseph, you did not ask me to cross the river with you —you did not ask me to come to jail with you—and do you think I would forsake you now? But I will tell you what I will do; if you are condemned to be hung for treason, I will be hung in your stead, and you shall go free." Joseph said, "You cannot." The Doctor said, "I will."

It was but a short time following this that there was a rustling at the door of the prison, the mob had arrived and was bent on taking the lives of the prisoners, which, as we all know, they wickedly did. The account of this tragedy is not to be related here. The reader is referred to the full account of the awful and bloody deed as it is recorded in the Documentary History of the Church.

INDEX AND CONCORDANCE

Prepared by Dr. Robert J. Matthews, chairman of the Department of Ancient Scripture, Brigham Young University.

Atonement, through blood of Christ, 58

Australia, opening of missionary work in, 178

Authority, divine, necessary to make ordinances valid, 274; of apostles next to Presidency, 105

Avard, Dr., false teacher in the Church, 127, 146

Backbite, do not, 155

Bag of sand, just as well baptize a, as a man, if not done with right intent, 314

Baptism, not necessary for telestial and terrestrial kingdoms, 12; essential for celestial kingdom, 12, 16, 198; need for, settles the question of all men's religion, 12, 264-65; of water is preparatory to reception of Holy Ghost, 148, 198-99, 263; not needed for little children, 197; of children, is not consistent with character of God, 197; is a sign of obedience, 198; is absolutely essential for salvation, 198-99, 262; is for remission of sins, 198, 262, 314; in name of Father, Son, and Holy Ghost, 201; derived from Greek "baptizo"—meaning immerse, 262, 314; necessity of, taught in Bible, 262; is only way for remission of sins, 262; sectarians differ in opinions concerning, 262; sectarian, is not valid, 192, 263; has always been a requirement for salvation, 264, 266; is a burial, 266, 314; of the children of Israel, 264; angels cannot perform, 265; there is no substitute for, 265; no salvation without, 265-66; necessary to fulfill all righteousness, 266, 274, 319; is the only door to mansions of bliss, 266; does not replace circumcision, 314; must be by immersion, 314, 262; of infants, not taught in Bible, 314; is useless unless done with view of remission of sins and receiving Holy Ghost, 314; by water only half a baptism, 314, 360; neglect of, lays foundation of damnation, 361; not to be performed for wives if husbands object, 87; cannot benefit murderers, 339

Baptism (for dead), practiced in ancient Church, 179; taught by Paul, 179; first taught (in this dispensation) at funeral of Seymour Brunson, 179; for dead relatives and friends, 222-23; is for those who would have believed had they heard gospel in mortality, 179, 201, 221-22; is for those who have received gospel in spirit prison, 179, 336; enlarges the scope of the gospel, 180, 192; is only way to become a Savior on Mount Zion, 191; is necessary for the salvation of the dead, 193; to be done in house of the Lord, 193, 308, 363; great numbers of, have been performed, 201; is supported by biblical evidence, 201, 310; practiced by Marchionites, 222; recorder and witness needed at, 260; to be testified of in Grand Council, 260; decreed before foundation of world, 308; taught in New Testament, 310; is the purpose for gathering of Israel, 130

Baptist, John. See John the Baptist

Barnes, Lorenzo D., funeral of, 294-97

Baurau, Hebrew term, meaning of, 348, 371

Be like God, to go where he is, 216

Beetle (figurative expression), 331

Beasts, of John's revelation, 287-94; of Daniel's vision, 289; use of, in the revelations, 288-89; represent degenerate and wicked kingdoms, 289; are not used to represent kingdom of God, 289; in heaven, 291-94; give glory to God in heaven, 291-92; God is glorified by salvation of, 291-92; saved from any worlds, 291; given power over inhabitants of earth, 293-94; image of, 291-92, 294

Beginning, gospel ordinances are from the, 59

Berosheit, Hebrew term, meaning of, 348, 371

Betrayal of brethren, a major sin, 156

Bible, he who reads it most often will like it best, 56; many important things taken from or lost before compiled, 10-11; erroneous belief that all revelation from God is in, 61; is not believed by the religious

Born again, comes by Spirit of God through ordinances, 162; comes by water and Spirit and is required for salvation, 12, 264, 360

Boys and the preaching of the gospel, 43

Brother to be against brother in last days, 161

Brown, Father, teachings concerning beasts of the revelation, 288-89

Browning, O. H. (attorney), the Prophet's letter to, from Carthage, 394

Buffetings of Satan, 301; traitors and false brethren delivered unto, 128; spirit of Elijah has power to deliver unto, 338

Burial, in land of Zion is desirable, 294-95; of Jacob and Joseph, 295; not to have honorable, is great calamity, 295. *See also* Burying place

Burned, world to be, 101, 337

Burnings, God dwells in everlasting, 347, 361, 367, 373; righteous to dwell in everlasting, 347, 361, 367, 373; immortal glory is everlasting, 347; flesh and blood cannot dwell in eternal, 367

Burying place, sacredness of, 294; sacredness of, mentioned in Book of Mormon, 294

Cain, offering of, not acceptable because not done in faith, 58; offering of, rejected because contained no blood, 58; authorized to offer sacrifices before his fall, 169; cursed for unrighteousness, 169

Called, many are, but few chosen, 142, 331

Calling and election, 150, 298, 305

Calling of the apostles, 74. *See also* Twelve apostles

Campbell, Alexander, practiced water baptism without Holy Ghost, 360

Canada, the Prophet's views on, 335

Captivity, comes through lack of knowledge of things of God, 217

Carlin, Governor, the Prophet's letter to, concerning favorable treatment in Nauvoo, 254

Carthage, events on way to, 380

Cause of God is a common one in which all should be interested, 231

Celestial kingdom, baptism of water and Spirit required for entrance to, 12, 16, 198; every man who reigns in, is a God to his dominions, 374; all who obtain fulness of will be Gods, 301, 374; vision of, 106-107; fiery gate of, 107; throne of God in, 107; streets of, appear to be paved with gold, 107; heirs of, 107; all children who die before age of accountability are saved in, 107; vision of Adam, Abraham, and the Prophet's parents in, 107; children to be born to parents in, 301; three degrees in, 301; eternal marriage necessary for highest degree of, 301; eternal increase limited to, 301; Alvin Smith in, 107

Celestial law, many will fail to abide, 331

Ceremonies, revelation of, 109-10

Chance, universe not by, 56

Chaos, result of absence of law, 55

Characterization of the Prophet, by himself, 304

Charity, sects lack, 192; world lacks, 240; greatness of, 228

Chastened by hand of God, saints have been, 253

Chastisement, man must be willing to receive, from the Lord, 194; God uses sickness and death as a, 194; corrupt men will not endure, 195; comes because of disobedience, 253; comes because of light regard for God's commandments, 253

Children, not to be baptized if parents object, 87; concerning death of little, 196; who die, are delivered from evil, 197; baptism of, a false doctrine, 197; all, are redeemed by Christ, 197, 314; resurrection of, 200, 368; to be born to parents in celestial kingdom, 301; have no sins, 314; baptism of, not taught in Bible, 314; value of a seal upon, 321; Saints may have to fight to protect, 366; must be sealed to parents, 368; should be obedient to parents, 87; who die, are saved in celestial kingdom, 107; hearts of, turn to fathers, 160, 337

Chosen, few are, 142, 331

Christ, is the Great High Priest, 158; presides over Adam, 168; is head of the Church, 318; second coming of,

29, 286, 341; brought the resurrection, 62; to present the kingdom to his Father at end of last dispensation, 169, 347. *See also* Jesus Christ, Son of Man, Son of God, Messiah, Savior, False Christs

Christian Godhead, strangeness of, 372. *See also* Godhead, Sectarian

Christianity, present day, is not the order of heaven, 48-49; professors of, inspired by Satan, 270; is sleeping, 14; apostasy evident in, 15; lacks faith, 270; does not believe in Bible, but rather in interpretation of Bible, 119. *See also* Sectarian, Sectarians

Church, compared to human body, 35, 231, 244-45; compact body, 244; parable of, in last days, 98; retarded by ignorance, 138; to be purged, 373; to prevail against all evil, 257; could give world universal peace, 392; at times lacks physical strength to defend itself, 392

Church, Catholic, 375, 293, 313

Church of the Firstborn, 12, 320; endowment, pertains to, 237

Circumcision, covenant of, made with Abraham, 264; practiced by Israel while in Egypt, 264; abandoned by Israel while in wilderness, 264; renewed by Joshua, 264; is not baptism, 314; was not replaced by baptism, 314

Circumstances, revelations are adapted to, 256; what is wrong under some, may be right under other, 256

Clark, man named, frozen to death while drunk, 108; the Prophet's comment concerning, 108-109

Columbus, anecdote concerning wisdom of, 304

Comforter, difference between first and second, 149-50; first, is the Holy Ghost, 149; effect of first, is pure intelligence, 149-50; second is Jesus Christ, 150-51; second, will manifest the Father, 151; various prophets had second, 151; doctrine of, recorded by John, 150

Commandments, only those who keep to end will be saved, 63; all of God's are binding upon us, 253-54;

of God deal with both spiritual and temporal things, 252-54; obedience to, brings happiness, 255-56; must be known to be kept, 256; man must obey present, before given more, 256; all of God's are right, 256; vary with the circumstances, 256; all of God's are calculated for man's happiness, 256; all who will not obey, will be damned, 199, 332

Commandments, Book of. *See* Book of Commandments

Common, not believe in having all things in, 119

Common consent, Church business to be done by, 75, 108

Common sense, plans of Jehovah are consistent with, 221

Compassion, the righteous have, on perishing souls, 241

Compulsion, exercise of, contrary to righteousness, 142, 341; is not in kingdom of God, 241

Condemned, man not, for disobedience if not taught, 220-22

Conference of April 1841, report of, 184

Confusion among nations, 252

Conscience, man should be free in matters of, 49, 326; remorse of, follows willful transgression, 50

Consecrated lives, meaning of, 127

Consecration, must be voluntary, 23; great particulars in inventory of, not necessary, 22; is required to become legal heir of the kingdom, 23; to be done with mutual consent, 23; true meaning of, 127

Constitution (of man), no change in since fall of Adam, 60; varied, among men, 299; man's, seems to be to set up stakes limiting progress, 321, 327; man's, seems to be to set up stakes limiting the Almighty, 320-21

Constitution (of the United States), a glorious standard, 147; founded in wisdom of God, 147; a true document, 148; guarantees civil and religious liberty, 185, 279, 317, 326, 331-32, 344; comments of the Prophet on powers of the, 278-79; contains provisions for making laws, 278-79; designed to regulate groups, not individuals, 279; not broad enough to cover the whole ground, 326-27; Joseph Smith, greatest advocate of, 326. *See also* Political motto

Contention, evil of, 43; in heaven, what it was, 357

Copyright, of Book of Mormon, 7; Book of Mormon, Doctrine and Covenants, and hymn book to have, in Prophet's name, 164

Corn-dodger (figurative expression), 331

Cornelius, received Holy Ghost before baptism, 199; could not receive gift of Holy Ghost until after baptism, 199; had to be baptized for salvation, 265

Corrections, scriptural. *See* Bible, corrections of

Corruption, earth now groaning under, 253; not to be condoned, 226

Council, Grand. *See* Grand Council

Council of the Gods, 348-49

Councils, strict order in, 69, 93-94, 307; importance and seriousness of, 69; instructions on proper decorum of, 69; difference between standing and traveling, 74. *See also* High council

Counsel, effects of disobeying, 42; for the exiled Saints, 144; Saints subject to divine, 254; value of aged men in, 299

Covenant, new, 12; of Christ, rejected by Jews, 14-15; with the Gentiles, 15; broken by the Gentiles, 15; of tithing, 70; with the fathers, 85; Melchizedek Priesthood is by, 323; made between personages in Godhead, 190

Covenants, fulfilling of, with Israel, 14; bring assurance of God's protection, 9; Jesus Christ endeavored to make, with Israel, 14

Cowdery, Oliver, blessed for constancy and steadfastness, 38; if faithful, to be helped out of many troubles, 38; must forsake evil, 38; made covenant of tithing, 70; harsh language of, to the Twelve, 106; accused Joseph Smith of being a fallen prophet, 270; mob action against, 271; ordained the Twelve in company with David Whitmer and Joseph Smith, 307

Create, means "form" or "organize," 181, 350-51; does not mean to make out of nothing, 350

Creator, God the First, 190

Creatures in heaven, varied, 291

Creeds of men, mix truth with error, 327; limit progress, 320-21, 327

Crimes are increasing, 48

Crown of righteousness, obtained through suffering, 64; Paul to receive a, 64

Cursed are those who fight against the Lord's anointed, 135

Cursings, rejected blessings become, 61, 308, 322

Damnation of hell, 198, 338; disobedient cannot escape, 198; explanation of, 198; rejecting revelation brings, 272, 298-99; rejecting offered blessings brings, 322; without revelation there is no escape from, 349; is awaiting the rebellious in Christendom, 298-99; neglect of baptism brings, 361

Damned, will everyone but Mormons be? 119; great many Mormons to be, 119; all who will not obey commandments will be, 199, 332, 335; does not come from believing too much, but because of unbelief, 374; the self-righteous to be, 277-78

Daniel, visions of, concerning Adam, 253; visions of, concerning distress of nations, 253; vision of, concerning beasts, 287; difference between visions of, and those of John, 290; visions of beast by, refer to kingdoms of earth, 260, 289-90

Darkness, spiritual, covers minds of people, 47-48; prevails on the earth, 90; is the condemnation of the world, 95

Daughter will oppose mother in great conflict, 161

David, a murderer, 188, 339; not resurrected at time of Christ, 188; not forgiven of murder of Uriah, 339; obtained promise that he would not remain in hell, 339; never did obtain fulness of priesthood, 339; priesthood and throne of, to be given to another by name of David in last days, and of his lineage, 339

Dead, proper respect due the, 120; no more incredible that God should save, than that he raise the, 191; God can use man as instrument to raise the, 120; the righteous, often pained knowing our thoughts and acts, 326; salvation of, is man's greatest responsibility, 356; at our departure we shall meet our, 360; all men shall rise as they are laid away, 368; Saints have not too much time to labor for, 330; the, worked for by the living, 338, 363

Dead, baptism for. See Baptism for the dead

Dead Sea waters to be healed, 286

Death, sometimes a chastisement, 194; as a warning voice for repentance, 196-97; of little children, 196-97; Joseph Smith predicts own, 225, 376; annihilation worse than thoughts of, 296; is last enemy to be conquered, 297, 305; the second, 361

Deathbed, man should not wait for, to repent, 197; danger of waiting till, for repentance, 197

Debts, man should pay, 22

Deceive, the devil's power to, 227

Decrees of God, are immovable, 197-99; the devil seeks to thwart, 297

Deeds, every man judged by his own, 218, 221, 237, 257, 311

Degrees of glory, greatness of the Prophet's vision of, 11; belief in, is beyond the narrowminded creeds of men, 11; Jacob's ladder a representation of, 305

Denial of Christ does violence to good judgment, 65

Destroying angels, to lay waste the inhabitants of earth because of wickedness, 87; to destroy workers of iniquity, 92; four, hold power over earth, 321; to go forth upon the earth, 330; to follow after the preaching of the gospel, 92

Destruction, coming upon world, 16; in the United States, 17; prepares way for return of lost tribes, 17; none but pure in heart shall escape, 71; follows rejection of gospel, 260, 271

Devil, exact destiny of, not revealed, 24; that he will be restored is false,

24; ought to be ashamed of traitors, 127; lays snares for the people of God, 130; uses his greatest efforts to afflict the Saints, 161; spirit of, now enraged, 161; is an orator, 162; is powerful, 162, 208; as an angel of light, 162, 204-205, 214; can speak in tongues, 162, 212; tempts all classes and nationalities, 162; has no power over man only as man permits, 181; has no body of flesh, 181; is pleased to steal body of man, 181, 298, 306; punishment of, is to be denied body of flesh, 181, 297; prefers swine's body to none, 181; cannot compel man to do evil, 187; all have power to resist, 189; spirit of, is an independent principle, 189; is pleased by man's ignorance, 203; detection of, requires more than human intelligence, 205; mysterious devices of, 205; to detect cunning and falseness of, requires priesthood, 205; often manifests zeal for God in order to deceive man, 205; gracious influence of, 205; holy garb of, 205; is willing to let persons think they worship God, while actually serving him, 205; is detected and unmasked by Spirit of God, 205; revelation required to detect, 205; control of, requires priesthood, 208; speaks both truth and falsehood, 214; has more knowledge than many men, 217; is subtle, 225; to curb, requires humility, 225; the innocent soul that resists evil cannot be overthrown by, 226; has great power to deceive, 227; can make righteousness appear strange, 227; retards human mind with self-righteousness, 241; opposes good men, 259; smooth, sophisticated influence of, 270; inspires professors of religion with false hope of salvation, 270; whole world is deceived by, 270; unlawful things sought by, 297; seeks to thwart decrees of God, 297; goes to and fro in the earth seeking whom he may destroy, 297-98; takes possession of man's body, 298, 306; often given the advantage by fools, 331; laid plans before Grand

and come to Christ, 43, 88, 306; difference between high council and, 76; are to clean skirts from blood of this generation, 76; duties of, 76-77, 86-87; not to teach children without parents' consent, 86; not to teach wives without husband's consent, 87; not to teach servants or slaves without master's consent, 87-88; to stand up boldly for the cause of Christ, 88; to teach in the name of the Lord, 88; to preach in meekness and sobriety, 109; aspiring, cause difficulty, 225; difficulty caused by "great big," 225; are to leave the mysteries alone, 292; are to teach as directed by the Spirit, 306; are to shun lightmindedness, 326

Elect, God to avenge the, 36; to be gathered to New Jerusalem, 84

Election, doctrine of, taught by Paul, 149; should be taught today, 149; explained, 189, 321; is based on obedience, 189; is taught in ninth chapter of Romans, 189; according to the flesh, 189; according to the seed of Abraham, 189, 321; is associated with the power of Elijah, 338; unconditional, not a true doctrine, 189

Election and calling, made sure, 149, 298, 299, 305-306, 321, 323, 366; is by the sealing power, 149

Elements, are eternal, 181, 351-52; can be purified by righteousness, 200; cannot be destroyed, 353

Elias, a man of like passions as other men, 89; with Savior and Moses, gave keys to Peter, James, and John, 158; spirit and power of, is to prepare the way for a greater work, 335-36, 340; difference between power of Elijah and power of, 335-36, 338, 340; John the Baptist had calling of, 335

Eliases, since beginning of world, have tried to establish principles of priesthood among the people, 159; prophesied of a day of God's glory, 159

Elijah (prophet), if not come, whole earth be smitten, 160, 356; last prophet holding keys of priesthood, 172; holds keys to administer all ordinances, 172, 337; revealed covenants of the fathers, 321, 323, 326; coming of, 330; held keys of sealing, 337-38

Elijah (spirit and power of), difference between power of Elias and, 335-36, 338, 340; deals with labor for living and dead, 337; has power to seal on earth and in heaven, 338, 340; was manifest in days of apostles, 338; can deliver to buffetings of Satan, 338; is not understood by the world, 338; places seals of Melchizedek Priesthood on the house of Israel, 340; cannot seal against unpardonable sin, 339; not possessed by David, 339; prepares way for the Messiah, 340

Eloheim, plural meaning of, 371-72

Embalmed, Jacob and Joseph were, after manner of Egyptians, 232; Jesus was partially, 232

Embalming, art of, known by Egyptians, 232; known by the Hebrews, 232; ingredients for, 232; hasty burial prohibited the, of Jesus, 232; art of, transmitted to American continent, 233

End, who endure to, are saved, 63, 199

End of world, meaning of, 98, 100-101; explained in parable of wheat and tares, 97-98, 100-101; alludes to human family, not to the earth, 101

Endowment (in Kirtland), 91

Endowments, are necessary for full spiritual power, 91; necessary to enable one to overcome all things, 91; given, 237; are only understood by spiritually minded, 237; proper place needed for giving, 237, 363-64; pertain to Church of the Firstborn, 237; needed to prepare disciples for mission into the world, 274; prepare men to become priests and kings unto God, 363; first given in 1842, 237; for the dead are same as for living, 363, 366

Endure to the end to be saved, 63, 199

Enemies, overcoming of, is salvation, 297, 305

England, progress of the gospel in, 174

Enoch, prophecy of, concerning gathering of Israel, 83-84; understood the plan of the Messiah, 84; quoted

241, 316; of men should not be spoken of behind their backs, 31; no man without, 258; even Jesus, were he here now, would not seem to be without, in the eyes of men, 258

Feelings, brethren should be careful of one another's, 24-25; God has respect for the Saints', 19; unkindness brings harsh, 240

Feet, washing of. See Washing of feet

Fig tree, parable of, 161

Fire, God dwells in eternal, 367; world to be burned with, 101, 337; flesh and blood cannot dwell in eternal, 326, 367; flesh and bones quickened by Spirit can dwell in eternal, 326; righteous dwell in, 326

Firstborn, Church of. See Church of the Firstborn

First Presidency, report of, at April 1841 conference, 184; Adam held keys of, 157; is dissolved when the President dies, 106

Flattery, is a deadly poison, 137; the devil uses, 241

Flesh, all, subject to suffering, 162; subject to death, 163; of righteous to dwell in eternal fire, 326, 367

Flesh and blood, cannot dwell in eternal fire where God is, 367; cannot go to place where exalted spirits are, but flesh and bones can, 326, 367

Flesh and bones, God has a body of, 181; there is no other God in heaven except that God who has a body of, 181

Follett, King, death of, 342; funeral of, 342-62

Fools, none but, trifle with souls, 137; devil has many, to help him, 331; seal up the gate to knowledge, 371

Ford, Governor, letter to, 378

Forgive, man ought to be ready to, a brother even before he repents, 155

Forgiveness, is a requirement, 155; the principle of, 238; of sins is conditional, 358; is withheld from murderers, 188-89, 339

Foster, Dr., apostate, 368; the Prophet's dream concerning, 368

Foxes, little, spoil vines, 258

Free agency, given to every person, 12; doctrine of, 49, 187; because of,

man must be responsible for own sins, 187

Freedom of religion guaranteed by the Constitution, 185, 297, 317, 326

French prophets, 208. See also False prophets

Friends, value of in times of trouble, 134

Friendship, a fundamental principle of Mormonism, 316; will bring unity, 316; weakened by oaths, 146

Fruit of the vine, Christ and the Saints to partake of at Second Coming, 65-66

Fruits of the kingdom, 273

Fullmer, John S., in Carthage, 383

Fulness of times, all things to be revealed in, 138; nothing to be withheld in, 138; gathering of all things in, 231-32. See also Dispensation of the fulness of times

Funeral sermons, Ephraim Marks, 215-16; Judge Higbee, 319-21; James Adams, 324-26; King Follett, 342-62; Lorenzo D. Barnes, 294-97

Futurity, John's vision of, 289

Gabriel, is Noah, 157

Garment (wedding), none to eat and drink with the Bridegroom without a, 48

Gate, the strait, 67; to celestial kingdom, 107; many shut up the, of knowledge, 371

Gathering, of all things in one, 231; of the elect, 84; of false reports, 144; God designed a, for every age of the world, 308; greater blessings attend the, than are possible through individual effort, 183

Gathering of Israel, a matter of greatest importance, 83; a subject considered by all the prophets, 83; one of the most important points of our faith, 92; American Indians are included in the, 85-86, 92-93; doctrine of, taught in parable of the sower, 94-95; is to prepare the world for burning, 101; every needful blessing will be given to those who labor for, 163; the greatest spiritual and temporal blessings attend the, 183; salvation not obtainable without the, 183; will precede the Lord's second coming, 183; purpose of, is for redemption of living and dead, 307-308, 310, 312; enables building of the house of the Lord, 308; a place for the, 144, 175; glory of, 183

Generation, punishment awaits this, 328

Gentile nations hardly warned before destruction comes, 87

Gentile sophistry, warning against, 156

Gentiles, received covenant of gospel in meridian of time, 15; broke gospel covenant, 15; repentant, to receive inheritance in America, 17; Saints to be gathered from among, 71; effect of Holy Ghost upon, 149-50; receive a new creation by the Holy Ghost, 150; the "stony," referred to as dogs, 319

German New Testament, most nearly correct, 349, 360, 364

Ghost, Holy. See Holy Ghost

Gift of the Holy Ghost and Holy Ghost, difference between, 199. See also Holy Ghost

Gifts, from God are just, 256; of the gospel, 224. See also Spiritual gifts

Gifts of the Spirit. See Spiritual gifts

Glories, degrees of, 12; different, 359; eternal, 374; vision concerning the, is a transcript from the records of the eternal world, 11. See also Degrees of glory

Glory, mankind ought to seek for the, of Abraham, Noah, Adam, and the apostles, 162; of gathered Israel is described in the 50th psalm, 183; laws of God enable men to advance in, 354

God (Jehovah), sees secrets of human action, 19; knows the hearts of all living, 19; has respect for feelings of his Saints, 19; to inquire of, is a serious thing, 22; is not to be approached on trifling matters, 22; laws of, are greater than man's laws, 50-52; justice of, in punishing the rebellious, 52; is the source of all good, 55, 57, 251; cannot lie, 55; is perfect intelligence, 55; he alone has sufficient wisdom to govern universe, 55; is source of all wisdom and understanding, 55; is

author of law, 56; is not inconsistent in character, 56; will reward servants according to their labors, 57; it is reasonable to expect revelation from, 56; reason and inspiration declare there is an intelligent, 56; has appointed a day of judgment, 62; hates traitors and false brethren, 127, 129; controls the devil, 132; the things of, require solemn thought, 137; thoughts of, are more dignified and noble than are man's thoughts, 137; is our shield, 139; is the author of Mormonism, 139; has a body of flesh and bones, 181, 312; does not compel obedience, 187; passes over no man's sins, 189; man must be like, to go where he is, 216; man is drawing toward devil if not drawing toward, 216-17; has fatherly care for the human family, 218; holds reins of judgment, 218; justice of, 128; reveals things differently than man expects, 224; man must be innocent to dwell with, 227; man must be pure to dwell with, 227; does not look upon sin with allowance, 240; makes allowance for sinners, 241; will punish evildoers, 239, 241; can be known through prayer, 247; government of, 248-54; all will fall who have not, as their leader, 253; governs in both spiritual and temporal things, 252; all requirements of, are right, 256; is very liberal and merciful, 257; is terrible to workers of iniquity, 257; detects every false way, 257; will judge men according to their deeds, 257; will withhold no good thing from the faithful, 257; is the same yesterday, today, and forever, 264; the things of, are known only by revelation, 292; judges men according to the use they make of the light he gives them, 303; deals with man as tender parent with child, 305; character of, understood by but few, 343; knowledge of, separates man from the brute creation, 343; to know, is necessary for eternal life, 344, 346; Bible teaches character and being of, 345-46; is an exalted man, 345; was once a man like us, 345; once dwelt on an earth like this earth, 345; upholds all worlds by his power, 345; does not trifle with mankind, 347; dwells in everlasting burnings, 347; is a self-existent being, 352; did not create himself, 354; has given laws to enable man to advance like himself, 354; views all men with an eternal perspective, 356; will save all except who commit unpardonable sin, 356-57; will not acknowledge that which he has not called and appointed, 168; there is no place where man can hide from, 367; is a consuming fire, 367; everlasting covenant made by, 190. See also Jehovah

God (sectarian), that which is without body, parts, and passions, is nothing, 181; there is no God in heaven except with flesh and bones, 181; sectarian doctrine of, not correct, 311, 181, 312; strangeness of, 372

God, house of, order in, always the same in all ages, 91; certain ordinances performed only in, 308

Godhead, writings of Abraham concerning, 190; three persons in heaven holding keys of power, 312, 370; one personage presides over the others, 312; proof that Father and Son are separate personages, 312; separate bodies of Father and Son, 312; Greek text teaches correct nature of, 372; a plurality of gods, 370

Godhead (sectarian). See God (sectarian)

Gods (plurality of), 369-73; many gods and lords, 311, 370-71; New Testament teaches plurality of, 370; Father, Son, and Holy Ghost distinct personages, therefore a plurality, 370, 372, 373, 376; to us, there is but one, 371; Hebrew text teaches plurality of, 372; Abraham reasoned concerning plurality of, 190, 373; our God has a father, 369, 373; a plurality of, is the plain teaching of the scriptures, 373-74; a plurality of, met in Grand Council, 347

Gog and Magog, battle of, is after millennium, 280

Good, God is source of all, 55, 251

Good men, there have been few since Adam, 303

Gospel, revealed to Abel, 59; preached to Abraham, 60; always preached in name of Christ, 60; always has ordinances, 60; preached to Israel in Moses' day, 60; man's most important duty is to preach, 113; has always been the same, 168, 264; destruction follows rejection of, 271; first principles of, 328; first principle of, is to know character of God, 345; purpose of, is to enable man to advance in righteousness and godliness, 354; all who will not obey, will be dammed, 355; obedience to, brings salvation, 357; to be preached to a witness in last days, 364; ordinances of, arranged before world was, 308, 367; to triumph over the earth, 394; unchangeableness of, 264, 308; duties of elders in preaching the, 87

Government established by God, 251

Government of God, 248-54; based on correct principles, 52-53; essential to exaltation, 51; requirements of, 51, 256; dissimilar to government of men, 248; promotes peace, unity, strength, happiness, 248, 250-51; characteristics of, 248; practiced by Enoch, 251; practiced by Abraham, 251-52; deals with both civil and ecclesiastical affairs, 252; is only way to universal peace, 252; conducted by revelation, 254, 256; without force, 241

Government of man, dissimilar to government of God, 248; has tended toward confusion, disorder, weakness, and misery, 248; Egypt, Babylon, Greece, Persia, Carthage, Rome, are examples of, 248; founded, conducted by force, violence, 248; rapid succession of, 249; has not brought peace or happiness to human family, 249, 252-53; unsettled conditions of, 250; has been tried for six thousand years, 252; will not bring worldwide peace, 252-54; is a departure from the Lord's government, 57.

Government of the United States, did not protect Saints from persecution, 317, 327, 332; gathers the

American Indians, 93. See also Constitution of the United States

Governmental authority necessary, 49

Governments, need laws to protect innocent and punish guilty, 49, 55; value of, 53; the Almighty is a lover of good, 187; ancient, have failed, 250, 252; all, ought to permit religious freedom, 344

Grace, Presbyterian and Methodist doctrine is incorrect, 338-39; falling from, 338-39

Grand Council, meeting of the Gods in, 348; creation of worlds contemplated in, 348-49; devil laid plans before, 357; Joseph Smith ordained in, 365; many ordinations, 365

Grandin, E. B., printer of Book of Mormon, 7

Grave, Jesus Christ gained victory over, 62; body does not grow in, 199-200; sacredness of, 294

Greek, 364; "baptizo," meaning of, 262, 314; Book of Mormon plates contained no, 299; New Testament text in, teaches plurality of Gods, 372

Greene, John P., at Carthage, 388

Guardian angel, 368

Guilty, bring sufferings upon the righteous, 34

Hades, 310. See also Hell

Hair, Satan detected by color of, 214-15

Ham, cursed by Noah, 193-94

Haman and Mordecai, 123; persecutors of the Saints likened to, 123

Hand of the Lord can not be stayed, 139-40

Hands, laying on of. See Laying on of hands

Happiness, is object of existence, 255-56; comes only by obedience to commandments, 255-56; every commandment is designed to bring, 256-57

Harris, Martin, bitten by snake, 71-72; failure of, to understand promises of God, 71-72

Hatred, Saints have no room for, 179

Haun's Mill, murder and persecutions at, 133, 141

Heart, necessity of members being of one, to do Lord's will, 24; honest in, to be brought out of sectarianism, 192

Hearts, God has power to soften the, of all men, 36; all men to be judged according to desires of their, 107; of all living known to God, 19; of children turn to fathers, and fathers to children, 160, 337

Heaven, must include more kingdoms than one, 11; to be shaken at Jesus' coming, 29; the Lord speaks from, 53; to be unfolded as a scroll, 29; kingdom of, in last days, 98-99; laws of, binding upon man, 52; revelation needed to know of, 160

Hebrew, biblical text of, teaches plurality of gods, 371-72; quotations from, 300, 348, 371; text of, more accurate than English version of Bible, 290

Heirs, in kingdom of God, 54; of the celestial kingdom are all who die who would have received the gospel with all their hearts, 107. See also Joint heir with Christ

Hell, not as strong as an honest man, 139; revelation needed to know of, 160; meaning of, 310; is a modern word, 310; is world of spirits, 310

Hell, damnation of. See Damnation of hell

Hemlock knots (figurative expression), 331

Heritage of the righteous is persecution, 260

Higbee, Chauncey L., apostate at Nauvoo, 368; the Prophet's dream concerning, 368

Higbee, Judge, funeral of, 319-21

High council, the Twelve apostles are a traveling, 74; difference between standing and traveling, 74; standing, not have authority abroad, 74; standing, only established in Zion and stakes, not in branches, 74; organized to administer spiritual affairs, 76; difference between duties of elders and, 76; to regulate affairs of Zion, 78; not to dictate to the Twelve, 92; not to try cases without both parties having opportunity to be present, 165; not to hear one's complaint previous to trial, 165; nonmembers not to bring members before, for trial, 286

High-mindedness, to be avoided by the Saints, 141

High priest, to administer in spiritual things, 21; not to exercise monarchial government, 21; duty of, is to be better qualified than elder to teach gospel, 21; is a presiding office, 109; holds the same priesthood as the Presidency, but not the same authority in the Church, 112; not to be a seventy, 111-12; bishop is a, 112; to take charge of churches, 164

Holy Ghost, given to those who obey God, 62; gives assurance that Jesus Christ has risen from dead, 62; follows the remission of sins, 81; none can preach gospel without, 112; gives hidden knowledge, 138; is the First Comforter, 150-51, 243; effect of, upon seed of Abraham, 149-50; effect of, upon Gentiles, 149-50; gives power of great speech, 155-56; no other sin to be compared to sin against, 156; difference between gift of, and, 199; convinced Cornelius of gospel truth, 199; needed to know Jesus is the Christ, 223, 243; is a witness-bearer, 243; leads to all truth, 243; brings past events to remembrance, 243; shows things to come, 243; holy men speak by, 243; various gifts come by, 243; dove is sign of, 276; is a personage, 276; cannot be transformed into a dove, 276; revelations of, show errors in Bible translations, 310; is God's messenger to administer in the priesthood, 323; cannot be received without revelation, 328; is a revelator, 328; cannot be conferred by Aaronic Priesthood, 335; was given by Jesus to John the Baptist's disciples, 336; carries conviction of truth to heart and mind, 342; one cannot commit unpardonable sin without, 357; constant companion of the righteous, 143; power of, directs the elders of the Church, 156. See also Holy Ghost, gift of; Holy Ghost, sin against; Holy Spirit

Holy Ghost (gift of), is received only by the laying on of hands, 148, 199, 212, 243, 314; has been discarded by modern Christians, 188; sign concerning, 199; difference between Holy Ghost and, 199; comes after baptism, 199, 212, 314; the world has various opinions concerning, 242; is needed to organize priesthood and call men to the ministry, 243; not all have the same powers in, 243; should be sought after, 244; must accompany the baptism of water to be complete, 314, 360. See also Spiritual gifts

Holy Ghost (sin against), is unforgivable, 219, 191; no other sin to be compared to, 156; is the unpardonable sin, 375, 358; makes men sons of perdition, 358; no repentance for, 358-60; brings second death, 361; how committed, 358. See also Unpardonable sin

Holy Spirit, manifests truth through prayer, 11; gives knowledge, 11; knowledge by, removes speculation, 11-12; knowledge of God obtained by, 11-12; of Promise, 149

Hope, is centered in resurrection of Jesus Christ, 62; in God brings purity, 64; Saints are assured of a better, than are their persecutors, 123; of the wicked shall be blasted, 134-35; should not mourn as without, 197; Latter-day Saints should have greatest, of any people on earth, 359

Hopes, disappointment of, at resurrection more painful than annihilation, 320, 325; when centered in the gospel are far above what man can conceive, 359

"Horn" made war with the Saints and overcame them, 159

House of God, order always the same in, 91; certain ordinances can only be performed in, 308

Howe's *Mormonism Unveiled*, 99

Humility, required of those who hold the priesthood, 155

Husbands, love for wives, 88

Hyde, Orson, letter to, on Palestine mission, 163; comment on the Negro, 269-70

Hymnbook, printing of, 176

Hypocrite, status of, 303

Ignorance, hinders the Church, 138; man cannot be saved in, 301; men too wise to be taught will die in, 309; of nature of spirits, 202-203

Imagination, beware of a fanciful and flowery, 137

Immorality, the curse of, 47

Immortality, of the spirit, 158, 352-54; dwells in everlasting burnings, 347, 361-62, 372; the infidel yearns for, when at point of death, 197

Imposter, how detected, 335; is likely to transcend his bounds and privileges, 335-36

Increase, the power of eternal, is confined to celestial kingdom, 301

Independent principles, there are three: Spirit of God, the spirit of man, and the spirit of devil, 189

Indians, American, are descendants of Joseph of Egypt, 17; Israelitish origin of, 92-93; being gathered by the U.S. government, 93; will be gathered by gospel, 93

Infants, taken at times through mercy, 196; baptism of, is false doctrine, 314

Infidel, yearns for immortality when at point of death, 197

Ingratitude of men, 309

Inhabitants, ancient, of America, perseverance and determination of, 299

Inheritance, right in sight of God for man to defend, 33

Inhumanity and cruelty against the Saints in Missouri is among worst of all history, 126, 131

Injury, most comes from little things, 258

Instruction, it is contrary for anyone to receive, for persons higher in authority, 21

Intelligence, has man increased in?, 249; is eternal, 354; God is perfect, 55; is not created, 158, 353; superior, is given to those who obey gospel, 67

Intelligences, some are superior to others, 373; Abraham's reasoning concerning, 373

Intemperance, is a curse, 47; evils of, 108

Irvingites, have perhaps counterfeited the truth nearest to any modern

sectarians, 210; teachings and proceedings of, 210-12. *See also* False prophets

Israel, gospel covenant not made with, in time of Christ, 14; tribes of (except Judah) to obtain inheritance in America, 17; purpose of gathering of, 307; God will keep covenant with, 14; lost tribes of, shall return from north country, 17; resides in America, says Book of Mormon, 93. *See also* Gathering of Israel

Jacob, 51; embalmed after manner of the Egyptians, 232; known as James in English New Testament, 349

Jacob's ladder, compared to degrees of glory, 305; angels descending on, 12-13

Jail, last night in Carthage, 383

James, with John and Peter received keys of priesthood, 158; in New Testament, should be Jacob, 349

Jaques, Vienna, letter to, 26

Jaredites, came to American continent from Tower of Babel, 267; lived in America more than 1,000 years, 267; covered whole continent from sea to sea, 267

Jasher, Book of, not yet disproved, 260; records persecutions of Abraham, 260

Jehovah, knows past, present, and future, 220; is acquainted with situation of all nations, 220; knows situation of both living and dead, 220; has made provision for the redemption of mankind, 220; is a wise legislator, 221; is more just than is man, 221; plans of, are consistent with common sense, 221; designs of, for government, 250-51; to stand at head of universe, 251. *See also* God

Jerusalem, the scriptures speak of two cities of, 94; the New, 85-86, 286. *See also* New Jerusalem

Jesus Christ, never broke a commandment or law of heaven, 67; none so pure, holy, perfect, or good as, 67; none other like, 67; went as ministering spirit to world of spirits, 191, 218-19, 222; ministered to

on earth, 290; with Peter and James, received keys of priesthood, 158; saw same type of vision as did Enoch concerning redemption of Zion, 84; quoted on marriage supper, 63; on second coming of Jesus Christ, 64-65; on becoming a king and a priest, 65; on God dwelling with men, 84; on Second Comforter, 150; on nature of spirits, 203; on what constitutes a prophet, 269, 312; on many mansions in heaven, 359; on plurality of gods, 373

Joint heir with Christ, to become, man must put away all false traditions, 321; to become, is to be like God, 347; to become, requires fulness of ordinances, 309; to become, is to have eternal power, 374

Jones, Dan, prophecy of Joseph Smith concerning, 384; in Carthage, 383

Joseph of Egypt, received knowledge of astronomy from the Lord, 251; taught astronomy to Egyptians, 251; patriarchal authority belongs to blood of, 151

Joseph Smith. See Smith, Joseph, the Prophet

Joshua the Jewish minister, 103; physical appearance of, 103; interpretations of Daniel by, 103-104; traveling under assumed name, 104-105; real name of, was Matthias, 105; claimed to be reincarnation of the apostle Matthias, 105; taught doctrine of transmigration, 105; may have been a murderer, 105

Joy, comes through knowledge of God, 51; in the resurrection, for the righteous, 295

Judah, to find deliverance in old Jerusalem, 17; must return before Christ comes, 286

Judas Iscariot, Satan entered into, 67; best friend of, was Jesus, 67; is example of an apostate, 67

Jude, was visited by Enoch, 170; cites prophecy of Enoch, 170

Judgment, will be according to works and desires of heart, 107; evils of hasty, 118, 358; doctrine of eternal, is among first principles, 149, 365; doctrine of eternal, is not understood by ministers of religion, 188-

89; Peter taught doctrine of eternal, 188; of man will be conditioned upon opportunities and circumstances, 218; according to deeds, 218, 221, 257, 311; of God is just, 218; according to use made of light given by God, 303; Zion to be redeemed by, 76; day of, appointed by God, 62

Judgment of God, ready to burst upon the earth, 16; rests upon people and nations that reject gospel, 271; to be poured out, 286; on mankind, 13-14; saints will not completely escape, 162; how to escape, 16

Just, Jehovah's plans are, 221

Just men made perfect, 325

Justice, for all the human family, 219; in each gift from God, 256; of the great lawgiver, 218; to neighbors, importance of, 303

Key, to understanding gospel principles, 181; to discerning of spirits, 204; to detecting false teachers and prophets, 269; to understanding scriptures, 276; to interpretation of the parable of the prodigal son, 277; to Peter's writings, 296; to mysteries of heaven is knowledge of Christ, 298; to understanding of John's revelations, 289; revelation is the, which unlocks the glories of celestial world, 298-99; to mysteries, faultfinding leads to apostasy, 156-57; signseeking indicates adultery, 157; to the Twelve, not sent to be taught, but to teach, 156; be vigilant and sober, 156; do not be a betrayer, 156

Key words, of the priesthood, 199; of Relief Society, 239

Keys, of sealing, 337-38; to endless life and how acquired, 322; of plural marriage, 323; of ministry are held by twelve apostles, 74, 109; of power and knowledge are held by the spirits of the just, 325; of kingdom, 21

Keys of priesthood, government and doctrine of Christ are vested in the, 21; sent from heaven, 157; held by Adam, 157, 167; are revealed from heaven by Adam, 157; held by Noah, 157; all who have held, must stand before Adam in grand council, 157; given to Peter, James, and John, 158; Enoch held, 170-71; Lamech held, 171; Elijah held, 172

Keystone of our religion is the Book of Mormon, 194

Kimball, Heber C., faithfulness of, 307

Kind, every plant, tree, etc., cannot come forth except after its, 198

Kindness, to animals, 71; should never be forgotten, 31; affection and, powerful influence of, 227, 240; lack of, harrows up harsh feelings, 240

King of kings, is Christ, 375

Kingdom, all things that offend shall be taken out of the, 101, 159; the Jews considered Christ to be least in the, 276; difference between the fruits and the, 273; requirement of the, 51; what is the, 271; of heaven, 63; men cannot be compelled into the, 241; of Satan set up in opposition to God, 365; vision of the celestial, 106-107; keys of, govern the Church in doctrine and principle, 21

Kingdom of God, set up on earth from days of Adam, 271; exists wherever the priesthood is, 271-72, 274; no salvation without, 272; was vested for a time with John only, 272, 276; difference between fruits of and, 273-74; cannot be established without a legal administrator, 274; seeing the, is not necessarily entering, 328; the devil sets up his kingdom in opposition to, 365

Kingdoms of glory, greatness of the Prophet's vision of, 11; the Prophet not permitted to reveal one-hundredth part of knowledge of the, 305

Kings and priests unto God, 65, 370

Kirtland, false spirits manifested among the Church at, 213-14; endowment at, 91

Knowledge, removes speculation, 11-12; elders should diligently seek, 43; is given by Holy Ghost, 138, 319; of spirits is lacking in the world, 205-206; of devil obtained only by Spirit of God, 205; of things of God obtainable only by Spirit of God, 202, 205, 246; man

saved no faster than he gets, of gospel, 217, 357; of God obtained only by revelation, 217; he who lacks, will be brought into captivity by the devil, 217; is power, 217, 288; as man approaches God he increases in, 51; correct, needed to end contention, 287; does away with darkness and suspense, 288; God has greater, than all other beings, hence more power, 288; Saints have, of resurrection, 296; principle of, is principle of salvation, 297, 305, 357; of Jesus Christ is key to glories and mysteries of heaven, 298; not all, is revealed at once, 297, 305; is revealed as man is able to bear, 305; is necessary for life and godliness, 305; is the power of salvation, 306, 354; a man of God needs, 311; purpose of revelation is to gain, 320; rejection of, brings damnation, 322; all, can be obtained by revelation, 330; of God is necessary for eternal life, 344, 346; God has placed man in a situation to advance in, 354; some seal up the gate of all, 371; condemnation of man without, 343; men are saved by obedience to, 217; of the gospel unlocks mysteries of the kingdom, 298; the consequences of unwillingness to learn, 331; Jesus had sufficient, as a boy to govern the kingdom, 392; men who are too "wise" to learn, will find their mistake in the resurrection, 309

Lamanites, to be blessed, 85; and Nephites, anciently, had very persevering nature in both wickedness and righteousness, 299

Lamb and lion to dwell together when men set the example, 71

Lamb's book of life, 9, 37

Lamech, held keys of priesthood, 171

Lands in Zion, not to be sold, 36

Language, of Jesus will be adapted to capacity of the learner, 162; of man cannot express importance of the gospel, 57; a pure, 93

Law, was given to Moses by Christ, 276; exaltation requires obedience to celestial, 331; full salvation requires observance of the whole, 331; of God is binding on man, 50

Law, William and Wilson: apostates at Nauvoo, 369; the Prophet's dream concerning, 369

Law of Moses, added to gospel, 60; given to Moses by Christ, 276; rites and ceremonies of, not to figure in restoration of all things, 173

Lawgiver, justice of the great, 218

Laws, are necessary for organized government, 49, 55; of man not equal to heaven's, 50-51; of heaven offer a guarantee beyond anything earthly, 50; comparison of earthly and heavenly, 50-51; man must be instructed in the, of God to endure celestial glory, 51; purpose of God's, are to prepare men for celestial kingdom, 54; are beneficial to promote peace and happiness among men, 55; of God are given to be obeyed, 56-57, 253; God influences men in the making of just, 57; governing spiritual worlds and beings were fixed in heaven, 325; the importance of man's understanding and subscribing to eternal, 325; of God are given to enable man to advance in glory, 354

Laying on of hands, has been discarded by world, 188; sick to be healed by, 198; gift of Holy Ghost received by, 148, 188, 199, 212, 243, 314; priesthood conferred by, 42, 264

Least in the kingdom of God, the Jews considered Christ to be, 276

Leaven, parable of the, 100

Legal administrator, only a, can set up the kingdom of God on earth, 274; only a, can perform valid ordinances, 274; wherever there is a, there is the kingdom of God, 274, 271; John the Baptist was, 273, 276, 318, 335-36; where the, is not, there the kingdom of God is not, 274; no salvation from the Bible without a, 274, 319; Jesus Christ was a, 319; Jesus came to John for baptism because John was a, 319

Lehi landed in America south of Isthmus of Darien, 267

Levitical Priesthood. See Priesthood, Levitical

Liberty, love of, 313; of conscience, 326; American, purchased with blood, 117

Liberty Jail, letter written from, 122-29; epistle written from, 129-48

Life, mortal is not all, 56; what is purpose of, 56-57; the source of, 56; how to obtain a long, 241; the spirit of, 281; the Son laid down his, 312; the Father laid down his, 312, 356

Light, those who do not receive more, shall lose, 94; man to be judged according to use he makes of the, that he has, 303, 227

Lightmindedness, elders and Saints should do away with, 326

Little evils, create the most injury, 258-59

Little foxes spoil the vines, 258

Living to work for the dead, 337-38, 363

Lord, promised a visit to Kirtland Temple, 19; requires that brethren honor one another more than selves, 25; hand of, cannot be stayed, 139; day of, rapidly approaching, 47

Lord's will, requires members be of one heart and mind, 24; cannot be known without revelation, 205-206, 256

Lost tribes of Israel will return from north country, 17

Love, perfect, is safeguard from falling from grave, 9; perfect, comes with testimony of name sealed in Lamb's book of life, 9; of God gives scope to the mind, 147; of God is without prejudice, 147; power of, over human mind, 240; is one of the chief characteristics of diety, 174; should predominate among the Saints, 178-79; one must give love to gain, 313; for enemies required, 313; of liberty, 313; no greater, than to lay down life for friends, 315; begets love, 316; is charity, 316

Loyalty to friends, 316

Lucifer, why he fell, 297. See also Devil, Satan

Lying spirits are abroad, 161

Malachi quoted, coming of Elijah, 356

Man, lives for himself, 12; mind of, capable of instruction and enlargement, 51, 354; is enlightened in proportion to diligence to God's laws, 51; needs preparation to dwell in celestial glory, 54; is unable to save himself, 58; no change in constiution of, since Adam's fall, 60; an honest, is stronger than powers of hell, 139; Jesus was the only perfect, 187-88; should serve God in days of health and vigor and not wait till deathbed, 197; to be judged according to deeds, 218, 221, 257, 311; to be judged with fairness, 218-23; must exert some labor himself for salvation, 227; must stand by himself for salvation, 227; must stand by himself, not leaning upon another, 238; is not able to govern himself wisely, 58, 250; no, is without fault, 258; a strong-minded, generally has coarse features, 299; can bear strong burdens by practice, 299; persevering nature of, brings either blessings or cursings, 299; to be judged according to use made of light given him, 303; must understand character of God to understand self, 343; is a self-existent being, 353-54; is in a situation to advance in knowledge, 354; will be own tormentor and accuser, 311, 357; cannot escape from God, 367; every, who reigns in celestial glory is a god to his own dominions, 374; body of, was made out of the earth, 353; laws of, are imperfect, 51; failure of the governments of, 248. *See also* Men

Man, Son of, 279, 287. *See also* Jesus Christ

Mankind, is naturally selfish and ambitious, 297; sets up bounds and stakes to the Almighty, 320-21; truth will unite, 313

Manufacturing, to be established in Nauvoo, 175; must be established for benefit of nonfarmers who gather, 175; is to be encouraged, 328-29

Many are called but few are chosen, 142, 331

Marchionites, practiced a form of baptism for the dead, 222

Markham, Stephen, in Carthage, 383

Marks, Ephraim, the Prophet's sermon at funeral of, 215-16

Marriage, early, after death of companion disapproved, 119-20; for eternity confined to celestial kingdom, 300-301; for eternity necessary for eternal increase, 301; entrance to highest degree of celestial glory requires eternal, 301; plural, 324

Marriage supper, parable of, 63

Masonry, secret of, 255, 329

Matter, eternal duration of, 301; all spirit is, 301-302; spirit, is fine and pure, 302

Maxims of the Prophet, man who turns away from friend without cause is not easily forgiven, 31; the kindness of man should never be forgotten, 31; extol the virtues and speak not of the faults of the man who willeth to do well, 31; the man who never forsaketh his trust should have the highest place of regard in our hearts, 31

Mediator, is Jesus, 12, 57, 320, 325

Meekness, meaning of, 270

Meetings, no gentleman will leave near close of, 287, 296-97

Melchizedek, held power of endless life, 322; ordained Abraham, 323; taught Abraham of Christ, 323-24; taught Abraham of the priesthood, 323

Melchizedek Priesthood. *See* Priesthood, Melchizedek

Members, how dealt with in transgression, 21; cannot be brought before high council by nonmembers, 286; privilege of, is to live long and enjoy health, 202; should show great liberality to nonmembers, 147. *See also* Saints

Men, are agents unto themselves, 12; are disposed to walk in own paths in preference to law of God, 27; most, are treacherous and selfish, 30; all, are equal in matters of conscience, 49; are dependent upon God for every blessing, 68; are quick to forget God, 68; must be pure in heart to judge others correctly, 69; must become harmless, 71; must worship for themselves, 241; cannot be compelled into the kingdom, 241; souls of, are very precious, 228; have strange notions of gift of Holy Ghost, 242-43; persistence of wicked, 259; good, are opposed by wicked men, 259; value of aged, in counsel, 299; handsome, are not apt to be wise and strongminded, 299; various natures of, 299; were very determined and persevering in ancient times, 299; not many good, since days of Adam, 303; some, are too "wise" to be taught so must die in ignorance, 309; all, must die, 324, 367-68; may become gods, 346-47; ordinations of, in Grand Council, 365; all, must enter eternity, 368; weakminded, pass over great truths, 374; is duty of, to protect their lives, 391; must stand before God to be judged, 62; are responsible to God for the manner in which they improve upon light and wisdom, 227, 303. *See also* Man

Mercy, should be exercised, 155; characterizes dealings of Heavenly Father with mankind, 165; of God is available to all except who commit unpardonable sin, 191; sisters should be armed with, 238; should be shown to sinners, 239; must be shown to one another, 240; must show mercy to obtain, 241; must accompany reproof, 241; is an eternal principle, 191

Messiah, mission and office of, 335, 340; organized world, 340-41; is greater than office of Elijah, 340; power of Elijah prepares way for, 340; is Jesus Christ, 65

Metals, art of working with, taught by revelation, 251

Mexico, 334

Michael is Adam, 39, 157, 167

Militia officers, interviewed by the Prophet, 381

Millennial Harbinger of A. Campbell carries derogatory article about the Prophet, 99

Millennium, day of, is coming, 29; not multitude of preachers but righteousness will bring, 42; rule of Christ during, 268-69; wicked men on earth during, 269; Christ and

resurrected saints may not dwell constantly on earth during, but will visit whenever necessary, 268

Mind, of man is capable of instruction and enlargement, 51, 354; devil retards human, with self-righteousness, 241; kindness has power over the, 240; outlines of a man's features, reveal something of the, 299; truth has power over the, 341; love has power over the, 240

Ministering spirits, purpose of their visits is to bring men up to the standard of their knowledge, 320, 325; sealing power of, 325

Ministers (sectarian), do not understand doctrine of eternal judgment, 188-89; why, do not get revelation, 217; oppose revelation because it makes known their wickedness, 217; do not claim to have Melchizedek Priesthood, 322; do not have authority, 345; ninety-nine out of one hundred, are false teachers, 345

Ministers, priesthood makes men, on earth and in eternity also, 157

Ministry, ordinations to, should not be hasty, 42; appointments to, can be lost by failure to magnify calling, 42; spiritual gifts are needed in the, 243

Miracles, are not all from God, 202-203; those most anxious to see, are least prepared to meet them, 247

Missouri, persecutions against the Saints in, among worst in all history, 126; innocent blood has stained, 131; extreme persecution of Saints in, 131, 302-303; corruption and evil deeds by officials of state of, 130, 133; murder of the Saints in, 302-303; ancient Nephite tower in, 122; Divine command to go to, 79

Mobbings, information and details concerning, to be gathered and kept, 31-32

Moon, to be turned into blood as sign of second coming of Christ, 160

Mormon, means "more good," 300; is of reformed Egyptian origin, 300; not of Greek or Latin origin, 299

Mormon, Book of. *See* Book of Mormon

Mormon political motto, 117

Mormonism, is truth, 139; will withstand all persecution, 139; God is author of, 139; grand principle of, is to receive truth from any source, 313; fosters friendship, 316; gathers truth, 316

Mormonism Unveiled, Howe's, 99

Mormons, will everybody be damned except, 119; great many, to be damned unless they repent, 119; do not believe in having all things in common, 119; have been persecuted by lawless, worthless, inhuman men, 125; persecution against, is among worst in all human history, 126

Moroni, a resurrected being, 119; deposited plates of Book of Mormon near Manchester, New York, 119

Moses, quoting on gathering of Israel, 84-85; with Savior and Elias gave keys to Peter, James, and John, 158; sought to bring children of Israel into presence of God, 159; held gift of discerning of spirits, 207; governed Israel by revelation in both civil and ecclesiastical affairs, 252; practiced the government of God, 252; Christ gave law to, 276; was a god to children of Israel, 375; Law of, was added to gospel, 60. *See also* Law of Moses, Book of Moses

Mother against daughter, in last days seen in vision by the Prophet, 161

Motto, Mormon political, 117

Mountains, to be laid low when Christ comes, 13

Mounts, Rocky, prophecy that Saints would be driven to, 255

Mourners, righteous have reason to rejoice, 359, 296

Mummies, found in Kentucky give evidence for Book of Mormon, 232-33

Murder, spirit of, is of devil, 358; spirit of, is not of God, 358

Murderer, no, hath eternal life, 188; David is a, 188, 339; cannot be forgiven until he pays last farthing, 189; prayers of ministers cannot close the gates of hell against a, 189; cannot be saved, 192; cannot have forgiveness, 339; not to be baptized for remission of sins, 339;

shall welter in hell for ages in torment, 359

Murmur, man should not, at dealings of God, 31, 32

Mustard seed, parable of, 159

Mysteries, do not strive over, 77, 292; likened unto pearls cast before swine, 77; a key to, 156; knowledge through Jesus Christ is key to, of heaven, 298; to be revealed when men are prepared, 309; keys of, revealed, 137; of godliness, known by the prophets, 12; of godliness, the Saints should search deeper into, 364

Narrow-mindedness, doctrine of degrees of glory is far above the, of man, 11

Nations, to be broken as potter's vessel, 16; heathen, that refuse to worship God will eventually be destroyed from the earth, 269

Nauvoo, prosperous condition of, 177; incorporation of City of, 177, 182; seminary of learning in, 177; name of, is of Hebrew origin, 182; meaning of, 182; description of land around, 182; University of, 186; Legion, 186

Negro, status of, 269-70; came into world as slave mentally and physically, 269; are subjects of salvation, 269; many are more refined than some whites, 269; should be confined by law to own species, 270; should be given national equalization, 270; Texas and the, 334

Nephite altar at Adam-ondi-Ahman, 112

Nephites, greatness of, 266; disposition of ancient, 299

Net cast into sea, parable of, 102

New Jerusalem, prophecy of Enoch concerning, 84; prophecy of Ether concerning, 86; men and angels to be co-workers in establishment of, 84; to be prepared for the gathering of the elect, 84; to be caught up, 86; to come down from heaven, 86; is not the Jerusalem of old, 86; Book of Mormon teaches that city of, should be built on American continent, 85-86

New Orleans, gospel preached in, 184

New Testament, comment of the Prophet concerning relative correctness of Greek, English, German, Hebrew, and Latin texts, 349, 360

New translation of the Bible, 25, 102; note 6, page 9

Noah, appointed to save seed of everything through the flood, 12; is Gabriel, 157; stands next to Adam in authority, 157; holds keys of priesthood, 157; obtained same covenant, power, and glories as were given to Adam, 171; became drunk, 193-94; cursed Ham and his posterity, 193-94; given design by revelation for building of ark, 251; baptism of, 264; was ordained by laying on of hands, 264

Nonmembers, attitude that Saints should have toward, 147; members should have great liberality toward, 147

Obedience, promises of God are conditioned upon, 19; strict, to all commandments is required, 27, 32, 332; to government is necessary, 49; to God's law brings reward, 61; blessings for, to law of heaven, 62; to knowledge is a saving principle, 217; brings happiness, 255-56; to the gospel ordinances is essential, 198, 308-309; necessary to be joint heirs with the Son, 54; necessary to be admitted into God's glorious kingdom, 62

Office, aspiring men seek for higher, in the Church, 223-24

Oldest man, is Adam, 157

"Olive leaf," revelation of the Lord's message of peace plucked from the tree of paradise, 18

One hundred and forty-four thousand, are saviors on Mt. Zion, 366; are accompanied by an innumerable multitude, 366

Opportunity, men must give account to God for their use of every, 68

Ordained, every man who administers in the gospel was, for that very work in Grand Council, 365; man must be, by laying on of hands, 42, 264

Order, value of, in government, 53; must prevail in councils of the Church, 75, 93-94; of heaven in receiving revelations, 111; of the house of God is same in all ages, 91; the Almighty is a lover of good, 187; the ancient, has been restored, 223; of Ancient of Days revealed, 237

Ordinances, always part of the gospel, 59-60, 264; Abel had the, 59-60; are to be the same forever and ever, 91, 168, 264, 308; are revealed and watched over by Adam, 168; must be kept in the very way God has appointed, 167; all, of every dispensation to be restored in last dispensation, 171, 173; of sacrifice to be restored, 172-73; must be administered by authority, 172, 274; obedience to, required to obtain gift of Holy Ghost, 199, 212; certain, are administered only in house of God, 308, 312, 362-63; of the gospel were instituted in heaven before foundation of world, 308, 325, 367; fulness of, necessary for full salvation, 309, 331; for the dead are same as for living, 363, 366; are required of each individual, 331; of the temple are necessary for celestial thrones, 362

Ordination, evils of hasty, 42; Paul cited on hasty, 42; is for the faithful men, 42

Organizations, all have certain problems, 238

Overcometh, he that, shall be clothed in white, 65

Overflowing scourge to come upon the earth, 17-18

Palestine mission, letters to Elders Hyde and Page, 163

Parables: marriage supper, 63-64; talents, 48, 68, 257; sower, 94-97; wheat and tares, 97-98, 100-101; of the church in the last days, 98; mustard seed, 98-99, 159; leaven, 100; treasure hid in field, 101; pearl of great price, 101-102; net cast into sea, 102; householder, 102; fig tree, 161; new wine in old bottles, 192; vine and branches, 194;

held keys of the kingdom, 263; had adequate knowledge about how to enter kingdom of heaven, 263; penned most sublime language of any of apostles, 301; secret of writings of, 304; quoted on resurrection of Jesus, 62; on Holy Ghost, 62, 81; on first principles, 81; on remission of sins, 81; on eternal judgment, 188; on situation of David, 188; on preaching in spirit prison, 219, 223, 309; on baptism, 263; on calling and election made sure, 298, 304-305; on nature of Godhead, 312; on no baptism for murderers, 339; on Pentecost sermon, 339

Phelps, W. W., 18, 24; to establish press in Zion (Missouri), 36; collect information of persecutions, 37; welcomed back into Church by letter from Joseph Smith, 165-66

Philip, had spirit of Elias, 338

Plan of salvation, man not able to devise his own, 58; all must be saved by the same, whether before or after time of Christ, 59-60; Abel was taught the, 59; was revealed to Abraham, 60; ought to occupy our strict attention, 68; is one of heaven's greatest gifts of mankind, 68; was formulated before the world was, 220, 325; harmonizes every principle of righteousness, justice, and truth, 218-21; puts all men on equal footing, 219, 223

Planetary system, was made known to Abraham, 118, 251; was made known to Joseph in Egypt, 251; was taught to Egyptians by Abraham and Joseph, 251

Planets, translated beings are ministering angels to inhabitants of other, 170

Plural marriage, instruction on, 324

Political motto, 117

Politics, the Prophet's views on, 275, 333-34

Poor, to inherit earth, 22; duty of bishop is to see to the, 23; how to bring, to repentance, 241; Relief Society to aid the, 229, 242; care of, 328-29

Popularity of a principle does not determine its truth, 332

Power, of wicked spirits restricted,

208; knowledge is, 217, 288; God had greater, than others because he has greater knowledge, 288; devil has more, than some men because he has more knowledge, 217; of salvation comes by knowledge, 306; of endless lives, 322; of love, 240; of kindness, 227, 240; of God, begins to fall upon the nations, 16

Pratt, Parley P., to remain in England, 176

Prayer, truth is manifest through, 11-12; should be in name of Jesus Christ, 11; knowledge is necessary to receive answer to, 226; of the Prophet for afflicted Saints in Zion, 37; necessity of, 247; Book of Mormon teaches, 247; God is known through, 247; of the righteous availeth much, 342; of the Prophet in Liberty Jail, 132; fasting and, could turn away sickness, 326; is best way to learn truth, 191, 325

Preaching, of gospel is most important duty, 113; to the guards at Carthage Jail, 382

Premonition of Joseph Smith, 382

Presidency, First. See First Presidency

Presidency of all dispensations is held by Adam, 169

Presidency of the United States, why Joseph Smith was a candidate for, 331-34

Pride, beware of, 43, 137, 155

Priesthood (Aaronic), rightly belongs to lineal descendants of Aaron, 112, 272; John the Baptist held keys of, 273; Zacharias held, 273; hereditary nature of, 319; was in active operation from Aaron to Zacharias, father of John the Baptist, 319; restoration of, to Joseph Smith, 335; does not have power to confer Holy Ghost, 335; office of bishop belongs to, 112

Priesthood (general), it is privilege of those who hold, to receive revelation from God, 112; offices of, likened to human body, 112; all offices necessary in, 112; the higher the authority in, the greater the difficulty of the station, 113; was first given to Adam, 157; is an everlasting principle without beginning of days or end of years, 157-58; keys of, brought from heaven, 157; no change of ordinances signifies no change in, 158, 308; has come down in regular succession from the beginning, 158, 173; there are two, spoken of, 166; power in, is conditioned upon righteousness, 169; sometimes becomes a cursing instead of a blessing, 169; power of translation belongs to, 170; many things pertaining to, have been hid from foundation of the world, 170; there are different portions of, 180; order of in temple building, 183; releases spirits of the dead, 192; key words of, 199; holds the power of discerning of spirits, 204-207, 213; ministers both in earth and in heaven, 222; the heavenly to unite with the earthly, 232; makes men to be ministers now and in eternity, 159; highest order and principles of, revealed, 237; relation between gifts of the spirit and, 243; gifts of spirit needed in order to call men to offices in, 243; God works within his own, on earth, 265; fulness of, must be obtained the same way Jesus Christ obtained it, 308; three grand orders of, 322; is a perfect law of theocracy, 322; gives laws to the people, 322; Holy Ghost administers in, 323; all who hold, should be qualified, 112, 142; doctrines of, shall distill upon soul of righteous, 142; Adam stands next to Jesus Christ at head of, 158; is given by laying on of hands, 42, 264

Priesthood (Levitical), was added because of transgression, 60; hereditary, 319; is without oath, 323; administers outward ordinances, 323; is also called Aaronic, 166

Priesthood (Melchizedek), is priesthood of the Son of God, 111, 167; has power to reprove and rebuke as well as to receive revelations, 112; is highest authority in kingdom of God, 166; is the channel of communication from God, 166-67; existed before world, 167; has power of endless lives, 322; all

priesthood can be denominated, 180; all prophets held, 181; is not by lineage, 323; is eternal, 323; is by oath and covenant, 323; fulness of not possessed by David, 339; true Church cannot exist without, 375; has power to marry for eternity, 300-301; those married by, have children after the resurrection, 301; purpose of, is to direct man in the right way of salvation, 364

Priesthood (Patriarchal), Joseph Smith, Sr., holds right and keys to, 38; Hyrum Smith holds right and keys to, 40; is the evangelical priesthood, 40, 151; right of, belongs to blood of Joseph in the last days, 151; knowledge of, received in temple, 323

Priests, should not be idle, 77; few even qualified to be, 112; if do duty, can have as much enjoyment as though members of Presidency, 112

Principle, popularity does not determine truthfulness of, 332; of knowledge is the, of salvation, 297, 305, 357; of religious freedom, 147

Prison, spirit. See Spirit prison

Procrastination of repentance is dangerous, 197

Promises, this generation cannot claim those, of the ancients, 12; are on conditions of obedience, 19; were given to the ancients, 65; are obtained by faith and diligence, 66; to others are not ours, 66; of God not to be trifled with, 71-72; were made by the Father to the children of Abraham, 163; are calculated to interest, awakened, and arouse the Saints, 163; of salvation were made before foundation of world, 356

Property in Zion, how to distribute, 23; consecration of, must be by mutual consent, 23; instruction concerning inventory of consecrated, 22

Prophecies should be studied, 12, 43

Prophecy, testimony of Jesus is the spirit of, 119, 160, 265, 269, 300, 312, 315; gift of, comes by Holy Ghost, 243; more sure word of, 288-89, 301, 303; of removal to

Rocky Mountains, 255; that Saints would be beyond enemies in five years, 333; to Stephen A. Douglas, 302

Prophet, is subject to weakness and frailties common to mankind, 89, 303, 315; the world is ignorant concerning the true nature of a, 89; every man with testimony of Jesus is a, 119, 160; what constitutes a, 269; is not always a prophet, 278; Joseph's answer to charge of being a fallen prophet, 194, 335, 365

Prophets, reveal the word and will of God, 12; mankind should rejoice that God gives the world, 12; know the mysteries of godliness, 12; false, often mistaken for true, 206; held keys of discerning of spirits, 207; ancient, were fired with zeal for building Zion, 231-32; speak by Holy Ghost, 243; the Twelve are, 109

Prophets, false. See False prophets

Proverbs of Joseph Smith, 317

Psalm, 50th, describes glory of gathered Israel, 183; 102nd describes city of Zion, 17

Pumpkin (figurative expression), 331

Punishment, of the devil is not to have a body of flesh, 297; of suspense, 287-88; of the wicked is to mingle with their own kind, 198; of the persecutors of the righteous, 134-35, 260-61, 359

Pure, to dwell with God a man must be, 227; the, have hope in God, 64

Pure in heart, man must be, to escape destructions, 71

Purged, the Church to be, 373

Purify, those who, themselves will see and know the things of God for themselves, 13; those who have hope in God will, themselves, 64

Purposes of God, are not understood by the world, 217, 220; are hastening to accomplishment, 223; were understood by Paul, 168

Purposes of Relief Society, 201-202, 229, 242, 259

Questions and answers, 119-21

Rainbow, given for a sign concerning end of world, 305; year in which, is seen Lord will not come, 340-41

Reason teaches there is a God, 56

Rebellious, to be cast out of the kingdom of God, 52

Rebuke, value of a righteous, 112

Records, importance of written, 72; are made of the acts of men, 69; of meetings are to be kept, 73; failure to keep, is sign of slothfulness, 73; are a protection against evil, 73; must be kept of baptisms for dead, 260

Redeemer, Christ is, of both men and animals, 290-92; God the Second is, 190

Redemption, plan of, 48, 57-58. See also Plan of salvation

Reincarnation is doctrine of the devil, 104-105. See also Transmigration

Relief Society, remarks of Joseph Smith concerning, 201-202, 223-29, 237-42, 257-60; rules of, must be observed by members, 201; not to receive unworthy as members, 201, 240; objective of, is to purge iniquity, 201-202; is a charitable organization, 226; members of, must be virtuous and of good report, 240; object of, is to reform people, 240; purpose of, is to relieve the poor, 229, 242; purpose of, is to save souls, 242; is to practice holiness, 259

Religion, is between man and God, 147; freedom of, is guaranteed by the Constitution of the U.S., 147, 185, 279, 344; freedom of, should be guaranteed by all governments, 344

Repentance, should be preached to old, young, rich, poor, bond, free, 81; should be accompanied by baptism and remission of sins, 81; is not to be trifled with, 148; is not to be procrastinated, 197; required to escape judgments, 16; to attend to needs of poor is the best way to bring them to, 241; Jesus associated with sinners on condition of their, 240; is as important in one age of the world as in another, 265; cannot come after sin against Holy Ghost, 358; a call to, 16, 361; should be preached, 292

Reports, false. See False reports

Responsibility, most important, is to preach gospel, 113; man's greatest, is to seek after dead, 356; is left upon parents who deny the gospel to children, 88; of the Jews in rejecting the gospel, 222; of the Jews for neglecting their dead, 222-23; of man to improve and use the light and knowledge given him, 227, 303

Restitution of all things, 101, 231

Restoration of ancient ordinances, 173, 237

Resurrected beings, do not die again, 347; do not have blood, 200, 367; differ in stature and size, 368; beauty and indescribable glory of, 368

Resurrection, of Jesus Christ is center-point of hope, 62; doctrine of, is an important point of our faith, 62; of the corporeal bodies of all the human family, 84; should be taught with the first principles and the doctrine of eternal judgment, 149; is greater than translation, 170; distinction between translation and, 171; the righteous continue their labors after the, 171; of children, 200, 368; of all people, 199-200, 367-68; is the reuniting of spirit with body, 207, 210; the Prophet's vision of, 295; joy for the righteous in the, 295; all losses to be made up in, 296; the Prophet's testimony of, 295-96; belief in, is insoluble to the children of men in the last days, 309; some will be raised to be angels and some to be gods, 312; exaltation to be obtained after the, 348; all do not have the same glory in, 366; glory of, is indescribable, 368; at the time of Christ, 188; of sons of perdition, 361

Revelation, Bible does not contain all, 61; spirit of, 151; no salvation without, 160; is needed to discern between false and true spirits, 205; without, none can understand either God or the devil, 205; the world is unwilling to acknowledge the principle of, 205-206; is not binding unless received from legally constituted authority, 21, 215; why modern priests do not get, 217; is opposed by modern Christendom, 217; the world has

been without for centuries, 242; design of ark given to Noah by, 251; is to come through the Presidency, 111; any officer in the Church may receive, for his particular calling, 111; without, man remains in ignorance, 206; is adapted to the circumstances, 256; is adapted to the capacity and language of person receiving, 162; we cannot be people of God without, 272; is given to Church in every age of world, 272; they who reject, cannot escape damnation of hell, 272, 298-99, 349; rock of, 274; things of God known only by, 292; of things kept hidden from before foundation of world, 309, 321; individual and first-hand, needed for salvation, 324; Holy Ghost gives, 328; one cannot receive Holy Ghost without receiving, 328; many have received knowledge by, 329; all knowledge can be received by, 330; one, from heaven is worth more than all the sectarian notions in existence, 338; is given to man's spirit independent of his body, 355; that which will save spirit will save body also, 355; is given with an eternal perspective of man's existence, 355; to Brigham Young, 118; the Prophet's fear to approach the Lord for, in trivial matters, 22; is not to be trifled with, 54, 61; never inquire of God for special, unless there is no previous one that would suit the case, 22; doctrine of, far excels the doctrine of no revelation, 338; is the most glorious principle of the gospel, 298-99; is the key that unlocks the mysteries of the heavens, 299

Revelation, Book of, portions of, explained, 287-94; the beasts of, 287-94; is one of the plainest books God ever caused to be written, 290; deals with events of the future and not the past, 290

Revelations, value of the, 7-8; are the foundation of the Church, 8; are a benefit to the world, 8; are worth the riches of the whole world, 8; are granted to man for his salvation, 8; tradition hampers the teaching of many of the, 70; should be searched, 11-12; former, are not always applicable to present-day conditions, 70; truth of the, manifested by Holy Ghost through prayer, 11; Saints should be careful not to betray, 156; no error in, 368

Revelator, Holy Ghost is a, 328; each of the Twelve is a, 109

Revolutionize, the Prophet's work will, the world, 366

Rewards, to be given to obedient, 54; law of heaven guarantees, 50

Rich are not to cast out poor, 22

Riches of earth, the revelations are worth as much as, 8

Riches of eternity are within the grasp of the obedient, 8

Richards, Willard, at Carthage, 383

Rigdon, Sidney, love of the Prophet for, 30; not capable of that pure love characteristic of a Church President, 30; selfishness of, 30; independence of mind of, 30; faults of, 30; great power of words of, 30; ability of, to gain friendships easily, 30; posterity of, to be sought after, 31; the Lord will watch over his generations, 31; unfitness of, to lead the Church, 382

Right, whatever God requires is, 256; that which is, under one circumstance may be wrong under another, 256; everything from God is, 256-57

Righteous, a crown for the, 64; often must suffer with the guilty, 34; to dwell in everlasting burnings, 347; to inherit glory, 12; blessed by departure into spirit world, 326

Righteousness, must be the aim of the Saints, 77; is not increasing, 48; to sweep the earth with a flood, 84; baptism required for, 266, 274, 319; of man is much less than that of God, 317; comes by obedience, 266

Ring, used to illustrate eternity, 181, 354

Rock, of revelation, 274; of ages, 41; unless we are looking for the Second Coming, we may be among the number calling for, to fall on them, 160

Rockwell, O.P., prophecy concerning, 285

Rocky Mountain Expedition, 332

Rocky Mountain prophecy, 255

Rocky Mountains, Saints to be driven to, 255; Joseph warned by the Lord to flee to for safety, 377

"Rosh," Hebrew term, meaning of, 348, 371

Rule of Christ in millennium, 268

Sacredness of burial grounds, 294

Sacrifice, a type of the Only Begotten, 58; Christ was the great, 58, 172; must be done with faith, 58; is to point mind toward Christ, 60; of all things is necessary to obtain keys of endless life, 322; meaning of Abraham's, 322; of animals to be restored in last dispensation, 172-73; is one of the duties of the priesthood, 172; to be offered by the sons of Levi, 173; ordinance of, necessary to make restitution of all things, 173; to be in temple, 173; priests received portions from, 172-73

Saints, the Prophet's prayer for the afflicted, 37; must love one another, 76; must overcome evil, 76; must keep unspotted from world, 76; to be crowned with glory at Christ's coming, 29; hated by world for testimony of Jesus Christ, 125; trial of, in Missouri, equal to that of Abraham, 136; should be willing to confess all their sins, 155; shall not escape all judgments, 162; should cultivate principle of unity, 174, 231; should bury every selfish feeling, 178; should let love predominate, 178-79; have no room for hatred, 179; are to live unto God, not unto themselves, 179; faith and trials of, 185; should be mindful to observe all commandments, 187; are to be patient, 187; should be a select people, 202; should be separate from the evils of the world, 202; should be choice, virtuous, and holy, 202; should not be divided by separate interests or exclusive designs, 231; proper attitude of, toward sinners, 241; must be long-suffering, 241; to be driven to Rocky Mountains, 255; to become mighty people in Rocky Mountains, 255; persecuted by wicked men, 259; should not shrink in day of trial, 261-62; in all ages of the world have been baptized in name of Jesus Christ, 266; should cultivate a meek, quiet, and peaceable spirit, 136; to shun lightmindedness, 326; should be sober, 326; have not much time to redeem their dead, 330; are sometimes slow to understand, 331; are often unwilling to learn, 331; gathering of, 143; are to become like Christ, 65; are in pathway of eternal fame if faithful, 163

Salem. See Shiloam

Salvation, gift of, 68; cannot come without revelation, 160, 272; is always administered by testimony, 160; must be on eternal principles, 181, 308, 325; plan of, made in heaven, 181; plan of, exhibits greatness of God's compassion, 192; for the dead, 192, 308, 355, 363, 366; plan of, not understood by human family, 217; now is day of, to such as repent, 238; comes only by obedience to commandments, 253, 357; cannot be found outside of kingdom of God, 272; no, without legal administrator, 274, 319; of beasts, 291-92; comes through knowledge, 217, 297; is to triumph over all enemies, 297, 301, 305; requires power over evil spirits, 217, 297; no, without a tabernacle of flesh, 297; is obtained by the same principles in every age of the world, 308; not in Bible without legal administrator, 319; could not come without the mediation of Jesus Christ, 323; to acquire, one must be subject to certain fixed rules and principles which originated before world was, 324; principles of, are unalterable, 324-25; fulness of, requires ordinances, 308, 331; requires total obedience, 332; requires just what God commands, no more, no less, 332; obedience to other than God's commandments will not bring, 332; available to all, except who commit unpardonable sin, 356-58; obedience to gospel brings, 357;

narrow concept of, held by sectarians, 11, 192. See also Plan of salvation

Satan, entered into Judas Iscariot, 67; influence of, activates apostates, 68; cannot be blamed for all of man's wrongdoings, 187; can appear as an angel of light, 204, 214; is the accuser, 212; priesthood necessary to detect cunning of, 204-205; can be detected by color of hair, 214-15; seen by Joseph Smith, 373; buffeting of, 338. See also Devil, Lucifer

Savior, 158. See also Jesus Christ

Saviors on Mt. Zion, how to become, 223, 330; one hundred and forty-four thousand, 366

Scepter of righteousness, 142

Sceva, modern sons of, 99

School of the prophets, Lord commanded organization of, 18

Scourge, an overflowing, to come upon mankind, 18

Scriptures, are for the good of man, 53; contain the will of heaven, 54; contain laws of God, 54; contain God's blessings, cursings, and teachings for the human family, 54; he who reads, oftenest will like them best, 56; canon of, not full, 121; say what they mean and mean what they say, 264; rule of interpretation, 276; key to understanding of, 276-77; revision of, 25, note 6, p. 9; should be searched, 11; knowledge of, revealed through faith and study, 11

Scriptures, corrections. See Bible, corrections

Seal, will secure posterity, 321

Sealed, in Lamb's book of life, 9; heavens are often, because of covetousness in the Church, 9

Sealing, taught by Paul, 149; in foreheads, meaning of, 321; keys of, held by Elijah, 337-38; necessary for family organization to continue into eternity, 368

Seaton, N.E., newspaper editor, letter from Joseph Smith to, 13

Second Comforter. See Comforter

Second coming of Jesus Christ. See Jesus Christ, second coming of

Second death is consequence of sin against Holy Ghost, 361

Secrecies, counsel against, 146

Secret combinations, proclamation of the Prophet against, 285

Secret of Masonry, is to keep a secret, 329

Secrets, of human action are known to God, 19; man ought to learn to keep, 195; ability of the Prophet to keep, 195; of God are revealed to his prophets, 265; of Peter's writings, 304; inability to keep, is reason why we do not get more revelations, 195

Sectarian baptism, is not valid, 192, 263

Sectarian doctrine of heaven, contradicts teachings of Jesus and Paul, 311

Sectarian God. See God, sectarian

Sectarian priests are blind and build on old revelations, 311

Sectarians, narrow concept of salvation of, is worse than atheism, 192; baptism of is not valid, 192, 263; lack correct knowledge of spirits, 203-204; manifestations of false spirits among, 203-204; lack key for discerning of spirits, 204; some have false notions of the justice and mercy of God, 220; conflicting creeds among, 221, 262; deny spirit of revelation, 312; do not profess to have Melchizedek Priesthood, 322; will be damned, 322; have false concept of God, 181, 311-12, 372; are inspired with a false hope of salvation, 270

Seers, know mysteries of godliness, 12; the Twelve are, 109

Selfish, mankind is naturally, 297

Selfishness, Saints should shun, 178; people are full of, 241

Self-justification, mankind persists in, 18

Self-righteous, the, Jews condemned Jesus, 240; are to be damned, 277-78; parables of lost sheep and lost coin pertain to persons who are, 277-78

Self-righteousness, beware of, 228; hinders progress, 241; is a doctrine of the devil, 241; must be done away with, 241; reproof of, 303-304

Serpents, protected by the prophet, 71-72; meaning of the Lord's promise concerning deadly, 72; the prophet's dream of, 368

Servants of God, will not have gone over the nations before destruction comes, 87

Seventh thousand years, government of God to rule in, 252

Seventies, are a traveling quorum, 68; to go into all the earth, 68; are subject to direction from the Twelve, 68, 112, 164; more to be called as needed, 76; are not to attend meetings of the Twelve unless invited, 75; to hold themselves in readiness to travel, 75; to be chosen from experienced elders, 75-76, 112; to be ordained by the first presidency of the seventy, 75; not a presiding office, 109; are called to preach the gospel rather than regulate the Church, 109, 164; to assist the Twelve, 109; High priests not to be, 111-12

Sherwood, Henry, conversation with, 379

Shiloam, Hebrew designation of Salem, meaning righteousness and peace, 321

Sick, to trust in God, 190; to call for elders, 190; to be nourished by herbs and mild food, 190, 229; to live by faith and not by medicine or poison, 190; are healed by faith, 224-25; administration to, by females, 224-25, 229; to be treated by simple remedies, 329

Sickness, Lord chastises with, 194; could be turned away by fasting and prayer, 326

Sign, baptism is, of obedience, 198; of healing of sick, 198; of gift of Holy Ghost, 199; of the dove, 276; of the dove—devil cannot duplicate, 276

Sign of Son of Man, comes after sun darkened and moon turns into blood, 279-80, 287; one grand, will be mistaken for a comet, 287

Signs, of coming of Christ have commenced, 160; God has set many, in heaven and earth, 198; of the gospel must be obeyed for salvation, 198; will follow the believer, 224, 262; a wicked and adulterous generation seeks for, 278

assembly of the patriarchs with Adam, 39; blessings of Joseph of Egypt to be upon, 39; to possess a celestial mansion, 40; to be had in honorable remembrance, 40; to be mighty in counsel, 40; death of, 177; directed that Hyrum should succeed him as patriarch, 177

Smith, Lucy, partaker of the blessings of her husband, 39; filled with benevolence, 39; to have eternal life, 39

Smith, Samuel, to be a teacher in the house of the Lord, 41; the Lord will mature his mind in judgment, 41

Smith, William, proud of heart, 41; neglects the more weighty matters, 41; rebellious heart of, 41; to be saved at the last by repentance, 41

Societies, temperance, 306

Solemn assembly, washing of feet in, 91; to be held in house of the Lord, 91; pure in heart to receive an endowment in, 91; Savior to be seen in the, 92

Solomon, God was source of wisdom possessed by, 251, 256

Son, has separate body from Father, 312; does what the Father did, 312, 345-46

Son of God, came to redeem world from fall, 12; to appear in all the glory of his Father, 42; only by merits of, can man obtain redemption, 58; opens door to God's presence, 58

Son of Man, to stand before Adam in Grand Council, 157; we must be looking for coming of, 160; the dead are to be looking for coming of, 160; sign of the, 279-80, 287; soon to come, 29, 132, 160

Sons of God, the faithful are, 64

Sons of Levi, were too prejudiced to receive priesthood from Jesus, 172; to offer sacrifice in last dispensation, 173

Sons of perdition, exact destiny of, not revealed, except to partakers thereof, 24; not to be restored, 24, 361; are those who sin against Holy Ghost, 358; many apostates of Church are, 358; resurrection of, 361

Sophistry, Gentile, warning against, 156

Souls, saving of, 77; compassion for perishing, 241; of men, only fools trifle with, 137

Sower, parable of, 94-97

Sows, man reaps what he, 195

Spirit, from God can appear only in glory, 162, 325-26; not every, is from God, 162, 203, 210; is pure, elastic, and refined substance, 207, 302; difference between body and, 207; resurrected bodies have, instead of blood, 199-200; can only be discerned by purer eyes, 302

Spirit of God, is being withdrawn from nations of the earth, 16, 231; will bear testimony to all who seek diligently for knowledge of God, 29; is needed to discern things of God, 202, 205, 242, 247; forsakes apostates, 67; all who have not, are in transgression, 78

Spirit of man, not created, 158, 352, 354; is material, 207, 301-302; exists independently of the body, 207; is self-existent, 354; is never too old to approach God, 191; revelations are to the, and not to the body, 355; revelations that will save the, will save body also, 355

Spirit of revelation, what it is, 151

Spirit prison, Jesus preached to spirits in, 219; Peter spoke of, 219, 309; gospel taught in, 366, 179

Spirits, lying, are abroad in earth, 161; to be a great manifestation of both false and true, 161; are eternal, 181, 203, 208; difference between angels and, 191, 325; minister to disembodied spirits, 191; Christ became a ministering, while body was in tomb, 191; of the dead released by priesthood, 192; discourse of the Prophet on, 202-15; false, manifested in apostles' time, 202; intelligence from God needed to discern, 202-205; world is ignorant concerning nature of, 202-203, 205; all kinds of, are manifested among all people, 203-204; false, manifested among sectarians, 203-204; false, manifested among Latter-day Saints, 204, 213; are governed by priesthood, 208; great

Temple ordinances, 362; always the same, 90, 91

Tenderness leads sinners to repentance, 240

Terrestrial bodies, translated beings minister to, 170-71

Terrestrial kingdom does not require baptism, 12

Testimony, of Joseph Smith about work of God in last days, 29; Holy Ghost bears, to all who work diligently for knowledge of God, 29; salvation always administered by, 160; of Jesus is spirit of prophecy, 119, 160, 265, 269, 300, 312, 315; of Jesus brought imprisonment, 123

Texas, Prophet's views concerning annexation of, 334; the Negroes and, 334; Great Britain and, 334; slavery and, 334

Things revealed to "babes" in last days, meaning of, is that God has chosen the weak and obscure, 137

Things too wonderful to utter, 304-305

Tithing, covenant of, 70

Title page of Book of Mormon was translated from original plates, 7

Tongue, man must guard the, 238-39; man needs double watch over, 238

Tongues, gift of, to be used with care, 25; Satan may deceive in regard to, 25, 229; given for preaching among those of another language, 148-49, 195, 247; not necessary to be taught, 149; devil can speak in, 162, 195; not to be done without interpretation, 162, 247; not to be exercised too frequently, 229, 247; anything taught by, not to be received for doctrine, 229; comes by Holy Ghost, 243; is least of the gifts, yet perhaps most sought, 246. See also Spiritual gifts

"Too wise to be taught," some men are, so must die in ignorance and then learn of their mistake, 309

Torment, is disappointment of hopes in next world, 357; of mind is like fire and brimstone, 357-61

Tormentor, man is own, 311, 357

Tower Hill, or Adam-ondi-Ahman, is place of Nephite altar, 122

Traditions, man must give up false, for they hinder spiritual progress, 70, 321, 331

Traitor, to be, is among greatest of sins, 156

Traitors, world uses, to afflict the Saints, 126; God hates, 127; we cannot love, 127; devil ought to be ashamed of, 127; God will not acknowledge, 375

Transfiguration, of earth shown upon the Mount of, 13; keys of priesthood given upon Mount of, 158

Transgression, man cut off from direct contact with God by, 57; all who have not the Spirit are in, 78; daily, is displeasing to God, 148; of Church members, 78; will bring disappointment, 357

Translated beings, continue their labor in ministry, 171; must still undergo change equivalent to death, 191; are designed for future missions, 191; are of terrestrial order, 170-71; minister to inhabitants of other planets, 170; are not taken immediately into God's presence, 170

Translation, is doctrine of the priesthood, 170; not as final as resurrection, 170; distinction between resurrection and, 171; obtains deliverance from pains of body, 171

Translation of the scriptures, 9; of St. John's gospel, 11

Transmigration of souls, doctrine of the devil, 105; false teachings of "Joshua the Jewish Minister" concerning, 105

Treason, Joseph and Hyrum jailed on charge of, 394

Treasure hid in field, parable of, 101

Trials, before high councils, 164

Tribulation, blessings come after much, 34; day of, fast approaching, 42; before blessings, 78; in last days, 160-61

Tried people, Saints to be a, 135

Trifle, not with promises of God, 72; only fools will, with souls, 137

Trifles, do not approach the Lord with, 22

Truth, cannot be understood by unrighteous men, 96; not understood because of lack of desire, 96; to sweep earth with flood, 84; Mormonism is, 139; will triumph, 133;

many kept from, only because they know not where to find it, 145-46; some are strangers to, 175; saves people, 191; by prayer is best way to obtain, 191; breaks down falsehood, 192; devil speaks both falsehood and, 214; sober thinking and sound reasoning men will listen to the voice of, 299; will be received from any source by Mormonism, 313; will unite mankind, 313; will cut its own way, 313; all sects have mixture of error and, 316; importance of eternal, 325; need for becoming subject to fixed principles of eternal, 324-25; of the gospel can be known through prayer, 325; cannot be reconciled with error, 326; power of, 341; weak-minded men pass over great, 374

Twelve Apostles, Council of, instructions concerning office of, 74; hold keys of the ministry, 74, 109; are to travel to all nations, 74, 109; differ from other offices of the Church, 74; are a traveling high council, 74; are not subject to standing high council, 92; are next to First Presidency in authority, 105-106, 190; subject only to First Presidency, 106; the Prophet's vision concerning, 197; are prophets, seers, and revelators, 109; are called to preach, not to preside over churches, 109; instructions to the, 155-63; not to exalt themselves, 155; a key to the, 156; sent to teach not to be taught, 156; are to act honestly before God and man, 156; to beware of Gentile sophistry, 156; must be careful not to betray the brethren, 156; no work on earth more important than that of the, 173; must practice virtue, faith, charity, and diligence, 173-74; are to counsel the Saints in regard to building of Zion, 254; were ordained by Oliver Cowdery, David Whitmer, and Joseph Smith, 307; the Prophet's characterization of, 307; to plan the western movement of the Church, 332

Unfaithfulness of men, 309

United States, to be scene of bloodshed, 17; has greater resources than any other nation, 249; is troubled with disunity and strife, 249; government of, should redress wrongs suffered by Saints in Missouri, 302-303

United States Constitution. See Constitution of the United States

Unity, greater blessings available through, 183; blessings of, explained, 174; makes burdens light, 231; is result of friendship, 316; comes through learning truth, 313

Universal resurrection, 368

Unpardonable sin, is against Holy Ghost, 156; has no forgiveness in this world or next, 191, 219, 356-57, 361; is to shed innocent blood, 301; is sin against light and knowledge, 358; man cannot be sealed against, 339. See also Holy Ghost, sin against

Unprepared, hundreds and thousands die, 14; the people are, to receive the full knowledge of the kingdoms of glory, 305

Valleys to be exalted, 13

Value, of tribulation, 134; of chastisement, 194-95; of a rebuke, 112

Van Buren, President, visit of Joseph Smith to, 302; comments of, concerning persecution, 302, 327

Vanity, all are subject to, 187-88

Veil, parted through perfect love, 9; parting requires one heart and mind, 9

Vengeance, comes through ignoring the word of the Lord, 54, 77, 322, 260-61

Vicious dispositions should be overcome, 71

Vine. See Fruit of the vine

Violence, offered to God when his teachings are ignored, 54; to good judgment to deny second coming of Christ, 65

Virtue, do not underestimate your neighbor's, 228; do not overestimate your own, 228; increase of, calls for enlarged views, 228

Virtuous are not to oppress sinners, 238

Vision, of degrees of glory, 11; only

that, seen by the eye is reliable, 161; when one sees a, he should pray for interpretation, 161; open, manifests more important things, 161; of mother against daughter and father against son in last days, 161; not every, is from God, 162; false, given by Devil, 213-14; of beasts must be accompanied by interpretation, 291; of the resurrection, 295-96; of the Twelve, 107-108; of the celestial kingdom, 106

Visions, personal intended only for the individual and not for the Church, 21

Voice of the Church, officers sustained by, 108, 75

War and bloodshed to come, 160

Warning, to unrighteous, 161; of nations not to be finished before angels of destruction begin work, 87

Warning voice, duty of elders to lift up the, 86; death is a, for repentance, 196-97

Washing of feet, a necessary ordinance, 90; to be done in solemn assembly, 91; only for official members, 91; to be done apart from world, 90; in Kirtland Temple, 111

Washings and anointings, necessary for celestial thrones, 362; must be administered in a holy place, 362; part of the endowment, 237

Wasson, M. L. D., nephew of Emma Smith, 200; baptized by the Prophet, 200; first of her kindred to join the Church, 200; accused Joseph of cowardice, 377

Water, existed in elementary state from eternity, 158; baptism in, useless without Holy Ghost to follow, 148, 314, 360; to come from under Jerusalem temple, 286

Western movement of the Church, the Twelve to investigate plan for, 332; purpose of, was for safety and security, 332; equipment for expedition, 333; prophecy of, within five years, 333

Wheelock, Cyrus, obtains list of witnesses for trial, 392; Hyrum's comments to, 392-93

Wicked, destruction of, at end of world, 100; suspense in punishment of, 288; righteous and, go to same spirit world, 310; during the millennium, 268-69

Wickedness of men, 47-48

Will of God, Church must be willing to obey, 253; deals with temporal as well as spiritual things, 252-54

Willful sin is unpardonable, 128

Wings, angels do not have, 162

Wisdom, man ought to learn by precept as well as by experience, 155; prayer is best way to obtain, 191; each must improve upon that given him from God, 227; of God needed to govern human family, 252; comes from God, 251; men of God should be endowed with, 311; should be sought by the Saints, 253

Wisdom, Word of, should be observed, 117. See also Word of Wisdom

Wise, it behooves us to be, 253; some men too, to be taught, 309

Witness, the gospel to be preached to a, in last days, 364-65; God the Third, 190

Witnesses, the three, ordained the Twelve, 307; needed at baptisms for dead, 260; of the doctrines of Christ, 262

Wives, love of, for husbands, 88; not to be baptized contrary to wishes of husbands, 87; duty to, 145; should greet husbands with a smile instead of an argument, 228; plurality of, only one man on earth at a time holds keys to, 324; practice of plurality of, must be directed by the Lord, 324

Woe to the unbelieving, 83

Women, do not have authority to organize the Church, 212; Paul on, ruling in Church, 209; false preaching of the, in Irvingite Church, 210-12; faithful may administer to sick, 224-25, 229; are to honor husbands, 226; charity and benevolence are natural with, 226; if pure and innocent, shall stand in presence of God, 227; to stimulate elders to good works by example, 226; not to tease husbands, 227; not to jangle, contradict, or dispute with husbands, 227; to be kind and

redemption of, 231-32, must be
built up by revelation, 254; all of
North and South America is, 362;
headquarters of, in center of land,
362; stakes of, to be established,
363; 102nd Psalm describes city of,
17; another people to be chosen
for, if Saints not faithful, 18